THE CURIES

Also by Denis Brian

The Unexpected Einstein: The Real Man Behind the Icon

Pulitzer: A Life

Murderers and Other Friendly People:
The Public and Private Worlds of Interviewers

The Enchanted Voyage: The Life of J. B. Rhine

The True Gen: An Intimate Portrait of Ernest Hemingway
by Those Who Knew Him

Fair Game: What Biographers Don't Tell

Genius Talk: Conversations with Nobel Scientists
and Other Luminaries

Einstein: A Life

THE CURIES

A Biography of the Most Controversial Family in Science

Denis Brian

WILEY

John Wiley & Sons, Inc.

Published by John Wiley & Sons, Inc., Hoboken, New Jersey
Published simultaneously in Canada

Photo Credits: Pages, 7, 18, 31, 118, 119, 161, 165, 173, 193, 202, 212, 221, 236, 244, 258, 263, 366: Archives Curie and Joliot-Curie; page 66: Courtesy of the Library of Congress. Photo: Henri Manuet, Paris; pages 182 right, 241, 251, 384: Library of Congress; page 186: Courtesy Robert Abbe; pages 260, 315: Courtesy Eve Curie Labouisse; page 285: Franklin Roosevelt Library

For general information about our other products and services, please contact our Customer Care Department within the United States at (800) 762-2974, outside the United States at (317) 572-3993 or fax (317) 572-4002.

Wiley also publishes its books in a variety of electronic formats. Some content that appears in print may not be available in electronic books. For more information about Wiley products, visit our web site at www.wiley.com.

Library of Congress Cataloging-in-Publication Data:

Brian, Denis, date.
    The Curies : a biography of the most controversial family in science / Denis Brian.
        p.   cm.
    ISBN-13 978-0-471-27391-2 (cloth)
    ISBN-10 0-471-27391-0 (cloth)
    1. Curie family. 2. Curie, Marie, 1867–1934. 3. Curie, Pierre, 1859–1906.
4. Chemists—Poland—Biography. 5. Chemists—France—Biography. 6. Physicists—France—Biography. I. Title.
QD22.C79B75   2005
540'.92'2—dc22   2005007001

Printed in the United States of America
10 9 8 7 6 5 4 3 2 1

Contents

Acknowledgments

Eve Curie Labouisse and her niece, Hélène Langevin-Joliot, were of enormous help in making sure this account of the extraordinary Curie family was accurate, and made no attempt at censorship. Dr. Langevin-Joliot read and commented on every chapter and Mrs. Labouisse read and commented on most of the manuscript until—at one hundred years of age—her eyesight began to fail. Even so, she kindly and meticulously checked the chapter on her tour of the battlefronts during World War II when she interviewed three Indian leaders, Nehru, Gandhi, and Jinnah. Our agreement was that she would answer my questions but not comment on the book for publicity purposes. I contacted Mrs. Labouisse by phone and corresponded with her by mail. I corresponded with Dr. Langevin-Joliot by e-mail.

I also received valuable information from Robert Abbe, Monique Bordry, Pierre Radvanyi, Bertrand Goldschmidt, Georges Charpak, Sidney Hook, Spencer R. Weart, Arun Gandhi, John Campbell, Larry Grimm, Sharon Broom, R. H. Stuewer, George Dracoulis, Phillipe Burrin, Per F. Dahl, Shirley A. Fry, Stanley W. Pycior, Ruth Long, Barbara Wolff, Richard Evans, Robert McCabe, Elisabeth Crawford, Nathalie Huchette, Virginia Lewick, Ginette Gablot, Regis Babinet, Martha Chapin, Richard Fraser, Robert L. Wolker, Andy Oppenheimer, Diane E. Kaplan, Ben Stein, Joe Calabrise, Edward O'Donnell, and Jack Eckert. Lenka Brochard supplied many of the photos from the Archives Curie and Joliot-Curie.

This biography was greatly enriched by the efforts of previous Marie Curie biographers: Eve Curie, Robert Reid, Rosalynd Pflaum, Susan Quinn, Françoise Giroud, Nanny Froman, Naomi E. Pasachoff, Sharon Bertsch McGrayne, Karin Blanc, and Barbara Goldsmith. And of the major Frédéric Joliot-Curie biographers: Michel Pinault, Maurice Goldsmith, and Pierre Biquard. Many thanks, too, to the helpful staffs at the Curie Museum and Archives, the Bibliothèque Nationale, the Library of Congress, the National Archives, the American Institute of Physics, Cambridge University, Columbia University, and Smith College.

I could not have hoped for a more caring, careful, and encouraging editor than Hana Lane, who edited my previous biographies, *Einstein: A Life*, *Pulitzer: A Life*, and *The Unexpected Einstein: The Real Man Behind the Icon*. My wife, Martine, my partner in much of the research, also translated the French, and her guiding hand is evident on every page.

CHAPTER 1

Pierre Curie

1859–1894

C ity workers in Paris removed a tree obscuring a view of Victor Hugo's home, placed baskets of flowers in front of it, decked the street with flags, and sanded it to prepare for a million marching feet. It was the writer's eightieth birthday in February 1881. Members of guilds carrying their banners gathered at the Arc de Triomphe before joining the enormous parade. The entire Sorbonne turned out, faculty and students. And each time the white-haired author appeared at his window he was greeted with a roar of approval.

In May of that same year, scientist and fellow Parisian Louis Pasteur achieved immortality and changed the course of medical history with a daring experiment on fifty sheep infected with the deadly anthrax. His successful work led to the birth of the sciences of immunology and bacteriology, whose advances have saved the lives of millions. Experiments were also under way in the Parisian art world. Claude Monet and Pierre Renoir, among others, tried to capture the effect of light on their subjects with short brush strokes and bright colors. Although critics dismissed their efforts as childish or myopic impressions of reality, the small band of artists pressed on to make the slur "impressionist" an accolade. No musician caused more of a stir in Paris at the time than Camille Saint-Saens, a short, ill-tempered dandy who spoke with a lisp and looked like a parrot. He composed operas, concertos, and symphonies, conducted orchestras, and gave piano and organ concerts. In his spare time he penned plays and poetry, and also studied astronomy, archaeology, and the occult.

Living in the same city as Hugo, Pasteur, Renoir, Monet, and Saint-Saens was a twenty-two-year-old physicist at the start of his career. Though Pierre Curie's achievements would eventually rival those of his remarkable compatriots in his own field, at that time he wondered if he could keep his modest job as a lab assistant. It seemed unlikely, judging by an entry in his diary. And, if it was a clue to his character, he was certainly in the wrong profession. He sounded more like a poet in distress heading for a breakdown than an experimental scientist on the way up. "What shall I become?" he wrote. "Very rarely have I (complete) command of myself; ordinarily a part of me sleeps. My poor spirit, are you then so weak that you cannot control my body? Oh, my thoughts, you count indeed for very little! It seems to me that my mind gets clumsier every day. Before, I flung myself into scientific or other [diversions]; today they don't hold my interest. And I have so many, many things to do! Is my poor mind then so feeble that it cannot act upon my body? And Pride, Ambition—couldn't they at least propel me, or will they let me live like this? I should have the greatest confidence in the power of my imagination to pull myself out of this rut, but I greatly fear that my imagination is dead."

In her brief biography of Pierre, his widow, Marie, tried to explain this diary entry. She believed that when not fully engaged in scientific research he felt himself incomplete and became depressed. It was during such a time, she implied, that he made the diary entry. Yet his devastating self-analysis was recorded soon after he and his brother, Jacques, had made a scientific breakthrough. They had discovered that pressure on certain crystals produced electricity—later known as piezoelectricity. And their modus operandi had been reported by Jacques's teacher Charles Friedel at an Academy of Sciences meeting on August 2, 1880. Meanwhile the brothers were pursuing further research in piezoelectricity, which resulted in the publication of eight more papers on the subject. Yet it was during this time, while fully engaged in his work, that Pierre had expressed his fear of failure.

What a glaring contrast in confidence and spirit to both his father and his grandfather. His grandfather, Dr. Paul François Curie, had been a surgeon in the Military Hospital of Paris until he realized that conventional medicine killed as many as it cured—prompting him to leave France for England to pioneer a daring new system of healing, called homeopathy, in a London hospital. Homeopathy was a natural pharmaceutical science that made use of plants and minerals to stimulate the sick person's natural defenses. He gave his patients small doses of a medicine that in large doses would cause symptoms similar to those they were experiencing. Dr. Curie taught an Irishman, Joseph Kidd, to use the same method of healing. Kidd returned to Ireland during the potato famine of 1847 to give homeopathic

Pierre's grandfather, Paul François Curie, a political radical and a daring and enterprising physician, practiced homeopathic medicine in England.

treatment to those suffering from the fever and dysentery associated with starvation. "During 676 days he treated 111 cases with 108 cured, 1 dismissed, and 2 deaths—a mortality rate of 1.8% compared to the 13.8% mortality rate in the local hospital." Later, for several years Kidd was British prime minister Benjamin Disraeli's doctor.

A fervent practitioner, Dr. Paul Curie dedicated his book *Practice of Homeopathy* to fellow physicians and appealed to their scientific integrity to test the new treatment.

Pierre apparently had inherited none of his grandfather's enterprise, self-confidence, and commitment, nor did he inherit any of his father's drive and audacity. His quick-tempered, somewhat autocratic father, Eugène, was a man of action, with a scar to show for it. A bullet had shattered his jaw when, as a medical student at the Hôpital de la Pitié in Paris, during France's revolution of 1848, he took care of wounded rebels. He eagerly supported this successful insurrection against King Louis-Philippe, whose government of mostly noblemen had ignored the appalling conditions of the poor. The new republican government gave Eugène a medal for his honorable and courageous conduct. He again showed his mettle as a young doctor when a cholera epidemic broke out in Paris. Other doctors fled in panic, but Curie risked his life to go to the dreaded area and treat the victims.

His wife, Sophie Claire Depouilly, five years his junior, was the daughter of a once wealthy cloth manufacturer in Puteaux. When she was a teenager her father lost his fortune in a financial crisis brought on by the 1848 revolution. But she remained cheerful and optimistic, a loving wife and mother.

The Curies already had a three-year-old son, Jacques, when Pierre was born in Paris on May 15, 1859. Their house on the rue Cuvier overlooked the Jardin des Plantes, a sixty-acre complex of botanical gardens, a zoo, and the National Museum of Natural History, where for a time Dr. Curie worked in the laboratories. Jacques welcomed the newcomer to the family—and the brothers would become close, affectionate friends for life.

Convinced that Pierre was too sensitive and introspective for the rigid, highly structured atmosphere of a French classroom, his parents, and later his brother, taught him at home. Throughout the elementary and high school years they gave him a grounding in biology, chemistry, physics, and geometry. He made up for his lack of schooling in literature and history by reading many of the books in his father's large library. In her biography of her husband, Marie Curie explained why it would have been hopeless to send Pierre away to school: he could only learn a subject thoroughly by intense concentration, which he found impossible in a disturbing environment. "It is clear," she wrote, "that a mind of this kind can hold great future possibilities. But it is no less clear that no system of education can be especially provided by the public school for persons of this intellectual type. If, then, Pierre's earliest instruction was irregular and incomplete, it had the advantage of [freeing his mind from] dogmas, prejudices or preconceived ideas. And he was always grateful to his parents for this liberal attitude." Pierre called himself a slow thinker. Years later, Marie would be more generous. She believed that "Pierre's intellectual capacities were not those that would permit the rapid assimilation of a prescribed course of studies. His dreamer's spirit would not submit itself to the ordering of the intellectual effort imposed by the school." In other words, he would resist being told what to do and when to do it.

When Pierre was twelve, his father again supported the workers, this time in the uprising at the end of the Franco-German War (1870–1871), which Napoleon III had launched to boost his fading popularity. During the siege of Paris by the Germans, the desperate French government had reluctantly allowed Parisians to form a national guard to defend their surrounded city—reluctantly, because the government justifiably feared the independent spirit of Parisians. In February 1871 the French army, led by corrupt and inefficient officers, surrendered to German troops—who then planned what would have been to most Parisians a humiliating triumphant march down the Champs-Elysées. News of the proposed march strengthened the will of the national guard. They refused to surrender and resolved to discourage the march with some two hundred cannon. But, having made peace with the Germans, the French government now regarded its own national guard as the enemy and set out to disarm them. Government troops sent to Paris to retrieve the cannon—and forestall a revolution—were driven off by the guards, who were joined by an enraged crowd that killed two generals.

The government retreated to Versailles, while many affluent residents fled to the country and the ailing emperor Napoleon III and his wife, Eugenie, sought sanctuary in England. The rebels then took over most of Paris, erecting barricades in the main streets in anticipation of a government counterattack. At the Hôtel de Ville on March 28, 1871, they proclaimed a revolutionary republican government known as the Paris Commune. During its brief regime, its supporters, Communards, canceled rents for the period of the fighting, created unemployment exchanges, allowed workers to reopen and run all factories deserted by their owners, and established day nurseries near the factories. Men who had pawned their tools to avoid starvation during the siege—when they had been reduced to eating rats—were allowed to retrieve their tools without charge. The rebels also instituted free education for all, including women.

Two months later government troops entered the city to take it back, and began a bloodbath unique in French history. In a week of savage fighting they butchered at least 30,000 Parisians and possibly as many as 100,000 for a loss of only 750 soldiers. They executed men, women, and children in groups of fifty or one hundred in the Jardin du Luxembourg, the Champ de Mars, and the Parc Monceau, and burned some six hundred Communards trapped in the Hôtel de Ville. They massacred rebels manning the street barricades and buried some alive in a ditch. The rebels also committed atrocities, shooting sixty-seven hostages, including the archbishop of Paris. They demolished entire streets of houses and torched the Louvre, the Palais de Justice, and the royal residence, the Tuileries Palace.

Although Pierre's father had not joined in the fighting, his heart was with the rebels. He converted the family apartment—they were now living on place de la Visitation—into an emergency hospital and sent his sons, Jacques, now sixteen, and Pierre, twelve, into the streets to bring back the most seriously wounded for him to treat. Despite the horrors the boys witnessed and the deadly risk they took by helping the rebels, for the next two years after the defeat of the Communards the Curies continued to live in a city under martial law and from which thousands were shipped to penal colonies, including Devil's Island. Some who had supported the revolt became informers to save their own lives. Archibald Forbes, a *London Daily*

News correspondent, saw such turncoats in action. "Yesterday," he reported, Parisians "had cried, 'Vive la Commune.' Today they rubbed their hands with livid currish joy to have it in their power to denounce a Communist and reveal his hiding place.* They have found him, a tall, pale hatless man with something not ignoble in his carriage. The crowd yells — "Shoot him; shoot him!' An arm goes in the air, and there is a stick in the fist. The stick falls on the head of the man in black. Men club their rifles, and bring them down on that head, or slash them in splinters in their lust for murder. A certain British impulse prompts me to run forward. But it is useless. They are firing into the flaccid carcass now. His brains spurt on my foot and splash into the gutter, whither the carrion is bodily chucked, presently to be trodden on and rolled on by the feet of multitudes and wheels of gun carriages."

Even if twelve-year-old Pierre Curie had never witnessed such killings in the streets, knowledge of them must have affected the ultrasensitive youngster. It explains in part why, in 1883, Dr. Curie moved with his family to Fontenay-aux-roses, and finally, about two kilometers away, to a small, old house on the rue des Sablons in Sceaux, a peaceful, leafy spot southeast of Paris, a paradise for bird lovers, with a range of ponds several miles long. But the move to the country did not improve Dr. Curie's finances. As an outspoken radical he could hardly expect to attract wealthy patients even had he wished to, which is doubtful. Instead, he held poorly paid jobs, first as a medical inspector for an organization protecting children and later as a school doctor. Fortunately, none of his family had expensive tastes. His sons' idea of a great vacation was to spend entire days at nearby Draveil on the Seine, where they walked for hours along the riverbank, cooling off with a dip in the river. At home they explored the country outside Paris. Sometimes Pierre went alone, becoming so enthralled by his surroundings that he lost all sense of time and arrived home late at night exhilarated but physically exhausted.

When Pierre was fourteen, his father realized that he was exceptional at math, especially spatial geometry, and hired Professor Albert Bazille to teach him advanced mathematics. Bazille inspired him to such intense effort that despite his early casual home schooling, he matriculated at the prestigious Sorbonne at sixteen. There, in just two years, he got a degree in physics. Then, at eighteen, because his financial help was needed at

---

* In those days the terms *Communist*, *Communard*, and *Socialist* were used indiscriminately and interchangeably.

Pierre Curie at nineteen, in 1878. The following year, a close female friend died—of a cause that remains a mystery—and he decided to be a lifelong bachelor and to devote his life to science.

home, instead of pursuing a doctorate, he began to work as a physics lab assistant at the Sorbonne. It didn't hurt that his brother, Jacques, was already employed as an assistant in the mineralogy department. As a pacifist, having seen the horrors of war, Pierre avoided military service, otherwise mandatory for eighteen-year-old Frenchmen, by agreeing to spend ten years working in public education—something he had already started to do as a lab assistant.

At this time he was deeply in love with a young woman he had known since childhood, but he was reticent, even guarded, about their relationship. In fact her identity has never been revealed. She may have become the mistress he obliquely referred to in his diary when he noted that the least distraction could seriously disturb him—such as when his mother kissed him. Though, strangely, he wrote that the kiss of a mistress was less "dangerous, because [it] can answer a purely physical need." Dangerous? Perhaps a less sensitive and introspective young scientist would have lightheartedly remarked that he welcomed his mistress's kisses more than his mother's. But to the easily distracted Pierre, apparently neither was welcome when he was engrossed in scientific speculation.

He explained this "weakness" in his diary, writing that to prevent his mind from flying away "on every wind that blows, yielding to the slightest breath it encounters," everything had to be motionless around him, or else, to overcome his surroundings, his mind had to be like "a humming top, the movement itself making me insensible to what is happening around me." He complained that his mother never seemed to understand this, adding, "Whenever, rotating slowly, I attempt to speed up [my mind], the merest nothing—a word, a story, a newspaper, a visit—stops me from becoming a gyroscope or top, and can postpone or forever delay the time when, with enough speed I might be able to concentrate despite my surroundings."

One welcome distraction was reading novels, and he was especially taken with Emile Zola's recent assertion in *The Experimental Novel* that novelists should adopt a scientific approach and become biologists of society. Zola had tried this by spending a few days in Lourdes on a fact-finding mission. He incorporated the facts and his impressions in a novel, *Lourdes*. In it he concluded that miracles, as such, did not exist, but that many people needed to believe in them—a rationalist view Pierre shared.

Yet it seemed something of a miracle that despite distractions and his despondency Pierre was able to marshal his "flying thoughts" to produce his first original work, in partnership with lab director Professor Paul Desains. They found a new, simple, and effective way to measure the wavelengths of heat waves, using a metallic wire grating and a thermoelectric element.

After that, Pierre's partnerships were invariably with his brother, Jacques, who shared his absorbing interest in nature and scientific research. They were so compatible, in fact, that they almost communicated telepathically. Or, as Pierre said, there was no need for them to speak to understand what the other was thinking. They also looked alike, dressed alike, sported beards, and wore similar rumpled clothes. They worked and played well together. The big difference between them was their relationship with their father. Jacques had such violent quarrels with him that it "scared their mother," said Pierre, who rarely raised his voice and would simply walk away from a potential quarrel.

The charming, intelligent parents imposed no religious strictures and encouraged their sons to think for themselves. Though nominally a Protestant, Dr. Eugène Curie did not follow any organized religion, believing, like his doctor father, that one should "do in this life that which Christianity expects only of the next life." He lived his beliefs, according to Marie Curie, being a loving husband and father, extremely unselfish, ready to help all in need, and completely uninterested in making money. Politically, the Curies subscribed to the republican ideal of "Liberté! Egalité! Fraternité!"

In his early twenties, Pierre Curie leans on the shoulder of his older brother, Jacques. His parents, Dr. Eugène and Sophie Claire, had realized that the ultrasensitive Pierre required an unorthodox education.

When Dr. Curie worked in the laboratory of the Museum of Natural History in Paris, he had imbued his sons with his own awestruck love of nature and the urge to bare its secrets. Although he wished to devote his life to full-time scientific research, he had to give it up in order to support his family as a physician. However, in his free time he investigated the possibility of using inoculations to prevent tuberculosis. His sons often headed for the fields and woods outside the city to bring back unusual plants, insects, and small animals for him to study and discuss with them. On these expeditions, Pierre showed a childlike reaction to almost everything he saw, appearing spellbound at the sight of a frog and staring with wonder at an elaborate cobweb.

These were therapeutic as well as delightful encounters, and he explained that when he was twenty he needed such trips to escape "from the thousand little worrying things that torment me in Paris."

Despite his scientific achievements, the unspecified torments in Paris overwhelmed him, so that at twenty-two he saw himself as a weak-willed failure lacking imagination and ambition. Another persistent torment was his inability to stop feeling guilty for the death two years earlier of the woman he had loved. He never explained how she died and why he blamed himself, and it continued to haunt him. Even when writing to his future wife, Marie, some fifteen years after the tragedy, Pierre couldn't bear to give her the details: "When I was twenty I had a dreadful misfortune. I lost, in terrible circumstances, a childhood friend whom I loved. I haven't the courage to tell you all about it. I was very guilty. I had and will always have a great remorse about it. I went through days and nights with a fixed idea, and experienced a sort of delight in torturing myself. Then I vowed . . . to lead a priest's existence. I promised myself to be interested only in *things* after that, and never again to think of either myself or of mankind. Since the tragedy I have often asked if this renunciation of life was not simply a trick I used against myself to acquire the right to forget."

Since the tragedy, he had struggled to resist the wiles of seductive women and his own natural inclinations, and he began to define his attitude toward women in poetic, tortured, and somewhat misogynistic terms: "Women, much more than men, love life for life's sake," he wrote when twenty-two. "Women of genius are rare. Also, when we are impelled by some mystic love to enter into a life opposed to nature, when we devote all our thoughts to some task that removes us from those immediately about us, it is with women that we have to struggle. The mother wants the love of her child above all things, even if it should make an imbecile of him. The mistress also wishes to possess her lover, and would find it natural to sacrifice the rarest genius in the world for an hour of love. The struggle is almost always an unequal one because it is in the name of life and nature that they try to bring us back."

How did he maintain the struggle for some fifteen years? He confided to his diary a need to eat, drink, sleep, relax, and love, "that is to touch the sweetest things in this life, and yet not succumb." To do that "one must make the anti-natural thought to which one has devoted one's life remain dominant. . . . One must make of life a dream, and of that dream a reality." So he lost himself in work that intrigued him, investigating, with his brother, crystals, one of nature's many examples of symmetry. Pierre had marveled at the near-perfect symmetry of flowers and snowflakes, as well as the eyes, ears, and limbs of humans and animals—the tiger's "dreadful" symmetry that inspired one of William Blake's greatest poems. Although Pierre had also occasionally tried his hand at poetry, it was as a scientist that he chose to focus on the properties and symmetries of crystals.

He and his brother already knew that crystals heated in a fire attracted ash and wood to their surfaces like magnets. And they had heard of the discovery by Scottish physicist Lord Kelvin that when he heated certain crystals they generated electricity. This became known as pyroelectricity. The question was whether pyroelectricity applied to all crystals. Jacques's mentor, Charles Friedel, believed that it did and asked the Curie brothers to test his theory. They did, disproving it. The Curie brothers then went one step further, trying to prove that pressure on some crystals had the same effect as heat. Starting in 1879 and using remarkably simple equipment— a jeweler's saw, tinfoil, hardened rubber, and a vise—they put various crystals to the test. The results confirmed their theory: under pressure some crystals produced electricity.

In 1881 the brothers also experimentally confirmed Sorbonne professor Gabriel Lippman's theory that applying electricity to a crystal distorted its shape and made it vibrate, a discovery that would eventually have tremendous significance.

Marie Curie emphasized that the enterprise was more sophisticated than it sounds. "Their experiment," she wrote, "led the two young physicists to a great success: the discovery of the hitherto unknown phenomenon piezoelectricity [as it became known, from the Greek *piezine*, 'to press'], which consists of an electric polarization produced by the compression of the expansion of crystals in the direction of the axis of symmetry. This was by no means a chance discovery. It was the result of much reflection on the symmetry of crystalline matter which enabled the brothers to foresee the possibility of such polarization. The first part of the investigation was made in Friedel's laboratory [of mineralogy at the Sorbonne, where Jacques was Professor Friedel's assistant]. With experimental skill rare at their age, the young men succeeded in making a complete study of the new phenomenon, established the conditions of symmetry necessary to its production in crystals, and stated its remarkably simple quantitative laws, as well as its absolute magnitude for certain crystals. Several well-known scientists of other nations [Roentgen, Kundt, Voigt, Riecke] have made further investigations along this new road opened by Jacques and Pierre Curie."

To measure the minute amounts of electricity produced, Pierre, who was clever with his hands, invented and built an instrument he called an electrometer. Though there was no other immediate use for it, time and fate would change that most dramatically. The nine papers on piezoelectricity that he and his brother eventually published exhaustively covered the subject. Their discovery is partly responsible for today's electronics industry and the ongoing search for additional uses of piezoelectricity in the growing field of solid-state physics. Piezoelectricity was used in World War I in a device called sonar, which created sound waves underwater able to detect enemy submarines, torpedoes, mines, and icebergs. These sound waves were reflected back as echoes by all objects in their path, and when the echoes were converted into electricity, an operator could determine the object's range, speed, and position. During World War II, the U.S. government used some fifty million quartz crystal elements for various purposes. And in 1954 a crystal was used to convert sunlight into electricity. Today, crystals are also used in microphones, electronic components, and quartz watches. A quartz crystal is stable even in extremes of temperature, so that a police officer using a two-way radio can move from a warm room to a freezing street and the crystals in the transmitter and receiver remain exactly on the correct frequency.

When Pierre was twenty-four, Jacques married and left to be head lecturer in mineralogy at the University of Montpellier hundreds of miles away in southern France, but they continued their joint research on crystals during their vacations. About the same time Pierre also quit the Sorbonne to take charge of the laboratory at the new School of Industrial Physics and Chemistry of the City of Paris. There, although able to conduct his own experiments, he also had to teach a class of thirty students. One of the most promising, Paul Langevin, recalled that his first impression of the new lab director was of a timid and awkward young man with a childlike laugh. But in time, though still shy, he became more assured and revealed "a flame of enthusiasm that inspired and encouraged his students." Then Langevin would return "with joy to [Curie's] laboratory, where it was good to work near him. He loved to stand in front of the blackboard and talk with us, to awaken interesting possibilities in us, and to speak of the work which was developing our taste for science." Once while he was teaching two students, either Pierre or his subject was so compelling that the trio lost all sense of time. And when they tried to leave, they found that the custodian had locked them in the second-floor room. To avoid spending the night on the floor, they all climbed through a window and down a drainpipe.

Pierre's opportunities to conduct his own experiments were extremely limited. In those days, he never had a proper laboratory entirely for himself and could use one only when students didn't need it. Otherwise he had to make do with a cramped corridor between a stairway and a classroom. Despite these restrictions, he formulated the principle of symmetry on which much of modern physics relies, invented and built the ultrasensitive scientific weighing machine, the "Curie Scale," and began to investigate magnetism.

First he tried to see if he could make diamagnetic substances more magnetic by subjecting them to intense heat, but he couldn't. He then collected ferromagnetics (highly magnetic materials such as iron, cobalt, nickel, and some alloys) and put them to the same test. The result was a scientific breakthrough. As he increased the temperature they lost their magnetic characteristics until they became paramagnetic—only slightly magnetic. Today this temperature is known as the Curie point or Curie temperature. He also formulated a fundamental law, called Curie's law, stating that the magnetic power of a magnetic material varies in inverse proportion to the absolute temperature (zero).

For a decade he had lived up to his vow to devote himself entirely to his work. Not that he became a hermit. He went to art galleries and concerts, and continued to write poetry. He had several male friends, among them a cousin, Louis Depouilly; Albert Bazille, an engineer and son of his former math tutor; and a young doctor, Louis Vauthier. But Pierre avoided any serious relationship with a woman, which partly explains how at thirty-two he had achieved so much in his scientific work.

Yet for all the prestige he brought to the new school with his scientific discoveries, his teaching skill, and his devotion to work, Pierre Curie got about the same wage as a skilled factory hand. Then someone said that he could get a salary increase by applying to replace a professor about to resign. The problem was that a candidate, like a politician, had to canvass for support from others. And the retiring, modest man despised the convention and dreaded the prospect. As he explained in a letter rejecting the opportunity: "I am not accustomed to this form of activity, demoralizing in the highest degree. I think that nothing is more unhealthy to the spirit than to allow oneself to be occupied with things of this character and to listen to the petty gossip people come to report to you."

Though money generally didn't mean much to Pierre, there was a time when he was not reluctant to make a little extra, judging by his note on March 29, 1882, to Georges Gouy, a friend who bought several instruments Pierre had invented: "Thanks to you Lyon will be the city where our most important firm will make its biggest profits." In a fiercely competitive world, he not only refused to compete but put the kibosh on a proposal by the director of the school to recommend him for a government decoration in recognition of his contributions to science: "I pray you do not do so," he replied. "If you procure for me this honor, you will place me under the necessity of refusing it, for I have firmly decided not to accept a decoration of any kind. I hope you will be good enough to avoid taking a step that will make me appear a little ridiculous in the eyes of many people. If your aim is to offer me a testimony of your interest, you have already done that, and in a very much more effective manner which touched me greatly, for you have made it possible for me to work without worry."

Although Pierre was hardly known outside a small scientific circle in France, an account of his work reached Lord Kelvin, the Scottish physicist of international renown. A major contributor to the laws of thermodynamics, Kelvin had published over six hundred papers on scientific subjects and patented seventy inventions. Both practical and gifted with a great imagination, Kelvin had directed the laying of the first successful transatlantic cable in 1866 and speculated that the germs of life on earth had come from another planet. He had also estimated the earth's age—the time it would take to cool from a molten state—as between 20 and 40 million years (the present-day estimate is 4.6 billion years).* A frequent visitor to Paris, Kelvin knew that the Curies' work competed with his. Having noted the effect of heat on crystals, Kelvin had expanded his research into their other properties. Now, reading of the Curie brothers' experiments, he realized that they had beaten him to it. To check their results he asked Pierre if he could send him an electrometer. Soon after Pierre sent one to him, as well as a piece of piezoelectric quartz, Kelvin responded on August 1893: "I thank you very much for having taken the trouble to obtain for me the apparatus by which I can so conveniently observe the magnificent experimental discovery of piezoelectric quartz made by you and your brother. I have written a note to the Philosophical Magazine, making it clear that your work preceded mine."

Two months later, Kelvin called on Pierre at his laboratory, where they talked shop for hours. This first of many visits led to their becoming friends, both having lost their innate shyness when discussing work. Had Kelvin claimed piezoelectricity as his discovery, Pierre would not have challenged him, according to Marie Curie, who characterized his attitude

* When Rutherford later estimated the earth's age to be billions of years (taking radioactivity into account), he had to present this result in a lecture. The story is that, discovering that old Lord Kelvin was in the audience, he searched for how to explain things without contradicting this most respected physicist. So he quoted Kelvin's calculations, adding, "Which naturally could not take into account an unknown source of energy." E-mail from Hélène Langevin-Joliot to the author, May 17, 2002.

as "that of a superior person who had reached the highest level of civiliza-tion," and his actions as those "of a really good man, full of understanding and forbearance, who was endowed with a strong sympathy for human nature." The work and the work alone was what mattered and not the indi-vidual. "What difference is there," he once said, "if I have not published the work as long as someone has?" He found competition so distasteful that he even opposed school examinations and ranking, as well as all dis-tinctions and honors. Not that he ignored the talent of others. He encour-aged and advised those he considered gifted and "was always disposed to aid anyone in a difficult situation and even to give of his time, which was the greatest sacrifice he could make." If Marie seems too partial, describ-ing Pierre Curie as a flawless, almost saintly, man, no one has contradicted her—at least on the record.

His reputation for helping others explains why, in the spring of 1894, a Polish physics professor, Joseph Kowalski, invited him and Marie Sklodowska to a tea party in his rented apartment. Kowalski first met Marie when she was a governess in Poland, and now, while on his honey-moon in Paris and doing some lecturing, they met again. Marie, at the start of her scientific career, had told him of her futile search for a place to conduct experiments. And Kowalski believed that his friend Pierre Curie, a thirty-five-year-old bachelor, was just the man to help her.

CHAPTER 2

Marie Salomea Sklodowska

1867–1894

U nlike Pierre Curie, Marie Sklodowska had grown up in a police state under the autocratic Russian czar Alexander II. Although known as "the Liberator"—he had emancipated Russian and Polish serfs—he was determined to enslave the intellectual and middle-class Poles who had opposed his rule, and to eradicate their language, culture, and history. Polish law courts were disestablished, Russian became the official language, Russian officials and teachers replaced Poles, and Poland disappeared from maps to reappear as Vistula Land. Even speaking Polish became a criminal offense. In 1864, the Russians had savagely suppressed a rebellion in which Poles wielding spades, scythes, and clubs had battled rifle-wielding Cossacks.

Marie's paternal uncle Zdzislav, twice wounded in the uprising, had escaped to France. Her maternal uncle Henryk was captured and sent in chains to Siberia along with tens of thousands of others. Five rebel leaders were publicly hanged in Warsaw, the city where Marie was born three years later, on November 7, 1867. Her parents, Vladislav and Bronislava, already had three daughters and a son: Sophie, six; Joseph, four; Bronia, three; and Hela, eighteen months. Marie's father, a professor and assistant principal of a boys' school, taught physics and mathematics, which he loved. Her mother was headmistress and director of a prestigious girls' boarding school nearby. She was a devout Catholic, while Marie's father, nominally a Catholic, was a free-thinking skeptic.

As a baby, Marie lived with her family in an apartment at the rear of her mother's private school on Freta Street. After her father was demoted,

Marie Curie's mother, Bronislava Sklodowska, a devout Catholic, had been headmistress of a girls' school in Warsaw. There was a good reason why she never kissed her children.

probably to be replaced by a Russian, he was transferred from central Warsaw to another school on Novolipki Street near the Jewish quarter, on the western outskirts of the city. There he was eventually promoted to under-inspector and his salary increased. Being more financially secure, Marie's mother gave up her career to be a full-time housewife.

Bronislava kept all her children at arm's length but her apparent coldness was an act of loving concern. It was the way she tried to protect them from the tuberculosis she had contracted soon after Marie's birth. Not understanding this, young Marie wondered why, that before she went to sleep, her mother gently stroked her forehead but never kissed her. And in the daytime, when Marie tried to take her hand or embrace her, she would be rebuffed and told to play outside in the fresh air. For months at a time Bronislava was separated from her family—and longing to return—seeking a cure in health spas in Austria and on the French Riviera. Marie, too, longed for her mother's return, as she missed her loving presence, which she felt was the soul of the house. Marie also missed hearing her play the piano while singing in a lovely, languid voice. And she admired how, when money was tight, her unpretentious mother taught herself cobbling and was not too proud to make her children's shoes.

Such economizing became essential when Vladislav was again demoted and had to leave his school-financed lodgings, either because he was

Despite their solemn expressions in this 1870 photo, the Sklodowski children (from left) Sophie, Hela, Marie, Joseph, and Bronia, were a lively bunch—their home was often alive with screams, arguments, and laughter.

too obviously a Polish patriot or to make way for a Russian. He eventually found another place to live as well as a new way to support his family. He established a boys' boarding school in the family home—to Marie's great regret. As she later explained, the family's "existence, once so peaceful and sweet, gradually suffered. The professor took two or three boarders at first—then five, eight, ten. He gave lodging, food, and private instruction to these young boys, chosen from among his pupils. The house was transformed into a noisy barracks and intimacy vanished from family life." To Marie it meant having to sleep on a moleskin divan in the dining room and be awakened at dawn, still sleepy, to allow the boarders to have breakfast there. After five o'clock tea, servants cleared the dining room to convert it into a study for Marie and her siblings to do their homework, with background noises from the nearby boarders. This was compounded by the antics of the adored family dog, Lancet, a massively overweight brown pointer that defied training and chewed the furniture, grabbed and ate any food within reach, and gave every new arrival a frantic, affectionate welcome.

When Marie was nine, one of the boarders caught typhus and fourteen-year-old Sophie was infected with the disease, which killed her. Marie was stunned by the death of her brilliant and high-spirited sister. She felt the loss as a violent physical blow, and throughout her life tragic events would always affect her this way. A talented actress and writer, Sophie had kept the family spellbound with her clever comedy sketches and fantastic stories. And she had been an affectionate and capable nurse-companion for her ailing mother during long trips abroad on a futile search for a cure. Too weak to leave the house, Sophie's heartbroken mother watched from her bedroom window as the funeral procession for her firstborn moved along dreary Carmelite Street to the cemetery. Marie, in a black dress, was among the mourners.

A year later, at ten, Marie left home to attend a private boarding school, where her teacher, Mlle Antonina Tupalska, doted on her. Though two years younger than most of her twenty-four classmates, Marie invariably beat them all in history, literature, German, and French. The daring and patriotic Mlle Tupalska taught Polish history in Polish—a practice forbidden by the Russian overlords. To avoid being caught using her native language, she arranged for the school porter to signal a warning—two long, then two short rings of an electric bell—should the government inspector appear unexpectedly. When the bell rang one morning, Polish-language books and papers were quickly loaded into the aprons of four girls, who took them to the dormitory and then returned to their desks. Moments later the uniformed inspector entered the room to observe twenty-five girls in starch-collared blue-serge uniforms at sewing class, calmly making buttonholes. Under interrogation Mlle Tupalska admitted that she had been reading from Krylov's *Fairy Tales* just before the inspector arrived. Of course, she said, it was in Russian, and she showed him the book. The Polish edition she *had* been reading was safely hidden in the dormitory with other forbidden Polish-language literature.

The inspector next called for a girl to face an oral exam exclusively in Russian. Marie, the smallest, youngest, and brightest student in the class, was often chosen. But she was a timid child whose first reaction was to hide. When Mlle Tupalska named her, she stood and anxiously waited for the inspector's questions. He asked for the Lord's Prayer, which she repeated in flawless Russian. Then, at his prompting, and speaking Russian throughout, she named all the Russian czars since Catherine II, as well as the names and titles of the reigning royal family, and replied to the inspector's final question: "Who rules over us?" with a reluctant "His Majesty Alexander II, czar of all the Russians." There was a huge sigh of relief the moment the inspector left. And when the grateful Mlle Tupalska kissed Marie on the forehead, the sensitive ten-year-old burst into tears.

Marie's happiest times were during family vacations, when, in her words, to escape "the strict watch of the police in the city, we took refuge with friends in the country. There we found the free life of the old-fashioned family estates, races in the woods, and joyous participation in work in the grain fields." Some areas of Poland that they visited were controlled by Austria rather than by Russia, so her family could even speak Polish and sing patriotic songs without fear of prison.

Marie treasured any time she could spend with the mother she idolized. "Her influence over me was extraordinary," she later recalled, "for in me the natural love of the little girl for her mother was united with a passionate admiration." When it became clear that her mother was dying, Marie prayed desperately for God to take her instead of her mother. Bronislava had grown skeptical of doctors' optimistic predictions and hoped for a miracle cure, confiding to a friend that God alone could restore her health. One day, just over two years after Sophie had succumbed to typhus, Bronislava Sklodowska called her husband and children to her room. As she lay in her bed, she barely had the strength to make the sign of the cross over their heads and to murmur that she loved them. She died the next day, aged forty-two. The loss of someone she loved most in the world sent Marie into a deep depression, and she often broke down and cried inconsolably.

Professor Sklodowski had been deeply in love with his wife and never remarried. A decade later, he remembered her in a poem as an angelic woman whose death turned his world into a graveyard. Now responsible for four motherless children and ten boarders, the professor hired a series of housekeepers. After a period of mourning, he resumed his active part in his children's studies and their free time. Every Saturday evening he read aloud to them and a few chosen boarders patriotic Polish poems and prose—in forbidden Polish—which fortified Marie's love of poetry and hatred of her country's oppressors. An exceptional linguist, he read in a pleasant, resonant voice the English edition of Dickens's *David Copperfield*, translating it effortlessly into Polish as he went along. At other times he showed the children a playful way to study geography by coloring wood blocks to represent countries, cities, mountains, and rivers, and by clipping relevant articles and photographs from magazines. He taught them military history by using the blocks as opposing armies, and imbued Marie, especially, with his love of science and nature. Naturally concerned with their health after the deaths of his wife and daughter, he made sure that they exercised frequently.

To pay for his late wife's medical expenses, Vladislav invested all of his savings in an enterprise recommended by a brother-in-law. He lost everything and felt that he had jeopardized his children's future for the investment. And he never forgave himself.

Although Marie still went to the church she had attended with her mother, she now experienced, as she later recalled, "the secret stir of revolt within her," and "no longer invoked with the same love that God who had unjustly inflicted such terrible blows."

There were welcome changes when the family moved from bleak Carmelite Street to a large first-floor apartment on colorful Leschen Street in a charming building with a quiet courtyard in the rear and a Virginia-creeper-covered balcony in front. It was large enough for the family to have four rooms to themselves and away from the noisy boarders in a fifth room. Marie did not always resent these boys. She and her sister Hela even fell desperately in love with the same boy, Vitold Romocki, who lived with them for six years. They fought and cried over him so fiercely that Hela thought of recording their passion in a novel titled *Sisters—Rivals*. But neither ended up with him and no novel appeared.

Meanwhile, the professor had fired the last of a succession of unsatisfactory housekeepers and his eldest daughter, Bronia, a high-school graduate with a gold medal for high marks, took over. Her brother, Joseph, also a gold medalist, started training to be a doctor at Warsaw's Faculty of Medicine. And Marie began, with trepidation, to attend a Russian-controlled high school on Krakovsky Boulevard. She hated its denigration of everything Polish and recalled that "the moral atmosphere was altogether unbearable. Constantly held in suspicion and spied upon, children knew that a single conversation in Polish, or an imprudent word, might seriously harm not only themselves but also their families. Amid these hostilities, they lost all joy of life, and precocious feelings of distrust and indignation weighed upon their childhood. On the other side, this abnormal situation resulted in exciting patriotic feeling of Polish youths to the highest degree." There were compensations: Marie loved several fellow students and had crushes on some Polish teachers. And she expressed her ambivalence to her best friend, Kazia Przyborowska, while vacationing in the country: "In spite of everything I like school . . . and even love it. I can realize that now. Don't go imagining that I miss it! Oh no, not at all. But the idea that I am going back soon does not depress me, and the two years I have left to spend there don't seem dreadful, as painful and long as they once did."

Kazia and Marie walked together to school every day, each carrying her lunch of bread, an apple, and two Polish sausages in a cloth bag. They took weekly dancing classes at Marie's home. One of the favorite haunts of the high-spirited fourteen-year-olds was the Saxony Gardens, where, on rainy days and wearing overshoes, they played the game of who could walk through the deepest pool without getting her feet wet. In another game each had to respond to the other by using a sentence with the word *green* in it, or by pointing out or touching a green object. For example, Marie might say she must buy a new notebook and wanted one with a green cover, and Kazia, to avoid paying a forfeit, might hand over a small piece of green velvet that she kept in her pocket for this moment. Then Marie might mention the time a teacher had turned green with embarrassment, and so on. The idea was to keep going as long as possible, a sort of verbal tennis volley.

Game playing didn't prevent them from expressing their revolutionary fervor. Whenever they passed a memorial to Poles faithful to the czar—whom the girls regarded as traitors—they always spat. And Mlle Mayer, the superintendent of studies, once caught them dancing joyfully in the classroom after hearing that Czar Alexander II had been killed by an assassin's bomb (on March 13, 1881, after several attempts on his life). When the brother of a friend was sentenced to death for revolutionary activity, Marie and her sisters, Hela and Bronia, and Kazia and her sister, Ua, sat up with the desperate girl throughout the night and prayed with her at dawn when the young man was hanged.

Mlle Mayer was a tiny woman who prowled the school corridors in slippers on the hunt for rule breakers and was Marie's bête noire. She took exception to what she called Marie's stubborn character, scornful smile, and disorderly and "ridiculous hair," once wielding a brush and trying in vain—being a head shorter—to reach up and straighten out the curls. As Marie stared down at her, the exasperated little woman exclaimed: "I forbid you to look at me like that! You mustn't look down on me!" To which Marie replied: "The fact is that I can't do anything else." Mlle Mayer could neither straighten her hair nor curb her spirit.

Marie graduated from high school at fifteen and at the top of her class on June 12, 1883, a sweltering day. As a gold medalist, and wearing a black dress with roses pinned at the waist, she followed in the footsteps of Bronia and Joseph. Her proud father watched Marie shake hands with her teachers, receive her medal from Monsieur Apushtin, grand master of education in Russian Poland, give a final curtsy, and collect several Russian books as her prizes.

Realizing that Marie was emotionally and physically exhausted, her father arranged for her to recuperate for a year in the country, staying with a series of relatives. After that she could think about a job. He agreed to pay a nominal amount toward her board and lodging, and she would help to earn her keep by giving occasional lessons to her younger cousins. Otherwise her time would be her own. It was just what she needed. In letters to Kazia—"My dear little devil" and "Kazia, my heart"—she said she had forgotten that geometry and algebra existed and that apart from giving a little boy an hour's French lesson, she hadn't done a stroke of work, not even finishing a piece of embroidery she had started.

I get up sometimes at ten o'clock, sometimes at four or five (morning, not evening!) I read . . . only harmless and absurd little novels. Sometimes I laugh all by myself, and I contemplate my state of total stupidity with genuine satisfaction. We go out in a band to walk in the woods, we roll hoops, we play battledore and shuttlecock (at which I am very bad!) cross-tag, the game of Goose, and many equally childish things. There have been so many wild strawberries here that one could buy a big plateful heaped high for a few groszy. Alas the season is over. I am afraid when I get back my appetite will be unlimited and my voracity alarming. We swing a lot, swinging ourselves hard and high; we bathe, we go fishing with torches for shrimps . . . Every Sunday the horses are harnessed for a trip to Mass, and afterward we pay a visit to the vicarage. The two priests are clever and very witty, and we get enormous amusement from their company. I was at Zwola for a few days. There was an actor there, M. Kotarbiński, [a leading thirty-five-year-old Polish actor, director, and author] who delighted us. He sang so many songs and recited so many verses, concocted so many jokes and picked so many gooseberries for us, that on the day of his departure we made him a great wreath of poppies, wild pinks, and cornflowers, and just as the carriage was starting off we flung it at him with shouts of Vivat! Vivat! M. Kotarbiński! He put the wreath on his head immediately, and carried it in a suitcase all the way to Warsaw. Ah, how gay life is in Zwola! There are always a great many people, and a freedom, equality, and independence such as you can hardly imagine. On our journey back Lancet barked so much that we didn't know what was to become of us.

While staying with her farmer uncle Xavier, who kept fifty thoroughbred horses on his estate, Marie borrowed riding breeches from a cousin and before she left was an accomplished horsewoman. She spent the winter with her father's brother, Uncle Zdzislav, a notary, near the snowcapped Carpathian mountains. He had a beautiful wife and four daughters, who were frequently convulsed with laughter. One of their many parties was a masked ball for which Marie, her aunt, and her cousins dressed as peasant girls. Then they rode to the ball through the snowy night in two sleighs, their way lit by torch-bearing young men on horseback, also dressed as peasants. Four Jewish fiddlers from the village also riding in a sleigh and bound for the ball caught up with them and played waltzes and mazurkas as they rode alongside for the rest of the journey. Afterward, Marie gave Kazia an excited account of the very handsome boys from Kraków at the ball, all great dancers, with whom she danced till eight next morning.

In July 1884, Marie had just returned home to Warsaw after a rejuvenating year away. A former student of Marie's mother, the young wife of Count de Fleury, called on Professor Sklodowski and invited Marie and her sister Hela to spend the rest of the summer at her country estate. The next day, the two young women headed by train for the countess's beautiful home. They were met at the station by a uniformed coachman, who drove them in a four-horse carriage toward the start of what Hela would never forget as the best and craziest summer she had ever spent. Marie would surely have agreed. Several weeks later, she told Kazia about the marvelous time when she was learning to swim and row in the nearby river and to "do everything that comes into our heads. We sleep sometimes at night and sometimes by day, we dance, and we run to such follies that sometimes we deserve to be locked up in an asylum for the insane." The follies included practical jokes inflicted on other guests. Marie was the ringleader, hanging from the rafters, with the help of a friendly gardener, all the contents of one young man's room, including his bed; putting poison ivy in his shoes; waiting until the count and his older guests were exploring the spectacular garden to grab and eat the pastries that were meant for them, and leaving a straw man sitting in the count's chair; stealing a big basket of gooseberries from the kitchen; and presenting their hosts, who were celebrating their fourteenth wedding anniversary, with an enormous bouquet of vegetables. Marie also recited a poem she had composed for the occasion, which ended:

> We expect a picnic
> Ask some boys for us,
> One boy for each of us,
> So that, following your example,
> We may climb as soon as possible —
> As soon as possible —
> Up the steps of the altar.

In the past eight weeks the countess had organized three balls, two garden parties, boating trips, and various charades. And in response to marriage-minded Marie's poem, instead of a picnic she announced a grand ball. Because Marie could not afford a new dress and new shoes for the ball, she altered an old dress to look different and bought shoes in which she danced until dawn, completely wearing away the soles.

When Marie returned to Warsaw in September, she joined her family in a smaller, cheaper apartment on Novolipki Street. After thirty years of teaching, her father was preparing for his eventual retirement on a small pension that would not allow him to support his children much longer. To help out, Joseph put an ad in a local paper saying that he was a medical student available for private tutoring and that Marie, "a young lady with diploma," was offering for a moderate price to give "lessons in arithmetic, geometry, and French." It was a frustrating and unrewarding experience for Marie, involving long walks across town in wintry weather to teach pupils who were either stubborn, lazy, late, or so disorganized that they forgot to pay her.

After a disappointing year, she decided to leave home to be a governess in a lawyer's family. Eve Curie points out in her biography of her mother that the naive eighteen-year-old had expected to love the family she was joining, hoping to find pleasant children and understanding parents. It was a disaster, and in a letter to a cousin, she gave a devastating critique of the family among whom she felt a prisoner:

> I shouldn't like my worst enemy to live in such a hell. My relations with [the wife] had become so icy that I could not endure it any longer and told her so. Since she was exactly as enthusiastic about me as I was about her, we understood each other marvelously well. It was one of those rich houses where they speak French when there is company—a chimney-sweeper's kind of French—where they don't pay their bills for six months, and fling money out of the window even though they economize pettily on oil for the lamps. They have five servants. They pose as liberals and, in reality, they are sunk in the darkest stupidity. And, although they speak in most sugary tones, slander and scandal rage through their talk—slander which leaves not a rag on anybody. I learned to know the human race a little better by being there. I learned that the characters described in novels really do exist, and that one must not enter into contact with people who have been demoralized by wealth.

Meanwhile, her elder sister, Bronia, had her own worries. Wanting to study medicine in Paris—women were barred from Russian-controlled Polish colleges—she had raised enough money for the journey and tuition. But when she reached Paris she hadn't enough left to survive on even in the inexpensive Latin Quarter. Marie longed to join her, so the two came to an agreement that made it possible for them both to study there, albeit one at a time. Marie would escape from her "prison" and accept another job she had been offered at a good salary, also as a governess. Her new employer, Mr. Zorawski, managed the estate and farmed the lands of the Princess Czartoryski, a hundred kilometers north of Warsaw. From her salary she promised to subsidize Bronia—to augment their father's small amount—until she graduated and got a job as a doctor. Then Bronia in turn would support Marie's stay in Paris until she, too, graduated.

As her father was about to see Marie off at the railroad station, she panicked. He was getting old. Would she ever see him again? And would this family be as bad as the horror she had just left? Had she made a terrible mistake? Facing a three-hour train journey, to be followed by five hours in a horse-drawn sleigh, she had never felt so alone, and wept part of the way. She arrived exhausted on a freezing night and was welcomed by her employers with hot tea and friendly greetings, after which Mme Zorawski led her upstairs to her big, quiet bedroom.

Compared with her recent experience, her early days here were idyllic. The oldest daughter, Bronka, about Marie's age, became more companion than pupil. After the lessons were over, Bronka and Marie's main charge, ten-year-old Andzia, joined her for walks in the countryside and to skate on the nearby ice-bound river. The other children at home were Stas, three, and six-month-old Martyshna. Two older sons were away at Warsaw University and a third was in boarding school.

As she later wrote, "I took the greatest interest in the agricultural development of the estate where the methods were considered as models for the region. I knew the progressive details of the work, the distribution of crops in the fields (mostly sugar beets); I eagerly followed the growth of the plants, and in the stables of the farm I knew the horses. In winter the vast plains, covered with snow, were not lacking in charm, and we went for long sleigh rides. Sometimes we could hardly see the road. 'Look out for the ditch!' I would call out to the driver. 'You are going straight into it,' and 'Never fear!' he would answer, as over we went! But these tumbles only added to the gaiety of our excursions."

Most evenings she devoted to her own studies—literature and sociology—but eventually decided that if she ever got to Paris she would focus on mathematics and physics.

After a month Marie had mixed feelings about her new job, confiding to her cousin Henrietta on February 3, 1886, that although she liked the Zorawski family, Andzia was disorderly and spoiled, and some guests for a Twelfth Night ball were "worthy of the caricaturist's pencil," and "the young people here are most uninteresting. Some of the girls are so many geese who never open their mouths, the others are highly provocative."

Bronka, apparently an exception, was "a rare pearl both in her good sense and in her understanding of life."

Marie had been premature in expecting a lot of free time. Now she was tutoring her pupils for seven hours a day. Some months later she updated her opinions. Mr. Zorawski was charming, she told Henrietta, but his wife had a bad temper and behaved tactlessly—perhaps because she had once been a governess herself. Andzia was proving a problem, being "one of those children who profit enthusiastically by every interruption of work. Today we had another scene because she did not want to get up at the usual hour. In the end I was obliged to take her calmly by the hand and pull her out of bed. I was boiling inside. You can't imagine what such little things do to me: such a piece of nonsense can make me ill for several hours. But I had to get the better of her."

And she missed intelligent conversations. No one was prepared to discuss her interest in positivism, a philosophy that stressed the importance of science and supported higher education for women. She doubted if her employers had even heard the word.* They seemed only interested in gossip about the neighbors and talk of dances and parties. Some girls she met were "intelligent, but their education has done nothing to develop their minds, and the stupid, incessant parties here have ended by frittering their wits away. As for the young men, there are a few nice ones who are even a bit intelligent." She still liked her male employer, who was "full of good sense, sympathetic and reasonable." And she modified her opinion of his wife, who was "rather difficult to live with, but when one knows how to take her she is quite nice. I think she likes me well enough."

Marie soon had the chance to put her progressive ideas into action. After speaking with illiterate peasant children in the nearby village of Szczuki, who said they'd like to read and write, she asked Mme Zorawski for permission to use her room to teach them history and the Polish language. To her surprise, she not only agreed, but offered to help, even after Marie warned her that if they were caught they might be sent to Siberia. Mr. Zorawski also approved the suggestion. So Marie converted

---

* Positivism is the philosophy of a Frenchman, Auguste Comte, who coined the words *sociology* and *altruism* and believed that science rather than religion could solve many of society's biggest problems. Polish positivists had much in common with humanitarians and socialists. As anti-colonialists, they regarded women as the political and social equals of men, and advocated female emancipation and education, educating peasants, being tolerant to Jews, and abolishing class distinctions. They thought that the way to build a better world was by improving the individual, no longer being preoccupied with an imaginary heaven, and by freeing social and political theory from theological dogma and superstition.

her bedroom into a schoolroom by borrowing a pine table and some chairs, then raided her savings to buy copybooks and pens. And then she awaited her pupils.

The stomping of boots and shuffle of bare feet on the stairs—leading directly from the courtyard to her room—announced the first arrivals. Ten students turned up for the daily two-hour class, during which Bronka and her mother helped to keep order. By the end of the year the class had grown to eighteen, and at times the class lasted for five hours. It was hard, tiring work. Sometimes illiterate parents stood at the back of the room to watch in wonder the achievements of their children, but Marie felt inadequate for the task and far too late in trying to educate the children. According to Marie's daughter Eve, "She thought of all this good will wasted, and of the gifts that perhaps lay hidden in these balked and defrauded creatures. Before their sea of ignorance she felt disarmed and feeble."

What Marie does not mention in her *Autobiographical Notes* is that she had fallen in love. Eve learned of it from Marie's sisters, Bronia and Hela, and detailed the course of the romance in her biography of her mother. The man who had captivated her was the slim, handsome, and fair-haired eldest son of her employers, Casimir Zorawski, home for a vacation from his mathematical studies at Warsaw University. How could she resist an attractive, intelligent, and spirited nineteen-year-old who danced, rode a horse, and drove a carriage superbly—and had asked her to marry him? She expected his family to be pleased. After all, Bronka adored her, his father enjoyed long walks with her, and his mother, despite earlier reservations, had apparently grown fond of her. And the families knew one another. Several times they had Marie's family stay with them as their guests.

But when Casimir asked for his parents' approval to marry Marie, his father hit the roof and his mother almost hit the floor. The idea of their son marrying a poor working woman was intolerable. "In one instant the social barriers went up, insurmountable," Eve writes. "The fact that the girl was of good family, that she was cultivated, brilliant, and of irreproachable reputation, the fact that her father was honorably known in Warsaw—none of that counted against six implacable little words: one does not marry a governess."

Subjected to his parents' disapproval, Casimir did not fight for the woman he loved. Heartbroken and humiliated, Marie wanted to leave immediately, but she felt unable to break the pact that she had made with her sister—to send almost half her salary to support Bronia's stay in Paris. So she continued on as the family's governess, trying hard to hide her anger and bitter disappointment.

That summer, having learned that the man who had proposed to her sister Hela had also broken the engagement under similar circumstances, Marie wrote to their brother, Joseph: "I can imagine how Hela's self-respect must have suffered. Truly, it gives me a good opinion of men! If they don't want to marry poor young girls, then let them go to the devil!" Disillusioned and disheartened, she told her cousin Henrietta in the winter of 1886 that her plans for the future weren't worth discussing and tried to deny that she had ever been in love. Which wasn't true. She still hoped to marry Casimir despite his parents' strong opposition.

A year later, again in a letter to Henrietta, Marie was denying rumors of an impending wedding: "That tale has been spread about, even in Warsaw, and though this is not my fault, I am afraid it may bring me trouble. My dream for the moment is to have a corner of my own where I can live with my father. The poor man misses me a lot, he would like to have me at home, he longs for me! To get my independence again, and a place to live, I would give half my life."

The following spring of 1888 she was still working for the Zorawskis, with another year to go on her contract with them. And hating it. When she sent her brother twenty-fifth-birthday greetings, she confided that but for having to think of Bronia, she would resign from her job immediately: "Ah, if only I could extract myself for just a few days from this icy atmosphere of criticism," she wrote, "from the perpetual guard over my own words, the expression in my face, my gestures!" But it was not only having to help support Bronia that made her stay. What she still hid from Joseph and everyone else was that despite her denials and the continued opposition of his parents, she still hoped to marry Casimir.

In October 1888, when her friend Kazia wrote to announce her engagement and expressed concern that she might sound ridiculously excited, Marie replied: "How could I, your chosen little sister, not take to heart everything that concerns you, as if it were my own?" But then she admitted that she was writing with some bitterness, because "you tell me you have just lived through the happiest week of your life, and I during these holidays, have been through such weeks as you will never know. The thing that softens the memory of them is that I have come through with my head high. (As you see, I have not renounced, in life, that carriage which brought me Mlle Mayer's hatred of old.) I often hide my deep lack of gaiety under laughter, something I learned to do when I found out that creatures who feel as keenly as I do, and are unable to change this characteristic of their nature, have to dissimulate it at least as much as possible."

At other times she did not disguise how she felt, then regretted that she'd lost control.

A month later she told Henrietta, "Everybody says that I have changed a great deal, physically and spiritually, during my stay at Szczuki. This is not surprising. I was barely eighteen when I came here and what have I not been through! There have been moments which I shall certainly count among the most cruel of my life. I feel everything very violently, with a physical violence, and then I give myself a shaking, the vigor of my nature conquers, and it seems to me that I am coming out of a nightmare . . . First principle: never to let one's self be beaten down by persons or by events. I count the hours and days that separate me from the holidays and my departure to my own people. There is also the need of new impressions, of change, of movement and life, which seizes me sometimes with such force that I want to fling myself into the greatest follies, if only to keep my life from being eternally the same. Fortunately I have so much work to do that these attacks seize me pretty rarely. It is my last year here; and I must therefore work all the harder, so that the children's examinations will go well."

The spring brought Marie good news. Her father had never forgiven himself for depriving his children of the money he lost in the failed investment. Apparently, in an attempt to make up for it, he had taken a grim and demanding job as director of a reform school near Warsaw. But it was so well paid that he was able to help his daughters, adding to the money Marie sent to support her sister in Paris. Then Bronia told their father she could live on thirty-two rubles a month and to save eight of the forty he usually sent her and give them to Marie instead, which he did. For the first time Marie was able to save toward her future life in France. And she gave up her idea to teach at a local girls' school. More good news followed. Bronia, now twenty-four, was in love with Casimir Dluski, a charming and intelligent fellow Pole ten years her senior. He was also studying to be a doctor.

By July 1890, Marie had left the Zorawskis with her head "so full of plans," she told her friend Kazia, "that it seems aflame." To get to her new job as a governess for the Fuchs family in Zoppot, on the Baltic coast,

Marie (left) at twenty-two, in 1890, with her sisters, Bronia (center) and Hela, and her widower father, Professor Sklodowski. Soon after, she went to study at the Sorbonne, in Paris.

involved five train changes before she reached her destination. After her employers met her at the station, they all drove to the Schultz Hotel for a brief stay before heading for their other home in Warsaw. The beautiful, elegant, and bejeweled Mrs. Fuchs took to Marie immediately, calling her "exquisite" and insisting that she attend all their tea parties and dances.

Marie had been working for the Fuchs family for less than a year when she got great news from her sister Bronia. She and her fiancé would soon graduate as doctors, after which they intended to marry. If Marie could save a few hundred rubles to pay for her fees at the Sorbonne, she could then live with them for free, meals included.

But Marie now had commitments that she couldn't break. She had recently promised to live with her fifty-eight-year-old father. As she explained to Bronia on March 12, 1890: "I dreamed of Paris as of redemption, but the hope of going there left me a long time ago. And now that the possibility is offered to me, I do not know what to do . . . I am afraid to speak of it to Father. I believe our plan of living together next year is close to his heart, and he clings to it; I want to give him a little happiness in his old age. And on the other hand my heart breaks when I think of ruining my abilities, which must have been worth something. There is also the fact that I promised Hela to find her a post in Warsaw and I feel it is my duty to watch over her." She also asked Bronia's help in getting a loan for Joseph to study in Warsaw to ensure his future. "With this help Joseph can become useful to society, whereas if he leaves for the provinces he is lost. I bore you with Hela, Joseph, and Father, and with my own wretched future. My heart is so black, so sad, that I feel how wrong I am to speak of all this to you and to poison your happiness, for you are the only one of us all who has had what they call luck. Forgive me, but, you see, so many things hurt me that it is hard for me to finish this letter gaily. I embrace you tenderly. The next time I shall write more cheerfully and at greater length—but today I am exceptionally unhappy in this world. Think of me with tenderness—perhaps I shall be able to feel it even here."

She soon recovered from her black mood and resolved to complete her job with the Fuchs family, live for a year with her father, earn enough to pay for her Sorbonne studies by giving private lessons, and then leave for Paris.

During the year Marie spent with her father, she jumped at the chance to work in a chemistry laboratory at 66 Krakovsky Boulevard, where her cousin Joseph Boguski directed "the Museum of Industry and Agriculture," a cover name for the so-called Floating University, where Poles, male and female, secretly studied in defiance of Russian restrictions. There, on free evenings and Sundays, Marie conducted physics and chemistry experiments, and was so excited "by a little unhoped-for success" that it kept her awake at night. She later expressed how she felt: "A scientist in his laboratory is not only a technician: he is also a child placed before natural phenomena which impress him like a fairy tale."

Marie delayed accepting Bronia's offer to support her in Paris, because she still loved Casimir Zorawski and was about to meet him on vacation at Zakopane in the Carparthians, hoping to renew their romance away from his parents' influence. As her father wrote to Bronia in September 1891:

[Marie] has a secret about her future, of which she is to speak to me at length . . . To tell you the truth, I can well imagine what it has to do with, and I don't myself know whether I should be glad or sorry. If my foresight is accurate, the same disappointments, coming from the same persons who have already caused them to her, are awaiting her. And yet if it is a question of building a life according to her own feeling, and of making two people happy, that is worth the trouble of facing them perhaps. Your invitation to Paris, which fell upon her in such unexpected fashion, has given her a fever and added to her disorder . . . If she does not come back to me completely cured, I should oppose her departure, because of the hard conditions she would find herself in during the winter in Paris . . . without even mentioning the fact that it would be very painful for me to separate from her, but this consideration is obviously secondary. I learned with great joy that Casimir [Bronia's fiancé] is doing well. How funny it would be if each of you had a Casimir!

But it was not to be. During their walks in the mountains Casimir merely repeated that he could not overcome his snobbish parents' opposition. And Marie made the final break with her parting shot, telling him that if he couldn't resolve the problem it was not for her to teach him how to do it.

That December, disillusioned and disheartened, she wrote to her cousin Henrietta that "I will get along as best I can and when I can do no more, will say farewell to this base world. Some pretend that I am obliged to pass through the kind of fever called love. This absolutely does not enter into my plans. If I ever had any others they have gone up in smoke. I have buried them, locked them up, sealed and forgotten them." Biographer Rosalynd Pflaum points out that "The letter's melodramatic hints at suicide indicate how thoroughly shattered" Marie was.

Casimir being a lost cause, Marie wrote to Bronia, now married and pregnant, saying that she would join her in Paris if her sister could feed her without depriving herself: "It would restore me spiritually after the cruel trials I have been through this summer which will have an influence on my whole life . . . I am so nervous at the prospect of my departure that I can't speak of anything else until I get your answer . . . I promise that I shall not be a bore or create disorder. I implore you to answer me, but very frankly."

A few days later, Marie was on a Warsaw railroad platform with her father, Joseph, and Hela, there to see her off on the forty-hour, twelve-hundred-mile steam-train journey to Paris. As she embraced her father, she promised to return in a few years, after passing a few exams, when they would live together and never be separated again.

Marie had sent ahead a mattress, bedclothes, and towels. She mostly traveled in a ladies-only, fourth-class carriage, bare as a freight car except for a bench on each of its four sides. She took books, food, and drinks to sustain her, blankets to keep from freezing in the unheated carriage, and a folding stool.

Did the young man who rejected Marie have any regrets? Biographer Robert Reid implies that he did, and that they endured. "Warsaw citizens still remember," he wrote in 1974, "that as an old man, professor of mathematics at Warsaw Polytechnic, he used to sit quietly and contemplatively in front of one of the statues" of Marie Sklodowska. Unfortunately no one seems to have persuaded him to record his memories of her. His loss, of course, was the world's gain.

When Marie arrived at the Gare du Nord station on a cold November morning, Bronia and her husband, Dr. Casimir Dluski, were there to meet Marie and to take her to their second-floor apartment on rue D'Allemagne nearby, an area populated by factory workers and slaughterers from the local stockyards. At first she was overwhelmed by her dynamic and fun-loving brother-in-law, a handsome, witty Pole with a social conscience who gave free medical treatment to the poor. He had an intriguing background. Suspected of involvement in the assassination of Czar Alexander II, he had escaped to Geneva, Switzerland, where he promoted the revolutionary cause before moving to Paris. There he studied at the School of Political Science before switching to medical school.

Marie began her studies at the Sorbonne's Faculty of Sciences on November 3, 1891, one of only twenty-three women among 1,825 students. Men outnumbered women almost a hundred to one. Most weekday mornings she traveled to the university by horse-drawn bus, then eagerly soaked in the words of professors, who were formally dressed in white ties and tails. But to her dismay, her French, which she thought perfect, failed her when a professor spoke quickly, and she could not grasp entire sentences. Not only that, but the physics and mathematics she had studied alone or in correspondence with her father was not up to the standard of her classmates educated in French schools.

Soon after Marie's arrival, Bronia went to Warsaw to see their father. And Marie, although anxious to improve her French and at least match the scientific knowledge of her fellow students, had little time for extra study because she was stuck with the housekeeping. A few weeks later, on March 17, 1892, her brother-in-law wrote to her father: "Dear and Honored Sir: Everything is going very well with us. Mademoiselle Marie is working seriously; she passes nearly all her time at the Sorbonne and we meet only at the evening meal. She is a very independent young person, and in spite of the formal power of attorney by which you have placed her under my protection, she not only shows me no respect or obedience, but does not care about my authority and my seriousness. I hope to reduce her to reason, but up to now my pedagogical talent has not proved efficacious. In spite of all this we understand each other very well and live in the most perfect agreement. I await Bronia's arrival with impatience. My young lady does not seem to be in a hurry to get home, where her presence would nevertheless be very useful and where she is much in demand. I may add that Mlle Marie is perfectly well and looks it." And, he might have added, determined to find time to study.

Marie complained in a letter to her brother that Casimir constantly disturbed her with his chatter when she was trying to study and that she had to put a stop to it. Things improved when Bronia returned from Warsaw and persuaded Casimir that they should move to a larger apartment near a park in La Villette, a Parisian suburb. To reduce expenses she and her husband shared an office where, at different times, she specialized in women's diseases and Casimir worked as a general practitioner. And both made house calls in the neighborhood.

Friends, mostly from the tight-knit Polish colony, were always welcome in their home, especially Boleslaw Motz, editor of the *Socialist Review*; Stanislaw Wojciechowski, about to become cofounder of the Polish Socialist Party; and microbiologist Jan Danysz, of the Pasteur Institute; as well as artists, actors, and musicians. Normally, Marie would have been thrilled to spend time with them, but she was absorbed in her studies and desperate to catch up with her classmates. Though she could have improved her French by befriending some of the natives, she was too shy to make the first move.

In the new apartment, Marie had a small room of her own at the end of a corridor, but it did not save her from Casimir's well-meant interruptions, once to insist that she and Bronia join him to hear the debut of his pianist friend. This was an interruption Marie did not resent or regret, for the redheaded pianist in a threadbare jacket was Ignace Paderewski (the future prime minister of a free Poland) and she was enthralled by his interpretation of Liszt, Schumann, and Chopin to a scattered audience in an almost empty hall. Paderewski also came to their apartment for a musical evening bringing a Mlle Gorska with him, whom he eventually married. Bronia recognized her as the young Polish woman she and her ailing mother had accompanied to a health spa several years before. And Bronia recalled with a laugh how her mother had jokingly said to Mlle Gorska that "she would never dare take you to a watering-place again, because you were too beautiful!"

The new apartment meant a longer journey to the Sorbonne, so Marie moved to a cheap attic room on the sixth floor of 3 rue Flatters in the Latin Quarter, with a high-flying bird's-eye view of Paris. From here she could reach the Sorbonne on foot in twenty minutes.

Living alone for the first time in her life, and in a foreign city, gave Marie a wonderful sense of freedom and independence. Though sometimes lonely, she was never depressed. Her usual state of mind, she recalled, "was one of calm and great moral satisfaction." To reach her attic room with its small skylight meant climbing more than a hundred wooden steps, sometimes while carrying a bucket of coal for her small stove. When the coal ran out, she studied in a nearby heated library until it closed at 10 P.M. and went home to try to sleep under a bundle of all her clothes, often to find next morning that the water in the washbasin had frozen solid. Living on a few francs a day, her usual meal was a cup of chocolate or tea heated over a saucer-size alcohol lamp, and a slice of buttered bread. For a special treat she had eggs or fruit.

Her friends joked that Marie didn't even know the ingredients for soup, which was true. And she didn't want to know, because even making soup would have been a waste of her precious time. Her furniture consisted of an iron folding bed, a stove, a white wooden table, and a kitchen chair. When friends or relatives called, she pulled out the trunk she used as combined wardrobe and chest of drawers for them to sit on. She describes those days in a poem that begins:

> Higher, higher, up she climbs,
> Past six floors she gasps and heaves.
> Students shelter near the sky
> Up among the drafty eaves.

And ends:

> Ideals flood this tiny room;
> They led her to this foreign land;
> They urge her to pursue the truth
> And seek the light that's close at hand.
> It is the light she longs to find,
> When she delights in learning more
> Her world is learning; it defines
> The destiny she's reaching for.

Of course, hundreds if not thousands of her fellow students in Paris lived in the same straitened circumstances. And like her, they would later call those years among the happiest of their lives.

She began to socialize with a small colony of politically aware Polish students who met in each other's rooms or on walks together to discuss their country's enslavement and what they should do about it. Then, as she became increasingly absorbed in her studies, she restricted herself to fellow science students and to discussions sparked by their extraordinary teachers, several of world renown, such as physicist Gabriel Lippmann, a Nobel Prize winner in 1908; Henri Poincaré, one of the greatest mathematicians of his time; math professor Paul Painlevé, twice to be France's prime minister; Emile Duclaux, a microbiologist who made science sound like poetry; and Pierre Puiseux, who taught analytical geometry and relaxed by climbing mountains.

In July she returned to Warsaw for the summer vacation and traveled with some of her family in Poland and Switzerland.

On her return to Paris she had experienced several dizzy spells and fainted once or twice, but she never realized that her near-starvation diet was to blame. When she came to play with her newborn niece, Hela, and Casimir told Marie that she looked exhausted, she put it down to overwork and changed the subject. One evening, she fainted in front of a friend, who then told Casimir. He hurried to her attic room, where he found Marie studying. After examining her he was surprised to find that the only "food" in the room was a packet of tea. She admitted that all she had eaten since the previous evening was a pound of cherries and a few radishes, and that she had studied until three that morning and slept for only four hours before walking to the Sorbonne.

Furious at himself for not having realized that she was on a starvation diet, he ordered her to take whatever she needed for the following week's study and insisted that she come home with him, where he told Bronia about the situation. In the evening, they made sure that Marie finished her meal of rare steak and fried potatoes. That night she slept at their apartment in her old room, where, at eleven, Bronia switched off her light. After several days and nights of supervised meals and sleep, Marie looked so much better that they let her return to her attic after she promised to take care of herself. But "the next day she began again to live on air" and to study with such concentration she seems not to have noticed that there were thirty thousand troops outside her window quelling a riot by a mob protesting a nudity ban in a local nightclub.

Though shy and almost aloof in her manner, Marie had a circle of friendly student admirers, mostly "grinds" (workaholics) and almost exclusively Polish. One, Jadwiga Dydynska, was so protective that she once threatened with an upraised umbrella an overexuberant group of men who had surrounded Marie. Another of the circle was a Frenchman named Lamotte, who hoped that their friendship would develop into romance. Marie held him at bay, telling him that after graduating she would return to Poland as a teacher. But they remained friends.

One Sunday in the spring of 1893 she gave herself a break from her studies and spent the day at Le Raincey, a village just outside Paris, walking under the blossoming apple and chestnut trees and breathing the lilac-scented air.

In fear and trembling she took her physics exam in July 1893. Failure meant what? Back to Poland and life as a governess? Several anxious days later she joined thirty other students and their families in the Sorbonne's amphitheater to hear the examiner read the results in order of merit. A sudden silence announced his arrival, then he spoke. And the first name with the highest score was Marie Sklodowska!

Never before in the Sorbonne's long history had a woman, and a foreigner at that, graduated at the top of the physics class. After her friends had congratulated her, Marie could hardly wait to share the extraordinary news with her family in Poland. She spent that summer with them, fed by her father and other proud relatives until, instead of being painfully thin, she was slightly plump.

Having concluded that mathematics was vital for all scientific endeavor, she was eager to return to the Sorbonne to get a master's degree in math. But her savings were exhausted, her father had already sacrificed too much, and Bronia, with a young child, couldn't be expected to extend their mutual-assistance pact for another year. Because the prospect of her returning to France seemed so remote, she was desperately disappointed. But, unknown to Marie, Mlle Dydynska, the young woman who had defended her with an umbrella, had successfully pleaded Marie's cause before the Alexandrovitch Scholarship Fund committee, which financed Polish students studying abroad. To Marie it was almost a miracle. The six hundred rubles was more than enough to support her in Paris until she got a math degree. (She surprised the fund's administrators some four years later by returning the money to help some other poor Polish student, something no previous recipient had done.)

By September 1893 she was reinstalled in Paris, again in a room on the sixth floor, but "in a clean and decent street," and with a wood floor that she expected to be warmer than the tile floor of her former attic, as well as a window that resisted drafts. "It was very hard for me to separate again from Father," she told her brother, "but I could see that he was very well, very lively, and that he could do without me—especially as you are living in Warsaw. And as for me, it is my whole life that is at stake. It seemed to me, therefore, that I could stay on here without having remorse on my conscience. I am studying mathematic unceasingly, so as to be up to date when the courses begin."

Marie again wrote to her brother in the spring of 1894, urging him to get his doctoral degree in medicine, agreeing that life wasn't easy for any of them, and concluding with, "We must believe that we are gifted for something, and that this thing, at whatever cost, must be obtained. Perhaps everything will turn out very well, at the moment when we least expect it."

Soon after that letter, she was hired by the Society for the Encouragement of National Industries to test the magnetic properties of various steels. But the Sorbonne's crowded physics lab hadn't room for the equipment she needed for the tests. A friend, Professor Kowalski, who had known her since her days as a governess in Poland invited her to meet someone he thought could help her.

CHAPTER 3

Pierre and Marie
in Love

1885–1895

As Marie arrived at Joseph Kowalski's apartment, she got her first enduring impression of Pierre Curie. There he stood, across the room, framed by a French window. He had auburn hair and large, clear eyes, like a "dreamer absorbed in his reflections," and looked much younger than thirty-five. She was immediately "struck by the open expression of his face and the slight suggestion of detachment in his whole attitude." She liked him almost at first glance and the feeling was mutual. Uncomfortable with small talk, he launched into his fascination with the world of crystals and she asked informed, intelligent questions. Curie had never before had a conversation about his work with a charming young woman, who understood the technical terms and complicated formulas he used. Although she was not yet fluent in French, they also managed to discuss social and humanitarian topics. His slow, calm speech, "grave and youthful," relaxed manner, and pleasant smile, put her at ease. "There was," she recalled, "between our native countries, a surprising kinship, no doubt attributable to a certain likeness in the moral atmosphere in which we were both raised by our families."

Women were rare in the world of physics; attractive women almost unknown. It was also Paris in the spring, and Pierre Curie's interest in her was obviously more than professional. For fifteen years, except for brief, superficial encounters, he had deliberately and persistently avoided attractive women. But this was a fellow scientist and a woman whose mind, personality, and looks all appealed to him. Their daughter Eve later re-created this fateful meeting from conversations with her mother.

Pierre, she wrote, "looked at Marie's [ash blonde] hair, at her high, curved forehead and her hands already stained by the acids of the laboratory. He was disconcerted by her grace, [and] absence of all coquetry. He dug from his memory all that his host had told him about the young woman. She had worked for years before being able to take the train for Paris, she had no money, she lived alone in a garret."

They met again at the French Society of Physics and at his laboratory. When Marie told him that after taking her upcoming math exam, it was her patriotic duty to return to Poland as a teacher and rejoin the struggle for Polish independence from the Russians, Pierre feared this might be their last meeting. And he surprised himself by asking if he could see her again, undeterred even when she said he'd have to face six flights of stairs to reach her attic. In Paris of the 1890s it was a scandal for a man other than a relative to visit a respectable woman alone in her room. Pierre and Marie didn't flout convention, they ignored it—one of the many things they had in common. So, Pierre climbed to the top floor of 11 rue des Feullantines in the Latin Quarter, favored by students for its cheap rents, where Marie was waiting for him. Mine "was a poor little room for my resources were extremely limited," she later wrote. "Nevertheless, I was very happy in it for I was now first realizing the ardent desire I had so long cherished of carrying on advanced studies in science." He showed sympathy for her current situation and an interest in her future. As for her past, she had not yet told him of her early days in Poland, how she had fainted from hunger during her student years, nor of the humiliations and torments she had endured to get this far.

Throughout the spring and summer Marie got to know Pierre Curie, son and grandson of doctors, as a reserved, absentminded, idealistic dreamer, a brilliant though personally unambitious physicist, almost unknown in France but highly respected abroad by his peers. He got to know her, this daughter of teachers, as romantic, high-spirited, ambitious, resilient, driven, sensitive, curious, stubborn, generous, compassionate, courageous, and exceptionally intelligent. Both were anticlerical freethinkers, humanists, nature lovers, and liberals who rooted for the underdog.

In an adoring biography of her mother, Eve Curie wrote: "Marie had built for herself a secret universe of implacable rigor, dominated by the passion for science. Family affection and the attachment to an oppressed fatherland also had their place in it. Thus she had decreed, the beautiful creature who lived alone in Paris and met young men every day at the Sorbonne and in the laboratory. Marie was obsessed by her dreams, harassed by poverty, over-driven by intensive work. She did not know leisure and its dangers. Her pride and timidity protected her, as did her distrust ever since the Zorawskis had rejected her as a daughter-in-law."

What Pierre did not yet know is that Marie had become something of a manhater. For seven years she had avoided any romantic attachment, convinced from one traumatic experience "that poor girls found no devotion or tenderness among men." And so, "stiffened by fine theories and bitter reflections, she clung fiercely to her independence."

Of the two men romantically interested in her, Lamotte, despite discouragement, had not given up, and Pierre was determined to marry her. For the first time in his life, in pursuing her, he later acknowledged, he had acted without hesitation, convinced that she was the right woman for him.

Lamotte longed to see her again, but knowing that she was frantically busy studying for her imminent exams, wished her a deservedly happy future and success in the exams and signed off with "one small word of reproach: you insisted that I would quickly forget you when I lost sight of you. I fear that you are mistaken. Without doubt, we won't meet again. However, if you ever should need it, remember that you have left somewhere a friend ready to do everything possible for you."

Though Lamotte seemed out of the picture, Marie and Pierre Curie were still only close friends. She had turned down his marriage proposal quite dramatically, saying that it would mean leaving her father and betraying her country. She had already teased her friend Kazia for being engaged to a foreigner—a German. But she still left Pierre with the hope that she might change her mind. He once suggested that by moving to Poland permanently she would be abandoning science. Marie sensed that he meant she would be abandoning him, and held his gaze for a while before quietly replying, "I believe you are right. I should like to come back very much." But that was clearly not a promise to return.

That summer of 1894 Marie took the exams for a mathematics degree along with France's brightest young mathematical minds—and scored second from the top. She then left for Fribourg, Switzerland, where her friend Professor Kowalski, who had introduced Pierre to her, taught physics. After visiting him and his wife she intended to join her family in Warsaw.

When she left Paris, Pierre feared he might not hear from her for at least two months and was overjoyed to receive a letter in ten days. He replied with his first love letter to her:

We have promised each other—haven't we, to be at least great friends. If you will only not change your mind! For there are no promises that are binding; such things cannot be ordered at will. It would be a fine thing, just the same, in which I hardly dare believe, to pass our lives near each other, hypnotized by our dreams; *your* patriotic dream, *our* humanitarian dream; and *our* scientific dream. Of all those dreams the last is, I believe, the only legitimate one. I mean by this that we are powerless to change the social order and even if we were not . . . we should never be sure of not doing more harm than good . . . by retarding some inevitable evolution. From the scientific point of view, on the contrary, we may hope to do something; the ground is solider here, and any discovery that we may make, however small, will remain acquired knowledge. But if you leave France in a year it would be an altogether too platonic a friendship, that of two creatures who would never see each other again. Wouldn't it be better for you to stay with me? I know that this question angers you, and that you don't want to speak of it again—and then, too, I feel so thoroughly unworthy of you from every point of view. . . . Believe me, your very devoted, Pierre Curie.

Her reply that she would return to Paris in October reassured him that he had not yet lost her. She also sent her photograph and invited him to join her in Poland and meet her father. Yet he declined, because, as he explained to her, he "was attacked by a sort of shame at pursuing you like this against your will; and the near-certainty that my presence would be disagreeable to your father and spoil his pleasure in your company. Now that it is too late, I am sorry I did not go."

As if he didn't realize that he was hopelessly in love, he wrote: "I don't know why I have got it into my head to keep you in France, to exile you from your country and family without having anything good to offer you in exchange for such a sacrifice." Then a step forward: "If you were French [by marrying him] you could easily manage to be a professor in the secondary schools . . . I showed your photograph to my brother. Was that wrong? He admired it [and said], 'she has a very decided look, not to say *stubborn.*'"

Marie returned to Paris for what she expected to be her final year in the city, living and studying in a small room adjoining Bronia's consulting office at 37 rue de Chateaudun, when she wasn't at the Sorbonne conducting experiments on steel's magnetic qualities.

Aware that time was running out, Pierre made two proposals to Marie that had an air of desperation. If she did not love him enough to marry him, would she rent an apartment with him—one he had already seen— that was divided into two separate units? They would then remain close, platonic friends and working partners. Or, if he left France and worked in Poland, would she marry him? He could teach French there and in their free time they could do scientific research as a team.

Moved by his willingness to leave his country for her, Marie discussed the proposals with Bronia. When Pierre somehow heard of this, he petitioned Bronia, who was so impressed that she went with him and Marie, as his champion, to meet his parents at their country home outside Paris. There, Marie felt immediate rapport for Pierre's doctor father, Eugène, and admired his "beautiful eyes of a clearness and brilliancy that were striking even in advanced age [that] reflected goodness and intelligence." When Pierre first mentioned his parents to her, he had called them "exquisite," and, having met them, she agreed. His mother obviously approved of his choice, because, during the visit, she took Bronia aside and whispered: "There isn't a soul on earth to equal my Pierre. Don't let your sister hesitate. She will be happier with him than with anybody."

But Marie did hesitate, for ten months. During that time she encouraged Pierre to complete a doctoral thesis in March 1895, titled "Magnetic Properties of Bodies at Diverse Temperatures." And then, with his father and several friends, attended his oral presentation before Sorbonne Professors Bonty, Lippmann, and Hautrefeuille. If Marie was not yet in love with Pierre, she certainly loved his mind, judging by her response to his performance: "I remember the simplicity and clarity of the exposition, the esteem indicated by the attitude of the professors, and the conversation between them and the candidate [and], it seemed to me, that day sheltered the exaltation of human thought."

Later that summer, having won over the trio of Sorbonne judges to award him a Ph.D., he finally persuaded Marie to marry him. As her daughter Eve understood the situation, by his gentle reasoning, "the protection he offered her, and by the deep, irresistible charm of his daily presence, Pierre Curie gradually made a human being out of the young hermit."

News of Marie's engagement reached her other suitor, Lamotte, as "a cruel surprise." He wrote to her on July 10 that he had not even known that he had a rival. Now, conceding defeat, he rejected as impossible her suggestion that they remain friends and insisted that they must "consider each other dead." He explained that he had hoped to win her by his "patient love [but] circumstances were against me. As the poet said, 'I came too late into a world too old!'" (Lamotte was quoting the response of the French poet Alfred de Musset to novelist George Sand after she had rejected his marriage proposal.) Her brother, Joseph, agreed that she was right to follow her heart, "and no just person can reproach you for it. Knowing you, I am convinced you will remain Polish with all your soul, and also that you will never cease to be part of our family in your heart. And we, too, will never cease to love you and consider you ours. . . . Tell [your fiancé] that I welcome him as a future member of our family and that I offer him my friendship and sympathy without reserve."

Marie explained her difficult decision in a letter to her girlhood friend Kazia: "It is a sorrow to me to have to stay forever in Paris. But what am I to do? Fate has made us deeply attached to each other and we cannot endure the idea of separating . . . I hesitated for a whole year and could not resolve upon an answer. Finally I became reconciled to the idea of settling here . . . Next year I shall bring [my husband] to Poland so that he will know my country and I shall not fail to introduce him to my dear little chosen sister, and ask her to love him."

CHAPTER 4

Mutual Adoration

1895–1898

Marie Sklodowska's watchword in planning her wedding for July 26, 1895, might have been *simplify*. She rejected the traditional religious ceremony and instead of the customary wedding dress chose one of navy blue, suitable to wear later in the laboratory. Only a few guests witnessed the civil ceremony in Sceaux's town hall: Marie's father and sister Hela, who came from Poland; her sister Bronia and brother-in-law, Casimir; Pierre's parents; and a handful of university friends. Then they all walked to the nearby Curie family home, where in the small, sunlit rose garden they enjoyed a lunch of turkey—carved by Pierre's father—and the largest peaches Hela had ever seen. Afterward, some guests played boules in a nearby field. As Pierre's mother had assured Bronia that her son would make Marie a wonderful husband, now Professor Sklodowski, speaking in flawless French, assured Dr. Curie: "You will have a daughter worthy of affection in Marie. Since she came into the world she has never caused me pain."

The couple posed for a photograph before starting on their honeymoon: a bicycle tour of the countryside for which Marie wore a black straw hat, a split skirt, and sensible shoes. The only festive note was a garland of flowers on her bicycle's handlebars. They left their bicycles in a farm worker's cottage and, with a compass and a bag of fruit, set off on foot to explore the area. Marie had shortened her skirt to walk more easily and wore a belt with pockets around her waist holding a knife, some cash, and a watch. Pierre led the way looking straight ahead and speaking his thoughts aloud about his ongoing challenging research on crystals and the mystery of their growth, while Marie, speaking to his back, made informed and helpful suggestions. She had high hopes for the future, and was con-

Pierre and Marie Curie in a flower-filled garden, about to set off on bicycles for their honeymoon in the summer of 1895.

fident that Professor Paul Schutzenberger, director of the School of Physics and Chemistry, would let her work in the same laboratory as Pierre.

When they broke through a thicket and reached a pond, Marie lay resting on the bank while Pierre walked along a fallen tree trunk to gather yellow walking irises and water lilies for her. Marie had almost dozed off when something cold and wet landed in her hand—a small, panting green frog. Pierre had put it there, and was shocked by her cry of protest. "See how nice it is!" he said. But she was unconvinced. So he took it back and placed it near the pond. Marie realized that he had not been playing a joke and had really expected her to enjoy holding the frog. They resumed their voyage of discovery, with Pierre still walking ahead and describing the apparatus he meant to build for new experiments, while Marie—carrying a bouquet of wildflowers—turned the monologue into conversation.

After their honeymoon they moved into a small three-room apartment on the fourth floor of 24 rue de la Glacière—its only charm the view below of a large garden. Their study was arranged to avoid distractions and discourage visitors, with bare walls and sparse furniture—a single white table and two chairs at either end of it where Pierre and Marie studied face to face. Uninvited visitors could tell at a glance that they weren't welcome in that room: there were no extra chairs. A woman came for an hour a day to wash the dishes and do heavy lifting. Otherwise Marie handled all the housekeeping. Housecleaning always baffled her, especially the kitchen floor. Discussing it with a woman contemplating marriage, she said, "I used to have my pail alongside me, with a cloth, but as soon as I moved it, everything looked as though it needed doing over again."

But she had learned to cook. The student to whom soup had been a mystery had secretly taken cooking lessons from Bronia's mother-in-law, though Pierre hardly noticed what he ate. He was oblivious to her efforts to serve chicken and fried potatoes, and to adjust the oven's gas jets with such precision that the roast meat wouldn't burn, or to prevent macaroni from sticking to the pan. She also annotated a cookbook recording her successes and failures, and experimented with her own invented dishes that required little preparation or simmered slowly and unattended for hours while she was away.

After dinner the Curies took their places facing each other at the study table, their books and papers lit by an oil lamp, a vase of flowers the only bright color in the room. They worked sometimes until three in the morning, Pierre on a detailed program for new courses at the School of Physics and Chemistry, Marie studying for an exam to qualify as a teacher at the newly created secondary school for girls.

She rose early each workday morning to shop for food, then returned to the apartment to make breakfast and prepare lunch, clean the floor, and make the bed, before leaving with Pierre for the nearby School of Physics. As she had hoped, Professor Schutzenberger allowed her to conduct experiments on the magnetic properties of steel in the lab with Pierre, where they spent most of each day. They returned in the evenings, arm-in-arm, buying milk and groceries for their dinner en route. At home, before serving dinner she entered the day's expenses marked "His" and "Hers" in a notebook. In fine weather they cycled to Sceaux every few days to visit Pierre's parents. If it rained, they went by train. But it hardly interrupted their work, because the Curies had provided them with two rooms equipped with everything they needed to continue their research. Their rare diversion was a Physics Society dinner, or a play by the great controversial dramatists of the day: Ibsen, Strindberg, and Hauptmann.

During August 1896, Marie took the exam for which she had been studying and received the highest mark. Now she was free to earn a living teaching physics at a secondary school. Pierre silently congratulated her by putting his arm affectionately around her neck and they celebrated with another bicycle tour—this time to Auvergue, riding through the fresh green fields of Aubrac and inhaling the pure air.

The following spring Marie was suffering through a difficult pregnancy. Though she wanted a child, she complained to her friend Kazia: "For more than two months I have had continual dizziness, all day long from morning to night. I tire myself out and get steadily weaker, and although I do not look ill, I feel unable to work and am in a very bad state of spirits. My condition irks me particularly because my mother-in-law is now seriously ill [with incurable breast cancer]." And she wrote to her brother: "I am afraid, above all, that the disease [of Pierre's mother] will reach its end at the same time as my pregnancy. If this should happen my poor Pierre will have some very hard weeks to go through."

In July, when Marie was seven months pregnant, her father invited her and Jadwiga Dydynska to join him at the Hotel of the Gray Rocks in Port Blanc, a fishing village in Brittany, where he was spending the summer. Jadwiga, a Sorbonne friend, had once defended her with an umbrella and helped her to get a scholarship. Pierre stayed behind to complete his teaching duties and help care for his dying mother until his brother, Jacques, was able to leave Montpellier to replace him. Then Pierre intended to join Marie.

This was the first time since their marriage that they had been separated for more than a few hours, and Pierre responded to a letter from Marie in the few words of Polish he knew, saying that when she left he missed his "little girl, so sweet, so dear, whom I love so much [that] my soul flew away with you." To which she replied, also in Polish, that she was well but very sad without him, because "I expect you from morning to night and I don't see you coming." She added that she was having trouble understanding a math book by her former teacher, the brilliant mathematical physicist Henri Poincaré, and wanted to reread the important parts with Pierre.

He missed her so much that he tried to convey his thoughts by thinking of her intensely. He wrote to tell her of this experiment and how he yearned for new faculties to make it possible. Theirs was a case of mutual adoration. She thought of him as "a man of infinite charm to which no one could remain insensible [and] almost unique through his detachment from any sort of vanity, and from those pettinesses which one finds in one-self and in others." And she believed he had no enemies, because "he never wounded anyone, even by accident. However, one could not turn him aside from a determined line of action, which made his father call him 'the gentle stubborn one.' If his attitude was that of a superior man who had attained the highest summit of civilization, his acts were those of a man truly good . . . full of understanding and indulgence. He was always disposed to aid any one in a difficult situation. [But] all affairs of a social life were entirely excluded from our existence." He was always pleased to meet childhood friends or to have meaningful discussions with fellow scientists, but, "if by chance he found himself drawn into a general conversation in which he felt no interest, he took refuge in a quiet corner and forgot those present in the pursuit of his own thoughts."

Pierre and Marie were separated for less than a month when his brother Jacques arrived to help take care of their mother, and Pierre then joined Marie at Port Blanc. She said she felt fine and, although eight months pregnant, she readily agreed when he proposed a bicycle tour. Their daughter Eve explained this as "the thoughtlessness of the insane—or rather of the scientist." And added that Pierre also "had a vague feeling that she was a supernatural being, who escaped from human laws." To be fair to him, he had asked her to check where the nearest doctor lived and how to reach him. The couple set off, but not for long. The baby was announcing its imminent appearance. They rushed to Paris where, on September 12, 1897, Pierre's father, Dr. Eugène Curie, delivered a six-pound, six-ounce baby girl. Pierre had reason to believe that Marie might be supernatural after all: she had endured the pain of childbirth silently, with clenched teeth. They named their baby Irène and celebrated with champagne.

Pierre's mother died two weeks later and he was so distraught he felt he would mourn her death forever. When, sometime later, he caught himself laughing, he was ashamed. Marie tried to assure him that he had not betrayed his mother's memory, but he was not easily consoled.

In time, Marie became overwhelmed by the demands made on her as wife, mother, housekeeper, cook, student, and experimental physicist. She couldn't bear the thought of giving up her work and Pierre wouldn't even consider it. Their work was "precious" to both of them, and as Pierre often said, he had in Marie "a wife made expressly for him to share all his pre-occupations." They eased the problem by hiring a nurse for Irène, though that didn't shield Marie from the occasional, irrational fear that her baby was sick or missing, a fear that would send her hurrying in a panic from the School of Physics and Chemisty to a nearby park or to her home to check that Irène was safe in her nurse's care. She also began to record, along with her research notes and expenses, important events in her daughter's life: when she first rolled over, held an object firmly in her hand, and showed fear of strangers and loud noises.

Pierre's father, now a widower, joined them soon after they moved from their small apartment to a two-story house, 108 boulevard Keller-mann, on the southern edge of Paris. He made himself useful, taking over when the nurse wasn't available, watching with delight as Irène took her first tentative steps in the garden, and becoming, according to Eve Curie, Irène's "first teacher and best friend."

Dr. Curie also enlivened family conversations as a vigorous political commentator on contemporary affairs and an impassioned defender of Alfred Dreyfus, a Jewish French army captain falsely accused of spying for Germany and sentenced to life on the dreaded Devil's Island. French rad-icals, socialists, moderate republicans, Jews, and most Europeans believed Dreyfus to be innocent, while much of the French army and population, especially Catholics and conservatives, blinded to the truth by their rabid anti-Semitism, were convinced of his guilt. The London correspondent of the New York *World* wrote that being a Jew, Dreyfus was "a convenient scapegoat," and announced, "A monster manifestation is preparing in Paris for tomorrow. Allegedly it is anti-Dreyfusian. Really it is anti-Semitic." Dreyfus's leading defender was the crusading writer Emile Zola, who ob-tained evidence proving his innocence and eventually published it under the title *J'Accuse*. Students paraded through the Paris streets shouting "Spit on Zola!" and "Death to the Jews!" and smashed the windows of a house they mistook for Zola's. (On January 13, 1998, the hundredth anniversary of Zola's cry for justice in *J'Accuse*, France's Roman Catholic daily, *Le Croix*, apologized for its anti-Semitic editorials during the Drey-fus affair.)

Dr. Curie and Marie usually took part in arguments among friends and colleagues, but Pierre invariably kept his thoughts to himself. Even when his views were challenged he refused to take the bait. Or, if accused of taking outrageous actions or events too calmly, he'd say that he wasn't good at getting angry. His rationale for rarely getting involved in politics, as he told his students, was that science would eventually solve many of society's problems. The Dreyfus case was an obvious exception. And Marie explained why this was "one of the few occasions on which Pierre Curie, coming out of his reserve, would grow impassioned in [discussing the] political struggle. He quite naturally took the part of the innocent and persecuted. He was to fight against an iniquity that filled him with horror, because he was a just man."

But nothing distracted him from his scientific pursuits for long. Late in 1897 in the hours free from teaching an in-depth course on the wonders of electricity—already replacing gaslights in Paris streets—he resumed his research into crystal growth. Meanwhile, Marie had completed her monograph on the magnetic qualities of tempered steel, for which she was paid fifteen hundred francs—what Pierre earned in three months, and a much needed addition to the family income. Then what? After discussions with Pierre, she decided not to seek a teaching job right away, but to study for a doctorate. If successful she would be the first woman in France, and possibly the whole of Europe, with a Ph.D. in physics.

Marie was so impatient to begin experimenting that she narrowed her field of interest to a thesis on recent discoveries about which there was little in print. Consequently she avoided spending time reading an exhaustive bibliography of scientific articles before getting down to the lab work.

Fascinated by the recent reports of William Roentgen on X-rays and Henri Becquerel on Becquerel rays, both she and Pierre considered them good subjects for her thesis. Roentgen, a darkly handsome fifty-year-old professor of physics at the University of Wurzburg, had discovered X-rays in 1895 while experimenting with high-voltage electricity. Working in his darkened lab, he sent an electric current through a cathode-ray vacuum tube. (Cathode rays are invisible streams of high-speed electrons—elementary particles—emitted by the negative electrode of a vacuum tube when an electric current is passed through it. Because they can be deflected and focused by electrical and magnetic fields, they are used today in the electron microscope and in the TV receiver's image tube.) Out of the corner of his eye he glimpsed a bright, greenish-yellow glow on a piece of paper on a nearby bench. He switched the electricity on and off repeatedly. The paper, coated with chemicals (crystals of barium platinocyanide) for another experiment, glowed only when the electricity was on. Roentgen was baffled. It was impossible for any known rays to have made the paper glow (phosphoresce). None would have been able to escape from the glass tube and reach the paper. What could it possibly be? Later, asked by a reporter to recall his thoughts at the time, Roentgen replied: "I did not think. I investigated."

He also almost went out of his mind.

As if possessed, torn between doubt and hope, he remained in his lab for seven weeks, speaking to no one except his wife, Bertha, and telling her that what he was studying would make people think he was mad. He had his meals brought to him and even slept in the lab. After many secret experiments he decided to share with the world what he had discovered about X-rays as he called them, X being the math symbol for the unknown. Appropriate, too, because much about them was still a mystery. Nothing deflected them from a straight path, so he knew that they weren't light rays or cathode rays. Though they did not go through lead or platinum, one amazing attribute was the ability of these invisible rays to penetrate paper, ebony, rubber, and thin layers of metal.

Then, totally by chance, he made another crucial discovery. While at work, he accidentally put his hand between the X-rays and a screen. And there on the screen was the image of the bones of his hand. The rays could penetrate flesh. Amazed and excited, Roentgen called his wife into the lab and took an X-ray photograph showing the bones of her hand and a silhouette of her gold wedding ring. Elated with the result, he hoped that it would pleasantly surprise her. Instead, she was scared by the sight of her own bones.

Roentgen quickly wrote a paper about his discovery, "On a New Kind of Rays," and mailed it with photographs of X-rayed hands to several leading scientists, including Henri Poincaré, the distinguished mathematician and physicist. Poincaré shared the exciting news with some of the seventy-eight members of the French Academy of Sciences at their weekly meeting in Paris on January 24, 1896. One of them, physicist Henri Becquerel, was specially intrigued by Poincaré's comment that Roentgen's X-rays had caused a green glow (phosphorescence) both on the glass wall of the cathode tube and on the chemically treated paper. Becquerel's father, also a physicist, had already found that light produced phosphorescence in some substances. And Becquerel decided to test his theory that phosphorescent substances were themselves emitting rather than just reflecting X-rays.

Just before Becquerel began his experiments, Roentgen came out of hiding to give his first public lecture on X-rays at a meeting of the Physical-Medical Association. There he took an X-ray photo of the hand of chairman Albert von Kolliker, clearly showing the bones. As it was passed around the hall, Roentgen was cheered and applauded. Having shattered the belief that physics had gone as far as it could go, that nothing new could be discovered, his breakthrough was reported throughout the world. This discovery, that X-rays were produced when cathode rays (later identified as high-velocity electrons) struck a material object, revolutionized medicine with amazing rapidity. Just over two weeks after his lecture, X-rays were used in the United States to locate a bullet in a patient's leg and to set the broken arm of a boy in Dartmouth, New Hampshire.

In 1897 a U.S. Army doctor reported "a case of X-ray burn which had no parallel in medical literature up to date, either in length of exposure [almost twelve hours] or in the extent [15.8 inches] and intensity of the resulting lesion . . . The most distressing feature of the case is the intense pain, which nothing but morphine will control . . . The slowness with which the apparently superficial denudation heals is almost incredible."

Within a year fifty books and some thousand papers on X-rays were published worldwide. One curious outcome was a proposed law by the Purity League in the United States to prevent theatergoers from using X-rays in their opera glasses. And clothing stores did a brisk business in X-ray-proof corsets and so-called modesty gowns. A contemporary English magazine, the *Pall Mall Gazette*, expressed a typically Victorian view: "You can see other people's bones with the naked eye. On the revolting indecency of this there is no need to dwell."

Edward Reid, professor of physiology at Scotland's Dundee University, enthusiastically put the X-rays to the test, and after directing them at an assistant for an hour, reported that "passage of the rays through the head of a laboratory boy of medium intelligence did not cause deterioration or improvement thereof." He then turned the rays on himself for four sessions of up to ninety minutes a time, and as a result temporarily lost all his hair and suffered severe dermatitis. Reid also used X-rays to probe for swallowed teeth "within the entrails" of a patient and to locate bullets "within the skulls of living men."

As his wife told a relative, Roentgen hated the uproar caused by his worldwide fame: "It is not a little matter to become a famous man, and people little realize how much work and unrest fame brings with it." Because Roentgen believed that no scientist should personally profit from his discoveries, he did not patent X-ray imagery, so that doctors, dentists, and businessmen were free to make use of it. But he paid for his principles. Although he got the first Nobel Prize for physics in 1901, he died in poverty at seventy-three.

Spurred by Roentgen's work and his own father's experiments, the French physicist Becquerel began to test his theory that phosphorescent substances themselves—stimulated by sunlight—and not cathode rays from a vacuum tube were the source of X-rays. He did not prove this theory, but he made a new remarkable discovery. He wrapped a photographic plate in two sheets of thick black paper to prevent daylight from fogging it, then placed a slab of uranium salts—known to have strong phosphorescent properties—on the plate and exposed it to sunlight for several hours. When he developed the plate, it showed a black silhouette of the salts.

Becquerel concluded that he had confirmed his theory—that having absorbed the sun's energy, the uranium salts were reemitting it as X-rays that penetrated the black paper and left the evidence.

What else, he wondered, other than the sun, could be the source of this energy? The long-established law of conservation of energy demanded that it come from somewhere. To confirm his findings he repeated the experiment, this time placing a copper cross between the salts and the photographic plate. As the Paris skies were overcast on February 26 and 27, 1896, he put the new material away in a light-proof drawer to await the sun.

On March 1, it was still a sunless city, but because Becquerel was impatient, or, as British scientist William Crookes, with him at the time, suggested, "with the unconscious prevision of genius," he developed the plate anyway, and was astonished to see a clear image of the cross. Believing, like his contemporaries, that energy can be neither created nor destroyed, he was baffled by its origin. As far as he knew, the uranium salts had been exposed neither to the sun—the ultimate source of the Earth's energy—nor to any other external energy source. The French physicist had, in fact, accidentally discovered spontaneous radiation, a nonsolar source of energy, something no scientist, including Becquerel, then believed possible. So he surmised that the uranium salts must have previously been "exposed" to an energy source. But what that source was remained a mystery.

According to Robert L. Wolke of the University of Pittsburgh, Becquerel was "in a sense correct. Today we know that the energy given off by long-lived radioactive elements such as uranium was indeed stored in them . . . some 20 billion years ago, when their atoms were created in the nucleogenetic processes that followed the 'big bang.' The energy was stored, not in the form of absorbed exciting radiation, but in the form of mass, which is today being re-emitted as electromagnetic and particulate radiation [minute separate particles]. Radioactivity, then . . . is returning to us some of the primordial energy of the universe. Becquerel's notion was not quite wrong after all." The rays emitted by uranium salts were at first known as Becquerel rays, or uranium rays.

Both Marie and Pierre were intrigued by accounts of a substance—uranium salts—that emitted radiations similar to Roentgen rays. The big difference was that Roentgen rays could be produced only in a vacuum tube and with the expenditure of energy (electricity), while uranium appeared to emit Becquerel rays spontaneously, continuously, and without expenditure of energy. And they were different from ordinary luminous rays because they could pass through black paper.

The Curies agreed that a fundamental study of the nature of uranium would be an engrossing subject for Marie's Ph.D. thesis. One of the many questions she hoped to answer was: Were any other substances capable of emitting Becquerel rays? To find the answer she had to do her own experiments. After a quick but careful reading of the sparse available material on the subject, she was eager to start. But instead of trying to replicate Becquerel's experiments with uranium salts by testing their effect on photographic plates, Marie was more adventurous and planned a new experiment. Becquerel had found that the radiation from uranium causes the air in its vicinity to conduct electricity. (Ionizing the air, as it is called, is the principle behind the Geiger counter, which measures the presence of radioactivity. When radioactive particles strike a Geiger counter tube, they close an electric circuit and cause an audible clicking.)

Marie hoped "to determine the intensity of the radiation, by measuring the conductivity of the air exposed to the action of the rays." She already had ideal equipment to measure weak electric currents with great precision: the electrometer that Pierre and Jacques had built, and a piezo-electric quartz crystal. They had been lying around for years and now she could put them to good use. All she needed was a place to work.

Pierre persuaded his boss, Professor Charles Gabriel, who had succeeded Schutzenberger, to let her use a small damp workshop in the engineering school on the rue Lhomond, which normally served as a warehouse for discarded equipment and pieces of lumber. She set up her equipment there in December 1897. As she later explained: "One of the most important properties of the radioactive elements is that of ionizing the air in their vicinity. When an uranium compound is placed on a metal plate A situated opposite another plate B and a difference in potential is maintained between the plates A and B, an electric current is set up between plates; this current can be measured with accuracy . . . and will serve as a measure of the activity of the substance." She was photographed conducting this experiment as Pierre and their assistant, Petit, looked on.

After several weeks Marie was thrilled to find that "the emission of rays by the compounds of uranium is a property of the metal itself—that it is an atomic property of the element uranium independent of the chemical or physical state." She also found that the intensity of this surprising radiation was proportional to the quantity of the uranium contained in the sample under examination, and that this radiation, which could be measured with precision, was very constant and never affected by external factors such as lighting or temperature. Marie herself, however, was certainly affected by the temperature, writing on February 6, 1898, along with her scientific notes, that the air in her workplace was just six degrees above freezing—followed by six exclamation points.

While most physicists fixated exclusively on uranium as the source of this unique energy, Marie wondered if it might exist in other substances as well, and undertook the enormous task of looking for it in all the metals, metallic compounds, salts, and minerals she could get her hands on. Pierre helped her to collect them from various sources: a friendly chemist, a large collection at the School of Physics, and Alfred Lacroix, head of the Museum of Natural History. Some specimens were extremely rare, the only ones in existence. Then she "simply put her substance on a metal plate, opposite which was a second metal plate forming a condenser, and used her electrometer to detect whether she could make an electric current pass through the air between the plates. In this way she could quickly test dozens of substances with the thoroughness that for her had already become an obsessional scientific method."

She called the rays Becquerel rays, but eventually coined the word *radioactivity* to describe the spontaneous emission of radiation. Further testing revealed that only minerals containing traces of uranium or thorium were very radioactive, thorium oxide surpassing even metallic uranium in its radioactivity. Cerium, niobium, and tantalum were slightly radioactive. She then stopped work on all inactive minerals, such as gold and copper, to concentrate on the radioactive ones.

Because neither she nor Pierre were members of the prestigious French Academy of Sciences, Marie's former teacher, Professor Gabriel Lippmann (who had also formerly approved Pierre's Ph.D. thesis), delivered her first paper on her research at the weekly meeting of the Academy, on April 12, 1898. Titled "Rays Emitted by Compounds of Uranium and of Thorium," it was printed within ten days, when it reached the scientific world at large. Biographer Robert Reid pointed out that Marie Curie did not yet fully realize the enormous importance of her discovery—that radiation was not caused by an interaction between molecules, or by atoms creating new molecules, or by molecules taking on "new shapes as in an ordinary chemical reaction when energy as heat or light is given out as a product of the reaction." She had shown that "the radiation energy has a different origin and must come from the atom itself, irrespective of what the atom is joined up with or how it is behaving; radiation must be an atomic property. From this simple discovery twentieth century science was able to elucidate the structure of the atom, and from it sprang all the practical consequences of a knowledge of atomic structure."

But instead of atomic structure, what had immediately grabbed Marie's attention was the wild results from testing pitchblende. Astonished to find that its radioactivity was four times more intense than justified by its uranium content, she naturally thought it must be her mistake, and repeated the measurements as often as twenty times. But each time she got the same results. A similar inexplicable discrepancy occurred with the radioactive mineral chalcolite. The Curies discussed the problem with other scientists, who, without exception, concluded that her experiments were flawed and advised her to take more care. But Marie and Pierre disagreed. They knew that she had been extremely careful, and came to the same explanation for the discrepancies. She confided this daring hypothesis to her sister, Bronia: "The radiation [from pitchblende] that I couldn't explain comes from a new chemical element. The element is there and I've got to find it. We are sure!"

Pierre was so excited by the prospect of discovering a new element that he abandoned his own work on crystal growth research, expecting eventually to return to it. But he never did. He was hooked. Now, as active, enthusiastic partners, Marie and Pierre began their quest, under the misapprehension that trace amounts of this mystery element might be as common as one hundredth part of pitchblende ore—in blissful ignorance of the fact that they were hunting for a needle in a large haystack—something that was a millionth part of the substance. In pursuit of material for Marie's Ph.D. thesis, they were about to undertake the most arduous and physically demanding task in the recorded history of scientific research. For both, this would be a dangerous but passionate labor of love.

On June 6, 1898, they brought in an unassuming red-bearded chemist, Gustave Bémont, to help with the chemical analysis of pitchblende. Following his advice, Marie ground pitchblende into powder, dissolved it in acid, and went through the almost endless, repetitive task of separating its different elements. At each stage of the separation and purification she became increasingly convinced that something in the pitchblende was more radioactive than uranium itself. Finally she had excluded every element except bismuth, to which she added hydrogen sulphide. The chemical reaction produced a solid that she tested for its radioactivity. Marie's Eureka! is indicated by her unusually bold and underlined handwriting in their joint lab notebook as follows: **150 times more active than uranium**.

Working beside her at the time, Pierre was heating a solution of bismuth sulphide when the glass test tube cracked. But a thin black powder remained on part of the glass. He measured the powder, which was 330 times more active than uranium. Three weeks later, Marie was getting similar extraordinary results. As they continued they found that the less bismuth in the mixture, the more striking the results. They now knew for sure that they had discovered a new element. Marie named it polonium in honor of her native land, and before their work was published sent an account of it to her cousin, Joseph Boguski, director of the rebel Floating University in Warsaw, where she had made her first science experiments.

Their joint report was presented to the Academy of Sciences by the man who had inspired it, Henri Becquerel. Titled "On a New Radioactive Substance Contained in Pitchblende," it partly read: "We obtained a substance whose activity is about four hundred times greater than that of uranium. We have sought again among the known substances to determine if this is the most active. We have examined compounds of almost all the elementary substances [about eighty] thanks to the kindnesses of several chemists we have had samples of the rarest substances. . . . We believe therefore that the substance which we have removed from pitchblende contains a metal not yet reported. . . . If the existence of this new metal is confirmed, we propose to call it *polonium* from the name of the country of origin of one of us." It became element 84. The report concluded: "Allow us to note that if the existence of a new element is confirmed, this discovery will be uniquely attributable to the new method of detection that Becquerel rays provide."

Impressed by Marie's work both on the magnetic properties of steel and on radioactivity, the Academy of Sciences awarded her the Gegner Prize but, because its members were male chauvinists, did not tell her. Instead, Pierre was asked to inform her that she had won the prize and with it three thousand eight hundred francs. Meanwhile, instead of boiling chemicals, Marie was at home boiling gooseberries to make fourteen jars of gooseberry jelly, duly recorded in her notebook along with a record of her daughter's progress: On July 20, 1898, ten-month-old Irène could "walk very well now on all fours. She says 'Gogli, gogli, go.' She stays in the garden all day at Sceaux on a carpet [and] can roll, pick herself up, and sit down." On vacation in the mountains of Auvergne, she "cut her seventh tooth down on the left . . . can stand for half a minute alone. For the past three days we have bathed her in the river. She cries, but today (4th bath) she stopped crying and played with her hands in the water. She plays with the cat and chases him with war cries. She is not afraid of strangers anymore. She sings a great deal. She gets up on the table when she is in her chair."

Because of Irène, the Curies no longer spent their vacations on bicycles but stayed put, usually in a remote village, where they lived simply and could hardly be distinguished from the natives. Marie remembered the surprise of an American journalist who found her seated on the stone steps of her house emptying the sand from her shoes, who then sat beside her and "began to set down in his notebook my answers to his questions."

In September, refreshed from their vacation, the Curies returned to work. Again helped by chemist Gustave Bemont, they isolated a product from barium that was nine hundred times more radioactive than uranium. To confirm that this was a new element, they submitted it for spectral analysis to spectroscopist Eugène Demarcay. He was an odd choice for work demanding good eyesight, because he had lost one eye in a lab explosion. Nevertheless, the Curies had great faith in his expertise even though he had tried and failed to find a new spectral line to confirm polonium's existence.

Demarcay first dissolved a sample of the barium product, then painted the solution on electrodes, across which he passed an electric spark. Then came the tricky part—to photograph the spark spectrum. The Curies continued to provide him with progressively purer samples of the solid, until he was able to produce a clear spectral line—an element's unique fingerprint. As it was different from that of any known element, it was evidence that the Curies had discovered a new radioactive element. Demarcay died a few years later and showed his affection for Pierre by leaving him his laboratory equipment in his will, including his "beloved spectograph."

The Curies' success was overshadowed by the departure of Bronia and Casimir, Marie's sister and brother-in-law, for Austrian-dominated Poland. They intended to start an experimental open-air sanatorium in the Carpathian Mountains for tuberculosis patients, a disease that had killed Bronia and Marie's mother. It was partly funded by fellow Poles, their pianist friend Paderewski, and their novelist friend Henryk Sienkiewicz, author of *Quo Vadis*. Despite her preoccupations, Marie missed them desperately, writing to Bronia on December 2, 1898: "You can't imagine what a hole you have made in my life. With you two, I have lost everything I clung to in Paris except my husband and child. It seems to me that Paris no longer exists, aside from our lodging and the school where we work." Soon after, Marie and Pierre paid them a brief visit.

At year's end the scientific world learned that with the help of a chemist, Gustave Bémont, the Curies had discovered a minute amount of another new radioactive element in pitchblende, which they called radium (Latin for ray). The most powerful radioactive substance ever discovered, it would prove to emit "a million times more intensely than uranium." But, as was the case with polonium, incredulous scientists demanded decisive proof. After all, spontaneous radiation would overthrow fundamental theories accepted as true for centuries. To satisfy the skeptical scientific fraternity that the two new radioactive elements, polonium and radium, existed, the Curies would have to isolate them from the bismuth and barium with which they were mixed, then "produce them in demonstrable amounts [and] determine their atomic weight." This seemed an impossible task because to obtain significant quantities of these elements, they would need literally tons of pitchblende—and that would cost a fortune.

CHAPTER 5

Spirits, Radioactivity, and the Price of Fame

1899–1904

U ndeterred by the almost impossible task and encouraged by Marie, Pierre Curie began to hunt for international sources of radioactive material. As well as potential suppliers in France, he tried Norway, England, Portugal, and the United States. Several responded with offers of pathetically small amounts of uranium. The most generous was from a member of the U.S. Geological Survey at the Smithsonian, who sent five hundred grams of it as a gift.

The Curies believed that minute traces of polonium and radium might still remain in slag heaps of pitchblende from a mine in Bohemia (now Jachymov in the Czech Republic) owned by the Austro-Hungarian government. The uranium salts already extracted from it had been sold to color ceramic glazing and tint photographs, and the residue had been dumped as useless in a nearby pine forest. Pierre contacted Professor Eduard Suess, a geologist at the University of Vienna, who said that this residue was probably available and the work already done on it, in the massive first stage of uranium recovery, would save Pierre and Marie months of effort.

Determined to get it, Pierre informed the relevant Austro-Hungarian official that the aim of their research was purely scientific, a sentence he underlined to stress the purity of their motives. But he shrewdly added that the result of "this research will benefit the Joachimsthal factory, [which] could [then] sell or exploit the otherwise valueless residues." The government agreed to provide several tons of the waste pitchblende at a moderate price, but still out of the Curies' reach. However, Professor Suess persuaded the Austrians to give a ton of it to a couple they apparently regarded, according to Eve Curie, as "two French lunatics who thought they needed" the useless stuff. The Curies simply had to pay the transportation costs. Fortunately, an unknown benefactor (almost certainly Baron Edmond de Rothschild) gave them enough to buy several more tons of pitchblende residue—mixed with pine needles from the forest where it had been dumped—and have it delivered to Paris in sacks.

The problem then was where to undertake the experiments. As their present lab was hopeless, they appealed to the bureaucrat in charge of the Sorbonne's many buildings, who turned them down. The new director at the School of Physics and Chemistry, the uptight, officious Professor Gabriel, was hardly more helpful. Pierre had already had a run-in with him over his rule that no visitor could call on the Curies without his permission. In a polite but firm letter, Pierre asked Gabriel to renew Schutzenberger's authorization for Marie to work at the school, and for permission to have visitors without anyone's authorization, and Gabriel caved. But when the Curies asked for space to work on pitchblende, his reluctant offer was almost an insult. They were shown, across from the school's courtyard, a dilapidated shed, once used as a morgue by the School of Medicine, where students dissected cadavers. Abandoned, it seemed not even fit for cadavers: the skylight's broken windows let in the rain and the dirt floor was roughly covered with a scattering of asphalt. It had a few battered kitchen tables, a blackboard, and a cast-iron stove with a rusty pipe. They would discover that the shed was an oven in summer and an icebox in winter. Despite the obvious drawbacks, they accepted it. German chemist Wilhelm Oswald, who saw the place after the Curies had moved in, called it "a cross between a stable and a potato-cellar, and if I had not seen the worktable with the chemical apparatus I would have thought it a practical joke."

Cornell University physics professor Ernest Merritt compared their immediate task to that of a detective searching for suspects in a crowded street. "Pitchblende," he wrote, "is one of the most complex of minerals, containing [up to] thirty different elements, combined in a great variety of ways. The problem had all the fascination of a journey into an unexplored land." Tracking down a new element would have been a tough job for an experienced chemist familiar with the varieties of behavior of all known elements. Yet, though neither Marie nor Pierre was a trained chemist, they were not discouraged.

Marie was ecstatic when the first load of pitchblende arrived early in 1899 and she and Pierre hurried from the shed to watch the sacks of it unloaded from a truck. Too excited to wait, she opened the nearest sack and eagerly plunged her hands into the mix of ore, dust, and pine needles. She then had the sacks moved inside, away from the spots where water dripped steadily during rainstorms. This, and subsequent loads, she would sort, grind, dissolve, filter, precipitate, collect, redissolve, crystalize, and recrystalize over and over again. Visitors were astonished to see the apparently fragile young woman wielding a hefty iron bar almost as tall as herself to stir a vat of the boiling solutions for hours on end—unprotected from the poisonous hydrogen-sulphide used in the purification process. Though unaware of it, the Curies were also inhaling a dangerous gas rising from the steaming caldrons. Radon was discovered that same year, in 1899, by New Zealand physicist Ernest Rutherford, who encountered this radioactive gas while experimenting at Cambridge University with Becquerel rays.

Georges Urbain, a young physicist with a large collection of minerals, visited Marie while she was working in this poisonous atmosphere. He was startled to see her vigorously stirring the hot, fuming liquids—a task that would have challenged a strong man. Urbain later felt that he had witnessed the birth of radium. She obviously loved the work even though, as she admitted, at the day's end she would be broken with fatigue. Marie chose this physically demanding aspect of the work despite Pierre's reservation, insisting that she could handle it. In the summer, when stifling heat drove them outdoors, they continued their work in the courtyard. Rainstorms or freezing weather in the fall and winter drove them back inside, where the rusty old stove did little to warm them. A few feet from it the air was as cold as outside. Marie soldiered on in a dust-covered, acid-stained smock, her eyes and throat stinging from the smoke and poisonous gases. Yet, she wrote: "In our poor shed there reigned a great tranquility. Sometimes, as we watched over some operation, we would walk up and down, talking about work in the present and in the future. When we were cold a cup of hot tea taken near the stove comforted us. We lived in our single preoccupation as if in a dream. We saw only very few persons at the laboratory; among the physicists and chemists there were a few who came from time to time, either to see our experiments or to ask for advice from Pierre Curie, whose competence in several branches of physics was well-known."

Marie still missed her father and the rest of her Polish family, but was otherwise pleased with life. She and Pierre felt healthy, were equally devoted to their intriguing work, and were delighted with their two-year-old daughter, Irène. Their marriage, too, was flourishing. As Marie told her sister, "I have the best husband one could dream of; I could never have imagined finding one like him. He is a true gift from heaven, and the more we live together, the more we love each other."

Eventually, overwhelmed by the work, Marie and Pierre began to make more use of a technician named Petit, who usually helped students at the School of Physics and Chemistry to set up their experiments. He was also supposed to clean up the Curies' shed before going home at night. But if he forgot, Marie, a stickler for a clean workbench, did it for him. Pierre also encouraged a young chemist at the Sorbonne, André Debierne, to join them whenever he was free from other commitments. Some believed this temperamental and somewhat inarticulate man was secretly in love with Marie.

He surely became the Curies' devoted friend and valued colleague, and almost one of the family. Working with them on the pitchblende in 1899 he discovered a new element, actinium (no. 89), the rare, highly radioactive silvery-white metal that, like radium, also glowed blue in the dark. Another young physicist, Georges Sagnac, who had once collaborated with Pierre to measure the electric charge of the secondary rays in X-rays, also became a close friend of the Curies.

They gained more friends by their generous spirit in responding to the requests of other investigators, sending samples of radioactive material to an Icelandic scientist, Adam Paulsen; physicist Ernest Rutherford in Canada; Lord Kelvin in England; and to others in Poland, Germany, Austria, and Denmark. They also gave a glass tube of radioactive barium to Becquerel, who for some reason kept it in his waistcoat wrapped in thick paper for about six hours. This caused a burn on his skin the shape of the glass tube. Yet he had felt no burning sensation. He told the Curies that this inadvertent experiment, with himself as guinea pig, had both delighted and annoyed him. In Germany, F. Giesel had written to Pierre that he, too, had observed the effect of radiation on his skin. Pierre then personally confirmed the possibly dangerous effect by intentionally inducing a burn on his own arm with the radioactive barium. Meeting fellow physicist Charles-Edouard Guillaume on the street soon after, Pierre rolled back his sleeve and said, "Look how this has begun to redden," showing him the developing sore. It took fifty-two days to heal, leaving a gray spot he believed indicated a deeper injury. Both he and Marie had already noticed that handling containers of radioactive material caused their fingertips to become hard and painful for as long as two months.

The experience spurred Pierre to collaborate with two doctors, Professors Charles Bouchard and V. Bathazard, to investigate radium's effect on animals. The positive results were promising. According to several French

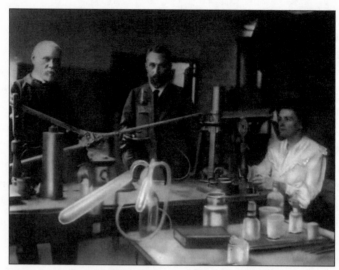

The Curie team in 1899. Marie measures radioactivity with a
piezoelectric quartz balance—devised by Pierre and his brother
Jacques—as Pierre and their assistant, Petit, look on.

doctors, the radium they had borrowed from the Curies cured or reduced
their patients' tumors, lesions, and some kinds of cancer. This radium
treatment became known as Curie-therapy.

But as for the Curies themselves, their continual contact with radium
under awful working conditions was beginning to have the opposite effect.
In March 1899 Marie wrote to her brother, Joseph, now a respected doctor with a wife and daughter, Manyusya, that Pierre was on a diet of milk,
eggs, and vegetables, plenty of water, and no red meat, to fight what was
thought to be extremely painful rheumatism. And she played down her
own visits to the doctor to check her lungs after fits of coughing and suspected tuberculosis. Baby Irène, she was pleased to report, was healthy.

Now that the Curies were becoming internationally known, they
sometimes shared news of their progress and problems with an indepen-
dently wealthy British chemist, Sir William Crookes. As president of the
British Society for Psychical Research, he also took a keen interest in the
spirit world. Consequently, he had his own wonders to report of both this
world and the next. In this one, as early as 1861, he had discovered a new
chemical element, thallium. As for the next, he claimed to have met a
ghost in the flesh. He insisted that during a spiritualist séance he had seen
and touched a woman returned from the dead—and he had a photograph
of the two of them together to prove it. Some of his peers responded with
derision, thought his name, Crookes, was appropriate, and regarded him
as a fool, a liar, or a lunatic. The evidence points to the conclusion that he

was either a dupe or in cahoots with a living woman who masqueraded as the "spirit" in white bedsheets. If Pierre Curie ever knew of Crookes's dalliance with a female ghost made flesh it is unlikely to have completely disillusioned him. Both he and his brother, Jacques, were interested in the paranormal and open-minded on the subject. Spiritualism was in its heyday and several reputable and notable scientists were seriously testing mediums and their purported communication with the dead, while conceding that many were frauds.* Pierre and Marie later investigated a famous Neapolitan trance medium, Eusapia Palladino.

In his more credible research, Crookes, like Marie Curie, was trying to extract radium from pitchblende by fractional crystallization, a method he had learned from a former student, André Debierne, now working for the Curies. Marie, too, had started to use this method and it was a race to see who would succeed first. Ernest Rutherford and Frederick Soddy at Montreal's McGill University were close behind, though focusing on different aspects of radioactivity.

Learning of the Curies' growing reputation, the dean of the University of Geneva arrived at their shed to tempt Pierre with the answer to most of his problems: an idyllic life in the Swiss mountains, his own laboratory equipped with anything he wanted, two full-time assistants, a generous salary of ten thousand francs, and an allowance for his residence. Marie was also promised an undefined position at the university. Not everyone knew that she was at least Pierre's partner if not the leading partner of the team. Marie apparently didn't take offense and agreed to consider the offer. In July 1900, Pierre wrote to a Swiss friend: "Your compatriots have been extremely kind and have insisted on having me. We are now going to Geneva to take a closer look at the situation. It seems to me it would be an excellent thing to live in your beautiful land of mountains." They went and were impressed. Their current income, augmented by occasional small grants and prize money, was not enough to meet even their frugal lifestyle. Pierre earned a measly salary of twenty thousand five hundred francs and their yearly rent alone was fourteen hundred francs. The Swiss offer would more than solve their financial problems.

Warned that the Curies might be lost to France, Henri Poincaré, the country's leading mathematician, pulled strings that resulted in Pierre being offered a minor teaching position at the School of Physics, Chemistry,

---

* Among them were British physicist Sir Oliver Lodge, French Nobel Prize–winning physiologist Professor Charles Richet, French astronomer Camille Flammarion, German physician Baron Albert von Schrenck-Notzing, Irish physicist Sir William Barrett, and American psychologist William James.

and Natural Science. Attached to the Sorbonne, it paid only a slightly higher salary than his present one. And Marie was offered a part-time job lecturing on physics at Sèvres, a teachers college for women in a Paris suburb, which had once been Mme de Pompadour's porcelain factory. If she accepted, Marie would be the first woman ever to teach there.

Later, during their summer vacation with Irène on the Brittany coast, the Curies rejected the fabulous Swiss offer, deciding that it would disrupt and delay their work on radium. Instead, though in dire need of money, they accepted the job offers in France. That, too, would delay their research, but not as much. So Pierre began preparing lectures for his two classes of mostly medical students or engineers, while Marie did the same for her twice-weekly classes at Sèvres, which she reached by train. Otherwise, almost every free moment they had was spent working in their shed.

Marie's early classes were a fiasco. The twenty-year-old students disliked her because the math she taught was over their heads, and she stuttered and spoke too fast, probably from nerves. Though her French was good, they ridiculed her slight Polish accent. According to former student Marthe Baillaud, the general reaction was epitomized in the mocking lyrics of a song they sang about Marie that ended:

> Wouldn't she be better off
> Cooking for her husband-prof
> Instead of talking in a stream
> To a class that's bored enough to scream.

Biographer Susan Quinn believed that another reason for their derision was that a woman in an "unfamiliar role made them uncomfortable." What a contrast to her next year's students. They couldn't wait for the bell to call them to class, impatiently looking from a window for her to appear in her little gray dress, walking toward them between two rows of chestnut trees. Then they eagerly rushed to their seats to await her entrance. Marie had taken the measure of these students and, as one recalled: "She held us with her simplicity, her desire to be useful to us, the sense she had of both our ignorance and our possibilities." Unlike the male lecturers, she allowed them to handle the experimental apparatus and welcomed questions with an encouraging smile.

At home, if there was no vital lab work, she might make clothes for four-year-old Irène from patterns of her own design—just as her mother had made shoes for Marie. And during the night she often responded to Irène's cries for her, staying until the child dropped off to sleep. When she returned, Pierre would invariably complain, "You never think of anything but that child!"—a reproach, as their daughter Eve remarked, that "was so unjust as to be comic." Pierre was not quite the saint "and true gift from heaven" Marie pictured in her memoirs. Still, she understood him, because she shared his obsession. For instance, one night after dinner, having corrected her students' homework and completed an account of that day's research and household expenses, she stayed with Irène until she was asleep. Then, when she rejoined Pierre downstairs she was greeted with the familiar, "You never think of anything but that child!" Marie knew that Pierre was at his happiest when concentrating on the one subject that gripped him. It had been crystals, now it was radium. Any distraction, which included little Irène, upset him. So she suggested that they go back to the "miserable old shed," as she affectionately called it. They had only left it a few hours earlier, after a hard day. Yet Pierre was all for it. Leaving his father in charge of the sleeping Irène, they strolled arm-in-arm past factories, tenements, and a wasteland where the local authorities permitted carpet beating, then crossed the courtyard to their decrepit laboratory. Once inside, Marie told him not to light the lamps. Instead, they stared for a while, almost lovingly, at their wonderland lit by the bluish glow from minute amounts of radium in glass bottles spread around the shed, and bright enough to read by.

Despite their heavy workload, the Curies also produced a detailed report on radioactive substances for the International Congress of Physics, part of an international exhibition in Paris from August 6 to 12 in 1900. It attracted an amazing fifty million visitors, Lord Kelvin among them, to see the latest scientific miracles. In their report the Curies highlighted the still enigmatic nature of radioactivity that not only, they wrote, "seemed to violate the first law of thermodynamics, i.e., that energy can be converted from one form to another but cannot be created or destroyed," while "radium just emitted energy without seeming to undergo any change."

As the months passed, the Central Chemical Products Company offered to take over the crude processes to refine the radium—without charge, though doubtless anticipating eventual profit. The inducement was that it would allow Marie to concentrate on the final stages. The Curies agreed, and their friend André Debierne supervised the factory's operations. He also collaborated with Pierre Curie.

In 1901 in their joint paper "On Induced Radioactivity and the Gas Activated by Radium," they mentioned "the deplorable situation in the lab, where everything has become radioactive. This does not seem to us to be explained by the direct radiation of radioactive dust spread about the lab; it is probably due . . . to the continual formation of radioactive gas."

Pierre was able to show that this gas was largely responsible for radium's intense radiation.

Ernest Rutherford, already showing signs of becoming the greatest experimental physicist of his time, knew that his biggest rivals in establishing the nature of radium were still the French. As he wrote to his mother on January 5, 1902: "I have to publish my present work as rapidly as possible in order to keep in the race. The best sprinters in this road of investigation are Becquerel and the Curies in Paris, who have done a great deal of very important work in the subject of radioactive bodies during the last few years."

Early in 1902 the Curies got a grant of twenty thousand francs from the French Academy of Sciences. This allowed them to buy more pitchblende residue, from which they hoped to produce enough pure radium to estimate its atomic weight. This alone would satisfy the scientific community that it was a new chemical element. On March 28, Marie believed she had produced a suitable sample. She took it to Eugène Demarcay and asked him to weigh it. It was so radioactive that it sent his electrical equipment haywire. But he kept trying and finally was able to tell her that it weighed just over one-tenth of a gram—enough for her to calculate its atomic weight. Working with her usual care and caution, after several calculations she wrote down its atomic weight as 225.93, remarkably close to the 226 on today's Periodic Table listing for radium. Here at long last was the evidence science demanded. It had taken them almost four exhausting years to produce, a process the Curies had expected to take a few weeks.

Marie immediately told her father, who was recovering from a serious injury caused when a Warsaw tram hit him. He replied with heartfelt congratulations, but expressed his disappointment that the work seemed to have no practical value. In fact, wrote biographer Pflaum, their discovery of radium "opened the doors to twentieth-century physics. Scientists now had a powerful source of radiation. Its study would enable them to witness for the first time the manifestation of atomic energy. Radium was the key to unlock the mystery of the composition of the universe, for it would help them explore and understand the structure of the atom, the base of all matter on earth." Or, as Paul Langevin speculated some forty years after its discovery: "It may have an importance for the future of civilization comparable to that which allowed man to discover the power of fire."

But Marie's father would never live to see it. Soon after his street accident, when Marie heard that he had been rushed back to the hospital for a gallbladder operation, she dropped everything and took a train to Warsaw. During the two-and-half-day journey she learned that he was dead, arriving just in time for his funeral. The coffin was closed, but she insisted that it be opened and then wept uncontrollably, not only because of his death, but because she felt guilty for abandoning the seventy-year-old man, who had counted on spending his last days with her. She stayed beside his coffin crying hysterically from guilt and grief, wrote her daughter Eve "until her brother and sisters put an end to the cruel scene." Later that year she briefly returned to Warsaw for a family reunion.

Her rigorous lifestyle, inadequate diet, exposure to radium, and loss of her father took their toll. One symptom of the stress was that she began to sleepwalk. Pierre's health, too, greatly concerned her and their friends. Hoping to ease his workload, they recommended him to head Sorbonne's mineralogy department, which would involve fewer and less demanding hours and a better income. He was well qualified, but someone else got the job. His disappointed friends then pressured him into being a candidate for the French Academy of Sciences, membership of which would enhance his chances of promotion, having his own lab, and receiving a livable salary. He reluctantly went through what he found demeaning, seeking approval from his peers, the academy's physicists, who unanimously approved his application. Then the entire academy, which included all disciplines, had to vote for him, or for one of his two rivals, Emile Amagat or Désiré Gernez. This entailed the process that Pierre found most humiliating: calling on the members to promote himself, name his achievements, and explain why he was the best man. He couldn't play the game and, instead, spoke of Amagat as more deserving and qualified than himself. Most seem to have taken him at his word, and on June 9, 1902, Amagat was elected with thirty-two votes to Pierre's twenty; Gernez got six. Pierre's only regret was the wasted time.

Wanting to help Pierre after his failure to be accepted by the academy, Paul Appell, the Sorbonne's new dean and Marie's former teacher, intended to recommend him for the prestigious Legion of Honor. Knowing that Pierre scorned public recognition, he enlisted Marie's help in breaking Pierre's resistance. Tell him, Appell wrote, that it would be to the greater glory of the faculty and could lead to practical advantages for Pierre, and that he need not wear the decoration. It didn't work. As Pierre saw it, instead of helping his research, the government was trying to fob him off with a medal and a scrap of colored ribbon. He asked Appell to thank the appropriate minister and "inform him that I do not feel the slightest need of being decorated but I am in the greatest need of a laboratory."

Even without a decent laboratory Pierre got remarkable results. Marie described his efforts as superhuman and rated all his investigations as fundamentally important. She pointed out that several had as their aim the study of "that strange gaseous body that radium produces and which is largely responsible for the intense radiation commonly attributed to the radium itself. Pierre Curie demonstrated by a searching examination the rigorous and invariable law according to which the emanation destroys itself, no matter what the conditions."

In March 1903 Pierre and Albert Laborde published their equally extraordinary findings that just one gram of radium spontaneously heated its own weight of water from freezing to boiling in an hour—a hint of its enormous potential energy. Pierre's longtime physicist friend Georges Gouy, among the first to grasp its threat and promise, wrote to him: "When an atom of radium explodes, sending off its parts with enormous speed and producing a significant heat, the constituents must be exposed, during this explosion, to colossal forces."

Albert Einstein would soon explain how an ounce of radium emitted four thousand calories an hour almost indefinitely. For two years he had been mulling over his momentous conclusion that all matter in the universe is a repository of enormous, latent energy. And in 1905 he revealed this secret of creation in six strokes of the pen, the equation $E=mc^2$.

The formula implied that mass is frozen energy, and predicted that converting a small amount of mass would release an enormous amount of energy—as eventually happened with the atomic bomb. Though Einstein neither revealed how to split the atom nor suggested the possibility, his formula would be used to uncover the mystery of how, through nuclear reactions, the sun and stars radiate light and heat for billions of years. Einstein also noted that this incredible energy was unknown until the Curies discovered radium.

In 1903 the source of the energy remained a tantalizing mystery. Pierre still thought that it must be external, while Marie wondered if it came from an interior source, with small violently agitated particles being expelled as energy. She had invited her Sèvres class of would-be teachers to watch Pierre use a Bunsen calorimeter to measure the heat produced by radium. One student was specially impressed by his clear explanations, his slow and serious manner of speaking, "by his luminous expression, and by the deftness of his long artistic hands, which operated before us with astonishing confidence." Back at the school Marie had her class repeat the experiment to measure the specific heat of a small sample of copper.

On Sundays, nominally the Curies' day off, visitors were usually fellow scientists from the School of Physics and Chemistry or the Sorbonne, and the discussions and arguments continued with them. On sunny days they gathered in the Curies' garden, shaded by sycamore trees and scented by lilacs bushes, to talk shop. Several would play important roles in the Curies' lives, especially their next-door neighbor Jean Perrin, an expert on cathode rays; Pierre's former student Paul Langevin, who had moved with his wife and children to a house near the Curies; Emile Borel, a distinguished mathematician and his fun-loving wife, Marguerite, who wrote novels under the pen name Camille Marbo; André Debierne; Georges Sagnac; and Aimé Cotton.

The Curies were also beginning to get important international attention. When Thomas Alva Edison's collaborator, William Joseph Hammer, lectured on radium at the New York Academy of Medicine on February 19, 1903, he quoted Pierre Curie's remark that: "[I] would not like to be in the same room with a kilogram of the substance, which would probably burn the side off [my] body and the eyes out of [my] head." The *New York Times*' report of the lecture was the first time the paper ever mentioned radioactivity. Four months later the *St. Louis Post-Dispatch*, in previewing the upcoming International Electrical Congress in St. Louis, announced that "a grain of the most wonderful and mysterious metal will be shown in St. Louis in 1904 . . . Its power will be inconceivable. By means of the metal all the arsenals of the world would be destroyed . . . It is even possible that an instrument might be invented which at the touch of a key would blow up the whole earth and bring about the end of the world."

Meanwhile, through the spring of 1903, Pierre worked on two more of his papers (by 1904 he had published twenty-six papers) and Marie put the finishing touches on perhaps history's most momentous academic thesis: an understated account of how she and Pierre had established the existence of a new, enigmatic chemical element that, unknown to them, would usher in the atomic age.

Shortly before Marie defended her doctoral dissertation before three professors, she and Pierre crossed the English Channel to London, where Pierre had been invited to lecture on radium at the Royal Institution to an audience of Britain's greatest scientists—among them Sir William Crookes, Lord Rayleigh, Sir Oliver Lodge, and Professor William Ayrton. As Pierre chose to give the lecture in French, he was advised to speak slowly and simply and to entertain the audience by showing rather than telling. Though he was so ill in fact that he had trouble changing into his worn and shiny formal clothes, he managed to make his way to the institution's large amphitheater. In his talk, as Marie listened sitting alongside their friend Lord Kelvin, Pierre mentioned four times her important role in their work. During the lecture Pierre raised his sleeve to show the audience the radium burn scar on his arm and said, "the action of radium on nervous centers may result in paralysis or death. They seem to act with particular intensity on living tissues in the process of growth." This early warning that radium was a health hazard may also explain the nature of his illness. But he stressed its possible therapeutic value, too, saying that researchers had used it to treat lupus and cancer, and that a Dr. Walkhoff claimed to have successfully treated some cancers with X-rays. Pierre thought that radium might be used "in a similar fashion."

Then the room at the Royal Institution was darkened and, in the words of biographer Robert Reid, "by the witchcraft of radium he discharged a gold-leaf electroscope at a distance, rendered a screen of zinc sulphide fluorescent, made impressions on photographic plates wrapped in black paper, and proved the spontaneous release of heat from the marvelous substance." Pierre must have accidentally spilled some radium, because fifty years later a decontamination team from Harwell's atomic research station was called in to clean it up.

Marie felt uncomfortably on display in London because so many seemed to regard a woman physicist as even more exotic than a tube of radium. But she warmed to Professor Ayrton's wife, Hertha, the daughter of a Polish Jew. She was also a physicist and could discuss the subject intelligently and in French. They agreed to keep in touch. The next day Kelvin hosted a luncheon in Pierre's honor, and that weekend the Curies were guests at crowded receptions ablaze and aglitter with high-society women. During one dinner, Marie amused herself by calculating how many labs they could build with the wealth from the precious stones the women wore. An astronomical figure, she told Pierre later, with a laugh.

Although they, too, could have been wealthy and Marie bejeweled by patenting the process to produce radium—factories were already preparing to exploit it—the Curies had agreed to give it to the world. They had discussed how the prospective money could provide for Irène's future, make their life easier, and allow them to build the laboratory of Pierre's dreams. But they decided that taking financial advantage of their discovery was against the scientific spirit, especially as radium might be used to fight disease. Consequently one Sunday morning, Pierre wrote to the American engineers who had asked for details about radium production and gave them all the answers. Twenty years later, Marie recalled: "This was a great benefit to the radium industry, which was enabled to develop in full liberty, first in France and then abroad, furnishing the scientists and doctors the products they needed."

Fifteen minutes after their irrevocable decision to eschew a fortune, they were on their bicycles headed for the woods of Clamart to gather wildflowers. And a few days later, on June 12, 1903, thirty-six-year-old Marie, three months pregnant with her second child, set off for the students' hall of the Sorbonne to defend her dissertation on radium. The atmosphere there was like the first night of a much-ballyhooed play. It was so crowded with scientists, students, and the public hoping for insight into the mysterious subject that there was standing room only and extra chairs were brought in. Bronia, there from Poland for the event, sat near the back with Pierre and his father. Besides several leading scientists, a few close friends such as Jean Perrin and Paul Langevin, there was a contingent of Marie's students from Sèvres.

She climbed the curving staircase and quietly entered the large, crowded hall, wearing a new dress that Bronia had persuaded her to buy for the occasion. Marie had insisted that it be black, intending to wear it later in the lab. She walked to a blackboard and stood waiting for the first question from the trio sitting at a long table and formally dressed in white ties and tails. They were all well-known to her: Professors Gabriel Lippmann—Marie's thesis advisor—Henri Moissan, who had supplied her with uranium, and Edmond Bouty. Two of them would become Nobel Prize winners: Moissan, in 1906, and Lippmann, in 1908. They, of course, had read her 132-page doctoral thesis in which she described with scientific objectivity how, helped by Pierre Curie, Gustave Bémont, and André Debierne, she had isolated two new radioactive chemical elements, polonium and radium.

During what resembled an easy, low-key, friendly conversation, Marie illustrated some technical answers with chalk on the blackboard, obviously more familiar with the subject than anyone else in the room. The interrogation completed, her examiners whispered their conclusions to Professor Lippmann as the audience held its collective breath. Finally, he turned to Marie to say: "The University of Paris [the Sorbonne] accords you the title of doctor of physical science." And the audience broke into thunderous applause for this, as biographer David Wilson put it, "remarkable breach of a male fortress." The examining committee also expressed its view that "the findings represented the greatest scientific contribution ever made in a doctoral thesis."

Some eighty-five years later, chemistry professor Robert L. Wolke of the University of Pittsburgh cast a critical eye on Marie's thesis. "The chemical separations and fractional crystallizations that they [the team] employed were nothing short of heroic in scale," he wrote. "'Courageous' is neither too strong nor too romantic a word to use for the woman who designed and led this incredibly difficult quest, ultimately giving up her life to a cancer [leukemia] born of the radiations in which she was continually immersed." But Wolke was disappointed to find no speculation in her thesis about the relationship of her experiments "to the great mystery that she and others [especially Rutherford] were struggling to solve. What is radioactivity, and what is the source of its energy?"

However, three years previously, while lecturing at the Sorbonne on June 14, 1900, she had suggested that radioactivity might be a unique chemical reaction that defies the long-held principle of atomic indestructibility. A no less embarrassing alternative hypothesis, she said, was that the law of conservation of energy did not apply to "certain molecular phenomena, and that radioactive substances possess the power of transforming ambient heat into work." She conceded that "this hypothesis strikes just as serious a blow at accepted ideas in physics as the hypothesis of the transformation of elements does at the principles of chemistry, and one can see that the question is not easy to resolve."

It was, however, as good as resolved two years later, in 1902, with Rutherford and Soddy's hypothesis of atomic transmutation. Professor Wolke concluded that although Marie's hypothesis of atoms that change was far from the Rutherford-Soddy hypothesis, it was "nevertheless an insightful speculation . . . which she was willing to express orally in a lecture, if not in print."

By coincidence, while Marie was defending her thesis, the ebullient Ernest Rutherford had just arrived in Paris with his wife. Informed by a long-delayed postcard from his partner, Soddy, in Canada, that Marie Curie wanted to meet him, he went to her lab and found it locked and empty. The Rutherfords eventually traced her to her home that evening, where Paul Langevin had arranged a celebratory dinner for her successful thesis, and they were invited to join the party. Langevin had been Rutherford's friend since their Cambridge days, when for several years the two men had worked in adjoining rooms at England's Cavendish Laboratory. The other guests were physicist Jean Perrin (a future Nobelist, who would confirm the atomic nature of matter) and his wife.

Langevin thought of Rutherford as a force of nature. Others called the New Zealander a magnetic personality, boisterous, full of infectious enthusiasm, and blunt to the point of being obnoxious.

Although several of Rutherford's close friends disliked Marie Curie, he took to her immediately. The man known as a "string and sealing wax" experimenter, because he got remarkable results with basic, sometimes handmade equipment, liked the simple way she dressed and her unpretentious manner. She liked his blunt honesty and admired the way he treated women as equals and encouraged them to pursue scientific careers. Like the Curies, he, too, had chosen not to make money from any of his discoveries. It was such a warm night that after dinner they moved to the garden to continue their conversation. Pierre brought the light with him, fascinating the group by taking a tube of radium from his pocket and holding it aloft like a lamp. It was bright enough for Rutherford to notice with concern that Pierre's hand was so raw and inflamed that he had difficulty in holding the tube. Rutherford may have escaped similar injuries by dealing in his research with weaker strengths of radium. Not that he thought radium was dangerous. When a colleague working on radioactive material said he could discharge an electroscope just by exhaling, instead of being worried that the man had inhaled radium fumes, Rutherford was delighted: it confirmed his theory that radium emitted airborne gases.

On his visit to the Curies, Rutherford had no idea how ill they were. Pierre, watched over by his desperately worried wife, had recently spent whole nights awake moaning in pain, and Marie was anemic and perpetually tired, and had lost ten pounds. That night they kept their troubles from him. But a young colleague, Georges Sagnac, who knew the Curies well, was so disturbed by Marie's changed appearance that in a frank, almost desperate ten-page letter he had urged Pierre to make a radical change in their lifestyle and stop perpetually thinking of science. Neither of them ate enough, he wrote. They must at least have a leisurely lunch and dinner, and not talk or read about physics during meals. Aware of how indifferent or stubborn Marie could be about her own welfare, Sagnac dared to suggest that she was a bad mother. (She was, in fact, loving and attentive.) "I can see the following objection," Sagnac wrote. "'[Marie] isn't hungry! And she's big enough now to know what she wants to do!' No, it won't do! *She actually behaves like a* CHILD! I am telling you this with all the conviction of my judgment and friendship . . . Don't you love Irène? It seems to me that I wouldn't prefer the idea of reading a paper by Rutherford, to getting what my body needs, and of looking at such an agreeable little girl. Give her a kiss from me. If she were a bit older she would think like me and she would tell you this. Think of her a little."

Did Pierre deliver Sagnac's heartfelt message to Marie? It was hardly necessary. Nature was about to force her to take it easy for several months. In early August 1903, during the fifth month of her pregnancy and while vacationing at Saint-Trojan, she miscarried and was devastated. As she wrote to Bronia: "I had grown so accustomed to the idea of the child that I am absolutely desperate and cannot be consoled. Write to me, I beg of you, if you think I should blame this on general fatigue—for I must admit that I have not spared my strength . . . and I regret this bitterly, as I have paid dearly for it. The child—a little girl—was in good condition and was living. And I had wanted it so badly!" Bronia had her own heartbreak to contend with, as her second child, a five-year-old boy, had died suddenly of meningitis. Hearing of it, Marie wrote to Joseph: "I can no longer look at my little girl without trembling with terror. And Bronia's grief tears me to pieces."

Four months later Marie was still recuperating from the miscarriage and too tired to accompany Pierre to England to collect their Davy Medal from the Royal Society. (Named for Sir Humphry Davy, a great eighteenth-century British scientist who experimented with nitrous oxide, or laughing gas, invented a safety lamp for miners, proved that diamond is a form of carbon, and discovered several chemical elements.)

At Cambridge, Pierre met Rutherford's mentor, Professor J. J. Thomson, chairman of the Physics Department at the Cavendish Laboratories. Thomson had discovered the electron, the long-sought "atom" of electricity, in 1897, for which he would receive the Nobel Prize in Physics in 1906. He must have been an inspiring teacher, because seven men who worked under him became Nobelists. Pierre Curie impressed him as "the most modest of men, ascribing everything to his wife, [and with] a most attractive simplicity of manner." Why did Pierre, who scorned French honors, accept a medal from the British? Apparently he had so enjoyed his previous visit that he welcomed the chance for a return trip. Besides, he didn't take the decoration seriously: on his return home, to the delight of his six-year-old daughter, Irène, Pierre gave her the gold medal as a plaything.

During that summer of grieving and physical pain, Pierre Curie was told that he was on the short list for a 1903 Nobel Prize. The list of nominees was normally kept secret and only the names of winners announced. But there was a special reason for warning Pierre in advance, as will shortly become clear.

Unknown to the Curies, they had both been nominated for the physics prize the first year it was awarded, 1901, by French pathologist Charles Bouchard. His vote was to prove of critical importance. That year the prize went to Roentgen of X-ray fame. The Curies were also unaware that the following year, Bouchard again nominated them and Becquerel. So did two others: Jean-Gaston Darboux, dean of the Sorbonne's Faculty of Sciences; and Emil Warburg, a German physicist. Physicist Eleuthère Mascart nominated Pierre alone. However, the 1902 prize went to Dutch physicists Hendrik Lorenz and Peter Zeeman for their research into the effect of magnetism on radiation phenomena.

Although support for the Curies had grown, in 1903 there was a mean-spirited and concerted attempt by four Frenchmen to prevent Marie from getting the prize. In researching the early history of the Nobel Institution, author Elisabeth Crawford found that Gabriel Lippmann, Jean-Gaston Darboux, Eleuthère Mascart, and Henri Poincaré, all members of the French Academy of Sciences, had signed a joint letter to the Nobel Prize selection committee. In it, they credited Pierre Curie alone with isolating polonium and radium and described Pierre and Becquerel as competing with foreign rivals for the radium supply and obtaining the "precious material" with great difficulty. They then concluded that because Pierre and Becquerel had studied together it was impossible "for us to separate the names of the two physicists and therefore we do not hesitate to propose that the Nobel Prize be shared between Mr. Becquerel and Mr. Curie." Not a word about Marie Curie! It was as if they were not even aware of her existence—or had completely discounted her work.

Lippmann and Poincaré especially knew for sure that she and Pierre had isolated polonium and radium as a team, with her, if anything, in the lead. Marie's papers, lectures, and thesis and the Curies' jointly kept notebooks were striking evidence of this. So what persuaded them to sign a letter they knew to be false? And what made Darboux change his mind after having nominated her the previous year? Was it that with so many male contenders to consider, the Frenchmen couldn't stomach the idea of a young woman—and a foreigner at that—getting the prestigious prize?

Then a Swedish mathematician came to Marie's rescue. Magnus Mittag-Leffler, a member of the Nobel Prize nominating committee, welcomed and encouraged women scientists, and when he learned of the plot against her, he wrote in confidence to Pierre warning him that he, but not Marie, was in the running for the prize. Pierre replied that if so, he wished Marie to be included. He mentioned her role in finding polonium and radium and asked: "Don't you think it would be more satisfying, from the artistic point of view, if we were to be associated in this manner?" It's puzzling why Pierre wrote *artistic point of view*, instead of: *She deserves the prize as much as, if not more than, I do.* Maybe his words reflected his customary disdainful attitude toward prizes and honors. And he surely consulted with Marie before he replied to Mittag-Leffler. On the other hand, the Nobel was one prize he did not disdain, having decided that accepting it was not "contrary to the scientific spirit."

But even with the influential Mittag-Leffler's support, how could she possibly share the physics prize for 1903? No one had nominated her for it. That seemed to make it virtually out of the question. Then during a brainstorming session, Swedish physicist Knut Angstrom found a possible loophole in the rules. They implied that a foreign member of the Swedish Academy of Sciences had permanent voting rights. Had any such member previously voted for Marie Curie? Yes, Professor Charles Bouchard, a French pathologist. So the committee simply updated Bouchard's 1902 nomination and made it valid for 1903. Marie was now at least in the running. Then they tackled the nominating language. Angstrom again had a helpful suggestion: they could credit the trio with opening up a new and important field for physics research, Becquerel, through his discovery of the spontaneous radioactivity of uranium that had inspired researchers to find more elements, and the Curies for their magnificent, methodical, and persistent investigations. While conceding that Rutherford and Soddy had surpassed the Curies in suggesting the possibility of transmutation, Angstrom asserted that this did not diminish the honor due to them for first discovering the phenomenon.

The committee then agreed to split the 1903 prize three ways, between Becquerel and both Curies. The Machiavellian plot to exclude Marie was foiled. But radioactivity research involved both physics and chemistry. For which category should the award be given? The committee's chemists eventually agreed on physics, because the language of the award was carefully crafted to leave open the possibility of a future Nobel Prize in chemistry in connection with radioactivity, which is what happened several years later.

And that's how Marie Curie would become the only woman scientist ever to win two Nobel Prizes—and for almost the same work. The French scientists who tried to deprive her of one Nobel Prize had made it possible for her to get two.

With everything settled, Professor Aurivillius, secretary of the Swedish Academy of Sciences, telegraphed the Curies on November 14, 1903, that they were to share the Nobel Prize for physics with Becquerel. He asked them to keep it secret until the ceremony, which they were invited to attend. Pierre replied five days later, grateful for the great honor but regretting that Marie was too ill and they both had too many teaching commitments to attend the ceremony.

At the Stockholm ceremony on December 10 (the anniversary of the death of Alfred Nobel, who had funded the prize), the king of Sweden handed the Curies' gold medal to their representative, French minister

Jean-Baptiste Marchand, a former soldier and explorer. The president of the Swedish Academy of Sciences, Dr. H. R. Tornebladh, summarized the work of Becquerel and the Curies as having "taught us that special forms of radiation that were only known hitherto by electric discharges through rarefied gas are natural phenomena of wide occurrence. We have gained knowledge of a property of matter quite new to us, the capability of emitting, spontaneously as it seems, these marvelous rays. We have gained new methods, infinitely superior in subtlety to any we had in this sphere, to examine under certain conditions the existence of matter in nature. Finally we have found a new source of energy, for which the full explanation is not yet forthcoming." The response of *Le Figaro* was to admonish the French people for not knowing who their great scientists were, and for leaving it to foreigners (the Scandinavians) to discover them.

Public recognition, however, was the last thing the Curies wanted. Yet the prize and the press made it inevitable. A day after the ceremony, a desperate Marie wrote to her brother that they had been overwhelmed by hordes of photographers and journalists, and "would like to dig into the ground somewhere to find a little peace." She said they expected the "huge sum" of seventy thousand francs [about twenty thousand dollars] as their share of the prize, and had an offer to lecture in the United States, which they meant to refuse however high the fee, and had declined the many banquets people proposed to organize in their honor. Strangely, for a woman now internationally famous, she ended her letter to her brother: "I implore you not to forget me."

When a *La Liberté* reporter told Pierre that he wished to write an article about him, he replied: "But we're not worth an article. We have only existed since yesterday." Not a bad quote, which the reporter used. A *Le Temps* reporter grumbled that he had to ring three times before the door of the Curies' home was answered by a maid (nurse), who told him that Pierre was working at his lab and Marie was teaching at Sèvres. So he sat waiting for them in a room without a fire—barely heated by a fire in the next room, the door between them being left ajar. He watched Irène eat her supper served by her nurse and later wrote the snide comment that: "Mlle Irène ate all alone, so that her mother could win the Nobel Prize." When Pierre arrived home he volunteered no information and gave the reporter only yes and no answers to his questions, which produced another snide remark: "I know people who have not invented radium who are better at the art of talking about themselves." Pierre complained to his friend Georges Gouy about this reporter, who published the conversation of Irène with the nurse. But it was not only reporters who kept Pierre from

The Nobel Prize–winning Curies were internationally famous in 1904 when the British magazine *Vanity Fair* featured this cartoon of them—with Pierre holding aloft a tube of sparkling radium.

his work. Eccentrics, inventors, beggars, autograph-hunters, and "snobs, worldly people, and sometimes [scientists] have come to see us in the magnificent setting of rue Lhomond," Pierre told Gouy. "With all this there is not a moment of tranquility in the laboratory and a voluminous correspondence to be sent off every night. On this regime I can feel myself being overwhelmed by brute stupidity. And yet all this turmoil will not perhaps have been in vain, if it results in my getting a professorship and a laboratory."

Getting a comparatively warm reception, a *La Presse* reporter described the Curies' home as "invaded by happiness . . . a dwelling illumined all at once by money and glory." According to him, as Marie looked on, Pierre answered his questions "gently and deliberately." But when he ran out of questions there was absolute silence, which he eventually realized was their polite way of telling him to leave.

A few newspapers gave Marie equal credit, but much if not most of the press could not, or did not, want to believe that Marie deserved the prize. To them she was either not worth mentioning or at best Pierre's assistant, "a devoted fellow laborer in her husband's researches (who) has associated her name with his discoveries . . . a collaborator, and the inspirer of her husband." Or perhaps that she was the woman who "fanned the sacred fire in him whenever she saw it dying out." Some even worried that she might be neglecting her duties as a wife and mother, but one at least implied that Irène was not neglected and called her adorable.

With the press publicizing the Curies' miserable working conditions in their cold, leaky, and ramshackle shed, the French government was shamed into creating a new professorship in physics for Pierre at the Sorbonne, with Marie as its laboratory chief, and giving them two assistants. But in fact there was no laboratory until eight years after Pierre's death — just a room shared with medical students and other researchers. This caused Marie's bitter words: "One of the best French scientists never had a suitable laboratory at his disposition although his genius had been revealed from the age of twenty." The *New York Times* was pleased to report that, as the Curies "had not profited financially from the work . . . their admirers will be delighted to hear of this windfall for them."

The prize money arrived on January 2, 1904, and allowed Pierre to follow a less rigorous schedule. Though Marie continued to teach at Sèvres, which she enjoyed, she insisted that Pierre quit his onerous teaching chores at the School of Physics and Chemisty. He was replaced by his friend and former student, Paul Langevin — also destined for greatness. Marie lent 20,000 francs of the prize money to her sister Bronia and brother-in-law, to sustain their tuberculosis sanatorium. She also lent or gave money to her brother, Joseph, and sister Hela; to several Polish students in need; to a childhood friend; to lab assistants; and to an impoverished student at Sèvres. Recalling with affection her childhood French teacher, Mme Kozlovka, who had long dreamed of revisiting her birthplace, Dieppe, Marie made it possible. She paid for her train journey from Warsaw to visit the Curies, then on to Dieppe and for her return home.

Two months after winning the prize Marie decided not to receive any more visitors, but they came anyway. As for the avalanche of letters, she couldn't resist reading many, had even replied to a few, and later was sorry she threw most away — among them poems about radium, spirit messages, inventors' pleas for financial backing, advice from philosophers, and an unrequited request from an American to name his racehorse after her. Marie didn't even buy herself a new hat with the prize money, but she did install a modern bathroom in their home and repaper a room. What cash was left, together with fifty thousand francs from the Osiris Prize awarded by the Paris Press Syndicate, the Curies invested equally in French and Polish government bonds.

To escape the demands of celebrity, whenever approached by a stranger asking, "Aren't you Madame Curie?" Marie steeled herself to reply as calmly as she could manage, "No, you are mistaken." It apparently worked. The Curies refused most social invitations, but made an exception when French president Emile Loubet invited them to dinner at the Elysées Palace. During the evening a woman asked Marie if she would like to be presented to the king of Greece. Marie, true to her motto "In science we must be interested in things, not in persons," declined politely but firmly, saying, "Why?" Then, recognizing that the woman, now in shock, was the president's wife, Marie blushed and stuttered, "But-but-naturally, I shall do whatever you please. Just as you please." It wasn't easy for her to stick to her principles.

Confiding in a friend that he longed for a life in which lectures were forbidden and newspapermen persecuted, Pierre reluctantly kept his promise to give a public lecture at the Sorbonne in February 1904. A *Philadelphia Evening Bulletin* reporter in the audience noticed that "the instant the professor put his foot on the platform he was trembling with shyness [perhaps the trembling was entirely or partly caused by the pains in his back and legs]; that he had probably never before worn an 'afternoon semi-dress suit'; that the massed thousands in the university amphitheatre were as terrible as lions to him, and that could he have escaped without disgrace he would have. But once he found his lips ready to respond to his thought, the modest professor captivated the throng by the lucidity of his explanations and the clarity of his experimentations."

Pierre also made clear that it was his twenty years at the School of Physics and Chemisty, and not at the Sorbonne, that had made the work possible, and that "it was among the former pupils of the school we found our collaborators and friends, and I am happy to be able to thank them all here." But he was much happier to escape from the crowd and head for his lab, where with coworkers he had recently demonstrated that radium emanations were deadly. They had subjected mice and hamsters to the radioactive gas that killed them all within four to nine hours. The stronger the emanations, the more rapidly the animals died.

Marie agreed with Pierre that their lives had been spoiled by honors and fame. And both yearned to return to their old life, especially in the spring, when Marie, now thirty-six, was pregnant. As Pierre told his friend Georges Gouy, "Never have we been less at peace. There are days when we have hardly the time to breathe. And to think that we dreamed of living like wild people far from other human beings!"

Pierre and Irène on vacation in the countryside outside Paris in 1904.

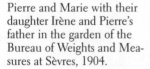

Pierre and Marie with their daughter Irène and Pierre's father in the garden of the Bureau of Weights and Measures at Sèvres, 1904.

On December 6, 1904, a month after they had moved their laboratory equipment to their makeshift lab at the Sorbonne, Marie gave birth to their second daughter, Eve Denise. The lively, blue-eyed, black-haired child with a radiant smile and a mind of her own delighted and reenergized Marie.

Pierre also took a keen and affectionate interest in both daughters, and was especially concerned with Irène's education, went for walks with her, and relished their chats together. Marie gradually resumed her active life, tending to her children, teaching at Sèvres, and spending much more time than Pierre at the laboratory. Some evenings she even found it possible to squeeze in a concert or an art exhibit, having persuaded her less energetic husband to join her. Then both did their utmost to avoid recognition by strangers.

Through frequent bouts of illness, Pierre prepared a new course of lectures for his Sorbonne students. He had been given a free hand, and with growing enthusiasm, he planned a wide-ranging account of the physics of crystals and how the laws of symmetry and the fields of vectors and tensors were relevant to the subject. And as a bonus he would tell them how radioactivity had brought about a revolution in science.

CHAPTER 6

Psychic Researchers

1905–1906

An unlikely friendship developed between the Curies and an American Folies-Bergère dancer, Loie Fuller. They had first glimpsed her spectacular performance at the Paris International Exhibition in 1900, where they attended the Congress in Physics to promote the wonders of electricity. Fuller had used the occasion to promote her own extraordinary enterprise. Dressed in voluminous silk skirts and veils, she danced on a pane of glass, illuminated from below by beams of colored electric lights and directed by thirty-eight lighting engineers. It made her an international sensation.

One evening she took the electricians and their elaborate lighting equipment with her to the Curies' home, converted the dining room into a stage, and gave a special performance for the Curies, and a few friends. Had she an ulterior motive? Much as Fuller admired the Curies, she also needed their expert advice. She had read that radium was luminous and planned to dance as a butterfly with the wings painted with radium. When she asked the Curies about it, they warned her that it was dangerous. Undaunted, Fuller and several assistants experimented with phosphorescent salts, until an explosion blew off their eyebrows and eyelashes and the phosphorescent wings went up in smoke. Only then did Fuller give up the idea.

Through Fuller the Curies met sculptor Auguste Rodin and took a greater interest in the theater, attending performances by the great Italian actress Eleonora Duse in Gorky's *The Lower Depths* and Lucien Guitry in *Nono*. During intermission of an Ibsen play, while in the foyer of the Théâtre de l'Oeuvre, the Curies met mathematician Emile Borel and his twenty-one-year-old wife, Marguerite, daughter of Gaston Darboux, the dean of the Sorbonne's Faculty of Science. Marguerite was so excited by the play that Marie hugged her impulsively, saying, "You remind me of the students of my youth. You're carried away like they were—like I was—in that far off day." The Curies also went to other modern plays, recommended by the university crowd, that depressed them for days. Pierre's father invariably greeted them on their return home with a mocking, "Don't forget that you went there for pleasure!"

After a wet and miserable winter, in the spring of 1905 the weather improved and Marie spent most mornings at home with her daughters, afternoons at the lab, and two mornings teaching at Sèvres. As for Pierre, his doctor had changed his diagnosis radically. Now, instead of rheumatism he attributed the pains to neurasthenia—a nervous condition caused by worry—gave him strychnine to fight it, and put him on a healthier diet. This seemed so effective that by early June Pierre decided to travel to Sweden with Marie to give his Nobel Prize lecture. As at his London lecture, Pierre brought samples of radium to demonstrate its effects and Marie again sat in the audience. Should anyone doubt her full partnership in their work, he mentioned her by name ten times and several times referred to "our" experiments. They were now at least prepared, he said, to consider the Rutherford-Soddy theory, which stated that the atom might consist of smaller elements. Or, as Pierre put it, "the existence of the atom is even at stake."

He also told his audience that radium rays had been used to treat lupus (a chronic inflammatory disease of various parts of the body), cancer, and nervous diseases, but warned that "in certain cases their action may become dangerous. If one leaves a wooden box containing a small glass ampule with several centigrams of radium salt in one's pocket for a few hours, one will feel absolutely nothing. But fifteen days afterwards a redness will appear on the epidermis and then a sore which will be very difficult to heal. A more prolonged action could lead to paralysis and death. Radium must be transported in a thick box of lead."

He never seems to have realized that radium might have caused his suffering. In fact, in a paper he and Becquerel had written titled "Physiological Effect of Radium Rays," published in *Comptes Rendus* in June 1901, they asserted that using lead as a shield made radiation harmless. However, there is no account of the Curies using lead to protect themselves during the years they worked in their lab. In his account of their work he focused on radium's positive aspects. They were confident enough, for example, to lend radium to a Dr. Danlos to treat his hospital patients. And Pierre described how he had worked with Professors C. Bouchard

(Marie's Nobel advocate) and V. Balthazard to test the effects of radiation on rabbits, and concluded not only that radium destroyed cancer cells, but that the reformed skin was healthy.

Having given his Nobel audience an idea of radium's therapeutic possibilities, Pierre warned: "One may also imagine that in criminal hands radium might become very dangerous, and here we may ask ourselves if humanity has anything to gain by learning the secrets of nature, if it is ripe enough to profit by them, or if this knowledge is not harmful. One example of Nobel's discoveries is characteristic: powerful explosives have permitted men to perform admirable work. They are also a terrible means of destruction in the hands of the great criminals who lead the peoples towards war. I am among those who think, with Nobel, that humanity will obtain more good than evil from the new discoveries." Pierre had reason to fear that radium might be used for military purposes: as early as 1900 a Captain Ferrie had asked him if radium could make gun sights and mine-safety catches luminous for night use.

The Curies were delighted with their warm reception in Sweden and their conversations with many of the country's leading scientists. They especially enjoyed the restful atmosphere—Stockholm was almost deserted, most of its populace being on vacation—and the unusual experience of being in Sweden when there was no night. Henri Poincaré once made the sour comment that Pierre Curie "rose to glory with the spirit of a whipped dog." But what he and few others knew was that Pierre was often exhausted, depressed, and wracked with pain. Even so, when the Curies returned from Sweden, Eleuthère Mascart, director of the Central Meteorological Office, persuaded Pierre to again endure the tedious and demeaning task of promoting himself for membership in the French Academy of Sciences. What apparently did the trick was Mascart's comment that being a member of the institute would put him in a position to help others, and that this time he was sure to make it. He did, by a slim majority of six. The election was secret, but for some reason he believed that Becquerel resented him and had voted for his rival, Désiré Gernez.

In late June 1905 the Curies waited at the Gare du Nord railroad station for Marie's sister Hela, a school principal, and her seven-year-old daughter, Hania, to arrive from Warsaw. Hela was overjoyed as her train approached the station, because, as she wrote in her memoir, "I was going to spend the whole summer with Marie and Pierre, whom I loved enormously; I was going to see them every day, to hear their melodious voices; and Hania was going to have little Irène for company! I was going to spend the summer at the ocean which I had never seen before."

Pierre greeted the visitors with a smile and halting Polish. He seemed to Hela to be slightly stooped but his usual calm self, and Marie was "very moved and joyous" to see her sister and niece. After a week of sightseeing in Paris they were off, together with a nanny for Eve and a cook, to the seaside village of Carolles on the Normandy coast. There, at high tide waves crashed against the front porch of their isolated, rented house, which at first scared Hela. At night, lights from lighthouses swept across the water. Marie had bought matching red outfits, swimsuits, and bathrobes for Irène and Hania and they swam every day.

Pierre and Marie spent several morning hours working before meeting the others on the beach. But his leg pains prevented him from walking on the wet sand at low tide. Hela recalled how she brought back rocks, seaweed, and "hermit crabs with stolen shells on their backs which contained colorful anemones." While she watched the crabs swimming in a basin of water, Pierre talked about them and the rocks she had collected and he impressed her with his wide knowledge of geology and biology. In August, on a day of the sun's eclipse, they visited Mont-Saint-Michel, a tenth-century Benedictine abbey, which was surrounded by water at high tide. Pierre had brought special lenses with him for them to see the eclipse up close. As they watched, and Irène and Hania bombarded him with questions, he explained it to them.

The two sisters spent a lot of time on the beach with their children, and invariably Eve attracted admiring remarks from strangers. Perhaps because Irène and Hania were ignored, it began to irritate the two women, especially Hela. When the next woman stared, entranced, at Eve and asked: "To whom does this superb baby belong?" Hela replied, with a straight face, "I have no idea. She's an orphan." When the woman left in a huff, Marie laughed until tears streamed down her cheeks. And afterward she sometimes caressed Eve saying, "My poor orphan!"

After the vacation Marie accompanied Hela and Hania to the railroad station to see them off. On their way, Marie confided that Pierre's pains were becoming so much stronger and more frequent that they prevented him from sleeping. She feared that he had some awful, incurable disease doctors didn't recognize. Hela tried to comfort her, and they were both crying as they said good-bye.

That same summer of 1905, Pierre had resumed his intense interest in the supernatural that had engaged him and his brother, Jacques, in their youth. He once told Marie that he thought that some aspects of spiritualistic phenomena "touch closely on physics." Possibly because his research with Marie had led them to hitherto unexplored territory, he was more open to entertaining uncommon ideas in other fields. On July 24, he persuaded Marie to return to Paris with him to attend a demonstration by an Italian medium, Eusapia Palladino.

Neapolitan Dr. Ercole Chiaia, who brought Palladino to the world's attention, described her in a letter to psychiatrist and criminologist Cesar Lombroso as an "ignorant, invalid woman of thirty who apparently is capable of defying natural laws. She floated in the air as if lying on a couch, then slowly descended to the floor. She grew taller or shorter at will (a real-life Alice in Wonderland). At times, what looked like flashes of lightning shot from her body; and distant musical instruments played as though she had only to think of music for them to come to life." For years Palladino had traveled to France, Britain, and the United States to be investigated extensively by some of the world's most respected scientists: Oliver Lodge, Alfred Russel Wallace, Charles Richet, Camille Flammarion, Baron Schrenck-Notzing, and Hugo Munsterberg, as well as investigators for the British and American Societies for Psychic Research. Harvard's William James told Swiss psychologist Theodore Flournoy that at Palladino's séances, which he attended about the same time as the Curies, she cheated by every means available when "allowed to do so." Most investigators agreed that she faked at times, but they were still completely baffled and intrigued by some of the phenomena she produced.

On July 6, 1905, Marie and Pierre sat around a table holding hands with Palladino and several people they trusted, to complete what they believed to be an unbroken ring. This was supposed to ensure that Palladino didn't use her hands to perform tricks. And to prevent her from using her feet, her neighbors on either side of her trod on them throughout the séance. Or so they thought. After Palladino appeared to go into a trance in the dimly lit room, the magic started. A table defied the laws of physics, taking off and floating in the air—all four legs off the floor. Luminous objects moved overhead apparently of their own volition and some mysterious objects touched and even caressed the sitters.

Pierre made notes afterward, sketching the positions of people and furniture at the séance, and describing the lighting and conditions as under his control. He wrote that the levitating table remained in the air for one second, then fell to the floor "the way an armature of an electromagnet would fall when one cuts the current." He mentioned that curtains were involved and that "some energy is accumulating behind the curtains, energy which sometimes acts violently and with apparent arms. After each phenomenon, generally, some time is necessary for the accumulation of new energy."

On July 24, 1905, he told his friend Georges Gouy: "It was very interesting and it doesn't seem possible to explain the phenomena we saw by
fakery. The table lifted off its four feet . . . hands punch and caress you,
luminous apparitions [appear] — all in a place prepared by us, with a small
number of spectators all known to us, and without any chance of the
medium using an assistant. The only possibility of fakery is if she is an
extraordinarily talented conjuror. But how do you explain the phenomena
when one holds her hands and feet, and the lighting is sufficient to see
everything that occurs? Eusapia is returning in November and I hope we
will come to a conclusion about the reality of these phenomena, or at
least about some of them. If they really exist one wonders how to study
them methodically . . . I wanted to see if the air was ionized [able to conduct electricity] around the medium. But the sound of a small fan which
stirred the air was enough to upset her and stop her working. Enough difficulty comes from the fact that she tries to cheat even if she knows how to
produce certain phenomena, because this is less tiring for her."

The Curies also tested Palladino's claim that she could move a very
sensitive balance by thought alone (telekinesis). For this they attached a
charged electroscope to the balance so that if she actually touched the
scale the electroscope would immediately discharge, giving her away. The
room was dimly lit, and Palladino had a handkerchief over her mouth to
prevent her from moving the scale by breathing on it. Then she put her
hands on either side of the scale without touching it. It went down. And
the electroscope did not discharge. However, Marie had noticed Palladino
make a suspicious movement. So the light was raised and an arch of thick
wire positioned in front of the scale as a barrier to prevent physical contact. In the now more brightly lit room, Palladino tried again, but this time
she failed to move the scale, which she explained by saying she was tired.
However, Marie suspected Palladino of using a fine thread to move the
scale on her first successful attempt. Her theory was tested and proved
plausible: a fine, almost invisible thread attached to the scale could move
it without discharging the electroscope. Consequently the scale was
painted so that a hair or thread would leave a mark on it. When Palladino
again tried to move the scale, she couldn't.

Published reports of the Curies' tests "in which monitoring instruments were used to register any improper physical movements, tell of
musical and telekinetic manifestations, of playful invisible hands untying
the savants' cravats and pulling their hair, and of a stool advancing on
Pierre Curie and making as if to crawl up his leg, and a small table floating prettily over his shoulder." Despite Palladino's failures, the Curies

remained interested, discounted the idea of an accomplice, and concluded that the medium had either produced genuine supernatural phenomena or was a brilliant conjuror. Pierre even considered including his notes on the séances in official accounts of his scientific research.

In the winter of 1905, he was buoyed by several events: a visit from Jacques, who incidentally no longer shared his interest in the supernatural; and the news that thanks to Pierre's recommendations, his colleague Georges Urbain won the Prix Hughes and his close friend Georges Gouy won the Prix La Caze.

January 1906 started well, too. As a member of the French Academy of Sciences, Pierre proudly presented to its members Marie's latest paper, "On the Diminution of the Radioactivity of Polonium over Time."

The Curies' mutual friend and Pierre's former pupil, Paul Langevin, could no longer support his wife and four children on his Sorbonne salary, so he took a second, part-time job at Sèvres where he, like Marie, taught young women training to be teachers. Langevin had become one of the regulars who congregated in the Curies' garden on Sunday afternoons. They usually included Jean Perrin and his wife, Henriette, Marie's best woman friend and next-door neighbor; Andre Debierne; Georges Urbain; Aimé Cotton; Georges Sagnac; Charles-Edouard Guillaume; and a few of Marie's students from Sèvres.

Their intense and lively conversations invariably touched on the mysteries and potential of radium. Pierre's father, Debierne, and Langevin occasionally changed the talk to politics, while at the end of the garden, Henriette Perrin read fairy stories to her daughter, Aline, and Irène Curie. Meanwhile Marie sat in the shade close to Eve in her baby carriage. On a typical Sunday afternoon, she would be mending clothes or sewing, enjoying the conversation and the teasing by Urbain about the plain way she dressed and her disdain for the flirtatious, breaking into laughter when Jean Perrin switched from discussing atoms to launch into a Wagnerian aria sung at full throttle.

Pierre was still without his own laboratory, which the French government had promised him to meet the needs of a developing research field. Meantime, he had to make do with a tiny lab on rue Cuvier—two rooms in the main faculty building and a small detached house. So he grasped at the offer from an anonymous, apparently wealthy woman, to build one for him. He replied to her on February 6, 1906, with stipulations. The lab, he wrote, must be in the country, "because it is of capital importance for us to live where we work. Children and a laboratory [require] the constant presence of those who take care of them. And, for my wife, especially, life is very difficult when the house and the laboratory are far from each other. At times the double task is beyond her strength . . . On the other hand, life in the middle of the city is destructive for children, and my wife cannot . . . bring them up under such circumstances. We are extremely touched by your solicitude with respect to us." The project came to nothing. Another unfulfilled promise.

Aside from rare outings, the Curies spent many evenings in their dressing gowns and slippers reading scientific journals or completing their notebooks. Life was somewhat easier for them now with a charwoman, a nanny–wet-nurse for Eve, and Emma, a combination maid and cook, who was frustrated by Pierre's indifference to food. One night she asked if he had enjoyed the beefsteak she had cooked and served. "Did I eat a beefsteak?" he asked casually, as if trying to recall the event. Then added: "It's quite possible."

Even with hired help, Marie was still very involved with her daughters. Both were distinct personalities. The fair-haired, green-eyed Irène, a shy, stubborn eight-year-old, though essentially healthy, was often seriously ill with, among other ailments, flu, whooping cough, and scarlet fever. Because of a persistent cough, her lungs were X-rayed and to Marie's immense relief found to be clear. When her cough was cured, Irène attended school in the mornings and classes in gymnastics, art, Polish, and music in the afternoons, all of which she enjoyed. At home, she demanded her mother's complete and constant attention—especially after sister Eve appeared on the scene—and her craving for hard-to-find orange pippin apples and bananas sent Marie on long journeys across Paris to locate and buy them. Marie was pleased with how quickly Irène had learned to ride a bicycle—and proud of her endurance—especially after she joined her parents on a ten-mile bike trip.

Eve, at just over one, was a physical contrast to her sister, with her dark hair, blue eyes, and a radiant smile. She was also unlike Irène in that she was outgoing, responding positively to all the Curies' friends and holding out her hand in greeting when asked for it.

As her mother's eventual biographer, Eve stressed the loving cooperation of her parents, writing that, "Ideas big and little, questions, remarks and advice were thrown back and forth at every hour of the day between Pierre and Marie. Compliments, too, and friendly reproaches. Between these two equals who admired each other passionately but could never envy, there was a worker's comradeship, light and exquisite, which was perhaps the most delicate expression of their profound love."

According to some lab workers who asked him to solve a tricky math problem, Pierre willingly conceded that Marie was his superior. It was beyond him, he said, and suggested that they wait for Marie, who was on her way. Because, as he explained, she "knew integral calculus better." When she arrived she solved the problem in minutes. George Jaffe, a research assistant in their lab in 1905, thought of the Curies as absolutely unique and was impressed by their extreme simplicity, modesty, extraordinary devotion to their work, and air "of unostentatious superiority." Although he knew of other distinguished scientific couples who collaborated, he believed that it would not be possible to find "a more distinguished instance where husband and wife with all their mutual admiration and devotion preserved so completely independence of character, in life as well as in science."

In the spring of 1906, Pierre wrote what would be his last letter to his friend Georges Gouy: "Happy to hear you are writing your memoirs and have found a good assistant. It's a rare happiness. I had a pretty good assistant, [Jacques Danne] but radium, journalism, and the dream of earning a lot of money, completely turned his head." Danne had traded on having once worked as Pierre's assistant to promote his own business enterprises, which included a radium factory and a journal he edited, *Radium*.

By this time Pierre had investigated several demonstrations by Palladino, some of which Jean Perrin also attended. Pierre, at least, seemed to be hooked, telling Gouy that

The result is that the phenomena really exists. It is not possible for me to doubt it any more. It's unbelievable, but that's the way it is. *It is impossible to deny it*, after the séances which we have had under conditions of perfect control. Strange, shapeless, fluid members are formed from the medium . . . separate from her own arms and legs, capable of pushing objects around. These are formed preferably under a piece of black material under her skirts . . . What is troubling is that one feels very strongly that by admitting to the existence of some of these phenomena one could, little by little, admit the ghosts of Crookes and Richet—and then one doesn't understand at all, any longer, how to explain that such transformations of matter can happen so rapidly and without using prodigious quantities of energy. I really would like you to be present at those kinds of séances and have no doubt that after a few good séances that you, too, would be convinced . . . You have such great intuition about phenomena, how would you explain that such a thing is possible? In my opinion there is here a world of entirely new facts, and physical states in space, about which we have no conception.

It's surprising that Pierre Curie didn't allow for the possibility, which he had at first entertained, that Palladino was a brilliant illusionist; had he lived a few years more perhaps he would have reached that conclusion. On April 17, 1910, Palladino was exposed as a fraud during a séance in New York—at that séance, two men in black tights crawled under chairs in the darkness and caught her trying to lift a table with her foot. She angrily told the investigators that it was up to them to stop her from cheating, her usual response after being caught in the act.

After mailing the letter about Palladino to Georges Gouy, on Easter Friday, Pierre left for the Sorbonne. At the same time Marie and the girls were about to leave for the railroad station. They meant to spend the Easter weekend at a country cottage in St. Rémy-les-Chevreuse, an hour from Paris. Concerned that Pierre was working too hard, she had made him promise to join them the next day. He agreed reluctantly and started to walk away. Then she reproached him for not saying good-bye to her. Because of their less than affectionate parting, though she sent Irène on her bicycle to meet his train next day, she wasn't sure he would be on it. He was.

The weather had turned cold and Marie, especially concerned for Pierre's fading health, lit a fire in the dining room. She watched him hold his hands before the flames and rub them together and then laugh when fourteen-month-old Eve copied him. These were precious moments for Marie that she would remember all her life.

Early the next morning they all walked to get milk from a nearby farm and Eve again made Pierre laugh as she tottered along, stubbornly trying to follow dried cart tracks. They decided to send Irène and their maid, Emma, for the milk and then, carrying Eve on their shoulders in turn, they wandered through the woods as far as the pond with water lilies they had seen the previous summer. Now it was dry and surrounded by brilliant yellow gorse. Later, lying on the grass in a sunlit meadow, while Eve yelled for their attention, the proud parents watched their graceful daughter Irène, in a girl's shirt and boy's shorts, gleefully chasing butterflies. When she caught one in a little green net, Marie persuaded her to let it go.

Back in Paris on Wednesday, April 18, 1906, Pierre and Marie attended the annual dinner of the Physical Society at Foyot's Restaurant. Pierre sat next to the great mathematician Henri Poincaré and explained how he and Marie were trying to measure radiation with great precision. (The Curie, as the agreed unit of radiation strength, was adopted internationally in 1912.) After discussing his determination to give both of his daughters a scientific education, he spoke of his and Marie's ongoing investigation of the paranormal. Poincaré was skeptical when Pierre admitted that Eusapia Palladino's strange powers had impressed him, but acknowledged that as expressed by Pierre's "original and lucid mind," displacement of objects from a distance certainly sounded interesting. The mild spring weather had suddenly changed. That night a chilly, windblown rain soaked the Paris streets.

CHAPTER 7

Pierre Curie's Last Day

1906–1907

I t was still raining early next morning when Pierre, on his way out, called upstairs to Marie and asked if she would join him later at the Sorbonne. But she was helping her girls get dressed and told him that she had a lot more chores at home and probably wouldn't have time. When he persisted, she replied impatiently, "Don't torment me!" Disappointed, he left, with a busy day ahead of him.

At midday, after working in his makeshift lab, he went to meet fellow members of the newly formed Association of Professors of the Science Faculties, a group of liberal iconoclasts, of which he was vice president. They hoped to change the hidebound education system that promoted teachers by seniority rather than by merit, denied girls a basic scientific education, and tolerated dangerous working conditions for lab assistants. Pierre joined the reform-minded group for lunch at the Hotel des Societies Savantes on the rue Danton. There, in an easygoing, noncontentious atmosphere that Pierre enjoyed, they discussed how to put their principles into practice. The occasion was especially meaningful to him because Polish physicist Joseph Kowalski was there. But for him Pierre might never have met Marie some twelve years earlier when she was a young student. Pierre's friends Jean Perrin and Paul Langevin were also at the lunchtime meeting, during which Langevin noticed how the once redheaded Pierre, now forty-seven, had become prematurely white and lost considerable weight. He attributed it to the pain Pierre silently endured. Yet Langevin had never known him in a happier or more lively mood. After shaking hands with the group and inviting several to his home for dinner that evening, Pierre left shortly before 2:30 P.M. to keep a proofreading appointment with his publisher, Gathier-Villars. As it was still raining, he opened

Marie's favorite photo of
Pierre, taken in 1905,
shortly before his death.

his umbrella and, joined by Perrin, headed for the publisher's office near
the Seine on the quay des Grands Augustins. But the door was locked:
Pierre had forgotten that the workers were on strike. Perrin headed for
home, but Pierre chose to drop in at the institute library, walking though
the driving rain along an unusually crowded street.

What happened next was described in a local police station by Louis
Manin, the thirty-year-old driver of a horse-drawn wagon loaded with military uniforms. Still in shock and crying, he sobbed out his testimony. He
was driving his team of horses in the right-hand lane of the rue Dauphine
when a horse cab going in the opposite direction began to pass him in the
left-hand lane. Suddenly, without warning, a man in a black suit and carrying a large umbrella appeared behind the cab and stepped into the path
of his left-hand horse. The man slipped on the rain-slicked street and, as
he fell, seemed almost to throw himself at the horse to grab its harness,
making the horse rear in panic. Horrified onlookers yelled for the driver to
stop and he desperately pulled on the reins, but, propelled by their own
momentum, the horses kept moving forward. The man lost his grip and
fell under the horses, where the driver lost sight of him. Other witnesses
told how, to their immense relief, it seemed that the man would survive,
as he had escaped being crushed by the horses' hooves and the wagon's two

front iron-rimmed wheels. But, to their dismay, its left rear wheel struck his head, shattering his skull and killing him instantly.

The police arrived in time to save the driver from an enraged crowd that blamed him for the fatal accident, and hailed several cabs to take Pierre's bloody corpse to the police station. But all the cabbies refused to have their upholstery stained with blood and drove on. He was finally carried off on a stretcher, provisionally identified by cards in his pocket, and definitely identified by Pierre Clerc, a lab assistant. Between sobs, Clerc said that he had often warned his absentminded employer to take more care when crossing streets. Meanwhile, a compassionate Dr. Drouet covered Pierre's crushed skull with a bandage and, as he washed his face, noticed to his surprise that it was untouched and appeared almost serene.

Later that afternoon Pierre's father answered the doorbell to a representative of the president of the Republic who asked to see Marie Curie. Told she was out, he left without another word. Two more visitors brought Dr. Curie to the door again: Paul Appell, the dean of the Sorbonne's Faculty of Science, and Jean Perrin, the Curies' friend and next-door neighbor. They arrived together and also asked to see Marie without explaining why. But their expressions were so grim that he guessed their mission. "My son is dead," he said. He seemed to take their confirmation calmly until they described how Pierre had died. Then Dr. Curie began to cry and murmur to himself, "What was he dreaming of this time?"

Having completed her work in the house sooner than expected, Marie had spent a pleasant afternoon with Irène and friends. She and her daughter arrived home at six in a happy mood, and then Paul Appell told her what had happened. She listened in frozen silence, then said repeatedly as if to herself, "Pierre is dead? Dead? Absolutely dead?" Her only request was for Perrin to ask his wife to take care of the girls for the next few days. She refused an autopsy and insisted that Pierre's body be brought directly to her. As she walked from the room to the garden she noticed with a pang that the flowers Pierre had brought from their St. Rémy vacation were still alive. Alone in the rain-soaked garden, she awaited her husband's corpse. There, someone first brought her the contents of his pockets: a pen, keys, wallet, his watch still ticking and its glass intact.

When the ambulance arrived at 8 P.M., André Debierne, who had accompanied the body, helped to carry it on a stretcher into the downstairs bedroom. There, Marie broke down, kissed Pierre's face, and clung to him so fiercely that she had to be forcibly removed while his body was prepared for burial.

That night the Establishment acknowledged its loss: the president of the republic, the president of the council, and senior members of the Sorbonne came to the Curies' home to offer their condolences. Pierre's brother, Jacques, arrived the next morning, and Marie again gave in to her feelings and wept. But she controlled herself enough to check if Eve's hair had been washed and combed, and to talk to Irène, who was playing in the Perrins' garden next door. She could not yet bring herself to tell Irène that her father was dead, saying instead that he had been hurt and needed to rest.

Eve, who would eventually share her mother's confidences more than anyone and become her informed biographer, believed that Marie never let anyone know how deeply and permanently Pierre's death changed her life. As Eve wrote: "From the moment when those three words, 'Pierre is dead,' reached her consciousness, Mme Curie, on that day in April, became not only a widow, but at the same time a pitiful and incurably lonely woman."

The *New York Times* reported:

Prof. Curie, the discoverer of radium, was run over and killed by a wagon on the place Dauphine this afternoon. Ever since the discovery of radium by [him] and his wife they have devoted their entire energies to further researches on the same lines and to the manufacture of the wonderful element that they found . . . The couple passed through many hardships together. Neither had any fortune, and with the few thousands francs which they earned it was by no means easy to make both ends meet . . . It was in the little laboratory in the rue Lhomond that the experiments which resulted in the discovery that has already revolutionized chemistry, and which may revolutionize the practice of medicine, were conducted . . . Prof. Curie said he could detect the presence of radio-active substance in such a minute quantity that it would require 5,000 times the amount to show it on the spectroscope . . . The professor was frequently forced to delay his tests for three or four hours, by reason of the fact that he had been exposed to radium and that his clothes had become so radio-active as to prevent him from going near his instruments. The Curies' laboratory became so thoroughly impregnated with radium that they had to move to another place for their experiments. Both the professor and his wife recently became ill through the effects of radium.

A French newspaper, *La Vie de Paris*, pointed out the irony of a great scientist who had "brushed up against death in his sparse laboratory, where the most dangerous experiments were conducted, and then died like an ordinary man by slipping under a horse wagon." Paul Langevin, his former student, close friend, and colleague, wrote of Pierre as a man who was "great because of his character and thoughts," and of how "physical forces affirmed once more their power over the most beautiful of all their creations, over human goodness and intelligence." The physical forces may well have included radium, because his difficulty in walking and his weakened condition might have been caused by radiation sickness and contributed to the tragic accident, though this is only speculation, since no doctor ever convincingly diagnosed his illness.

Lord Kelvin, among the first to express his sympathy, cabled to the thirty-eight-year-old widow: "Greatly distressed by the terrible news." Gabriel Lippmann mourned the loss of someone he considered "a brother." Pierre's young lab assistant, Charles Cheveneau, said that after his own family, "Pierre was one of the people I loved best. His immense kindness extended even to the humblest of assistants, who adored him. I have never seen more sincere and harrowing tears than those they shed when told of his sudden death." Jean Perrin: "His devotion to science was unyielding and disinterested. There have been few lives more pure and more justly famous." Henri Poincaré, one of the last to see him alive, noted how "a stupid fate has just reminded us what little place thought takes in the face of a thousand blind forces which meet around the world without knowing where they are going, and crushing everything in their way." As for Pierre himself, Poincaré recalled his surprise "that so much gentleness concealed an uncompromising soul. He did not compromise those principles on which he was nourished, nor the moral ideal he had been taught to love, that ideal of absolute sincerity, too high, perhaps, for the world in which we live." Ernest Rutherford: "Our scientific connection has been so close that I feel as if I had lost a personal friend as well as an esteemed colleague."

Marie's sister Bronia and brother, Joseph, arrived from Warsaw to comfort their inconsolable sister. At her request, on the morning of the funeral she sat alone beside his flower-covered coffin in the downstairs bedroom. She had wanted a simple funeral and for Pierre to be buried in the cemetery at Sceaux, but news of his death had reached the public and a crowd gathered at the site, including one prominent uninvited mourner, Aristide Briand, cofounder of both France's socialist party and socialist newspaper, *L'Humanité*. (Briand would become France's prime minister for six terms and in 1926 won the Nobel peace prize.) Marie arrived heavily veiled, leaning on the arm of Pierre's father. She had placed Pierre's favorite photo of her in the coffin and when it was closed covered it with periwinkles from the garden to go with him into the grave. After a short service she dropped more flowers, one by one, onto his coffin, then rejoined Dr. Curie and together with him and Pierre's brother, Jacques, walked slowly away.

Eve was not old enough to understand, but the day after the funeral Marie went to her neighbors, the Perrins, to tell nine-year-old Irène that her father was dead. She and the Perrins' daughter, Aline, were playing together. "Sixty years later, Aline still remembered how pale and icy Marie looked—in black from head to toe. Irène acted as if she did not hear what her mother was saying and continued to play." Marie then turned to Mme Perrin and said: " 'She is too young to understand.' And left. But Irène was not too young . . . Marie was barely out of the Perrins' front door when Irène burst into tears and asked to be taken home." An hour later her mother found her sobbing.

That night Eve, who *was* too young to understand, stayed with the Perrins, while Irène slept with her mother. Marie recalled how Irène woke in the morning and, half asleep, searching for her mother with her arm, "said in a plaintive voice, and using Marie's nickname, 'Me [pronounced May] is not dead?'" Except for asking for a photograph of her father that had been taken from her bedroom window, she did not mention him again that day and Marie believed she would soon forget him.

Two weeks after his death, on April 30, 1906, Marie began, through her private diary, a one-sided, heartbreaking conversation with her dead husband. It only became available to the public almost a century later. Previous biographers have wondered why this woman who tenaciously guarded her private life and destroyed many personal letters did not destroy this revealing document. Could it be that with it, she could at least keep her memory of Pierre vividly alive?

Her diary starts: "Dear Pierre, whom I'll never see again. I want to speak to you in the silence of the laboratory where I never thought I would live without you. And first I want to remember the last days we had together." After recalling their recent almost idyllic family vacation at St. Remy, she wrote that on their return,

> We were talking about education which interested us so much . . . It was to give children a great love of nature, of life and the curiosity to explore them. You thought like me and felt that we shared a rare and admirable mutual understanding.

Marie remembered their last night and morning together:

> Eve was ill. I made you take your shoes off to avoid noise. At night Eve woke and I had to rock her in my arms. Then I put her down between us . . . you

kissed her several times. She went to sleep soon after . . . In the morning you went out in a hurry . . . You left, and asked me from downstairs if I was going to the laboratory. I answered that I had no idea and I begged you not to torment me. And this is how you left. And the last sentence I spoke to you was not a sentence of love and tenderness. And I only saw you again dead.

After her account of the return of his body, she described how

They brought you to the bed in the downstairs room and I kissed you again . . . They told me to leave so they could take your clothes off. Stunned, I obeyed and I don't know how I could have been so crazy. It was up to me to take off your bloody rags . . . Pierre, you're here calm like a poor wounded man who rests while sleeping with his head bandaged. And your head is still sweet and serene, it's still you enclosed in a dream you can't get out of . . . I told you that I loved you and had always loved you with all my heart. I promised you that I would never give another the place you have occupied in my life, and that I would try to live as you would have wished . . . Pierre, calm came to me, an intuition that I would still find the courage to live. Was it an illusion, or was it an accumulation of energy coming from you . . . as an act of kindness on your part? . . . We were made to live together. Our union was fated. Alas, it should have lasted longer. Your coffin is closed after a last kiss and I can't see you any more . . . We take you back to Sceaux and we see you go down in the deep hole which must be your last bed . . . All is over. Pierre sleeps his last sleep under the earth. It's the end of everything, everything, everything.

Marie revealed the extent of her enormous grief when she asked her sister Bronia to join her in her bedroom. Though it was a warm day, a fire was blazing in the grate. After locking the door conspiratorially and saying, "I need your help," Marie took a bundle from a cupboard, and, to Bronia's astonishment, as she unwrapped it, out fell the bloodstained clothes Pierre had worn when he was killed. Marie began cutting them into pieces with a pair of scissors and throwing them into the flames. When only a few scraps were left, she covered them with kisses, until Bronia grabbed the lot and threw them and the wrapping paper into the fire. "I couldn't bear to have anyone touch them do you understand?" Marie sobbed, as Bronia embraced and tried to comfort her.

She was not only concerned with her own bereavement. Worried about Irène's future prospects, Marie wrote in her diary on May 1, still as if addressing her husband:

The loss of her father will weigh on her existence, and we will never know how much harm this will have done to her. Because I dreamed, my Pierre, and I often told you so, that this daughter, who promised to resemble you in her serious, calm thoughtfulness, would become your workmate as soon as possible. And that she would owe the best of herself to you. Who will give her what you could have?

She also mentions the "horror and misery" of burning Pierre's clothes with "the bloody parts and bits of his brain on them," and how she kissed "what was left of you in all this." Then she adds, "In the street I walk as if hypnotized. I shall not kill myself. I have not even the desire for suicide, but among all the vehicles is there not one to make me share the fate of my beloved?"

The day before Pierre's brother, Jacques, returned home, he "maneuvered Marie, on a pretext, back into the laboratory," knowing that "her work would help her to survive. . . . It was too much for her. Nevertheless, like a rider remounting a horse which had just thrown him, Marie had taken the first steps back to a normal existence." Feeling the need to justify her return to work in the laboratory, she explained to Pierre: "How many times did I tell you that without you I wouldn't work any longer? I put in you all my hope for scientific work and here I am daring to take it on without you. You used to tell me that 'if you didn't have me any longer you might still continue working, but you would be a body without a soul.' But where would I find a soul when mine has gone with you?"

Eighteen days after his death Marie continued her one-sided conversation:

My Pierre, life is atrocious without you . . . a nameless anxiety, a bottomless distress, a limitless desolation since you're not here any longer. Yesterday for the first time since the terrible day, something funny Irene said made me laugh, but I was hurting while I was laughing. Do you remember how you reproached yourself for laughing . . . after your mother's death? Oh, the longing to see your good smile, your sweet face, to hear the grave and sweet voice and to embrace each other. . . . Pierre, I don't want to bear this life . . . To see you sacrificed in this way, you the most harmless, the most just, the most benevolent, the most devoted. I will never have enough tears to weep for this . . . I do not understand that from now on I have to live without seeing you, without smiling to the sweet companion of my life, you my so tender and devoted friend. Yesterday I went to the cemetery and I couldn't understand the words 'Pierre Curie' engraved in the stone. The sun and the beauty of the countryside hurt me and I put my veil back so I could see everything through the crepe. My Pierre, how my heart contracts when I remember the dear image, it seems to me that the pain should be enough to break it and to end my life which you have left. My beautiful, my good, my dear beloved Pierre . . . I try to start living again. I think it is an illusion . . . I realize, however, if I am to have the least chance of success in my work I must not think any more of my misery by working . . . But the very idea of it revolts me. It seems to me, after having lost Pierre I will never be able to laugh from the heart till the end of my days.

When Marie woke five days later, on the morning of May 11, after sleeping "pretty well" she felt relatively calm for about fifteen minutes, then, as she wrote, wanted to "howl . . . like a wild beast."

The French government offered her a pension, which she refused, saying that she was young enough to support herself and her daughters. And she soon began to spend long days working in the lab. The prospect of a woman, even Marie Curie, assuming Pierre's place as chair of a department was too much for the Sorbonne to contemplate. Instead, she was asked to continue his work without his title. She accepted, and on May 13, 1906, was officially appointed Pierre's successor, as chief of research in the Faculty of Science of the University of Paris (the Sorbonne) with a yearly salary of ten thousand francs.

She discussed her feelings with Pierre in her diary the next day:

> I also want to tell you that they nominated me for your chair and some imbeciles congratulated me . . . I cannot conceive of anything which would give me real personal happiness, except perhaps scientific work, and not even that, because, if successful, I would be distressed that you didn't know about it. This laboratory gives me an illusion of keeping the remains of your life . . . I found a little picture of you near the scales, with such a lovely smiling expression that I can't look at it without sobbing, since I will never again see that sweet smile.

To be nearer Pierre's grave, Marie moved to a rented house in Sceaux and hired her brother Joseph's sister-in-law, Marya Kamienska, as her daughters' governess. When she asked Dr. Curie if he would prefer to live with his son Jacques in Montpellier, to Irène's delight, because she had grown to love him, he chose to stay.

Two months after Pierre's death, on June 10, 1906, Marie confided to her diary: "I cry much less and my pain is less sharp . . . The household, the children and the laboratory constantly preoccupy me, but at no time do I forget that I have lost Pierre . . . I do not have a happy or serene soul by nature and I latched onto Pierre's sweet serenity in order to find courage. And this source has gone." Then she again addressed the man she had lost: "Before meeting you I had never met a man like you, and never since then have I seen as perfect a human being. If I hadn't known you, I would never have known that it was possible to know of it."

In November 1906 Marie faced the ordeal of replacing Pierre at the Sorbonne. To give herself courage, she went to his graveside before heading for Paris to be "the first woman among Masters," as Catherine Schulof, one of her students at Sèvres, put it. She would be the first woman ever to teach at the Sorbonne. The unique situation of a widow replacing a physics professor at the Sorbonne attracted an excited crowd as if to a sensational murder trial or the highlight of the social season. When the doors opened at 1 P.M., they rushed into the amphitheater and quickly filled the two hundred seats. Jean Perrin and Paul Appell, dean of the Faculty of Sciences, made it inside, as well as Countess Greffulhe, a patron of the arts. Marie's advanced class from Sèvres had reserved seats in front. Other students, many Polish, jostled for room with reporters, professors of various disciplines, and the public. Marie had prevailed upon the authorities to skip the customary formal inauguration. So, moments before she was due to speak at 1:30 P.M., Paul Appell stood, silenced the hubbub, and simply announced that Marie Curie would be teaching Pierre's physics course.

As a prelude to the lecture it was traditional to laud the triumphs and talents of one's predecessors. *Le Journal* had headlined her promotion as "A Great Victory for Feminism." And quipped that "if a woman is allowed to teach advanced studies to both sexes," it challenged the pretended superiority of man, and foreshadowed the rapidly approaching time, "when women will become human beings." Doubtless some in the audience hoped Marie would take her cue from this and lambaste the Sorbonne for discouraging women for so long. The more romantic perhaps expected her to give a tearful and loving account of Pierre's life and work. In fact, it was the audience she moved to tears.

She entered unobtrusively, almost apologetically, to lively applause. Her inevitable black dress emphasized her pallor and ash-blonde hair. A *Figaro* reporter described her face as "strange, ageless; her eyes clear and profound seem weary from having read too much and cried too much." When she reached a table covered with physics apparatus, she placed her watch and papers on it, and, holding onto the edge, waited for the applause to fade.

Her eyes met those of her adoring Sèvres students in the reserved front row and she started to speak—picking up exactly where Pierre had ended his last lecture: "When one considers the progress that has been made in physics in the past ten years, one is surprised at the advance that has taken place in our ideas concerning electricity and matter."

Although her voice was level and unemotional, the crowd knew what she had endured, and many women and some men were evidently moved. After completing her lecture on electricity, atomic disintegration, and radio-active substances, Marie gathered her watch and papers, and, as the crowd applauded, left as quietly as she had entered. No one could have guessed what an ordeal it had been for her.

But she described it in her diary entry next day, speaking to Pierre:

> You would have been happy to see me as a professor at the Sorbonne, and I myself would have so willingly done it for you. But to do it in your place, my Pierre, could one dream of a thing more cruel . . . I really feel that all my will to live is dead in me, and I only have my duty to bring up my children and also to continue on the path I have accepted. Perhaps, also the wish to prove to the world and especially to myself that the one that you have loved so much really has some value. I also have the vague hope . . . that you might know about my life of pain and effort and that you would be grateful. And so that I might, perhaps, find you more easily in the other life if there is one.

For six months she didn't make another diary entry. Then, on the anniversary of Pierre's death, April 18, 1907, she wrote: "I live for your children, for your old father. The grief is dull but always there . . . How sweet it would be to sleep never to wake again. How young my poor darlings are! How tired I am. Will I still have the courage to write?" It was her last diary entry.

Around the same time she received a letter from Pierre's brother, saying that he believed it would be many years before she got over her loss. Yet he wrote, "I hope . . . that you have found the energy to overcome your despondency; you are the center of a little world and your responsibility is great. You must revive and carry on in spite of everything."

CHAPTER 8

Rescuing Langevin
from His Wife

1906–1911

E very workday morning the grieving Marie Curie left her rented home at 6 rue du Chemin de Fer in Sceaux and at 7:55 entered the same shabby second-class train carriage for the half-hour journey to the Paris railroad station, from which she walked to the Sorbonne to lecture or continue her research. Invariably she stayed until late in the evening, working with almost obsessive intensity as if under an imminent deadline or on the verge of another great discovery.

Meanwhile, her daughters were cared for by an affectionate governess and their grandfather, Dr. Eugène Curie. Already a strong influence on Irène, he imbued her with his humane, freethinking, and liberal principles. She eventually shared his passion for scientific research, a love of nature, and the works of Victor Hugo. As a child, intrigued by dinosaurs, she decided to question her grandfather about them because, she said, "He's old. He will have seen one." When she came across a Rembrandt print of a wrinkled old crone, she cried out, "Oh, the poor old woman!" and burst into tears. Like both her parents, Irène was shy and introverted. Though they were little concerned with what others thought of them, Irène simply didn't care. Her personality most resembled her father's in that she was incapable of and bored by small talk. Awkward in company, except among close friends and family, she would clam up in front of strangers, a childhood habit she never lost. This even extended, later in life, to her staff and colleagues in the lab, where she often arrived each morning without a word of greeting, as if unaware of their existence.

Dr. Curie never revisited Pierre's grave after the burial, "refusing to be tortured by a ghost." By not dwelling on his own bereavement, this eighty-year-old stoic and rationalist, perhaps more than anyone, brought laughter back into their lives and prevented Marie from a complete breakdown. His light touch was evident in a letter he wrote to Irène in the summer of 1906, while she was staying with friends. He enclosed a written message from the not-yet two-year-old Eve that read "Eu, eu, eu, eu," and explained, "My dear Irène, my dear big grandchild, this letter from Eve is thanking you for your postcards. I think you will recognize her style."

What also helped Marie's recovery was the mission she undertook: to build as a monument to Pierre the well-equipped laboratory he should have had, where future generations would develop the young science of radioactivity.

Marie never let her daughters see her cry and never told them of the nightmares that ruined her sleep, but she couldn't always protect them from the symptoms of her distress. As a young child, Eve was left with an indelible memory of watching her mother stare into space with unseeing eyes, and at other times rub her fingertips together obsessively, as if trying to erase the scars from radium burns. Once, when Eve came in from playing with a turtle and two cats on the garden lawn, she saw her careworn mother faint and fall to the dining-room floor. Hers was not a happy childhood, but she grew to be much more outgoing and sociable than Irène.

Marie's niece and namesake, Maria Sklodowska, her brother Joseph's daughter, came to live with the Curies at this time while studying in Paris. She recalled how Marie usually arrived home in the evening tired and silent, moving around "almost without a sound, in her soft, gray wool robe like a nun's habit." Yet she was very involved with household affairs, from fitting the girls' dresses to making preserves. But Marie admitted to her Polish friend Kazia that her "good, sweet and rather pretty" daughters could not "awaken life in me," though she was "making great efforts to give them a solid and healthy development."

As the daughter of dedicated teachers, Marie had strong views on education. She believed that French schoolchildren were overworked and trapped for too many boring hours in badly ventilated classrooms. Instead of subjecting her daughter to that endurance test, she asked Dr. Curie and a succession of governesses to give both girls an hour of stimulating schoolwork in the morning and let them spend the rest of the day in the fresh air, gardening, walking, or exercising on the crossbar, trapeze, flying rings, and climbing rope that she had installed in the garden. Irène recalled that "my mother tried to give us every chance to exercise. We swam, rowed, and skated. We did gymnastics, cycling, and riding on horse-back." On weekends Marie often joined them on cycling trips in the countryside. She also trained them to overcome the terror of thunder-storms, burglars, and disease that she had endured as a child. Eve explained how "Regarding thunderstorms—she got us interested in what thunderstorms consisted of—teaching us, for example, to count the num-ber of seconds which elapsed between the lightning and the thunder's noise: this enabled us to estimate at what distance from us the thunder-storm was actually happening. In other cases [burglars, diseases] . . . I sup-pose her own daily behaviour was what influenced us. She had always taken chances to accomplish what she intended to do and she was not, by nature, a prudent person."

Despite Pierre's fatal street accident, when Irène and Eve had each reached about the age of eleven, Marie let them walk in the busy streets and travel unescorted. They were taught to cook and sew and encouraged to be self-reliant. Although neither was baptized, when they were old enough to understand Marie told them that they were free to think about religion for themselves. But neither became formally religious. Irène, strongly influenced by her anticlerical grandfather, never entered a church, not even to see a great work of art.

Worried about their further education, Marie wrote to her sister Hela: "I sometimes have the feeling that it would be better to drown the chil-dren than to shut them up in the sort of schools we have now." She solved the problem by persuading several Sorbonne professor friends to join in a unique experiment. To avoid sending their offspring to an uninspiring, underfunded, state-run school, they agreed to teach them in their own homes or laboratories.

Consequently, some ten boys and girls, Irène among them, spent one day at a chemist's laboratory, the next in a mathematician's study, the third in the home of a historian, and so on—learning the subjects from brilliant men and women at the peak of their professions. Jean Perrin taught chem-istry; Paul Langevin, mathematics; Henriette Perrin, French history and literature; Alice Chavannes, English, German, and geography; Henri Mou-ton, the natural sciences; and Monsieur Magrou, a sculptor, drawing and modeling. Some classes were within walking distance of the children's homes. If not, they took the slow train to their destinations. On one such journey of many local stops, Irène entertained the group with her sponta-neous French translation of the Polish novel *Quo Vadis*, a talent inherited from her maternal grandfather. At times, instead of going to classes, the children went to museums or art galleries.

On Thursdays Marie taught them science and made it fun. She showed the class how to test the law of falling bodies by watching ball bearings they had dipped in ink as they rolled down an inclined plane. She challenged them to find the best way to keep a pan of boiling water hot. After rejecting several ingenious or complicated suggestions, she simply put a lid on it. Marie also taught them to make instruments, including a working thermometer. As in her lab, she insisted on absolute cleanliness. Should a student make a mess, Marie would sternly interrupt any excuse with: "Don't tell me you will clean it *afterward*. One must *never* dirty a table during an experiment." Each lesson was followed by a feast of rolls, chocolate bars, and fruit.

Not everyone approved of this educational experiment. One mocking newspaper account told of children who could hardly read or write being allowed to construct apparatus and conduct experiments in a Sorbonne laboratory. The reporter quipped that although the building had not yet been demolished by an explosion, there was still hope.

Often on Sundays Marie's friend and colleague Debierne turned up at the Curies' home with candy or cookies for the girls and entertained them by drawing elephants and Irène's favorites, giraffes. When she was bored by the sketches, Irène, who was mad about mathematics, would eagerly tackle algebra problems. Her incomparable education lasted two years, at the end of which, to prepare her for the conventional demands of the university, Marie enrolled her in a private school, the Collège de Sévigné, where Eve, too, eventually completed her secondary education.

Before Irène's school term at Sévigné started, Marie tutored her and her friend Isabelle Chavannes at home in an upstairs room. At one math session, Marie uncharacteristically lost control and Irène gave a dramatic demonstration of her own self-control. Marie had asked her a math question and when Irène, her mind elsewhere, failed to answer immediately, she grabbed her daughter's notebook from the desk and threw it out of the window. Without a word, Irène stood up, walked downstairs, retrieved her notebook, returned to the room, sat down—and calmly answered the question.

As Eve remembered, her mother did not tolerate anyone raising his voice "whether in anger or joy." However, she never used physical punishment and never deprived them of anything, no matter how annoying or disobedient they had been. But once, when Irène had been impertinent, Marie didn't speak to her for two days. Her influence on her daughters was enormous, wrote biographer Giroud: "She toughened them, she educated them in all sorts of fields, she developed their special aptitudes without going against their different temperaments and tastes. Irène was never made to say hello when she met people and she never did learn to do it, whereas Eve was charming [to] everyone. Both girls learned to speak foreign languages, cook, ski, sew, ride horseback, and play the piano. She protected them without crushing them, she loved them without smothering them, and she treated them both exactly the same."

Eve acknowledged their mother's positive influence on both of them: "She permanently imprinted upon us: the taste for work—a thousand times more victorious in my sister than in me!—a certain indifference toward money, and an instinct of independence which convinced us both that in any combination of circumstances we should know how to get along without help."

Marie herself lived up to these principles by rejecting the advice of Drs. Curie and Gouy, who urged her to make the radium she had produced, worth a million francs, her personal property. They stressed that she needed it to assure the financial future of her fatherless daughters. It was, in fact, hers. But the idea of anyone living in luxury was distasteful, even shocking to her. She said that her daughters would be able to support themselves, and donated the radium to the laboratory. However, her indifference toward money did not apply to funding for scientific research, which is why she welcomed the support of Scottish American multimillionaire Andrew Carnegie, an advocate of the simple life—at least for others—who briefly met her in Paris and donated fifty thousand dollars to help build and staff a laboratory for radioactivity research. It was also to honor Pierre's memory and to be known as the Curies Foundation, created by Andrew Carnegie, for which he stipulated that Marie should be in full control. With this new source of money available, she recruited a group of young scientists, especially women, to work with her.

Things were looking up until August 9, 1906, barely four months after Pierre's death. Then, a disturbing letter from his admiring friend Lord Kelvin appeared in the *London Times* challenging the Curies' credibility and reputation. Radium, he wrote, was probably a molecular compound of lead and helium, and the Curies were mistaken in calling it an element. The devastating implication was that she and Pierre got the Nobel Prize under false pretenses. Rutherford quickly came to the Curies' defense in *Nature*, asserting that "radium has fulfilled every test required of an element," and that Kelvin's lead-helium compound was unknown to chemistry. Although considered Britain's greatest physicist, Kelvin had once called Roentgen a charlatan and X-rays a hoax. Marie responded by saying that she saw no reason to attempt to refute Kelvin, but that's exactly what she did.

Distressed by his attack, she aimed to prove beyond doubt that her atomic hypothesis of radioactivity was valid. It meant even more laborious work than in the past, but she tackled it in her usual dogged and determined manner. And, after a long, sustained effort, she produced the required evidence: perfectly pure radium chloride.

But Kelvin was no longer around to apologize, having died in 1907, the same year when he had questioned her work. Some critics had also expressed doubts about polonium being an element. Marie put those to rest after more intense and sustained effort, with Debierne's help, by producing enough polonium to identify it positively—from its spectrum—as an element.

She usually continued working in Paris during the long vacations, making brief visits to her daughters, who were spending the time with friends or relatives and kept in touch with her by mail. She saved all their letters, in which they addressed her as "Darling Me [rhymes with May]," "My sweet darling," "My sweet," or, most often, "Sweet Me." One of nine-year-old Irène's earliest letters to her was in August 1907, when she and Eve were vacationing with the Hornois family in Arromanches-les-Bains. It reads:

Sweet Me,
Eve and I are well and I have been swimming as much as possible . . . I only missed once since you left. These days the sea is rough but I still swim. It's fun. I couldn't answer problem no. 2, the 2 equations with 2 unknowns, but I'm sending you nos. 3 and 4. Mr. Hornois helped me with 3, but I did 4 by myself. I have a good appetite. The sea bathing keeps me healthy. On Tuesday I went to the farm where Mrs. Hornois gets her butter and had fun in the hay that they were putting in a loft. Are you well? I love you, Your daughter, Irène.

Occasionally the Langevins, the Perrins, and the Curie girls vacationed together, with Marie making brief appearances. As early as 1907, she saw signs of trouble in the Langevins' marriage. It was the same year that thirty-five-year-old Paul Langevin made a great breakthrough by applying the electron theory to magnetism. The couple had married young, when he was twenty-six and she was twenty-two. Langevin's wife, Jeanne, resented his reluctance to seek better-paid work in industry to support their four children—two boys and two girls—in a more comfortable lifestyle. She also complained that he was harsh. He said she was insolent and, according to him, smashed a bottle on his head and called him the son of an alcoholic who would die insane. After one squabble with her, he threatened to kill himself. Their friends sympathized with both, but mostly with Paul. They believed that his wife and his mother-in-law, who lived with them, did not appreciate the charming genius. Women especially admired Paul Langevin's brilliant mind and beautiful brown eyes, and noted how his face lit up when he discussed his enthusiasms: literature, philosophy, politics, as well as science.

In 1908, while Marie was still teaching the world's only course in radioactivity, the Sorbonne promoted her from assistant professor to full professor. Overwhelmed with work, she quit teaching at Sèvres. And Paul Langevin, encouraged by his wife to take on the extra job, replaced her.

Later that summer, Eve and Irène were on vacation at Saint-Palais-sur Mer, with their aunts and the Langevin family. Eagerly awaiting her mother's appearance, on August 19, eleven-year-old Irène wrote to her:

My dear Me,

1) I want to know the exact date of your arrival here.
2) Will my uncle Jacques soon be in Sceaux?
3) Write and tell me if my palm tree is doing as well as my araucaria [a Chilean pine also known as the monkey puzzle tree]. If the palm has any new leaves?
4) Have Filou and Tigrette [perhaps two stray cats] escaped? If they're still at home it's a miracle. If you see them, tell me: 5) if they're fat; 6) if they are being fed.
7) Are the peaches in my garden ripening?
8) What plants have been put on Pe's [her father's] grave ?
9) Which of them are flowering?
10) Is André [Debierne] coming to Sceaux or is he on vacation?

I saw yesterday a very rough sea beating magnificently against the rocks at the puits de L'Auture. I had sent a postcard of it to grand-pere some time ago; he can show it to you.

I asked you ten questions. Answer all of them when you write to me.

I kiss you, Irène.

While Irène showed a talent and fervor for math, Eve had become a promising pianist and a singer with perfect pitch. She had taken singing lessons from Mme Chavannes and at three years and four months played "Au Clair de la Lune" on the piano. At four she could play thirty tunes including the "Marseillaise." After hearing a new tune once, she played it almost flawlessly.

Irène, being older, was more often away from home, when she loved getting letters from her grandfather, which amused her and bolstered her self-confidence.

Though pleased with her daughters' progress, Marie was dissatisfied with her own situation—the Sorbonne having failed to keep its promise to fund a new laboratory for her. So she threatened to leave and join the Pasteur Institute headed by her friend Dr. Emile Roux. The threat worked. The university agreed to provide the land and four hundred thousand francs to build a laboratory for chemical and physical research into radioactive elements under Marie's direction. A noted medical researcher, Professor Claude Regaud, was to direct research into the medical uses of radioactivity—colloquially known as Curie-therapy—in an adjoining building funded by the Pasteur Institute. The two buildings would be known collectively as the Radium Institute.

With that situation resolved, though the building would take years, her father-in-law became Marie's main preoccupation during the freezing winter of 1909. At eighty-two he had contracted life-threatening pneumonia. She recorded in her notebook: "Irène is concerned, takes care of him, stays near him. She is devoted and affectionate." Marie herself also spent all her free time with the difficult patient, invariably arriving back from Paris with an illustrated magazine or a special delicacy for him. When Dr. Curie died at the end of the year, Marie noted that Irène's "pain is deep. She saw her grandfather dead and was present at his burial. She worried about losing me, too, attached herself to me even more than ever. She suffers and matures." Two months later, in the early spring of 1910, Marie saw Irène crying and asked if she was thinking of her grandfather. "Yes," she said. "I am thinking that he also loved the sun and flowers."

At the funeral, Marie had told the gravediggers to dig up Pierre's coffin from the frozen ground, place his father's coffin in the spot, then replace Pierre's above it. When she died, she said that she intended her coffin to be above Pierre's.

The strain of caring for Dr. Curie and grief over his death had taken its toll, judging by the reaction of Pierre's brother, Jacques, after Marie sent him a family photo. "The two girls were a pleasure to see," he wrote, "but you look so sad. My wife cried so much when she saw how thin and drained you were. You must rally, if it is only for your children who need you to live a long time."

But later in the year, when she visited her friends the Perrins and Borels, they saw a striking change in her. The light had returned to her eyes, and instead of the customary black dress, she wore a white blouse with a red rose at the waist. Pleased but puzzled, they discussed her rejuvenation and concluded that the forty-three-year-old widow had fallen in love with Paul Langevin, five years her junior, Pierre's former student, and

The widowed Marie Curie in 1908 with her daughters. She was devastated by Pierre's accidental death and called him the most perfect human being she ever met.

his successor at the School of Physics and Chemistry. He had met Albert Einstein, who called him "the only Frenchman who understands me," and said that if he hadn't invented special relativity, Langevin would have done so.

With growing frequency of late, Paul had arrived at the homes of friends after a fight with his wife and mother-in-law. Once he turned up with a bruised face and said that during a quarrel his wife, mother-in-law, and sister-in-law had joined forces to hurl an iron chair at him. Marie and other friends feared that his disintegrating thirteen-year marriage was jeopardizing his scientific career, if not his life. A highly strung man with chronic indigestion, he had developed a stomach ulcer and several times had threatened suicide after stormy sessions with his enraged wife.

In July 1910 he rented an apartment near the Sorbonne in his own name, then renewed the lease under the pseudonym Grosnier. He and Marie referred to it as "our place," and frequently lunched together there. Had their friends known of it, they would not have suspected these to be romantic encounters. They knew that Langevin was estranged from his

Physicist Paul Langevin married Jeanne Desfosses in 1898, when he was twenty-six and she was twenty-two. He was to become Pierre's student and a close friend of both Curies.

wife and that he and Marie had been close friends for years, sharing the same scientific interests and liberal views. He had been a leading member of the League of the Rights of Man, which fought for Alfred Dreyfus's freedom from unjust imprisonment on Devil's Island. And when not complaining of his disastrous marriage or his stomach ulcer, he was great company, enthusiastic, and informed about music, art, politics, and literature.

During the summer of 1910 Marie sent her daughters on vacation with friends and relatives, intending to join them later, which accounts for Irène's letter in August: "My sweet Me, WHEN ARE YOU COMING TO JOIN US? . . . I shall be so happy when you arrive because I badly need to hug someone."

Marie joined her daughters soon after and then wrote a very affectionate letter to Langevin, who was still in Paris: "I spent yesterday evening and night thinking of you, of the hours that we have spent together and of which I have kept a delicious memory. I still see your good and tender eyes, your charming smile, and think of the moment when I will experience again the sweetness of your visit." (This is an extract from one of several letters printed by the gutter press — comparable to today's tabloids — in 1911 when Marie was being portrayed as a scarlet woman. As none of the original letters have survived, the complete accuracy of published accounts is suspect.)

Paul Langevin fought a
duel over Marie Curie.

In another letter Marie warned Langevin that it would end their close
relationship if his wife had another child, because, she explained, although
she would risk her life and position for him, "I couldn't accept this dis-
honor." Perhaps, she added, if his wife realized this, she would try to get
pregnant immediately, "and someone may suggest it to her."

Were Marie and Langevin lovers? He, at least, was behaving suspiciously, by renting an apartment under an assumed name and telling
Marie that his wife might not only have him followed, but was using one
of his sons to spy on him.

Jean Perrin soon became involved in the situation. After vacationing
with his family at the Brittany seashore in August, Perrin had returned to
Paris to complete work for an upcoming conference in Brussels when
Marie called on him. She had not heard from Langevin for several days
and was concerned that her recent letter to him might have been intercepted and misunderstood. It was essentially a scientific communication,
she assured Perrin, though couched in affectionate terms. In fact, Marie
had sent Langevin what could only be interpreted as a love letter. And in
one of his replies to her, he called her "my darling," wrote of her "dear
eyes," and discussed their future together.

Perrin went to the Langevins' home as the sympathetic mutual friend
of all concerned, to assess and try to calm the situation. It was immediately

clear that after Marie's letter had been mailed to Langevin's apartment, his wife somehow got hold of it. Greatly agitated, she threatened to cause a scandal in the newspapers and in Perrin's presence asked her eleven-year-old son, Jean, if he, too, intended to have a mistress.

For four days running Perrin visited the Langevins and finally believed he had persuaded Mme Langevin to behave reasonably. But as he was about to return home around midnight, he was astounded to see Marie Curie hurrying toward him. Mme Langevin and her sister, Mme Bourgeois, had met her in the street, she said, where they insulted her and threatened to kill her if she didn't leave France. She had been waiting for several hours in the dark for Perrin to appear, because she was afraid to return to her own home in Sceaux.

"I will never forget the emotion I felt," Perrin's wife, Henriette, later testified, "seeing the distress which this illustrious woman had suffered . . . wandering like a beast being hunted."

Perrin returned to the Langevins' home several times, but Madame Langevin was unable to keep her promise to be reasonable, once shouting that if Madame Curie didn't leave France within eight days she would kill her. Eventually Perrin met with both of the Langevins and Mme Langevin's brother-in-law, Henri Bourgeois, an editor of the disreputable *Petit Journal*. At the meeting, Langevin agreed never to see Marie again for any purpose, and his wife promised to stop threatening Marie and to keep the scandal out of the papers.

Langevin never publicly admitted to a love affair with Marie Curie. He later explained that both Pierre and Marie had been his friends since he was seventeen. His sympathy for her as a widow, as well as the work they had in common, drew him to her with brotherly affection. Over time he had told her about the problems of his marriage and sought from her the affection he didn't get from his wife. It was the cliché of the misunderstood husband. In a biography of his father, his son André confirmed that his parents had a miserable marriage and implied that the romance was inevitable. "Why should anyone think it unnatural," he wrote, "if Paul Langevin considered it his duty to encourage and assist Mme Curie in her misfortune? . . . Isn't it natural enough that a few years after Pierre Curie's death this friendship enhanced by mutual admiration should have gradually grown into a passion and resulted in a love affair?"

Marie did not let personal problems jeopardize her work. After touching home base with her daughters, in mid-September 1910, she joined Jean Perrin and her friend Ernest Rutherford (a Nobel Prize winner for physics two years earlier) at a contentious meeting of the World Congress on Radiology and Electricity in Brussels, Belgium. Radium's growing use in medicine, industry, and research had made it vital to have a uniform measurement for the element, and the aim of the congress was to choose an International Radium Standard.

Although Marie's friends had thought her transformed by love, Rutherford had a very different impression. Comparing her with the lively, witty, and lighthearted Perrin, Rutherford wrote to his mother, at forty-three, Marie was "wan and tired. And much older than her age. She works much too hard for her health. Altogether she was a very pathetic figure."

The meetings were confusing—in three languages—and on the third day the chairman lost control and was greeted with jeers, boos, and whistles. Eventually, the congress adopted the word *Curie* for the measurement, without establishing whether this was to honor Pierre, Marie, or both of them.

One evening Rutherford escorted Marie to the Opéra theater but she felt ill, so that at the first intermission he took her back to rest at the Hôtel du Grand Miroir. She appeared at the conference the next day, insisting that if the measurement was to be a "Curie," she must be allowed to define it as the amount of emanation (radon) expended by one gram of radium in one second.

After more arguments, her definition was adopted and she was appointed to "prepare the primary standard." This, as she later explained, "was a very delicate operation, as the weight of the standard sample, quite small [21.99 milligrams of pure radium chloride] had to be determined with great precision. It was accepted by the Commission and deposited in the International Bureau of Weights and Measures at Sèvres, near Paris." Subsequently, Marie wrote, "In France the control of radium tubes, by the measurement of their radiation, takes place in my laboratory, where anyone may come to bring the radium to be tested."

Marie returned from Belgium to Paris with Jean Perrin, then took the train to Sceaux for a few days of rest with her daughters before completing a massive undertaking, titled *Treatise on Radioactivity*, which covered the subject in two volumes and 971 pages. It had a photograph of Pierre opposite the title page. Ernest Rutherford read it and wrote a positive review in *Nature*. It was a friendly gesture, apparently, because, in a letter to an American radiochemist, Bertram Boltwood, Rutherford presumably said what he really thought: "She makes a mistake of trying to include all the work, old and new, with very little critical discussion of its relative importance . . . She has been reasonably generous in the recognition of those outside of France . . . I have not been neglected. In reading her book I could almost think I was reading my own with the extra work of the last few years thrown in to fill up . . . It is very amusing in parts to read where she is very anxious to claim priority for French science, or rather for herself and her husband . . . Altogether I feel that the poor woman has labored tremendously, and her volumes will be very useful for a year or two to save the researcher from hunting up his own literature." Sour grapes? Hardly. But although Rutherford felt great affection for Marie Curie, he was also an extremely ambitious and competitive man.

In late September 1910 Marie joined her daughters and sister Hela with her daughter, Hania, at L'Arcouest on the rocky Britanny coast, sharing a house with the Perrins. While there, Marie confided in the Perrins that despite Mme Langevin's threats she hoped for a future with Langevin—even though he had agreed never to see Marie again in any circumstances. Marie also told Henriette Perrin that Langevin had once said to her that, "Without your affection, I can't live." She then asked Henriette, "When you know that a man is one of the most intelligent there is . . . should you refuse to do what you can to help him?"

Despite the danger of Mme Langevin exposing the affair—especially as her brother-in-law was a newspaper editor—Marie still risked public scrutiny, especially by the press. Having followed Pierre's example and declined the Legion of Honor, in December 1910 she emulated him again by competing for membership in the Academy of Sciences, an institution that had an enormous influence on the support and direction of French science. This move would inevitably attract press coverage.

Although the Academy of Sciences had only sixty-eight members, interest was so intense in a woman trying to invade the all-male bastion that 163 members of the Institute de France—the umbrella organization representing several academies—turned up to vote. Among them were Baron Edmond de Rothschild, the prince of Monaco, and Prince Roland Bonaparte. Marie seemed a sure bet, supported as she was by the prestigious newspaper *Le Figaro*, which called her the nation's most famous physicist, as well as a pure, noble, and beautiful woman. One major obstacle, however, was the reluctance of some members to break with tradition and allow a woman to join them.

An irreverent *Le Figaro* reporter recorded their arrival to vote on January 4, 1911: "I see wrinkled old gentlemen go by with gray handkerchiefs in their hands; their shoulders are covered with dandruff, their pants are twisted around thin shanks . . . There is something both laughable and pitiful about the men that file by, some of them eminent figures but more of them simply decrepit." Unexpectedly, most voted to allow a woman to be a candidate, and to challenge the two other aspirants, Edouard Branly and Marcel Brillouin. Marie even seemed a possible winner, despite the published protests of a popular woman novelist, Marie Regnier, that women were made for love.

A loose but lively coalition of conservatives, Catholics, chauvinists, misogynists, and anti-Semites went on a ferocious attack. The most rabid anti-Semite—who still called Dreyfus a traitor despite compelling evidence of his innocence—claimed that Marie's application for the academy seat had been engineered by a Jewish-Protestant cabal to deprive two Catholic candidates of the honor. One right-wing rag suggested that with a name like Sklodowska, Marie must be Jewish herself—and was certainly a free-thinker—and consequently unfit to defeat her devout Catholic rivals. Others asserted that Pierre had been the only scientific genius in the fam-ily and that her Nobel Prize was undeserved. To prove her inadequacy a L'Intransigeant reporter attended her weekly lecture, scoffed at the applause that greeted her entrance, and declared that he was bored by Marie's talk about her "dear radium." Even some scientific colleagues at the Sorbonne joined the opposition, especially physiologist Professor Lapicque, who valued women as assistants but not as partners. Now the opposition seemed so powerful that the Paris correspondent of London's Truth predicted that the members of the academy would not defy the Napoleonic code and elect a woman.

Support mostly came from the more restrained liberal press and influ-ential friends, especially Nobelist Gabriel Lippmann.

The biggest blow to Marie's chances was on January 11, when the scandal sheet Excelsior filled much of its front page with what looked like police mug shots of her, giving the impression that she was a wanted crim-inal. This impression was reinforced by damning pseudoscientific charac-ter assessments from a handwriting expert, based on a sample of her writing, and from a physiognomist, based on the shape of her skull.

Inflammatory and skewed press reports fueled unusual public interest in the upcoming vote. And on January 23, 1911, institute members, re-porters, and the curious made such a frantic rush to get into the building that one man fainted in the crush. Nonscientists impatiently waited for members to read their scientific papers: one had discovered a new star, and Guillaume, Pierre's friend, spoke of a new metal. Ushers then appeared

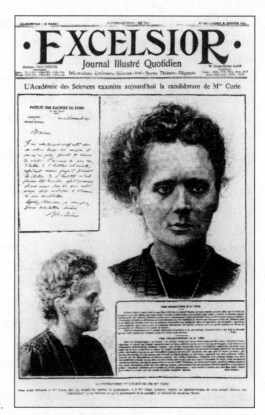

What looks like two police mug shots of Marie on the front page of the right-wing magazine *Excelsior* was part of its successful smear campaign to prevent her election to the prestigious Institute de France.

with ballot boxes and members lined up to choose their favorite among the three candidates. The votes were quickly announced: Branly, 29; Curie, 28; Brillouin, 1. Despite the devastating press campaign against her, Marie lost by only one vote. Because the vote was so close, a second vote was taken. This time, Branly picked up the one needed to win decisively.

Marie had remained in her laboratory and received the news of her defeat by phone. She returned to her work without a word. But lab workers soon got the news and quietly hid the bouquet prepared for what they had thought, despite the press onslaught, was a possible win. Another vote was taken soon after her defeat—when all institute members were invited to participate—to decide whether a woman would *ever* be admitted. They voted 90 to 52 to bar them for eternity.

Eternity turned out to be sixty-eight years: the first woman was admitted in 1979. But Marie would never again try to join.

Georges Gouy said she had won a moral victory. Georges Urbain wrote: "You are too noble to be affected in the least by this affair at the

Institute . . . In telling you that the best academy is a circle of devoted friends and enthusiastic students, I would be preaching to the converted." Charles-Edouard Guillaume felt that she had been treated abominably and unjustly and that "the election of M Branly was achieved by methods that would make monkeys blush."

Press distortions and outright lies had played their part in her defeat. In the following months, by exposing her private life in lurid and slanted detail, the same newspapers almost killed her.

CHAPTER 9

Battered by the Press

1911

In the spring of 1911, Mme Langevin's brother-in-law, Henri Bourgeois, a newspaper editor for *Le Petit Journal*, called on Marie Curie with alarming news. Someone, he told her, had entered Langevin's apartment, opened his desk, and discovered a cache of affectionate correspondence between her and Paul. Mme Langevin later identified herself as the "someone," admitting to the wife of scientist Marcel Brillouin: "When my husband was ill [at home] I went with his keys to his apartment and found the letters, as well as intimate feminine toilet objects there."

Langevin had promised his wife he would stop seeing Marie. But now that Mme Langevin possessed the compromising letters indicating that their romantic relationship had apparently continued, Bourgeois's message was clear: Marie's life was again at risk. Distraught, she sought advice from Jean Perrin, a charming man of the world whose wife, it was believed, tolerated his infidelities. He had seen the bruises Mme Langevin had apparently inflicted on her husband and had also taken her death threat to Marie seriously, so he advised her to leave town immediately.

She soon got the chance, without appearing to be on the run. Two friendly acquaintances, Emile and Marguerite Borel, were about to attend a scientific conference in Genoa, Italy. He was vice-president of the Ecole Normale Supérieure, where the nation's top professors taught the nation's top students to become teachers. She was a talented novelist and daughter of Paul Appell, dean of the Sorbonne's Faculty of Sciences. When they invited Marie to join them, she eagerly accepted, taking both daughters and Walcia Valentine, their Polish governess, with them.

They all stayed in the same small seafront hotel at Santa Margherita Ligure and went sightseeing together in the mornings, when fourteen-year-old Irène peppered Emile with questions about almost everything they saw and enthusiastically discussed mathematics with him. And Eve enchanted everyone they met. In the afternoons, when Emile and Marie were at the conference, the girls played on the beach, watched over by their governess and Mme Borel.

One night while Emile was preparing for the next day's conference, Marie invited Marguerite into her bedroom. As she rested on the bed and Marguerite sat at the foot, she spoke with great emotion and concern about Paul Langevin's miserable home life, calling him a genius who was being pressured by his wife to quit pure science to make more money in industry to support his family. She implored Marguerite to help "save him from himself. He is weak. You and I are tough. He needs understanding, he needs gentleness and affection." Marguerite listened sympathetically, surprised and pleased to find that "under the austere scientist, [was a] tender and lively woman capable of walking through fire for those she loves."

After their return to France, André Debierne urged Marguerite to stop Langevin from tormenting Mme Curie "with his disillusionment. He is worrying her. She can't bear to see him so despondent." When Marguerite said that Langevin also complained to her, Debierne replied, "Complaining to you is not as dangerous."

While Marie had been hiding in Italy, Langevin spent his nights with the Perrins rather than at his apartment, until the youngest of his four children became ill with enteritis and he returned home. Mme Langevin called the boy's illness the start of Langevin's deserved punishment, and made sure the punishment continued and intensified. She repeatedly threatened to ruin him and Marie by publishing the stolen letters. After she insulted him at dinner one evening, he called her a rotten cook and slapped her face. She rushed out in tears and shut herself in her bedroom. Having promised to take his two elder sons for a vacation in England later that summer, he decided to leave with them immediately. She then publicly charged him with abandoning his home and taking their sons with him.

Marie had only stopped briefly in Paris before leaving for Leiden, Holland, to study the behavior of radioactive bodies at very low temperatures with Heike Kamelingh Onnes. She couldn't have gone to a better place: Onnes had made the city the world center for low-temperature research. (In 1913 he would win the Nobel Prize for physics for his pioneering work on low-temperature physics and his production of liquid helium.)

Still wary of the formidable Mme Langevin, instead of returning to Paris, she planned to go from Holland to Poland and to introduce her daughters to her relatives and her country. It would be their first visit. She had already sent them ahead to stay with her sister Bronia and brother-in-law Casimir, in Zakopane. From there, soon after her arrival, Irène wrote Marie that she already loved Poland, the Poles, and the Polish language, because they were her mother's country, countrymen, and language, but that she loved France more. When Marie joined her daughters she took them on a hiking trip in the mountains and was impressed by six-year-old Eve's endurance and disposition.

They returned to Paris in the fall, but again Marie stayed only a few days, having accepted Ernest Solvay's invitation to an all-expenses-paid conference of world-class physicists in Brussels, the Belgian capital. Solvay, a wealthy industrialist and philanthropist, asked them to focus on the crisis in physics sparked by the astonishing work of Max Planck and Albert Einstein, and proposed radiation and quantum theory as the conference theme.

Photographs of the occasion show Marie as the only woman among the twenty scientists at the Solvay Conference, as it was known. They included Albert Einstein and Max Planck, Jean Perrin, Marcel Brillouin, Henri Poincaré, James Jeans, Ernest Rutherford, Kamelingh Onnes (with whom she had recently worked), and, despite his promise to his wife not to see Marie again, Paul Langevin. Group discussions at the Hotel Metropole presided over by Hendrik Lorentz and monitored by two scientific secretaries—an Englishman, Frederick Lindemann (later Winston Churchill's scientific adviser), and a Frenchman, Maurice de Broglie—began on October 30, 1911.

Marie complained of severe headaches and abruptly left several committee meetings. But her obvious discomfort didn't prevent her from a careful appraisal of Einstein's paper, "The Actual State of the Problems of Specific Heats," in which he explained the anomalies of specific heat at low temperatures. When he said that he was up for the chairmanship of mathematical physics at Zurich Polytechnic (where he had once failed the entrance exam), she offered to give him a reference after the conference, which he gladly accepted.

It read: "Mathematical physicists are at one in considering his work as being in the first rank. At Brussels, where I took part in a scientific conference he attended, I appreciated the clearness of his mind, the shrewdness with which he marshaled his facts and the depth of his knowledge. If one considers that M Einstein is still very young [thirty-two], one is justified in basing great hopes on him and in seeing in him one of the leading theoreticians of the future. I think that a scientific institution which gave M Ein-

The Solvay Conference in Brussels, 1911, when Marie was accused of eloping with Paul Langevin. She and Henri Poincaré are studying the same document. Langevin is standing far right, next to Albert Einstein. Their mutual friend Ernest Rutherford stands fourth from the right.

stein the chance to do the work which he wants to do, by appointing him to a chair . . . would render a great service to science." He got the job.

Ernest Rutherford, another friendly presence at the Solvay Conference, discussed with Marie the nature of Beta-rays (streams of electrons or positrons emitted by a radioactive nucleus with great penetrating power, at velocities sometimes exceeding 98 percent of the speed of light). One night Rutherford stayed in her hotel suite until midnight trying to decide where to keep the Curie, the international unit of radium to measure radioactivity. She intended to seal this precise amount in a glass tube and keep it permanently in her laboratory. Others wanted it located elsewhere. "For sentimental reasons I quite understand [her point of view]," Rutherford reported. "I am sure it is going to be a ticklish business to get the matter arranged satisfactorily as Mme Curie is rather a difficult person to deal with. She has the advantage and at the same time the disadvantage of being a woman."

Marie eventually, agreed to keep the Curie at the Office of Weights and Measurements in Sèvres.

Reporters waving newspapers waylaid Marie in the lobby of the Metropole Hotel on the morning of November 4 as she was on her way to a session of the conference. One thrust a copy of the big-circulation Paris paper *Le Journal* into her hand and asked what she thought of being called a husband snatcher. Stunned, she hurried past them without a word.

That afternoon she had a chance to read the two-column item headed "A Love Story: Mme Curie and Professor Langevin." Obviously aimed at the scandal-sheet's 750,000 mostly female readers, it told how "The fires of radium which so mysteriously warm everything around them, had a surprise in store for us: They have just kindled a blaze in the hearts of the scientists who are studying their behavior with such tenacity—and the wife and children of one of these scientists are in tears." The piece included Fernand Hauser's interview with Mme Langevin's elderly mother, Mme Desfosses, who spoke of letters that proved the love affair to be a fact and called the whereabouts of the lovers a mystery.

Marie responded in a letter to the more reputable Paris newspaper *Le Temps*, scorning the rumors of an elopement as pure fantasy and pointing out that it was well known in Paris where she could be found. *Le Petit Journal* got an interview with Langevin's wife, which was hardly surprising. Her brother-in-law, Henry Bourgeois, was one of its editors. Under the headline "A Novel in a Laboratory—The Affair of Mme Curie and M Langevin," Jeanne Langevin was reported to have known of the illicit relationship for three years, and had obtained proof of the affair eighteen months ago but kept quiet, hoping for a reconciliation with her husband. She was quoted as saying: "If I had been the sort of woman they have tried to make me out to be in certain places, stupid, jealous, and insane—I would have talked. I would have cried out that my husband had betrayed me and that that woman had destroyed my home. [But] I waited, always hoping for a reconciliation, for my husband to return to his senses. Perhaps I would have remained even longer in this horrible situation, knowing I was being ridiculed and hatefully deceived, if a decisive event hadn't taken place last July 25."

She began to sob as she described how her husband, dissatisfied with a dish of stewed fruit she had cooked for him, hit her, then disappeared with their two sons. In later testimony, Emile Borel disputed Jeanne Langevin's account, saying that she knew where the trio were all the time—in England in August and living with the Borels during most of September. Langevin said that he had left his wife simply to get away from her jealous outbursts.

The Solvay scientists read the newspapers, and if Einstein and Rutherford were typical, regarded the reports as ridiculous. Rutherford called
them "rubbish," but couldn't get confirmation from Marie because she
had skipped the last session and was on her way home, leaving a note saying that she would like to have shaken his hand before leaving, but was
too ill to stay any longer.

Einstein also ridiculed reports of a romance between Curie and Langevin. (Later, while married, Einstein had an affair with his cousin Elsa, then
divorced his wife and married her.) He thought their liaison was completely implausible. On his return to Prague on November 7, 1911, he told
a physician friend, Heinrich Zangger that he had been enchanted with
Perrin, Langevin, and especially Madame Curie, who had promised to visit
the Einsteins with her daughters. He called her honest and unpretentious,
and said that despite her heavy burdens and responsibilities, she had displayed a sparkling intelligence. As for "the horror story that was peddled in
the newspaper, [it] is nonsense. It has been known for some time that
Langevin wants to get a divorce. If he loves Mme Curie & she loves him,
they do not have to run off, because they have plenty of opportunities to
meet in Paris." (Einstein of course knew nothing of Mme Langevin's
death threats.) However, the pair had not given him the slightest impression that there was anything between them other than an innocent friendship. Though aware of Marie's passionate nature, he thought that she was
not attractive enough to be a danger to anyone.

Pierre's brother damned her journalistic detractors as rabble and filthy
swine, advised her to sue them, and suggested that Langevin should have
left his wife years ago. He wrote to the press that Marie Curie had made
his brother happy during their marriage, and that it would be almost impossible to imagine two people who were so completely compatible, that
their mutual affection was real, and that he regarded her as a true sister.

This did not prevent Leon Bailby from publishing an open letter in the
newspaper L'Intransigeant, addressed to Monsieur X, physicist, obviously
referring to Paul Langevin, with the challenging assertion: "The woman
who was once your confidante is now quite obviously your mistress."

Marie Curie took fast preemptive action to prevent any newspaper
from publishing the stolen Curie-Langevin correspondence, warning
them through the friendly Le Temps that she would sue anyone who
printed documents attributed to her, and use the money for scientific
research. This scared Le Journal's reporter Fernand Hauser, who had first
exposed the affair, into apologizing for his "detestable act" and for relying

on unreliable sources (which included Mme Langevin's mother). He wrote of being tortured by the harm he had done her, concluding, after more mea culpas: "I am left with only one consoling thought—that such a humble journalist as I am could never, by any of his writings, tarnish the glory that halos you nor the esteem that surrounds you . . . Yours, very distressed, Fernand Hauser."

Marie forwarded Hauser's sycophantic apology to *Le Temps*, the paper she read every afternoon, which printed it verbatim. In America the *New York World* published a cautious version of the drama headed "Mme Curie Denies Indignantly That She Is an Eloper." She was quoted as saying, "The attack upon me is absolute madness," and Langevin backed her up with: "I have been forced to separate from my wife because of daily scenes created by her jealousy. I have been associated with Mme Curie in scientific work, but our relations have never had any other significance."

The *World* apparently believed them, concluding that the sensational "rumor's falsity was established today by statements of those familiar with the case. [It] briefly amazed the scientific world, but there it found small credence. The general opinion [in Paris] is that the strong friendship existing between Mme Curie and Prof. Langevin has been solely the friendship of two scientists engrossed in their work, and that Mme Langevin cannot understand such friendship." To justify its claims to fair play, the paper gave Mme Langevin's rebuttal: "I am not an insanely jealous wife, causing needless trouble. In silence I allowed my home to be destroyed but I have been forced to act to protect my children. My husband has been unfaithful. I have proofs which have compelled me to take legal action to secure possession of my children."

The day after the *World* report, Marie received a telegram. Anticipating another threat that more details of her private life were about to be exposed, she anxiously opened it to read instead: "You have been awarded the Nobel Prize in Chemistry. Letter follows, Aurivillius." This one, for chemistry, was hers alone, unlike her first Nobel for physics, which she had shared with Pierre and Becquerel. And it would make her unique, as the world's only scientist with two Nobel Prizes.

But the news was overshadowed by the nonstop press onslaught. Fortunately, as well as the loving support of her family and Pierre's brother, she had the help of several influential and loyal friends. One, Charles-Edouard Guillaume, wrote to her on November 11: "We share your sadness and your joys. We were with you during the painful days you have just gone through: we still are with you. There are people who cannot forgive your superiority: they proved it during your presentation at the academy. The same base jealousy has animated them again . . . The campaign the last few days is proof that the same people have not given up yet."

By lucky chance, her legal adviser, Raymond Poincaré, who within a year would become France's president, was also attorney for an organization of powerful press barons, the Paris Press Syndicate. He asked the syndicate members to impose a moratorium on the Curie-Langevin story. On November 16, he had good news for Marie. The leading French newspaper editors had agreed to hold their fire, with one glaring exception, *L'Action Française*, an extreme right, nationalist newspaper that had led the attacks on Alfred Dreyfus and regarded Protestants, Jews, Freemasons, the liberal intelligentsia, and scientists as the enemy.

Literate, often witty, and always provocative, it encouraged supporters to keep "Paris in an uproar by battling Socialists in the streets and persecuting unpatriotic professors at the Sorbonne." One contributor, Léon Daudet, according to author Gordon Wright, was "intent on turning the scandal into a new Dreyfus affair," again with disputed letters involved, and portrayed Marie Curie as a foreigner who had destroyed the home of a blameless Frenchwoman. The paper reported that Mme Langevin had begun legal proceedings against an unnamed woman (almost anyone who could read knew who she was), that a police investigation was under way, and that Paris's police chief had agreed to sequester all the incriminating documents still in Mme Langevin's possession until the December 8 trial.

The vital question was the ultimate fate of the letters. Would their contents ever be disclosed to the public?* Unknown to Marie, who remained in Sceaux, accompanying her girls to their classes past gawking onlookers, some newspapers already had copies of the letters and were anxiously debating what to do with them.

As André Debierne wrote to Georges Gouy on November 17, Marie was ill and "very worried about the future and particularly fears that the threats made on her will occur . . . This story is not over and it will bring many painful moments for Mme Curie. The letters of affection and sympathy she gets from people like you are very precious to her and do a lot to comfort her."

The story, as Debierne expected, was kept aflame by among others *La Libre Presse*, its chauvinistic motto "France for the French." The paper

---

* In a March 3, 2002, e-mail to the author, Marie Curie's granddaughter, Hélène Langevin-Joliet, who married Langevin's son, stated her opinion that the original letters were probably destroyed by Jeanne Langevin or by someone else after her death, and that copies of the letters quoted in the press had been distorted by alteration or omission.

published a provocative front-page article headed "Will Mme Curie Remain a Professor at the Sorbonne?" Obviously hoping she wouldn't, it hinted at the contents of the controversial letters: They "will dumbfound people when they become known. And they will not fail to become known because they will be produced in the presence of the audience. As is our custom, we would have said nothing about this if it involved only the private lives of the people concerned. But . . . Mme Curie occupies a public teaching position that gives her students and their families the right to demand that the teacher be what the English call 'respectable.'"

The suspense was over on November 23, when Gustave Tery, editor of L'Oeuvre, risked Marie's threat to sue. He was an ugly, aggressive little man with a goatee and chronic indigestion, and his paper was "a salacious, quasi-intellectual scandal sheet, virulently anti-Jewish, zenophobic, and seeing traitors in France in every foreign or Jewish bed." Strangely, Tery and Paul Langevin had been friendly acquaintances as students at the Ecole Normale. After graduating, Tery became a philosophy teacher, but he had been dismissed because of his extreme political views. He then sought to express them through journalism. Boasting that he held his pen "in a hand which does not tremble," he set about destroying the couple in a twelve-page indictment daringly titled "The Truth About the Langevin-Curie Scandal." He wrote of Marie Curie as "the vestal virgin of radium" who "deliberately, methodically, scientifically, set about alienating Paul Langevin from his wife and separating her from her children. All this is either cynically recounted or unconsciously admitted in the letters which remain Mme Langevin's only defense now."

Tery claimed that to protect the sensibilities of his female readers, he would not reproduce the letters. Then he quoted long extracts from the legal writ issued against Langevin by his wife, which included Marie's urgent plea to him, "not to make me wait too long for you to stop sleeping in her bed." Tery ridiculed Langevin as a cad who hid behind a woman's skirts. And he previewed the imminent writ of separation to be read in court, which accused Langevin of adultery. The editor skillfully shaped his partial account to make it seem that only Mme Langevin's good breeding had stopped her from catching the pair in flagrante delicto. Even worse for Marie were Tery's implications that she had dishonored the name of Curie, that her affair with Langevin probably began while Pierre was alive, and that the words of the driver of the horse carriage—that he practically threw himself at the horse—fueled the rumor that Pierre knew of the affair and because of it had committed suicide.

None of these innuendos has ever been established as true, despite their wide and enduring currency. And her absolute fidelity to Pierre Curie is reflected in the diary she kept after his death, as well as in the testimony of all who knew her best. However, the public could only judge from the sensational press accounts—of a blameless mother of four betrayed by her husband, of a Frenchman enticed to leave his French wife by an immoral, scheming foreign woman. Tery's invective spurred a hostile group to gather outside Marie's home in Sceaux, one of them shouting, "Get the foreign woman out!" and another yelling, "Husband snatcher!" And someone threw a stone at the house.

Having read Tery's incendiary account, Jean Perrin and André Debierne hurried to the Borels' apartment at the Ecole Normale and handed the newspaper to Marguerite Borel. After reading it quickly, she concluded that the frank Polish expressions that Marie used in her written French, together with Tery's crafty editing of the letters, had distorted their sense. And that his calling Marie "an ambitious Pole who had ridden to glory on Curie's coat-tails and was now trying to latch on to Langevin's" as a mean-spirited lie.

The Borels decided to shelter Marie and her girls in their apartment on the university grounds, safe from public harassment. So Marguerite and Debierne took a cab to Sceaux to collect them. Elbowing their way through the mob at the gate, they found Marie alone with seven-year-old Eve. Irène was away at gym class.

Marie was reluctant to leave right away, worried about her fourteen-year-old daughter having to face the angry crowd on her return and finding the home deserted. But Debierne promised to collect Irène from school and to drive her directly to the Borels' apartment. Reassured, Marie hurriedly packed a change of clothing for herself and her daughters and left the house. She held Eve's hand as they walked past the hostile crowd to the waiting cab, her face, Marguerite recalled, white as a statue.

When Debierne reached Irène at her school, she was holding a copy of L'Oeuvre and looked shocked. Her schoolmate friend Isabelle Chavannes had seen the paper with the names of Curie and Langevin on the front page, thought they had made a scientific breakthrough, and showed it to Irène. She had glanced at the paper and almost fainted. Debierne took her to join her mother at the Borels', where she stayed close to her side as if afraid they would be separated. But that night Irène slept at the Perrins' home with their daughter, Aline—as she had done when her father died.

Furious when he learned that Marie Curie was staying in an Ecole Normale apartment, Theodore Steeg, minister of public education, summoned Emile Borel to his office and accused him, as the school's vice president, of discrediting the institution by sheltering a woman involved in a scandal. If Borel persisted, Steeg warned, he would be fired. "All right," Borel replied, "I will persist." Stymied, the minister gave him time to think it over and to discuss it with his wife, Marguerite. But she had her own problem to deal with—her father, Paul Appell, dean of the Sorbonne's Faculty of Sciences.

Because Appell had been the first person to tell Marie of Pierre's death, and later was her sponsor for membership in the French academy, Marguerite expected him to sympathize with Marie's plight. So that when he asked his daughter to see him at once, she thought it was to discuss how to help Marie. She was in for a surprise.

He stopped putting on his shoes when she entered the room and, eyes flashing with anger, forbade her to shelter a woman who was ruining the Sorbonne's reputation. He interrupted her frantic protest to say that he'd done everything he could for Marie Curie, "but I cannot hold back the flood now engulfing her." Everything was settled. He intended to fire Marie as Pierre's successor and advise her to resign from the Sorbonne and return to Poland. She will have "a chair and laboratory in Poland," Appell said. "She can leave at her own pace. . . . Her situation is impossible in Paris."

This was the first fight Marguerite had ever had with her father. Trembling with emotion, she begged him to change his mind, but he refused— until she said: "If you give in to that idiotic nationalist movement and insist that Marie should leave France you will never see me again!" Exasperated, he hurled his shoe at the wall. But she prevailed. By the time Marguerite left, he had promised to do nothing to harm Marie Curie.

Others, especially journalists, responded to the situation even more fiercely than Appell. As Marie's champion, Henri Chervet, an editor of *Gil Blas*, fought "several fierce bouts" with swords against her detractor, Léon Daudet, of *L'Action Française*. Photographers recorded the fight, which Chervet won by inflicting a deep gash on Daudet's elbow. The British press largely ignored the duel, preoccupied with politics and foreign policy: Irish demands for freedom from British rule, militant suffragettes agitating for votes for women, pogroms in Russia, and the danger of war with Germany over Morocco. But the French, German, and American press relished the affair. The *New York Times* headed its account

"Editors in Duel over Mme Curie" and described her as "the most prominent woman to-day in the scientific world." Which, of course, she was.

There were more duels to come. Gustave Tery challenged Pierre
Mortier, the chief editor of *Gil Blas*, for criticizing his publication of the
Curie-Langevin letters. They also fought with swords, in the Parc-des-
Princes Stadium, usually the site of bicycle races. Mme Langevin's brother-
in-law, Bourgeois, was one of Tery's seconds. The fight ended when Tery
twice bloodied Mortier's arm. The *San Francisco Examiner* titled its brief
front-page account "Another Curie Duel."

While the duels were still being ridiculed at home and abroad, Paul
Langevin called at the Borels' apartment to say that he knew it was idiotic,
but he had to fight Tery, his former school friend, for calling him a cad
who hid behind a woman's skirts, and a Polish woman's stooge. Instead of
swords they chose pistols, and at 11 A.M. Langevin appeared, also at the
Bicycle Stadium, with his distinguished seconds, mathematician Paul
Painlevé, a future Socialist prime minister of France, and Albin Haller,
director of the School of Physics and Chemistry. Two doctors hovered
nearby and a group of reporters sat in the stands.

Wearing bowler hats and dark suits and sporting similar waxed mus-
taches, the two men held loaded pistols as they faced each other twenty-
five paces apart. Tery had mixed feelings, which he later shared with his
readers: He could have killed Mme Langevin's husband, he wrote, but
that might harm her cause, and he would also be depriving French science of a brilliant mind. Having decided to let his opponent live, he simply pointed his pistol at the ground. Langevin could hardly fire at a man
who was not threatening him, so he, too, refused to fire. The seconds took
their pistols, fired them harmlessly into the air, and the duel was over. The
Los Angeles Times thought it was a hoot and headed its two-paragraph
report from the A.P. "Pistol Duel Pantomine [*sic*]: Principals Let Seconds
Do the Shooting and No Blood Is Let."

Marie was aware of none of this, because friends were isolating her
from the outside world. She stayed in her bedroom with Eve where they
took their meals, and Henriette Perrin kept newspapers from them. Her
sisters, Bronia and Hela, and her brother, Joseph, arrived to give her their
moral support, and, seeing her so distraught, begged her to leave France
permanently and return with them to Poland. She told no one at the time,
but she was contemplating suicide.

Pierre's brother, Jacques, sent words of sympathy and encouragement.
So did Paul Langevin, through a friend. The pianist Paderewski came to

lunch. And Albert Einstein, who knew what it was to be misquoted by the press, wrote to tell her how he admired her spirit, energy, and honesty, and rejoiced in the existence of genuine people like her and Langevin and advised that if the rabble continued to be occupied with her she should simply stop reading the drivel.

Perhaps the most succinct summary of the situation seen from an American perspective was the *San Francisco Examiner* headline (with an unlikely quote from Marie) for November 26: "Mme Curie Madly in Love. The Wife in the Triangle?—'An Idiot' She [Marie] Declares." (Presumably referring to Mme Langevin!) When years later Eve undertook a biography of her mother, she did not name the Langevins as any part of the uproar. Instead, she wrote that

> A perfidious campaign was set going in Paris against this woman of forty-four, fragile, worn out by crushing toil, alone and without defense. Marie, who exercised a man's profession, had chosen her friends and confidants among men. And this exceptional creature exercised upon her intimates, upon one of them particularly, a profound influence. No more was needed. A scientist devoted to her work, whose life was dignified, reserved, and in recent years especially pitiable, was accused of breaking up homes and dishonoring the name she bore with too much brilliance. It is not for me to judge those who gave the signal for the attack, or to say with what despair and often with what tragic clumsiness Marie floundered. Let us leave in peace those journalists who had the courage to insult a hunted woman pestered by anonymous letters, publicly threatened with violence, with her life itself in danger. Some among these men came to ask her pardon later on, with words of repentance and with tears. But the crime was committed. Marie had been led to the brink of suicide and of madness.

On the other hand, she had the loving and loyal support of her family, especially Pierre's brother; a circle of devoted and influential friends; and, as well as a slew of poison-pen letters, hundreds of letters of encouragement from strangers. There was also the great news from Sweden announcing her second Nobel Prize, although that, as well as her life and work in France, was now in jeopardy.

Largely unknown to Marie, those responsible for awarding her the second Nobel Prize and those who knew her were in an urgent correspondence to determine if the scandalous press reports were true, and if so, what to do about it. On November 5, the day after Marie learned of her award, Christer Aurivillius, secretary of the Swedish Royal Academy of Sciences, sent a telegram to the Swedish ambassador in Paris, August Glydenstolpe, asking outright if Marie Curie had left Paris with a married man.

The ambassador replied that people in the know denied it, but he would keep the academy fully informed of the latest developments in what was now known as "L'Affaire Langevin."

On November 7, Gustaf Retzious, a Swedish academician, asked Charles Bouchard, a foreign member of the Academy of Sciences—who had unsuccessfully nominated both Curies for a Nobel Prize in 1901 and Marie again in 1910—"What's going on with L'Affaire Langevin?" Bouchard replied: "When these horrible accusations broke out I had not the shadow of hesitation about completely denouncing the slander . . . absolutely convinced [of her innocence]. But last Monday . . . a friend . . . affirmed that it was all true, and he knew it from a reliable source—a magistrate at the Palais who had some letters from Mme Curie and testimony from people which left no doubt . . . What I have told you is only secondhand. Make up your mind and communicate one way or the other to the academy." He ended by writing that he only had "feelings of respect and admiration for this unhappy woman."

Spurred by his narrow-minded wife to discourage Marie from appearing, Retzious replied, "It would be very desirable that Mme Curie should not come to Stockholm to receive the prize from the hands of King Gustave. It could bring a lot of unpleasantness to the Academy and Science and mostly to herself."

Retzius sent Bouchard's information to Olaf Hammarsten, president of the Nobel committee for chemistry, who replied on November 15: "You gave me very sad news . . . Aurivillius [had] told me about several leading scientists who guaranteed . . . that Mme Curie was completely innocent. So I believed that it was all over and was very surprised to learn from your letter that this is not so. . . . I have nothing against her receiving the prize since the prize is given for the work and not for the person. But if we put our Royal house as well as ourselves in a difficult situation—because of what might happen during the ceremonies I would feel terrible."

A week later Urbain wrote to Svante Arrhenius. "In Mme Curie's letter to Langevin, who was so unhappy at home, she gives him advice on how to free himself. I think that Perrin or myself could have given him the same advice, but the fact that it was given by a woman and that the woman used affectionate terms are a sign of guilt in the eyes of the world. Taking this into account, how would she be received in Stockholm?" He again wrote to Arrhenius on November 29: "I am very sorry about the general cowardice I see. Among Marie Curie's greatest admirers are those who throw stones at her today."

Three days before he wrote that letter, news of the scandal reached the Swedish public when a German newspaper, *Berliner Tageblatt*, distributed in Sweden published a report from its Paris correspondent headed "The Langevin-Tery Duel. The Letters of Marie Curie." The obviously biased reporter described Marie Curie as having a masculine face full of lines and looking much older than her forty-four years, provided extracts from the Langevin-Curie letters, and quoted Tery as saying, "The world will be astonished to see how Mme Curie acted methodically in her hatred and cruelty . . . [Even] these few extracts cannot fully show the cold-bloodedness and unlimited selfishness in [Marie Curie's] long letter [to Langevin advising him how to handle his wife]."

Having read the diatribe, Svante Arrhenius—one of the two men who had nominated Marie for her second Nobel—wrote to her on December 1: "The situation was made much worse by M Langevin's ridiculous duel. It gives the impression, I hope false, that the published correspondence was true. All my colleagues replied that they do not want you to come here on December 10 . . . I, too, beg you to stay in France; because nobody can predict what would happen during the prize-giving . . . The honor, the esteem for our Academy, as well as for Science, and for your fatherland, seem to demand that under such circumstances you abandon idea of coming here to get the prize."

Marie Curie replied on December 5: "I must act according to my conviction. The course you advise me to take seems to me a big mistake on my part. In fact, the prize was given to me for the discovery of radium and polonium. I think there is absolutely no connection between my scientific work and the facts of my private life, which uninformed and disreputable people use against me. I cannot accept the principle that the appreciation of the value of a scientific work can be influenced by the distortion and slander concerning a private life. I am very hurt that you yourself should not share this opinion. When you receive this letter I will already have agreed to appear in Stockholm for the ceremony. However, I feel so ill that I don't know if it will be possible for me to travel."

Urbain forwarded the letter that Arrhenius had written to him—explaining why Marie should not come to Sweden—to Paul Langevin for his response. Langevin wrote directly to Arrhenius on December 6:

One cannot judge . . . , the correspondence which is reproduced in a distorted fashion—by alterations and omissions . . . if one does not know the condition in which I lived for thirteen years, nor from what kind of people these attacks came . . . It hurts me to have to shout with all my strength that such a woman did not do what she is accused of . . . When all my friends interested in the future of science got to know of the difficulties that I, sadly, had to endure for thirteen years, they wholeheartedly supported the advice Mme Curie gave me in a time of anxiety for her, after being threatened with death . . . by a jealous, violent woman. . . . However, I did not follow her advice, and tried with complete sincerity to stay with my family. A year ago, before the published correspondence was stolen, when Mme Curie was a candidate at the Academy of Sciences, Mme Langevin's brother-in-law, [Bourgeois] her advisor in all this business, was not afraid to write . . . shameful and anonymous letters to dirty Mme Curie's name. This man, a low journalist, immediately took the stolen correspondence to the editor of his paper without asking for any explanation from those who wrote it. . . . I must not, nor cannot say anything about my wife, but you will realize the terrible situation she has put me in. Either I must let her sully an irreproachable woman who is to be crucified for trying to save me, at my request, and in the name of friendship, for what she saw as my scientific future. Or, I must say, in order to defend her [Curie] in a public trial, what my whole married life had been like, which my children could reproach me for later.

If, despite her ill health and the warnings, Marie braved the Nobel ceremony, she would be introduced to the gathering by the president of the Swedish Royal Academy of Sciences, E. W. Dahlgren. In his 1994 memoir he recalled the desperate eagerness of the French ambassador to Sweden, Emile Thiebaut, for Marie to attend—for the glory of France, of course. To persuade Dahlgren that the rumors about her running away with a lover were ridiculous, the Frenchman said to him: "If you had seen what Mme Curie looks like and how she behaves, you would understand that she could never entice anyone into an escapade." And he was certain, he told Dahlgren, that if Mme Curie did come, there would be no hostile demonstration from the sophisticated Swedes, especially in the presence of their king. However, if Mme Curie did not turn up, as the French ambassador he would be expected to receive the prize in her name. Instead, he said, he intended to leave the prize in the king's hands and turn away. And what a scandal that would be!

Of course, it never happened.

Sick, worn, and worried, Marie Curie made the exhausting forty-eight-hour journey to Sweden, comforted by the presence of her sister Bronia and her fourteen-year-old daughter, Irène. "Suffering though I was," she wrote in her *Autobiographical Notes*, "I went to Stockholm to receive the prize. The journey was extremely painful." But the warm reception made up for it. Instead of the possible boos, insults, and even physical attacks, she was received with respect and affection, "especially by the women of Sweden." Three hundred of them honored her at a banquet hosted by the Swedish Association of University Women.

At the formal banquet with King Gustaf, she described radioactivity as "an infant that I saw being born, [which] I have contributed to raising with all my strength. The child has grown. It has become beautiful."

In the Nobel presentation speech, Dahlgren said that Madame Marie Sklodowska Curie was getting the prize in chemistry "in recognition of the part she has played in the development of chemistry: by the discovery of the chemical elements radium and polonium; by the determination of the properties of radium and by the isolation of radium in its pure metallic state; and finally, by the research into the compounds of this remarkable element." He explained that the discovery that one element could be transmuted into another had revolutionized chemistry, and that "the theory of the absolute immutability of chemical elements no longer holds good. The theory of transmutation, dear to the alchemists, has been unexpectedly restored to life in an exact form, deprived of any mystical element; and the philosopher's stone with the property of inducing such transmutations is no longer a mysterious, elusive elixir but is something which modern science calls energy." Dahlgren also touched on the promising use of radium to treat cancerous growths and lupus, and mentioned that "during the eleven years in which Nobel Prizes have been awarded, this is the first time that the distinction has been conferred upon a previous prizewinner."

Standing in the Stockholm Concert Hall on December 11, 1911, to give her Nobel lecture titled "Radium and the New Concepts in Chemistry," Marie was conspicuous in her customary simple black dress among the fashionably gowned and bejeweled women listening to her. She acknowledged that she and Pierre had jointly made the discoveries of radium and polonium. "I therefore think I am correctly interpreting the thoughts of the Academy of Sciences when I say that the high honor coming to me is a result of the work we did together and is thus an homage to the memory of Pierre Curie." She gave credit for their contributions to Becquerel, Rutherford, Ramsay, Soddy, Debierne, Hahn, Boltwood, and others. But, as if responding to those who dismissed her as Pierre's assistant, she emphasized that she alone had carried out many important discoveries, measured the activity of a number of minerals, named the activity "radioactivity," furnished proof for her own hypothesis, and repeatedly determined the average atomic weight of the metal through spectral analysis.

She concluded: We are "accustomed to deal currently in the laboratory with substances the presence of which is only shown to us by their radioactive properties but which nevertheless we can determine, dissolve, re-precipitate from their solutions and deposit [by electrolysis]. This means that we have here an entirely separate kind of chemistry, for which the current tool we use is the electrometer, not the balance, and which we might well call the chemistry of the imponderable."

The only disturbance in the hall was a storm of applause.

That same day, the *New York World* reported that Mme Langevin and her husband, "whom she accuses of being Mme Curie's affinity," had "amicably" agreed on a legal separation during which he would pay her alimony of $140 a month. Almost as an afterthought, the paper reported that Mme Curie had received a forty-thousand-dollar Nobel Prize. Six days later, the *New York Times* announced: "The Langevin divorce case—which appears to have created a more painful impression in England and America than in France—is now in the process of adjudication in the Paris Courts. Mme Curie, who is named as corespondent, has been described as 'the cleverest woman in the world.'" The *Times* was wrong: it was a legal separation, not a divorce, and Mme Curie had not been cited as a corespondent. The paper went on to say that the "little dark woman, with great eager eyes, and hair drawn back dowdily from a broad brow, short in stature, and wearing a nondescript gown," was "entirely unspoiled by success" and that her appearance gave "little indication of her remarkable faculties."

On her return to Paris she was greeted by an article in Téry's *L'Oeuvre* deploring the invasion of foreigners at the Sorbonne and other Paris university laboratories and charging that the female students were simply husband hunting. And in the right-wing *L'Action Française*, Maurice Pujo crowed over the triumph of the virtuous defenders of rock-solid French morality over a scandalous foreign woman and her Sorbonne supporters, whom he characterized as half-breeds and Jews.

Far from being defeated, Marie was acclaimed and revered throughout the rest of the world as a unique two-time Nobel Prize winner. She continued to lecture at the Sorbonne and to work in her laboratory. And all her friends, including Langevin, stuck with her.

But at the end of December 1911, she was in excruciating pain and shivering with fever from a serious kidney infection—possibly a symptom of radiation sickness. Under an assumed name, she was taken on a stretcher to a private clinic and not allowed visitors for several days, until she was out of danger. Then, as Jean Perrin explained in a letter to Rutherford:

"Mme Curie's fever has gone down and they won't have to operate on her right away. Something we were very worried about, because of her state of exhaustion. The separation decree between Langevin and his wife makes *no mention* of Madame Curie but the 'wrongs' are attributed to Langevin (who did not take the precaution of finding witnesses to the wrongs he could have accused his wife of without bringing Madame Curie's name into the trial). The two boys eat lunch with Langevin every day. The four children sleep at their mother's except for every other Thursday and every other Sunday. From the age of nineteen the boys will live with him. Lastly, he retains 'the intellectual control of the four children' . . . Langevin has appreciated your friendship very much. Mme Curie has also been very touched by your attitude."

After devoting so much time to solving his friends' problems, Jean Perrin was anxious to get back to work, which paid off with a Nobel Prize for physics in 1926. Perrin's study of the Brownian motion of minute particles suspended in liquids confirmed the atomic nature of matter.

Langevin would eventually return to his wife, though apparently only for the sake of their children. They never divorced, but she tolerated his having a mistress, Eliane Montel, a former student at Sèvres who had become his secretary, with whom he fathered a son, Paul-Gilbert.

Marie Curie and Paul Langevin remained lifelong, affectionate friends.

CHAPTER 10

Surgery and Suffragettes

1912–1914

Too weak to survive an operation on her infected kidneys, Marie Curie was released by her doctor in January 1912, the surgery postponed until she was stronger. The *Times* of London, which ignored the Langevin-Curie scandal and only briefly mentioned her second Nobel, mistakenly reported her illness as appendicitis. On her few attempts to resume work at the Sorbonne, the journey from Sceaux alone proved so exhausting that she reluctantly moved with her daughters into a spacious third-floor apartment in an eighteenth-century building on the Ile St. Louis, one of the loveliest parts of Paris, overlooking the Seine and a short walk to her laboratory.

Secrecy about her illness had backfired and caused malicious rumors. The hospital manager and its mother superior warned her of one recently published that had her in the hospital's maternity ward expecting Langevin's child. Normally their patients' medical records were sacrosanct, but the pair were so incensed by this libel they offered to make her records an exception. She accepted and *Le Temps* published her doctor's diagnosis—kidney infection—effectively refuting the rumors.

The Paris apartment was an ideal location for when she returned to work, but her sister Bronia, still with Marie after accompanying her to the Nobel Prize ceremony, thought that she also needed a quiet place in the country to convalesce. They settled on a small house in Brunoy, a village close enough to Paris for the girls to stay with Marie on the days they were out of school. Both now attended the Collège de Sévigné. To avoid being harassed by strangers and hunted by the press, Marie had Bronia rent the house in her married name, Dluska, and only Marie's closest friends and colleagues were given the address. Marie also reverted to her maiden name, Sklodowska, in a further attempt to keep her identity and where-abouts a secret.

She returned to her city apartment in March, hoping to attend an important meeting of the International Radium Standard Committee. They had already accepted her suggestion to measure the activity of a radioactive substance as the amount of radon in radioactive equilibrium with one gram of radium—and named that amount the Curie. Since then Marie had presented her own meticulously prepared sample to represent the standard for pure radium.

However, Stefan Meyer, an Austrian physicist, claimed that his own sample was more accurate and the committee was about to decide which to accept. As a courtesy, its members first lunched with Marie in her apart-ment—she was still not fit enough to attend the subsequent meeting—then left for the Sorbonne laboratory. Debierne, representing Marie's interests, had already arranged the apparatus to put the two samples to the test. Meyer's sample proved not to be more accurate than hers. In fact, they were virtually identical. Rutherford was at the meeting and called on Marie to discuss her triumph. As nuclear-age pioneers they probably also talked of his latest experiments, which supported Jean Perrin's 1901 theory that every atom had one or more positive suns and small negative planets.

Rutherford's ongoing tests indicated that Perrin was on the right track, that within the atom was a minute but massively dense nucleus, a positive proton, orbited by negatively charged electrons. They clearly spent little time discussing her illness, because he came away mistakenly thinking she had tuberculosis.

Later that month she had the delayed surgery. The aftereffects were devastating. Marie was in such agonizing pain and lost weight so rapidly—from 123 to 103 pounds—that she thought she was dying. She confided her fear to Georges Gouy and sought his advice about her daughters' futures and the fate of the Radium Institute. She told him where to find the radium she controlled and how to dispose of it. He assured her that it was natural to be depressed after a major operation, and that he was sure she would eventually recover. But, to console her, he promised to carry out her wishes if necessary.

Irène waited until it was clear that Marie was out of danger and recov-ering before taking a train south to Montpellier to spend two joyful weeks with her uncle, Jacques Curie, and his extended family. She went for long walks and bicycle rides in the country with his son, her cousin, Maurice Curie, who was eight years her senior, and became very fond of him.

Even though Marie was recuperating at Brunoy incognito, Debierne persuaded her to see a deputation of Polish professors headed by Henryk Sienkiewicz, the Nobel Prize–winning author of *Quo Vadis*. They urged her to quit France and return permanently to Poland to head a radium institute, which the Scientific Society of Warsaw wanted to build for her. "We are losing confidence in our intellectual faculties," their petition read. "We are being lowered in the opinion of our enemies, and we are abandoning hope for the future . . . Possessing you in Warsaw we should feel stronger, we should lift our heads now bent under so many misfortunes. May our prayers be granted. Do not repulse our hands which are stretched out to you."

It would have solved many of her problems. But she was committed to heading the Radium Institute nearing completion in Paris, and her daughters' futures were obviously more promising if they remained in France. Anxious not to disappoint her countrymen, she offered to send two of her brightest Polish assistants, twenty-five-year-old Ludwik Wertenstein and twenty-eight-year-old Jan Danysz, to run the institute in Warsaw under her direction from Paris. The deputation accepted the idea. So did the two young Poles.

Marie was so eager to be fit enough to return to work and impatient with her uncertain recovery that she went with a friend, Alice Chavannes, to a health spa in Thonon-les-Bains, near the French Alps. And every day she made detailed notes of her physical condition, comparable to her records of scientific experiments: her temperature, her intake and output of mineral water, the appearance of her urine, and the duration and intensity of the frequent attacks of pain. She also went to elaborate lengths to avoid being recognized. Instead of addressing letters to "Irène Curie" and so possibly betraying her own identity, Marie sealed them inside envelopes addressed to Debierne and asked Irène, when she replied, to address them to Mme Sklodowska. Extremely proud of being a Curie, Irène was naturally ambivalent about this, but she sympathized with her mother's plight. She was, after all, in hiding.

Fourteen-year-old Irène's frequent charming letters included accounts of helping Eve to mount a bicycle without falling off, her own walking and cycling trips, math problems she was tackling with enthusiasm, and political situations that puzzled her. In all of them there was a sense that she adored her mother and was deeply concerned about her health. On July 19, she confided: "Yesterday I read in *Le Matin* of the death of Henri Poincaré. I believe . . . he died after an operation. The idea that there could possibly have been a similar article about you sent a shudder up my scalp."

She and Eve had celebrated July 14—Bastille Day—by watching a fireworks display from their Paris apartment with the Perrins and their two children. On the way there from Brunoy, they had called on Paul Langevin—a sign that the scandal had not destroyed Marie's friendship with him.

In another chatty letter to Marie, Irène wrote on July 27, 1912: "Last evening, André [Debierne] had dinner with us. He brought a large loaf of bread, a roast duck, and a box of cookies, to be sure he wouldn't die of hunger." In the morning she had worked on a math problem and in the afternoon rode her bicycle for an hour "along the magnificent roads from Paris to Melun and back." In the evening she indulged her passion for reading. "You know darling," her letter continued, "that one of my needs is to read. When I have a book I devour it. Imagine what torture it is to have books and not know what's in them. So I started very courageously to read several books simultaneously," switching from a chapter of *David Copperfield* to two or three stories by Shakespeare arranged for children, on to Giraudoux's *Ondine*, to a poem, "The Ancient Mariner," then back to Dickens, with English and German dictionaries at her elbow for the difficult words. "Ah! At the beginning of the year, other than for homework, you would not have found me reading English or German books. The first thing I read in English without being made to was at Easter and it was a Kipling story."

Next day, Irène wrote: "I'm still interested in politics but there are a few things I can't understand. For example, the causes and consequences of the Turkish government are too complicated for me. I vaguely understand that it had something to do with dysentery in the Turkish army and the War or Navy Minister's resignation. Anyway, since the Turkish government fell the day M. Poincaré died, I concentrated more on what was said about M. Poincaré than the rest of it. I also saw that almost every day a British minister risked being killed by the British suffragettes. But it seems to me that it isn't a very clever way of proving they are capable of voting."

Marie didn't stay long in Paris, having accepted an invitation to be Hertha Ayrton's guest in England. A brilliant, vivacious, and outspoken Englishwoman, the model, it was said, for Mirah in George Eliot's novel *Daniel Deronda*, Ayrton first met the Curies when they visited London's Royal Institution in 1903. She and Marie had a lot in common. Besides being physicists and the widows of physicists who had encouraged them in their work, each had two daughters and were "outsiders" in their adopted countries—Marie as a Pole in France, Hertha as the daughter of a Polish-Jewish watchmaker in England. Hertha, however, was much more politically active than Marie.

She had once sent Marie a petition to sign demanding the release of three imprisoned British suffragettes on a hunger strike who were force-fed through their nostrils. In a covering letter, in the spring of 1912, Hertha explained: "I am a member of the association whose leaders are now in prison, and I know those leaders personally and look on them as persons of the utmost nobility of mind and greatness of purpose."

Marie replied that she "was very touched by all that you told me of the struggle of English women for their rights. I admire them very much and I wish for their success . . . I accept your using my name for the petition because I have great confidence in your judgment and I am convinced that your sympathy must be justified."

Hertha doubtless would soon be able to inform the puzzled Irène why suffragettes used violence. She had recently marched with 120 of them through London streets demanding the right to vote in national elections and smashing store windows with hammers. Reaching 10 Downing Street, the residence of the prime minister, Henry Asquith, they threw stones at the building until the police drove them off. Asquith had frequently lied to suffragettes about taking their demands seriously and they felt the need to resort to violence to get his attention. Their leader, Emmeline Pank-hurst, and her daughters, Christabel and Sylvia, kept up the pressure by angrily interrupting the speeches of political candidates, including Winston Churchill. Their opponents responded by setting rats loose at suffragette meetings. One of the most desperate, Emily Wilding Davison, released from prison after trying to blow up the prime minister's house, committed suicide by throwing herself in front of the king's horse during a famous horse race, the Derby. Taking part in another protest march, Hertha Ayrton tried to enter the prime minister's home to speak with him, and a policeman grabbed her by the neck and almost strangled her.

As Pankhurst explained: "We had to discredit the Government and Parliament in the eyes of the world. We had to spoil English sports, hurt business, destroy valuable property, demoralize the world of society, shame the churches, upset the whole orderly conduct of life. [So] a number of putting greens were burned with acids, telegraph and telephone wires were cut in several places . . . windows in various of London's smartest clubs were broken, and the orchid houses at Kew were invaded and a showcase broken. The residence of HRH Prince Christian and Lambeth Palace, seat of the Archbishop of Canterbury, were visited and windows broken. The refreshment house in Regents Park was burned to the ground . . . a country house which was being built [for] Lloyd George, [Chancellor of the Exchequer] was partially destroyed, a bomb having been exploded in the early morning before the arrival of workmen." (Britain gave some women the vote in 1918, and all women in 1928.)

Hertha Ayrton knew that many believed the myth that she and Marie had ridden to scientific fame on their husbands' coattails. So when the *Westminster Gazette* had attributed the discovery of radium to Pierre Curie, she had complained in a letter it published: "Errors are notoriously hard to kill, but an error that ascribes to a man what was actually the work of a woman, has more lives than a cat."

She and Marie had corresponded since their first meeting in London, and Hertha had visited her in Paris and knew of the Langevin scandal and of Marie's surgery. Feeling great affection and sympathy for her, she had offered her and her daughters rest and refuge in England. In August, Marie crossed the Channel on the Calais-Dover ferry. Hertha met her at Dover and escorted her—still ill and fragile—to an old mill house at Highcliffe-on-Sea in Hampshire, separated from the ocean by a small wood.

The Curie girls meanwhile were on vacation in L'Arcouest, a small fishing village on the magnificent Atlantic coast in northern Brittany, well worth the four-and-a-half-hour train journey on the *rapide* from Paris-Montparnasse to Guingamp, then a local train ride of fifty minutes to Paimpol, and, finally, twenty minutes by car. Sorbonne academics had made it their informal summer place. So had the foreign editor of the London *Times*, Wickham Steed. It would become a favorite refuge and playground of the Curies and eventually the Joliot-Curies. Irène was spending her fifteenth birthday there with Eve and their Polish governess.

A few days later, the girls left L'Arcouest to join Marie at Highcliffe-on-Sea, where Hertha had even provided an English governess for them to continue their studies. Eve arrived with a minor illness, quickly cured by a dip in the cold sea. Marie and Hertha went for long walks on the beach and on the cliffs, and in the evenings, Hertha, who thought the girls very interesting, accompanied Eve on the piano as she sang French songs and discussed mathematics with Irène. And the governess helped Irène to improve her English, a language she had grown to love.

While in England, Marie wrote to tell chemist George Jaffe, who had spent a year in her laboratory, that she intensely regretted not being able to "play an active part in the life of the laboratory that we all love." A month later, she informed Hendrik Lorentz that if she did attend the next Solvay conference in October, she would not want to talk on general ideas, because she'd lost the habit. And, perhaps, the energy. In fact there was no conference that year.

Marie stayed on when the girls returned to France in late September, and she risked being recognized to spend several days with Hertha at her London home, 41 Norfolk Square, Hyde Park West. But although the servants did recognize her, they were discreet and no mention of her visit appeared in the press.

As she had not been named in the Langevins' separation decree, there were no more duels to defend her honor, and the press had lost track of her, the Sorbonne administration quietly accepted the return of the world's only two-time Nobel Prize winner.

She was back at her laboratory desk in October, writing to Ernest Rutherford with good and bad news. She was delighted with Ernest Solvay's decision to give a million francs to finance future Solvay conferences and research into the medical use of radium in Paris hospitals. The bad news was Sir William Ramsay. Marie believed that this Nobel Prize–winning Scot and Britain's leading chemist, who had discovered an entire family of elements (helium, neon, argon, krypton, xenon, and radon), was invading her territory. She explained to Rutherford that Ramsay had recently published "some work on the atomic weight of radium. He arrives at exactly the same result as I did and his measurements are less consistent than mine. In spite of that he concludes that his work is the first good work on the subject!!! I must say that I was astounded. Moreover [he] made some malicious and incorrect comments [about] my experiments on atomic weights."

Ramsay often denigrated women scientists, once telling a *Daily Mail* reporter that "all the eminent women scientists have achieved their best work when collaborating with a male colleague." In other words, males, such as Pierre Curie and William Ayrton, were responsible for much, if not all, of the work attributed to their wives. In fact, Ayrton thought his wife was a genius, and Pierre had acknowledged Marie's gifts. Rutherford could do little but sympathize with Marie for defending her turf, aware that she was one of many infuriated by Ramsay's provocative public statements.

In November she went to Warsaw to dedicate the Radium Institute built in her honor and to lecture on science for the first time in her native tongue. The condition of the country struggling, in her words, to "defend its moral and intellectual life" under the "barbarous" Russian domination still outraged her. She was especially outraged by the treatment of her young nephew, her brother Joseph's son, a factory worker imprisoned for fifteen days for writing a few innocuous lines of patriotic poetry.

Early in the spring of 1913, Marie resumed teaching at the Sorbonne, walking unobtrusively to and from her nearby apartment, dressed in her customary black. Even before the foundation for the Radium Institute had been completed, she arrived on the scene and insisted on establishing a garden of trees and flowers between her projected building and the companion Pasteur Institute. On hands and knees she planted rambler roses and watered them daily. She carefully selected healthy young lime and plane trees and supervised their planting, all without the approval of the architect, Henri-Paul Nenot. But she did confer with him, contractors, and construction foremen about the features of the actual building. She even sometimes climbed the scaffolding to check that there was room for large windows from which the lab workers could look out on trees, grass, and flowers. And she made sure that a gardener was included in the estimated expenses to run her institute.

Her preoccupations didn't prevent her from inviting Albert Einstein and his wife, Mileva, to stay with her when they were due in Paris in March. Einstein, who called Paul Langevin the only Frenchman to completely understand the special theory of relativity, had accepted his invitation to address the French Society of Physics in the French capital. The Einsteins and Curies hit it off so well that they agreed—despite Mileva's rheumatism and congenitally dislocated hip, which made walking painful—to spend their summer vacation hiking through the Swiss Alps together.

After the visit, Einstein wrote from Zurich, where he was chairman of mathematical physics at Zurich Polytechnic, to tell Marie he was very grateful to her and her friends (which included the Perrins) for allowing him to participate in their everyday, natural, and uncomplicated lives and witness their marvelous camaraderie. Despite his poor French, he wrote, they never made him feel like a stranger. He apologized for his rough manners, if they had made her uneasy, and reminded her of the trip to the mountains they had arranged to take together at the end of the semester.

Before that vacation, Irène and Eve spent several weeks at L'Arcouest, their favorite Normandy fishing village. The girls were fed by their cook, Walecia, and encouraged to study by their governess, Jozia, while Marie continued her work at the Sorbonne as well as supervising the growing Radium Institute. Before she joined her daughters, a steady flow of letters between her and Irène kept the girls and their mother in almost constant contact. And practically every one mentioned math, such as Irène's, in which she remarked: "The derivatives are coming along all right; the inverse functions are adorable. On the other hand, I can feel my hair stand on end when I think of the theorem of Rolle, and Thomas's formula." Earlier she had called this formula "the ugliest thing I know."

The Curies and the girls' English governess arrived at Zurich in July for two weeks of hiking in the Alps with the Einsteins and their eldest son, ten-year-old Hans Albert. They had left their younger and ailing son, Eduard, at home with friends. Hans Albert later recalled that during their walk across the Maloja Pass, as his father and Marie inspected the glaciers, Einstein had speculated about the forces that had created such deep vertical wells, and that Marie challenged his father, who, she claimed, was technically a Swiss, to name every mountaintop within sight. He didn't say if his father succeeded.

Eve's biographer wrote that she "was amused at the way Einstein circulated absentmindedly among the boulders, so deep in conversation [in German] that he walked alongside deep crevasses and toiled up the steep rocks without noticing them. One day the three young people howled with laughter when Einstein suddenly stopped dead, seized Marie's arm, and demanded, peering intently at her: 'You understand, what I need to know is exactly what happens to the passengers in an elevator when it falls into emptiness.' The imaginary fall in an elevator posed problems of transcendent relativity—there would be no gravitational pull so they would float—and he was struggling with the problem of discovering a mathematical entity with which to represent gravitation."

In describing this trip to his cousin Elsa Lowenthal, Einstein called the scenery beautiful and the break from work refreshing, but he had a surprisingly poor view of the company, especially of Marie and Irène. He found Marie very intelligent but as cold as a fish, because the only time she expressed her feelings was to complain about something. Irène, he wrote, was even worse—behaving like an infantryman. He did concede, however, that Irène was extremely gifted. Not a word about his wife, Mileva, Hans Albert, or Eve.

Marie noted in her diary that Eve, who had been unwell, walked a lot and looked marvelous. Einstein was hardly an impartial witness and had a motive for disparaging Marie and Irène. At the time, he was no longer in love with his wife and had started an affair with Elsa, whom he eventually married. Naturally he wouldn't want her to think that he had spent time with two females attractive enough to be her rivals.

During September, while Irène was studying for the second half of an entrance exam to the Sorbonne, Marie traveled to England to visit Rutherford and for a meeting of the British Association in Birmingham, where the city's university was to award her an honorary doctorate. En route, she stayed with Hertha Ayrton at her London home, from which she wrote a birthday letter to Irène, who was sixteen on September 12, 1913. The letter included a trigonometry problem for her to solve, which pleased Irène, and news that delighted her: she could resume addressing her letters to "Mme Curie." As Marie explained, after two visits to Ayrton's home, the servants knew her identity and could be trusted not to go to the press.

She was amused by the ceremony and parade for her honorary degree, telling Irène that they had dressed her "in a beautiful red robe with green facings, as they did my companions in misery. That's to say, the other scientists who were receiving doctorates."

Rutherford's friend and eventual biographer, A. S. Eve, who attended the British Association meeting, saw Marie as a "shy, retiring, self-possessed and noble woman everyone wished to see, but few were successful. The press were eager for interviews, and Madame skillfully parried their questions by singing the praises of Rutherford. 'Dr. Rutherford,' she said, 'is the one man living who promises to confer some inestimable boon on mankind as a result of the discovery of radium. I would advise England to watch Dr. Rutherford; his work in radioactivity has surprised me greatly. Great developments are likely to transpire shortly, in which the discovery of radium is only a preliminary step.'" Hendrik Lorentz, Lord Rayleigh, James Jeans, and Niels Bohr were also among the brilliant scientists in Birmingham. During a discussion of radiation, Jeans spoke of the application of Bohr's quantum theory to the problem of atomic constitution. Bohr, a Danish physicist, had combined Rutherford's model of the atom and Max Planck's quantum theory to produce his own description of the still mysterious atom.

There had been no Solvay Conference in 1912, but Marie went to the second conference in 1913, the suggested theme of which was "The Structure of Matter." It was again attended by the admiring Einstein and the frank and ebullient Rutherford. Strangely, she and Rutherford were the only ones concerned with his experimentally based support for the theory of an atomic nucleus. Rutherford had said that the atom could be divided into an external and an interior part, which Marie later defined as "a central positive nucleus of small dimensions surrounded by a distribution of electrons."

Back in Paris, Marie often braved rainstorms and muddy walkways to make weekly visits to the incipient Radium Institute, where planners and workers took her suggestions as orders. The building was to be divided into two sections, one for research in physics and chemistry to be headed by

Marie, the other for research in medicine and biology to be directed by Claude Regaud, one of France's leading scientists. His assistant, Antoine Lacassagne, met Marie when he visited the site on her forty-sixth birthday, November 7, 1913. She seemed to him very young, and he was struck "by the charm and gentleness of her expression." Regaud, he recalled, listened to Marie "as though he were her pupil," while Lacassagne himself "felt like a small child as he looked down on the frail invalid . . . dressed all in black and very pale."

She had shown extraordinary resilience. Almost dying in the spring, by year's end she had moved to a new home, traveled to Poland and England, hiked through the Swiss mountains with the Einsteins, attended the second Solvay Conference, supervised the building of the Radium Institute, and created its garden. No longer in hiding under her maiden name, she had resumed her research and teaching at the Sorbonne.

At the end of July 1914, the Radium Institute, built to honor the memory of Pierre Curie and devoted to the study of radioactivity, was at long last ready. The trees in the courtyard were alive and well, the rambler roses were in bloom. Carpenters had installed shelves in Marie's office, and equipment was about to be moved from the old rue Cuvier laboratory.

But two days later, only Marie and one elderly lab assistant with a weak heart were available to take over the building. The rest of her staff had been called up to defend their country. Germany had declared war on France. It was the start of World War I.

CHAPTER 11

"Little Curies" and World War I

1914–1918

A nineteen-year-old Serbian assassin provoked European nations into World War I, but Germany was ready and eager to launch the attack, hoping to dominate Europe and enlarge its empire. So on August 4, 1914, a massive German army quickly smashed its way through neutral Belgium, which bravely but briefly resisted, and headed for Paris. Having promised to defend Belgian neutrality, the British joined the battle against the invaders. Casualties were enormous. French soldiers in their regulation red pants proved ridiculously easy targets for enemy gunners, but so were the German troops, because they advanced in close formation. As they came closer, hundreds of thousands of Parisians fled in overloaded trains and filled the streets leading out of the city.

Marie Curie remained. She had already written to her daughters vacationing in Brittany's l'Arcouest, when sure that war was imminent, telling them to stay put, encouraging them to be calm and courageous, and promising to bring them home when it was safe. But it was hard for the girls to be calm when the locals in the fishing village stared at them suspiciously, mistaking them for Germans because they spoke a foreign language—Polish—to their servants.

Charles Seignobos, a charming and notable Sorbonne historian, also there on vacation, tried to help by assuring villagers that the Curie girls were French. Since they had been mistaken for Germans, Irène had given daily French lessons to Eve's Polish governess, Walcia. "It's all the more important for us," Irène explained to her mother, "because you yourself were accused of being a foreigner, and we have nobody in the army. [Her cousin Maurice Curie would soon join the artillery.] I am, anyway, very annoyed that we rented the house in Brunoy under a foreign name and a borrowed name at that [Dluska]. I hope that you won't demand that our letters be sent there in the name of Sklodowska . . . It seems that I have been away from you for a century."

Determined to play an active role in the war, Marie offered her services to the president of the National Aid charity, Paul Appell—her friend's father, who had once tried to kick her out of the Sorbonne. He felt sorry for this exhausted woman with "her pale face and her eyes so big [and who] was all flame," but instead of recruiting her suggested that she take things easy for a while. Soon after, a leading radiologist, Dr. Antoine Béclère, gave her the answer she was looking for. During their conversation he spoke of a critical shortage of X-ray equipment in Paris hospitals. That was it. Within ten days of the outbreak of the conflict, Marie got permission from the war minister, Alexandre Millerand—one of her attorneys in the Langevin affair—to try to solve the problem. In an exhaustive tour of Paris she collected unused X-ray equipment from various sources: university laboratories, including hers; the offices of doctors not using theirs because they were away in the army; and patriotic manufacturers of scientific instruments. Then she delivered the lot to the city's hospitals.

On August 28, 1914, she warned her daughters that as Paris might soon be under siege, they would be cut off from one another. "If that should happen," she counseled sixteen-year-old Irène, "to endure it with courage, for our personal desires are nothing in comparison with the great struggle that is now under way. You must feel responsible for your sister and take care of her if we should be separated for a longer time than I expected."

The next day, Marie again wrote to Irène: "I'm afraid you're going to worry because of my letter of yesterday . . . We cannot foresee for sure how far the Germans can advance . . . which doesn't mean we cannot hope for France's final victory. So, courage and confidence. Think of your role as the older sister, which is high time that you take seriously . . . I'm burning to kiss you. The days go by without giving me that chance." Two days later she responded to Irène: "I have just received your sweet letter . . . and I wanted so much to kiss you that I almost cried. Things are not going very well and we are all heavyhearted . . . We need great courage, and I hope that we shall not lack it. We must keep our certainty that after the bad days the good days will come again. It is in this hope that I press you to my heart, my beloved daughters."

But Irène and Eve were more disturbed by ignorant local villagers than by the advancing German troops, especially when a drunk called at their vacation home, accused the Polish governess, Wilcia, and Polish cook, Josia, of being Germans, and ordered them to leave the country. Irène got the drunk's name from her landlord and resolved, she told her mother, to ask the mayor to talk to "the boor," unusually enterprising for a sixteen-year-old girl. "I didn't mention this before," Irène continued, "because I didn't want to hurt you, but I have often been hurt that they could take me for a foreigner, because I have the misfortune to be with foreigners." She followed through next day and protested to the mayor. He promised to talk to the drunk who had scared the two Polish women. But what bothered Irène much more was the local gossip about her. "For example," she wrote her mother,

> they say I'm a German spy, and that when I go out with a little dish to collect blackberries that I'm bringing food in the pail to a hidden German spy. They also say I am a German man dressed as a woman, etc. If they send the police to us we have nothing to fear. We could even put an end to the stories. But as long as people just talk there's nothing we can say. I'm a little bit frightened by all this, but very hurt. In Paris, at least, nobody would mistake me for a foreigner since I never go around with Wilcia [Eve's Polish governess] there. It hurts me that people take me for a foreigner when I am so profoundly French and love France more than anything. I can't help crying every time I think of this, so I'll stop so that you can read my letter.

To ease the situation, Irène continued to teach Wilcia French, and she obtained an identity card for Josia that gave her permission to travel throughout France.

The Germans were now so close that Parisians saw flashes of artillery guns on the horizon, and on September 2, expecting the city to fall within two days, the French government left for Bordeaux. German troops were within thirty miles of the city when the French government realized that Marie's radium was a national asset and instructed her to take it to Bordeaux for safety. So she left with the one gram of radium encased in lead—too heavy for her to lift alone—on a government-requisitioned train heading south.

When she arrived at the coastal city, a stranger helped her carry the bag to a room in which she slept with it at her side. Next morning she left the radium with Professor Bergonie of the University of Bordeaux's Faculty of Sciences. Marie returned to Paris on a much-delayed military train, in which a soldier shared his sandwich with her.

When she arrived, Paris was almost within the grasp of the German invaders led by General Alexander von Kluck—until what some considered miraculous occurred. Instead of taking Paris, he ordered his men to skirt the city and drive the retreating French troops in a southeasterly direction, hoping to overwhelm and destroy them in open country. French general Joffre took advantage of this tactical mistake to attack the exposed German flank, and the city's spirited military commander of Paris, General Gallieni, rushed some five thousand reinforcements to the rescue in every available vehicle, including scores of taxicabs. By September 9, with British support, they had the Germans on the run and Paris was safe. According to Winston Churchill, "The advance of the British Army . . . decided the immense battle which saved Paris." But at what a cost! Over 747,000 Germans and 854,000 Frenchmen had been killed or wounded in the first six weeks of war.

Marie continued to stay in Paris, while her daughters remained on the Brittany coast with their cook and governess. Her entire staff in the new, almost empty laboratory consisted of Louis Ragot, a technician with a weak heart, and a tiny charwoman. The rest were on war work. Now, as Marie walked through the almost deserted city, she noticed that "the glorious architectural treasures seemed to be particularly dear to those who remained in it."

Irène was almost frantic to return to Paris to help her embattled country, and Marie advised her that if she couldn't "work for France today, to work for its future. Many people will be missing after the war; it will be necessary to replace them. Do your physics and mathematics the best that you can." A few weeks later, in early October 1914, when the city seemed safe from German attack and Irène had recovered from an injury—a rock fell on her foot at the seashore—Marie sent for her daughters.

Irène immediately began to train as a Red Cross nurse, and Eve resumed her schooling at the Collège Sévigné. Wondering what more she could do for the war effort, Marie responded to a government appeal for gold and silver to pay for the war by offering her medals, including the Nobel Prize medal. But her offer was declined. Then, after discussing it with Irène, she used most of her Nobel Prize money—her daughters' future inheritance—to buy war bonds, knowing that at war's end they'd probably be worth much less.

But she could be helpful in another way. When Marie had taken X-ray equipment to Paris hospitals, she had learned that many wounded soldiers who might have survived were dying because it took too long to get them medical help. The entire French army had only one mobile

X-ray station, and few emergency stations at the battlefront had the electricity needed for X-rays. Marie decided to tackle the situation. She had lectured on X-rays at the Sorbonne but had no practical experience, so she took a cram course in anatomy and X-ray technique from Dr. Béclère at his Hospital Saint-Antoine and persuaded several colleagues to join her.

After completing the course, she asked War Minister Millerand for a second favor: to supply ambulances for service at the fighting front. She would transform them into mobile X-ray stations complete with electric power. He asked army chief General Joffre to consider her idea. Joffre had no ambulances to spare, but he gave Marie permission to provide and operate her own X-ray-equipped ambulances. The Sorbonne freed her for the duration—though she still occasionally taught there—and then, as director of the French Red Cross's radiological service, she set to work.

The Union of the Women of France gave her enough money to buy a Renault touring car and to have a body shop convert it into a quaint-looking hybrid ambulance. Officially known as "Car E," it had no front doors, so that driver and passenger were exposed to the elements, and was painted regulation gray, with a red cross and the words *Service Radiologique* painted on either side. Its engine powered a 110-volt, 15-ampere dynamo that supplied the electric current to produce X-rays. Her second vehicle was a gift from an architect named Ewald. The third and fourth came from the wealthy Marquise de Ganay and Princess Murat.

Marie talked them into donating their expensive cars for the duration by assuring each that after the war, "truthfully, if it's not useless by then, I shall give it back to you!" These were the prototypes for a fleet of sixteen more similar X-ray-equipped ambulances that she eventually provided. Soon a familiar sight to the troops, who affectionately nicknamed them "Little Curies," each had a driver and an X-ray technician on board.

Evidently her friendship with Paul Langevin, now an army sergeant, was still intact, because he was among the first she told of her plans. "The day I leave is not fixed yet, but it can't be far off," she wrote in a January 1, 1915, note to him. "I have had a letter saying that the radiological car working in the Saint-Pol region has been damaged. This means that the whole north is without any radiological service! I am taking the necessary steps to hasten my departure. I am resolved to put all my strength at the service of my adopted country, since I cannot do anything for my unfortunate native country just now, bathed as it is in blood after a century of suffering."

Marie was as good as her word. Her first call, on November 1, 1914, was to a military hospital at Creil, and she took Irène along as her assis-

Marie Curie devoted herself to helping the wounded during World War I. She drove this Renault—known as a "Little Curie" after its conversion into a radiological unit—to the various battlefronts to X-ray war casualties.

tant. From then on she was always on duty. Advised by a surgeon's urgent phone call or telegram, she would grab her cloak, a worn yellow leather bag, reading glasses, and felt gloves, which she believed would protect her from radiation, and hurriedly climb into the front passenger seat of Car E, then head for the various battlefields at a steady twenty miles an hour. Steady, that is, until the inevitable sentries stopped the vehicle with orders to forbid women to enter dangerous territory. If Marie couldn't talk her way past the sentries, she took a different route to reach her destination.

There Marie improvised a darkroom with curtains she had with her, then signaled her driver to start the power to the machine. Within half an hour she was usually ready for the first patient. When he was placed on the X-ray table, Marie focused the apparatus to show the damaged bones and organs and dark masses indicating embedded bullets or shell fragments. Sometimes there were scores of wounded men to be X-rayed, and she worked at it almost nonstop for days. She reassured frightened patients that it was just like being photographed—and converted some skeptical surgeons. Before leaving the field hospital she usually installed a permanent X-ray room and left a trained technician behind to continue her work. Then, as Eve Curie wrote, after packing up her equipment, "she would climb into the front seat of her magic chariot and start back to Paris." To be more self-reliant Marie learned to repair as well as to drive

Car E, and was seen in freezing weather cranking the engine, using the jack to change a tire, and once "cleaning a dirty carburetor with scientific gestures, her brows furrowed with attention."

In late January 1915, with her loyal friend Jean Perrin temporarily assigned to work with her, she headed for Boulogne to establish a base there for a Little Curie. After fixing two burst tires and surviving a head-on encounter with a tree, they finally made it. While there, Perrin wrote to their mutual friend Paul Langevin:

> Here we are at a semi-luxurious hotel drinking tea that is too strong at a shaky table . . . We're getting a good welcome everywhere, particularly because of Mme Curie's presence . . . We think you must hurry to put into practice your acoustic methods [sonar]. Meantime Weiss's method will be useful and I hope and think that in perhaps two months your more profound and precise idea . . . will be much more useful. We are going through such a hard time that a man like you must hurry to give the help that he alone can give. You can and must do a lot . . . You haven't been using your intelligence as a PHYSICIST. That and your courage will eventually be more useful than a thousand sergeants—despite our admiration for that honorable rank. Seriously, it seems to me that your great duty is to find ways to help us win. ALL the other duties take 20th or 25th place! Give it everything and neglect all the rest. Forgive me for "advising" you but it's precisely because I admire your intelligence.

Marie wrote on the back: "Dear Friend, I have just read Perrin's letter to you and I think in fact that you have lovely work ahead of you. For my part I should be very happy if this happened. It really seems that the war will be long and painful. One can hope to be of service with a well-researched invention. As for my service here I don't know yet what has to be done beside testing Perrin's car. Let's hope it behaves effectively. All the best."

The previous day, in one of Marie's frequent letters to Irène, she told her: "Some German aeroplanes dropped bombs at Dunkirk; a few people were killed, but the population weren't very scared. At Poperinghe, too, such incidents happen, but less often. We can hear the cannon rumbling almost constantly. It is not raining, but it has frozen a little. I was received with extreme cordiality at the hospital. I have a good room and they give me a fire in a stove . . . I embrace you tenderly."

By the spring, to his great relief Paul Langevin had switched from reluctant army sergeant with the Croix de Guerre back to physicist. He was working in his laboratory at the Ecole de Physique, trying to fine-tune ultrasound to detect enemy submarines. After briefly driving a Little

Curie in Boulogne, Jean Perrin was put in charge of National Defense Research in Paul Painlevé's Ministry of Inventions. There, like Langevin, he experimented with sound, but to locate night-flying or cloud-hidden airplanes instead of submarines. Her friend Albert Einstein, separated from his wife and courting his cousin Elsa in Berlin, was now in charge of the Kaiser Wilhelm Institute for Physics. But, being in enemy territory, he was unable to communicate with Marie. As a pacifist he had "speculated that future generations would be astonished that such a monstrous war could ever have occurred. He called Berlin a lunatic asylum and wished that he could move to Mars to observe the inmates through a telescope."

The Germans justified Einstein's scorn on April 22, 1915, when they resorted to using poison gas at Ypres, firing chlorine-gas shells that killed and maimed French and British troops. Two of Marie's friends were soon engaged in countering this new indiscriminate method of warfare: André Debierne was named director of the Chemical Warfare Service, and her English friend Hertha Ayrton invented a fan that cleared poison gases from the trenches.

Meanwhile, Irène and Eve continued their studies, knitted sweaters for soldiers they had "adopted," and kept track of the fluid war fronts by pinning little colored flags into a map on their dining-room wall. They also persuaded Marie to let them stay in their warm beds during bombing raids by cigar-shaped Zeppelins, instead of sheltering in the building's cold basement.

During her missions of mercy, Marie's sole protection from enemy attack was the red crosses on her ambulance. But the only war injury she sustained—other than exposure to X-rays—was caused by her driver. As Eve recalled, her mother once came home "a little less agile than usual . . . and shut herself into her room to sulk . . . because on her way back from the hospital at Forges, a sudden twist of the wheel by the driver had thrown her car into a ditch. The automobile overturned and Marie . . . seated among her apparatus, was hurled underneath the crashing cases. She was very vexed . . . to think . . . that her radiological plates must be shattered. But underneath the cases, which were gradually crushing her, she could not help laughing just the same when she heard her little driver, who had lost all his presence of mind and all his logic, running around the wrecked car inquiring in a whisper: 'Madame! Madame! Are you dead?'" She kept the accident to herself and hid her wounds, which were slight. However, Marie's daughters realized she had been injured when they came across bloodstained bandages in her dressing room. But before they could question her, she was on her way out on another mission.

Her affectionate nephew, Maurice Curie, an artilleryman, hoped in vain to spot her on one of her trips, and he wrote to her of sticking his "nose into every medical car that passes along the road." And later, still on the lookout for her, he wrote: "Dearest Aunt . . . I'd willingly give away my blanket for an hour at the window of your apartment on the Quai de Bethune . . . I go off again this evening, for three days we think, to a firing position along with my old chum, my 90 mm gun. How I love you. Maurice." He would survive the war. But to Marie's great distress, her favorite former assistant, the Franco-Polish codirector of the Radium Institute in Warsaw, Jan Kazimierz Danysz, who returned to France and volunteered for the army, was an early fatality.

With Paris no longer in imminent danger, she returned to Bordeaux to retrieve the precious gram of radium much in demand for medical purposes. Back in her laboratory she used an electric pump to collect radium's gaseous emanation, radon, easier and safer to handle than radium and just as effective. This was a technique pioneered by Dublin's Dr. John Joly. Sealed in glass tubes, the radon was delivered to military and civilian hospitals. There, wrote biographer Rosalynd Pflaum, "doctors encased the tubes in platinum needles and positioned them directly within patients' bodies, in the spot where [the radiation] could be most effective."

In all her work Marie had a willing and capable helper in Irène, whom she regarded, as she told her, as a friend and companion. It was Irène who hired a horse-drawn buggy to make hurried trips with her mother to cannibalize the abandoned laboratory on the rue Cuvier, partly to equip the all-but-empty Radium Institute on the rue Pierre Curie. Irène also taught, along with Marie and Marthe Klein, the first class of twenty nurses to become X-ray technicians. The six-week course at the institute included hands-on experience at a hospital recently renamed for Edith Cavell, in honor of the courageous British nurse shot by the Germans for helping Allied soldiers in German-occupied Belgium to escape. Eventually, 150 graduated from the course. To Marie's great delight, a former chambermaid proved more skillful than many highly educated students and developed her first "radiographic plate like an artist." Another student, Irène noted, ominously "tried to leave the course because of harmful effect of rays (???)" From her question marks, Irène apparently had her doubts about the danger.

While still just seventeen, Irène, as a Red Cross nurse, began accompanying her mother to the front line in radiological Car E, positioning the wounded men to be X-rayed and recording such details as: "Bullet in the forearm . . . Numerous shell splinters and fracture . . . Ball shrapnel in

A Red Cross nurse at the early age of seventeen, Irène Curie, pictured here with two assistants, drove this car of the French army's Radiological Service in World War I. She used the equipment on board to take X-rays of wounded soldiers.

right hand . . . Rifle bullet in left buttock. Depth of wound 10.9 cm. Examination of cranium. Rifle bullet in central region viewed in profile." Taking notes may have helped to distance themselves from the horrors they witnessed and that Marie vividly recalled in her *Autobiographical Notes*: "To hate the very idea of war, it ought to be sufficient to see once what I have seen so many times, over those years: men and boys brought to the advanced ambulance in a mixture of mud and blood, many of them dying of their injuries and many others recovering but slowly, in the space of months, with pain and suffering." Or as Eve Curie put it: "The memory of the thousands of hacked-up bodies she had seen, of the groans and shrieks she had heard, was to darken her life for a long time."

Despite the positive results, some older doctors were dubious about the value of X-rays, particularly the powerful inspector general of the Military Health Service, whom Irène had heard her mother call "difficult." When one day he arrived to inspect some radiological posts, Irène could hardly suppress her laughter as she watched her mother butter him up by saying with a straight face that the posts had been installed with his "gracious authorization."

Irène resisted going on the customary summer vacation in Brittany, but Marie insisted that her daughters take a break for their health. While there, Irène was somewhat reconciled to her exile by brief visits from Marie and the gratitude of shorthanded local farmers when she and Eve helped to harvest their wheat. On their return to Paris, Eve resumed her studies at preparatory school and Irène her war work.

Marie had such confidence in Irène that she put her in sole charge of the X-ray department of an Anglo-Belgian hospital at Hoogstade. And her daughter was not yet eighteen! When someone expressed astonishment at this, Irène responded, "My mother had no more doubts about me than she doubted herself." Temperamentally, Irène resembled her father, not her mother, and this, she believed, explained why she and Marie were so compatible.

Irène's work at Hoogstade wasn't always overwhelming. Luckily, her eighteenth birthday, on September 12, 1915, happened to be a quieter day, and, she told her mother, she spent the morning X-raying a soldier's hand, in which she located four bomb fragments, the afternoon watching a soccer match, the evening at a little concert, and that night, "slept [in a tent] under a beautiful starry sky."

They had both learned from firsthand experience how to handle doctors who resisted new ideas, especially from women. At Hoogstade, for example, as Marie recorded, Irène "had only been in the hospital for a short time when she located [through an X-ray] shrapnel that had shattered a man's thigh." She advised a Belgian surgeon, Van Meeven, to probe for the shrapnel from the side indicated by the X-ray. Instead, he stubbornly and persistently probed from another direction—through the soldier's open wound—and found nothing. He then reluctantly took Irene's advice and immediately located and extracted the shrapnel.

Marie was proud of Irène's triumphs over surgeons who seemed ignorant of elementary geometry, and of the way she outwitted obstructive bureaucrats—such as the time when a substitute took over from Irène at Hoogstade and Marie entrusted her daughter with driving an ambulance to a military hospital in Amiens, north of Paris, that the Germans had briefly occupied at the start of the war. Irène's job was to collect and install an X-ray unit in the hospital. The heavy equipment had been sent ahead by train. After driving alone in a Little Curie to pick it up at Amiens's railroad station, she was rebuffed by officials who told her that it would be at least three days before they could unload it. Emulating her mother's take-charge tactics, eighteen-year-old Irène persuaded an army sergeant and a young medical student to accompany her, ignored the officials, and got the equipment unloaded and into her ambulance in two hours.

With the Amiens radiology unit established, Irène wrote to her mother in October 1916: "I asked for curtains to make the X-ray room darker. Dr. Boucharcourt is very sweet but clumsy beyond all words. I fight so that he doesn't mess up the apparatus: he probably finds me clumsy as well. This morning under my supervision we had just found a bullet in a skull. It didn't go very well because D. B. gave some misinformation which led to a misunderstanding which prolonged the operation, but fortunately I was helping and it was fixed. Dr. Laval was furious with Dr. B. I kiss you darling."

Six months later, in April 1917, a five-day frontal attack by the British at Ypres gained five miles but cost them 160,000 casualties. Fortunately massive reinforcements from the U.S. Army, now in the war, arrived at this perilous time and assured final victory.

Most of Marie's friends and colleagues were still involved in the war effort: Henriette Perrin and Alice Chavannes as nurses, and Marguerite Borel as a hospital director. Ernest Rutherford, like Langevin, at work on how to detect silent submarines by echoes, was invited to lecture on the subject at France's Ministry of Inventions. After making the Channel crossing from England, he reached a Paris hotel where he began to check his notes for the lecture, when, to his delight, "a taxi driven by a soldier turned up in which were Perrin, Langevin, Mme Curie, and Debierne, who took me to lunch and treated me in royal fashion."

That afternoon he went with Langevin and Marie to inspect her laboratory and noticed, as they sipped tea at a lab bench, how, "rather gray and worn and tired," she looked. "She is very much occupied with radiology work, both direct and for training others," he wrote to his wife. Her daily exposure to radiation for years, as well as her punishing, self-imposed regimen, surely accounted for her appearance.

Despite the demanding work, she occasionally found time to include among the papers in her battered leather case some flower seeds and herbs she had collected whenever she got the chance to enhance the garden of the Radium Institute. One Saturday morning in March 1918, she and Irène were on such a quest, shopping for plants in an Ile de la Cité flower market, when they heard what sounded like a bomb dropped from a plane, followed by more explosions at regular intervals. When they returned to the nearby institute they learned that the explosions were caused by shells from four "Big Berthas," as they were known. These were enormous German guns with an amazing range of seventy-five miles that fired from secret emplacements and that now had the city well within range.

The shelling continued at exactly fifteen-minute intervals. However, it didn't prevent Marie and Irène from spending the rest of the day planting the flowers they'd bought. Allied planes sent up to hunt and destroy the guns couldn't find them, they were so well camouflaged.

On Sunday, the day after the Big Berthas' shells first reached Paris, a formation of twin-engine German planes bombed the Paris church of St. Gervais, killing seventy-seven worshippers and wounding eighty. Irène and Eve were so sleep deprived by the bombs, shells, and howling air-raid warnings that while Marie was in Italy at the Italian government's invitation to search for sources of pitchblende, Irène and Eve slept at the little house in Brunoy, returning to the city in the daytime. Irène wrote to her mother not to worry, that they were both intact, that she had been for some lovely walks, one in the morning and one in the evening, and to her great delight had just received her first pay ever.

In July 1918, what the Curies mistook for distant thunder was a thousand enemy guns launching another attack on Paris. German troops were within forty miles of the city when Marshal Ferdinand Foch, now commander in chief of the Allied armies, ordered a counterattack. Fortified by massive American reinforcements Foch rallied the collapsing Allied armies, which drove the enemy back. Paris was safe again.

That summer, twenty-year-old Irène was awarded a bachelor of science degree in physics, and the Sorbonne appointed her Marie's temporary assistant, with time off for research on her doctoral thesis—a study of polonium's alpha rays.

Marie Curie and a colleague, Marthe Klein, her former Sèvres student, were in the laboratory of the Radium Institute at 11 A.M. on November 11, 1918, when a roar of cannon fire from the Invalides—the church where Napoleon is buried—signaled the end of the war. They rushed out to buy French flags, but the stores were cleaned out. So Marie had her charwoman, Mme Bardinet, stitch some red, white, and blue material into primitive flags, then flew them from the Radium Institute's windows.

Eager to celebrate with the excited crowds in the streets, they invited an assistant in a nearby classroom to join them. He drove the two women in the battered old Car E as far as the place de la Concorde, where the crowds were so dense they had to stop. There, a dozen Parisians climbed onto the roof and remained, cheering, weeping with joy, and singing "La Marseillaise."

It was a double victory for Marie. The Allies had won the war, and her beloved Poland was freed from 150 years of enslavement. The Germans had attacked Poland as well as Russia, and with Germany's defeat, the revolutionary new Soviet Socialist Republic recognized Poland's independence. General Jósef Pilsudski, son of a poor Polish nobleman, after banishment to Siberia and imprisonment in Germany, returned to his country to head the Second Polish Republic.

For four years Marie had taken her Little Curie, Car E, to battlefields at Amiens, Calais, Dunkirk, Furnes, Poperinghe, Verdun, Nancy, Lunéville, Belfort, Compiègne, and Villers-Cotterets. Because of her determination, and the fleet of twenty ambulances she had provided, over a million wounded men had been X-rayed, and at a moderate estimate she had helped to save many thousands of lives. Irène, too, had been enormously enterprising and courageous, both as her mother's helpmate and later, when, only eighteen, she was left in sole charge of radiology at various military hospitals.

A grateful French government awarded Irène a Military Medal. It gave Marie Curie nothing.

CHAPTER 12

A Gift of Radium from the United States

1919–1923

I t was hardly surprising that Marie Curie despised the ninety-three intellectuals in Germany who, during the war, had signed a manifesto supporting the invasion of neutral Belgium as a military necessity. Far from conceding the brutality involved, the manifesto, titled "Appeal to the Cultured World," stated that not a single Belgian or his property had been harmed by a German soldier, characterized the enemy as Russian hordes allied with Mongols and Negroes unleashed against the white race, and warned that without the German military, German culture would have been wiped off the face of the earth. Among those who signed the audacious piece of fiction were the poet Gerhart Hauptmann, theater producer Max Reinhardt, and fifteen scientists, including the highly respected Max Planck. It was published in leading German newspapers, translated into ten languages, and distributed worldwide. Yet German records reveal that on the second day of the war, Belgians who showed invading soldiers disrespect or slowed their advance—including some fleeing refugees—were shot by firing squads.

Einstein and his friend Dr. George Nicolai, a German heart specialist, produced a countermanifesto, "Appeal to Europeans," calling for an end to the war and a united Europe. They invited a hundred intellectuals to sign it. Only two did: astronomer Wilhelm Forster, who had originally supported the prowar appeal and had a change of heart, and a Dr. Otto Beck. Toward the end of the war, Nicolai—in danger because of his pacifist views—had made a daring escape from Germany by plane.

After the war, when Marie Curie again met foreign scientists, she invariably asked if they had signed the "Appeal to the Cultured World," known as "The Manifesto of the Ninety-Three." If they had, she treated them with barely concealed disdain, or what she called polite reserve. With those who had not signed, and she knew they included Einstein, which further endeared him to her, she was friendly and talked freely of science, as if the war had not taken place. Although, wrote biographer Anna Hurwic, she "did not think that great minds could remain 'above the battle,' there were certain acts in which she could not acknowledge the intellectuals' right to complicity." Which included lying, even in wartime. And she had a definite, practical view on how to treat the defeated enemy. According to her daughter Eve, she believed that: "Either the Germans have to be exterminated down to the last man, which is unthinkable, or else they have to be given a peace they can tolerate."

Not that she was for peace at any price. So that when Romain Rolland, whose novels she admired, asked her to join Albert Einstein, Upton Sinclair, Heinrich Mann, and other intellectuals in signing a petition to outlaw war, she declined. Rolland, a quixotic idealist, had called for France and Germany to respect truth and humanity throughout World War I and in 1915 had received the Nobel Prize for literature.

In her carefully considered response to Rolland, Marie wrote:

I entirely share your aspirations for the reign of peace and fraternity. Certainly I have a horror of war and I deplore, like you, the subjection of intelligence to brute force [which she had also experienced in Poland]. But the highest cultivation of intellect is not a guarantee of a just view of national and social problems . . . Men whose minds deal in abstractions on the highest level and who produce admirable work have shown that they are ready to side with all kinds of banditry committed on behalf of their country. A scholar who signs the Manifesto of the Ninety-three is humanly more remote from me than a simple citizen who is capable of seeking justice not only for himself but for others . . . The difficulty that I have with your form of appeal is that it does not require the signers to be in agreement on certain elementary principles of international and social justice. Thus the agreement would be illusory because differences would reappear at the moment of the first conflict . . . For a useful common action, there needs to be a minimum of agreement on precise problems—invasion of Belgium, torpedoing of the *Lusitania*, devastation of France, reconstitution of Poland, independence of Ireland, etc.

Her argument was irrefutable. And Einstein proved her point many years later when the Nazis threatened the civilized world during World War II and he, the former poster boy for pacifists, urged the United States to build an atomic bomb. Again, when the existence of a newly created Israel was threatened by Arab armies and a fellow member of the War Resisters International asked him, "Don't you agree that Israel should recognize the status of conscientious objectors?" Einstein answered yes, but with an important reservation: he would not presume to advise people who had overcome what seemed to be insurmountable obstacles to save their nation.

Since the spring of 1919, the U.S. Army had been paying Marie seventy-five dollars a week to teach American army officers waiting to be shipped home how to use X-ray equipment. Irène's participation was an added appeal for the soldiers, who, according to Marie, "studied with much zeal the practical exercises directed by my daughter."

Despite a lack of makeup, a long-sleeved black smock down to her ankles, and a curt manner, twenty-one-year-old Irène could not conceal her attractive green eyes and obvious intelligence. But the American soldiers who tried to flirt with her were met with a surprised, cold stare, a far cry from her behavior with friends. Among them she engaged in good-humored banter—especially with her cousin Maurice—and indulged her craze for dancing far into the night. To Eve, who had an almost entirely positive view of her sister, Irène was always calm and good-humored, never said "a bad thing and, to my knowledge, never lied in her life. She is exactly what she shows us, with all her merits and demerits, without embellishing anything to please us."

Though they had radically different personalities, Marie loved and treated her daughters equally. Yet at times Eve felt neglected. Many evenings on returning to their apartment she found Marie at work, not at her desk but sitting on the floor. As Eve recalled, her mother "had to have limitless space to spread out her documents and her sheets of graphs. [Once she was so] absorbed in a difficult theoretical calculation, [that] although she had noticed [my] return, she did not lift her head." On another occasion, Marie was so focused on her work that she failed to notice that Eve had double pneumonia. It took a doctor friend who was visiting Marie to realize that Eve was seriously ill and to call for an ambulance. Afterward, of course, her mother felt guilty, Eve recalled, and spent a few days with her at the hospital.

Sharing her mother's scientific preoccupations and dedication, Irène was more understanding of her behavior. Although Eve said that she did

Because Irène had inherited her father's personality, Marie found her to be a great working partner as well as an outstanding scientist.

not feel jealous of the time her mother gave to research, accepting it as part of Marie's routine, she must at times have resented her treatment—and shown it. Which explains why, when Marie returned from their summer vacation ahead of them, she wrote to Irène: "I hope our Evette will love us more in Paris than she did in L'Arcouest." Adding, more optimistically, "I often think of the year of work that is opening before us. I think also of each of you, and of the sweetness, joys and cares you give me. You are in truth a great fortune to me, and I hope life still holds for me a few good years of existence in common with you."

However, when Irène returned from L'Arcouest impatient to work with her mother, they were both frustrated by lack of modern equipment and a limited amount of radium. The one gram they had—barely a thimbleful—was in constant demand from doctors and medical researchers. An appeal through the press might have helped to raise funds for more radium and equipment, but with her painful memories of reporters, Marie had adopted a way to keep most at bay. Everyone sent to break her resistance was told that she was available on Tuesdays and Fridays, but only to discuss scientific matters and never to talk of her personal life, which, of course, was what many reporters wanted.

This was the disappointing answer she gave American journalist Marie Mattingly Meloney, despite her impressive background, persuasive manner, and apparently philanthropic intentions. The *Delineator*, a popular women's magazine of which she was editor, had financed war relief work in Europe. And she had recently had no trouble interviewing in England such celebrities as H. G. Wells, Bertrand Russell, and Arnold Bennett. To break Marie's resistance, Meloney sought the help of Stephane Lauzanne, editor of *Le Matin*. But he discouraged her: "She will see no one," he said. "She does nothing but work. Few things in life are more distasteful to her than publicity. Her mind is as exact and logical as science itself. There are but two things for her—her family and her work."

Meloney, who had been the *Denver Post's* bureau chief in Washington, D.C., and the first woman to get a seat in the Senate press gallery, had not reached her prominent position by taking no for an answer. Help came from an unlikely source: a womanizing Frenchman, Henri-Pierre Roche, eventually author of the autobiographical ménage-à-trois novel *Jules and Jim*, which was eventually filmed by François Truffaut. Attracted to Meloney, a slight, dark-haired, bright-eyed, and dynamic woman who walked with a slight limp caused by a riding accident, Roche offered to introduce her to the elusive Marie Curie and to act as translator for their first conversation. (He and Marie probably first met at sculptor Rodin's studio.)

Through his recommendation Marie agreed to see her, but only for a few minutes. Anxious not to waste a moment of the interview, Meloney recalled how she waited with Roche "in the small bare office which might have been furnished from Grand Rapids, Michigan. Then the door opened and I saw a pale, timid little woman in a black cotton dress, with the saddest face I had ever looked upon. Her well-formed hands were rough. I noticed a characteristic, nervous little habit of rubbing the tips of her fingers over the pad of her thumb in quick succession. I later learned that working with radium had made them numb. Her kind, patient, beautiful face had the detached expression of a scholar." There was no need for Roche to translate, because Marie immediately revealed what was on her mind in clear, Polish-accented English. The United States had almost cornered the radium market, she said, possessing some fifty grams worth millions of dollars. And she knew where much of it was: four grams in Baltimore, six in Denver, and seven in New York. Yet in the whole of France there was only one gram of radium—and that was in her safe.

"You have only one gram?" Meloney exclaimed.

"I? Oh, I have none," she corrected. "It belongs to the laboratory." And was earmarked for medical purposes. Her greatest wish was for another gram of radium to continue her researches. But, Marie explained, she couldn't buy it, because it was too expensive.

Meloney suggested that the cost of the radium could be covered by Marie's patent rights to radium production. "There were no patents," she replied. "We were working in the interests of science. Radium was not to enrich anyone. Radium is an element. It belongs to all people." Now Meloney had the hook for her article: a great woman who needed help for a great cause. As she would tell her *Delineator* readers, Marie Curie "has contributed to the progress of science and the relief of human suffering, and yet, in the prime of her life she [is] without tools which would enable her to make further contribution of her genius."

Knowing that the radium Marie wanted would cost at least a one hundred thousand dollars, Meloney might have commiserated with her and changed the subject. Instead, she decided on the spot to get the money from affluent American acquaintances.

Either Meloney had extraordinary powers of persuasion or Marie Curie trusted her on sight. Perhaps both. Meloney even got her assurance that if the fund-raising drive succeeded, Marie would consider going to America to accept the radium or the money to buy it. What did the trick was Meloney's promise that the American press would not rehash the Langevin scandal—a seemingly impossible task, which she achieved because of her remarkable influence with major newspaper editors. Indeed, she must have hypnotized Arthur Brisbane of Hearst's New York *Evening Journal*. After she spoke to him, he handed her not only his paper's complete file on the Curie-Langevin affair, but also one hundred dollars for the radium fund.

Within days of her return home, Meloney had organized an advisory committee of scientists, including the president of the American Medical Association. As the appeal was to be from women to women, she also formed another all-female committee to run the campaign under her direction, which included Mrs. John D. Rockefeller, Mrs. Calvin Coolidge, and Mrs. Robert Mead, founder of the American Society for the Control of Cancer. At first she tried to get ten super-rich women to part with ten thousand dollars apiece, but not one responded. However, the widow of poet-playwright William Vaughn Moody, one of whose poems ironically was titled "The Faith Healer," gave a generous amount. So did Herbert Hoover, the chief Allied relief administrator during World War I and a future U.S. president. Meloney then changed her tactics, asking for one- or five-dollar donations from her readers. And it began to work. College women responded by taking up campus collections, and children who heard of the campaign from their mothers mailed in their nickels and dimes.

Before her anticipated trip to the United States, Marie handed over control of the lab to Irène, then took her first real vacation since before the war, traveling with her colleague Marthe Klein through Provence to Cavalaire, a hillside village on the Mediterranean near St. Tropez. They stayed in a small, nondescript hotel—deserted but for a few English tourists—where Marie completed her book *Radiology and the War*, swam in the warm sea, and for several nights slept on the hotel's terrace under the stars.

She returned refreshed and recharged, only to be inundated with letters, many from America, asking her to lecture, endorse products, make public appearances, send her autograph and photo, or give advice. She junked most, but after conferring with Professor Claude Regaud, an expert on radium's medical potential, replied to people interested in radium as a cancer cure. This involved a pleasant break when she left her office and strolled through the garden she had created to speak with Regaud in the adjoining building.

She also sought the advice of Dr. Robert Abbe of New York City, a plastic surgery pioneer who had introduced radiation therapy to the United States. Abbe had visited the Curies as early as 1903 when he briefly took part in their research, then brought back a supply of radium to use in his surgical practice at St. Luke's Hospital in New York. Abbe became so fond of the Curies that he named two swans in the pond of his Bar Harbor, Maine, summer home Pierre and Marie. Over the years he had collected postcards, photographs, news clippings, and letters from Marie, and when the museum run by the College of Physicians of Philadelphia asked her to donate some equipment for their collection, she took Abbe's suggestion to send the electrometer she and Pierre had used for their radium experiments.

An enthusiastic member of Meloney's "Marie Curie Radium Fund" committee, Abbe wrote in a book titled *Mme. Curie*: "We witness in [her] research one of the most complete pieces of detective work that ever unearthed a hidden mystery . . . It is the privilege of the women of this country to lay this tribute at her feet—a gift of radium—instead of a wreath of laurel—with which she can and will give back to them a thousand fold more in value, a hoped-for revelation of the medical power, when its forces can be tamed and used in cancer—that dread scourge."*

Thanks to Meloney's efforts, four major publishers—Macmillan, Scribner's, Dutton, and Houghton—were competing for Marie's autobiography, and Meloney advised her to ask for royalties of 20 percent—twice the going rate—which, she said, Theodore Roosevelt had recently received. (Macmillan published the book in 1923.)

When Meloney told Marie that the one hundred thousand dollars had been collected, Marie was expecting to stay in the United States for two weeks, but Meloney urged her to emulate recent visitors, the king and queen of Belgium, and to make it six. Marie replied that she would miss her daughters, so Meloney encouraged her to bring them, too. She had even arranged for President Warren Harding to hand Marie the gram of radium.

At the prospect of an unexpected vacation in America with her mother, Eve, the only one of the trio with a sense of style, talked Marie into buying a couple of new dresses—both black, of course—and to leave her worn and faded clothes at home.

Soon after, Stephane Lauzanne, the editor-in-chief of Le Matin, was surprised when told that Marie Curie was on the line. He had only spoken to her once before and wondered, "What extraordinary event—what tragedy, perhaps, might this mean?" He immediately recognized her voice as she began: "I am going to America. It was very hard for me to decide to go, because America is so far and so big. If someone did not come for me, [Meloney] I should probably never have made the trip. I should have been too frightened. But to this fear is added a great joy. I have devoted my life to the science of radio-activity and I know all we owe to America in the field of science. I am told you are among those who strongly favor this distant trip, so I wanted to tell you I have decided to go, but please don't let anyone know." It was strange to call an editor with news, then ask him to keep it to himself. Apparently he did—until after the fact. What also puzzled

---

* Abbe's great grandnephew writes: "Dr. Abbe experimented with radium therapy on my father. In those days, this was done by embedding particles of metallic radium in a plastic disk about the size of a silver dollar. My uncle strapped one of these to my father's neck for a period of time in hopes of removing my father's tonsils. The result was a brown radium burn about the size of a silver dollar. The tonsils proceeded as before, with no effect. My father died of natural causes at age 95. Dr. Abbe always carried a sealed vial of radium in his jacket pocket and died of leukemia in 1928. We assumed it was caused by his use of radium." Robert Abbe in a letter to author, April 24, 25, 2003.

Lauzanne was that "This great woman—the greatest woman in France—was speaking haltingly, tremblingly, almost like a little girl. She, who handles daily a particle of radium more dangerous than lightning, was afraid when confronted by the necessity of appearing before the public."

When Marie's niece, Hela, living in Chicago, picked up the *New York Times* and read an inaccurate report of Marie's imminent visit, headed "Radium Gift Awaits Mme. Curie Here," she wrote to the editor to put the record straight. "I am closely related to Mme Curie-Sklodowski [Sklodowska], who is the sister of my mother [Bronia] . . . I wish to correct some misstatements made in the article . . . Mme Curie-Sklodowski was born in Warsaw fifty-two years ago. Her father, as stated in the *New York Times*, was a Professor of Physics at the University of Warsaw. He was a Pole, not a Jew, as stated in your paper, a descendant of an old Polish family, so was not 'converted to Catholicism shortly before the birth of his daughter,' as he was born into a Catholic family for many centuries. Also, the mother of Mme Curie-Sklodowski was not a Swede. Her maiden name was Boguska, and she was also a descendant of an old Polish family. Mme Boguska was for many years the principal of one of the most prominent Polish schools for girls at Warsaw. She, therefore, held a position which hardly could have been trusted to a foreigner; especially in Poland under the Russian yoke, where the school was the only stronghold of nationalism against the Russian anti-Polish policy. These few remarks I am sending to you, knowing that Mme Curie-Sklodowski is very proud of her Polish nationality, and although married to a Frenchman, never ceased to be a Polish patriot."

After the French learned that the U.S. president intended to present Marie with a gram of radium, the French minister of public education offered her the Legion of Honor, which she declined. However, she did agree to attend a bon voyage celebration at the Paris Opera House to benefit her Radium Institute, on April 27, 1921. Sponsored by the journal *Je Sais Tout* (I Know Everything), actor-playwright Sacha Guitry produced the entertainment, with former French president Aristide Briand as one of the guests.

Lively applause greeted Marie's arrival at the auditorium with her daughters and Meloney, followed by tributes from her scientific friends Jean Perrin and Claude Regaud, a recitation of "Ode to Madame Curie" by the aged superstar Sarah Bernhardt, and a performance of two acts of Sacha Guitry's play *Pasteur*.

Marie had only a vague impression of what was happening onstage. She hid from almost everyone the frequent humming in her ears (tinnitus) and her increasingly clouded vision caused by double cataracts, which she suspected might have been due to exposure to radium. Meloney, one of the few in whom she confided, had arranged for her to consult an eye specialist in Manhattan.

Before they set off for America, the Curies befriended Harriet Eager, a young, French-speaking American in Paris, who accepted an invitation to join them on their trip.

As Marie boarded the *Olympic* at Cherbourg on May 4, 1921, the White Star Line's president escorted her to the bridal suite she was to share with her daughters. Being treated like royalty or a movie star was too much for Marie, who knew this was Meloney's doing. She grimaced disapprovingly at the luxurious rooms and later at the elaborate meals, writing about it to her friend Henriette Perrin: "I left France to go on this distant frolic, so little to my taste and habits." But in case Henriette misunderstood her reservations, Marie added that Meloney "is more of a friend than I can tell you, and I don't think she's doing this for personal advantage; she is an idealist and seems very disinterested."

One day aboard ship, when Marie was late joining the others for lunch, Harriet Eager went to look for her. She found her in the bridal suite facing an open closet. She seemed to be staring at her dresses, including an evening gown that she had worn to receive her two Nobel Prizes and intended to wear to receive the radium from President Harding. But she wasn't, it turned out, considering what to wear for lunch. Instead, to avoid wasting electricity, she was trying to find the switch that turned off the closet light. Harriet explained that a switch automatically extinguished the light when the door closed. "Show me where that switch is," Marie asked. Harriet searched, but also failed to find it. When it was obvious that Marie would not leave until she knew for sure that the light went out when the door was closed, Harriet suggested a practical experiment. If Marie went inside the closet, she would close the door on her. Then Marie could see for herself what happened. Marie agreed, and stepped inside the closet. Harriet shut the door, then opened it. A smiling Marie Curie emerged. "You are right, Harriet!" she exclaimed happily, as they walked arm-in-arm toward the lunchroom.

The rough, bone-chilling crossing of the Atlantic left Marie dizzy rather than seasick. Much of the time she stayed in her suite, comforted by thoughts of the coming summer in L'Arcouest, of swimming in its calm, blue sea, dotted with small islands, and of pottering in the small garden that awaited her there.

As the *Olympic* docked at New York City, Marie began to tremble at the prospect of giving her first American-style press conference. Tired and

Marie Curie (seated right) dreaded the boat deck interview she endured when she arrived in New York in 1921 to receive a gift of radium worth one hundred thousand dollars from the American public. Marie Meloney stands near her, wearing a hat and bow tie.

bewildered, she sat in a large armchair on deck, obeying the imperious commands from a semicircle of some forty men to look this way, then that, up and down, here and there, and responding to questions yelled at her from various directions. Her daughters and Meloney stood silently nearby: twenty-three-year-old Irène, like her mother making no concession to fashion, in sensible shoes and black cotton stockings; sixteen-year-old Eve in silk stockings, high-heeled shoes, and a flowered hat. A reporter catching Eve's lively glance named her in his account "Miss Radium Eyes."

"Radium is a positive cure for cancer," a *New York Times* reporter quoted Marie as saying. "It has already cured all kinds of cancers, even deep-rooted cases . . . Those [doctors] who have failed do not understand the methods." Unaware of her poor eyesight and fragile health, the same reporter wrote that, "Although 53 years old, she is energy personified, walking with a quick step. Several of those at the pier spoke of the clearness of her eyes, and the lively interest she took in everything she saw."

The lively interest and quick step were doubtless expressions of her attempt to make a fast getaway from excited fans waving American, French, and Polish flags, their voices mingling with brass bands playing three national anthems. Hundreds of women from the Polish American

Society carrying red and white roses mobbed her along with a large French contingent of Girl Scouts, members of scientific committees, and masses of other admirers.

A group of New York Camp Fire Girls handed her a red leather bag, a dozen people presented bouquets, often along with little speeches, and scores grabbed and shook her hand until it ached. Marie escaped into one of two limousines sent by Andrew Carnegie's widow, which took her and her entourage to Meloney's Greenwich Village home at 31 West Twelfth Street. To reach the front door, they had to negotiate a pathway of roses left by a horticulturist whose cancer had been cured by radium. Many more bouquets crowded the house, all of which Meloney eventually sent to a children's hospital.

Marie woke next day to read a front-page *New York Times* headline, "Mme Curie Plans to End All Cancers," a misquote repeated in the text. Meloney assured her that it would be corrected, and called the paper to make sure it was. "What Mme Curie said was that radium was a specific for many forms of the disease. She did not wish to be understood as asserting that it could effect a cure in every case." (The mistake was on page 1, the correction on page 16.)

That problem settled, another quickly arose. While discussing the several colleges intending to award Marie honorary degrees, Meloney remarked, "Naturally you've brought your cap and gown. They are indispensable for these ceremonies." In fact, she had never worn academic garb. Sorbonne's male professors did, but as a unique member of the group, the only female professor ever, Marie had been allowed a certain independence. Averse to display, she went without, and hadn't thought to bring a cap and gown with her. Meloney immediately phoned a nearby tailor, who agreed to take on the "emergency" assignment, and soon appeared carrying a black silk gown with velvet facings. But when Marie tried it on, she hated it, complaining that the "sleeves embarrassed her, that the gown was too hot—and above all that the silk irritated her poor fingers, ruined by radium." Meloney persuaded her to accept it, but she adamantly refused to wear a mortarboard, which, she grumbled after trying it on, looked hideous and kept falling off.

Next morning, Friday, a coach awaited the Curies and their escorts to drive them to Smith College, the start of their formidable itinerary, which included visits to Wellesley, Simmons, Radcliffe, and Bryn Mawr.

When Marie arrived at Northampton, a reporter noted that "she seemed dazed. Her arms hung lifelessly, her features were ashen gray, contrasting strongly with the simple black tailored suit she was wearing.

Marie Meloney (far left) took care
of the Curies when they arrived
in New York. Not willing to face
a several-weeks-long separation
from her daughters, Marie brought
Irène (on her right) and Eve with
her. She became so exhausted that
at times they represented her at
functions.

Marie Curie and her
daughter Eve, on arrival in
the United States in 1921.

Later she smiled from time to time wanly and patiently, and there was an
occasional gleam in her blue-gray eyes. The deep lines on her face, however, showed how seriously the unaccustomed strain of her whirlwind visit
to America has affected her."

At Smith, Marie was greeted by hundreds of students, all in white
dresses with red, green, purple, or yellow sashes. She was escorted across
the campus by Smith president William Neilson, walking from the library
steps to the chemistry lab between a guard of honor—a double row of
juniors in white dresses with red sashes, while a student played "The Marseillaise" on the college chimes. Meloney followed close behind, bur-
dened with a huge bouquet of roses from Marie's Polish compatriots in the
area, and lilies of the valley from the French Club. Students who had ser-
enaded her at the library joined the procession to the chemistry laboratory,
where Marie spent an hour inspecting the work of its students. Then, after

a tea break, a ceremony followed, characterized by a local paper as one of the most impressive in the history of the college.

Marie sat on a platform in John M. Greene Hall facing an audience of two thousand, listening to Professor Albert Schinz, head of the French department, compare her favorably with great French females throughout history. He also repeated a story about Marie Curie to which she would eventually respond. Then Professor H. D. Wells, head of the chemistry department, gave a detailed account of her life and work, followed by Professor Neilson, who described her as a "first among women of all ages for [the] brilliance, magnitude, and significance of her scientific discovery, the peer of the greatest benefactors of mankind in the unselfishness, [with] which she has devoted the results of her researches to the service of humanity." That said, Marie stood, and, as the crowd cheered and applauded, two women professors of chemistry placed the academic robes of a Doctor of Science over her shoulders.

Marie murmured her thanks to Professor Neilson, then turned to the audience and said in English: "I am very grateful to the college for this beautiful and graceful reception. I thank you for the honor you have done me." Then she responded to a story Professor Schinz had told to illustrate Marie Curie's ability to be totally absorbed by her work. He had described how when she was engrossed in her lab and a maid had rushed in crying out that she had swallowed a pin, Mme Curie replied, "Never mind, here's another." "It's a very good story," she said, "but unfortunately it never happened."

After a chorus sang the Smith alma mater, Marie was escorted to the library for an informal reception where she spoke with students and faculty. Everywhere she went, Meloney, Professor Neilson, and others formed a bodyguard, preventing any of the dozen reporters from approaching her for an interview, which didn't prevent them from discussing her among themselves.

The *Springfield Republican* printed their gloomy conclusion: "Doubt has been expressed by several who saw Mme Curie yesterday of her ability to complete this itinerary without a nervous breakdown."

She endured the same mass adulation the next day at Mount Holyoke and then at Vassar, where she emphasized the unexpected outcome of pure research. "When radium was discovered," she said, "no one knew that it would prove useful in hospitals. The work was one of pure science. And this is a proof that scientific work must not be considered from the point of view of the direct usefulness of it. It must be done for itself, for the beauty of science, and then there is always the chance that a scientific discovery may become like radium a benefit for humanity."

The *Springfield Republican* expected her to quit the tour, reporting: "A quarter of a century of painstaking research work in the field of chemistry has left the world's foremost woman scientist in complete possession of all her keen faculties. The first two hectic days of her two weeks' tour [it would be extended to six] of this country, following immediately after a seasick voyage from France, have transformed her into a listless being, tired nigh to death, and obviously ill."

But on Monday, after a catnap at Meloney's home, she appeared as guest of honor of the American Chemical Society at the Waldorf-Astoria, where cancer researcher Dr. Francis Wood told the six hundred members that she had done more to comfort human beings than any other scientist of her time.

Marie left the Waldorf-Astoria for receptions at the National Academy of Sciences, the American Museum of Natural History, and the New York Mineralogical Club. Eulogists included her friend Dr. Robert Abbe and Columbia University's Professor Michael Pupin, the physicist son of illiterate parents who won the 1924 Pulitzer Prize for his autobiography, *From Immigrant to Inventor*.

The next day she stepped on stage at Carnegie Hall to applause from thirty-five hundred members of the International Federation of University Women that lasted several minutes. Among the invited guests were the French and Polish ambassadors and her old pianist-politician friend, Ignace Paderewski, who heard Dr. Florence Sabin of Johns Hopkins Medical School praise Marie for proving that a woman could do laborious scientific work and also be a wife and mother. He was followed by a line of the country's most promising female science students. One by one, they approached Marie, bowed, and handed her a flower—one a rose, the next a lily, a third an orchid, and so on. The record-breaking celebration concluded with the fifty-strong Vassar choir singing "The Star Spangled Banner."

Watching Marie at one Manhattan function, a reporter judged her to be shy, weary, and uninterested. He was doubtless right. Staggering with fatigue and suffering from a sprained wrist—caused by a fan's too fervent handshake—now bandaged and in a sling, she took a doctor's advice to rest. Rather than disappoint hostesses who had contributed to her fund, she prevailed upon Irène and Eve to represent her at some parties and receptions. They proved a winning team: Eve loved the parties and charmed the guests, while Irène, though uncomfortable among strangers, still proved a good substitute by talking science like the professional she was.

At Meloney's home the night before they were to leave for Washington and the White House, Marie found a serious flaw in the deed giving her possession of the gram of radium. Under her control it would be used strictly for scientific research, but there was no provision for the fate of the radium after her death. Meloney discussed an amendment to remedy the omission with the group, including Mrs. Coolidge, who agreed that it could wait for a week or so, and certainly until after the imminent White House ceremony.

But Marie emphatically disagreed. "Not next week. Not tomorrow. Tonight," she said. "The act of gift will soon be valid, and I may die in a few hours." It was already late, but she insisted on rewriting the deed that night. Attorney Cecil Wahl, reportedly aroused from sleep, agreed to Marie's request. He drafted another document precisely according to her wishes, but before signing it, to make sure it was exactly what she wanted, she had it translated into French.

The new deed stated that she had control of the radium's present use and destiny. The following day Vice President and Mrs. Calvin Coolidge escorted her to the East Room of the White House.

There, while hundreds of French, Polish, and American officials, leading scientists, and philanthropists looked on, the French ambassador, Jules Jusserand, the first Pulitzer Prize–winning historian, introduced Marie to President Harding. He welcomed her as "an adopted daughter of France, our earliest supporter among the great nations. We greet you as a native-born daughter of Poland; newest, as it is among the oldest, of the great nations, and always bound by the ties of the closest sympathy to our own Republic. . . . We greet you as the foremost among scientists in the age of science, as leader among women in a generation which sees woman come tardily into her own."

After more in this vein, he placed a ribbon over her shoulder. A golden key hanging from the ribbon would unlock the lead-lined, mahogany box on a nearby table. Only a few knew that it was completely empty. For safety and security the radium was at the Bureau of Standards, whose officials had agreed to package it and deliver it to the ship on which Marie would return to France. President Harding had no problem with offering Marie an empty box and pretending it contained a hundred thousand dollars' worth of radium. (No stranger to subterfuge and fooling the public, he had at times concealed his mistress in a nearby cupboard.) He charmed Marie, calling her "the soul of radium" and a "noble woman, a devoted wife, a loving mother who, along with her crushing work, performed all the duties a woman must perform."

Marie replied in part: "You, the chief of this great Republic of the United States, honor me as no woman has ever been honored in America

At a White House reception, President Warren Harding (center) takes Marie Curie's arm. Also pictured are Irène (fourth from right), Eve (second from right) and Marie Meloney, who made the American trip possible (far left).

before. The destiny of a nation whose women can do what your country-women do today through you, Mr. President, is sure and safe. It gives me confidence in the destiny of democracy. I accept this rare gift, Mr. President, with the hope that I may make it serve mankind. I thank your countrywomen in the name of France. I thank them in the name of humanity which we all wish so much to make happier. I love you all, my American friends, very much." In no other photograph of her taken on this trip is she smiling more happily than on the arm of President Harding.

Though not yet in possession of the radium, she was keen to visit the Canonsburg Company in Pennsylvania that had produced it. Executives there told her about the enormous task. At first, some three hundred men in a desolate region of southern Colorado dug in the earth and dynamited rocks to load wagons with a radioactive mineral called carnotite. Burrows transported the bright yellow sandlike material eighteen miles to a mill. There, five hundred tons of it were chemically treated and crushed into tons of powder. This was sent in hundred-pound sacks sixty-five miles to a railroad depot at Placerville for a final twenty-five-hundred-mile train journey to the radium-extraction plant at Canonsburg. There, for several months, two hundred men used acids, water, and coal to boil and filter the carnotite into a few hundred pounds, then it was sent under guard to the research laboratories of the Standard Chemical Company in Pittsburgh. It took a year's labor to produce a few radium crystals from the original five hundred tons of carnotite. These crystals were kept in ten small tubes inside a lead-lined mahogany casket, which was locked and guarded and would soon be shipped to Marie.

For three hours she toured the mill and discussed the work with the men in charge, pleased to hear that they used the same method she had first introduced to extract the radium.

Absent was the charismatic and dynamic Joseph Flannery, a former funeral director, who had created the company. He certainly valued the product, having told a local newspaper that radium would cure "insanity, tuberculosis, rheumatism and anemia and a lot of cancers." But it failed him. Two years before Marie's arrival he had died of radiation sickness.

The Standard Chemical Company of Pittsburgh, Pennsylvania, had won the contract from the Radium Fund Committee to supply a gram of radium for one hundred thousand dollars. Though Marie wrote that "more than one hundred thousand dollars" were collected, that would include contributions earmarked for other purposes, such as modern equipment for her lab.

A day or so later both Marie and Meloney collapsed and canceled their planned trip to the West Coast. They rested and recuperated in Meloney's Manhattan home. Marie was suffering from hypertension and a kidney infection. Meloney had discovered that she might have a malignant tumor—a fact she hid from Marie. But the tour continued, with Harriet Eager taking over from Meloney, and the girls representing their mother—even doubling for her.

Both occasionally borrowed her university gown to face various academics apparently praising Irène or, at times, Eve, for her magnificent work and life of toil. Then each daughter replied, in accepting the honorary degree, as if she were indeed Marie Curie. It was less awkward for Irène, already a promising scientist, who, when invited to give lectures on radium, did so on three occasions and in English. Sixteen-year-old Eve, with little scientific knowledge and no scientific ambitions, aware of the absurdity of the situation, carried off the masquerades without laughing, and generally had a great time.

In her biography of Marie, Eve recalled that "when they were not representing their over-famous mother, the girls were sometimes offered amusements suited to their age; a party of tennis or boating, an elegant week-end on Long Island, an hour's swimming in Lake Michigan, a few evenings at the theater, and a night of wild delight at the colossal amusements park at Coney Island."

When Marie's condition improved, Meloney persuaded her to visit the Grand Canyon with her daughters and Harriet Eager. But the crowds who stared at Marie en route unnerved her. She began to leave trains, Eve recalled, "by the back way to escape, by leaping over rails in order to avoid the excited crowd that awaited her on the platform." At Sante Fe, where they were to change from a private compartment into a public car, according to biographer Reid, Harriet Eager found Marie with her head in her hands and trembling. "I cannot go on there," she whispered to Harriet. "I cannot go in and be stared at like a wild animal." But after a while she steeled herself to walk to her seat.

By contrast, as Eve vividly remembered, everything amused or astonished her and Irène on that trip: "The three days on the train by the Santa Fe line; across the sands of Texas; the exquisite meals in solitary little stations under a Spanish sun; the hotel at the Grand Canyon . . . of which the first sight, grandiose and almost terrifying leaves the spectator voiceless."

They returned via Chicago, where Marie received more degrees and was present at three lively receptions. The last, Eve reported, "surpassed all the others in fervor. [It was] in the Polish quarter of Chicago for a public entirely composed of Poles [where] men and women in tears tried to kiss Marie's hands or to touch her dress."

To avoid the crowds expected in Buffalo, which Marie still dreaded, the travelers got off the train one station earlier, at Niagara Falls, hoping to visit the famous waterfall in peace. But she couldn't escape the crowds. A large reception committee in Buffalo heard where Marie was and soon arrived in a caravan of cars and surrounded her.

She got a much cooler reception at her next stop, in Cambridge, Massachusetts. The academic community there was not uniformly wild about Marie Curie, especially Harvard's physics department. Although Harvard president Lawrence Lowell compared her with Isaac Newton, ex-Harvard president Charles Eliot believed that she had done nothing of importance since the death of her husband. Her former student, radiologist William Duane, now at Harvard, agreed with Eliot, but thought she deserved an honorary degree anyway. The rest of Harvard's physics department had voted against her.

Yet she paid Harvard a visit—to see Dr. Duane—and went on from there to New Haven, where Bertram Boltwood, Yale's professor of radiochemistry, a manic-depressive bachelor, anticipated her arrival with trepidation. When he first met her in 1908, he had found her a cold and uncooperative woman who "apparently has the idea that anyone associated with her laboratory is a sort of holy person." Now, thirteen years later, his college had voted to give her an honorary degree and he had been told that she wanted to meet him. He had warned the Yale authorities that he didn't want the "honor" thrust on him and that it was up to them to entertain her. Nevertheless, when she did visit his Sloane Laboratory for a couple of hours, he was "pleasantly surprised," he told his friend Ernest Rutherford, "to find that she was quite keen about scientific matters and in an unusually amiable mood, although she is in very poor physical condition and was on the verge of a breakdown. She has learned a lot of English since we saw her in Brussels and gets along quite well in conversation. I felt sorry for the poor old girl, she was a distinctly pathetic figure . . . and she seemed frightened by all the fuss people made over her."

Her friend Albert Einstein, now of relativity fame, had visited Yale the previous month, and Boltwood was pleased that the college hadn't given him an honorary degree, though he conceded that if Einstein "had been over here as a scientist and not as a Zionist it would have been entirely appropriate." (After a nervous breakdown, probably caused by overwork, Boltwood committed suicide in 1927.)

The American tour had been an overwhelming success. The one disappointment was that the Manhattan eye specialist Meloney had recommended had not helped Marie, and because of her worsening cataracts she feared that she was going blind. As she said good-bye to Meloney, she was overheard to say, "Let me look at you one more time, my dear, dear friend. This may be the last time I will ever see you." And as they embraced, they wept. Entering her cabin on the new French liner, *Paris*, Marie found it full of telegrams and flowers.

On July 2, 1921, the Curies' boat train arrived at the Gare St. Lazare after their triumphant American tour. Instead of cheering crowds, only four men waited for them: two reporters, their friend Jean Perrin, and a young Curie lab researcher, Marcel Laporte. But there was not a taxicab to be found. Apparently most drivers and most other Parisians were listening to loudspeakers in the streets relaying an account of a world championship fight: France's Georges Carpentier versus America's Jack Dempsey. Perrin and Laporte helped to unload the lead-lined casket of radium from the carriage, while a reporter asked Marie: "What do you think of the Carpentier-Dempsey match?" "I regret," she replied, "that I have no opinion on the subject."

Moments later, in the fourth round, Dempsey knocked out Carpentier.

With no bus or cab to take them home, Marie welcomed Laporte's offer to carry the radium to the laboratory and Perrin's offer to escort the Curies to their Quai de Bethune home. After taking his very heavy and valuable burden to the institute, the unfortunate Laporte found the gates locked. He had to sit outside guarding the radium until two in the morning, when the concierge arrived from his night out and let him in.

At the end of the month Meloney reported to Dr. Anson Stokes, secretary of Yale, the outstanding success of her mission. "Madame Curie," she wrote, "returned to France with her gram of radium and $22,000 worth of mesothorium and other valuable ores, bringing the precious package up to the value of $162,000. [She also] had in cash awards of scientific societies in this country $6,884.51. There is $52,000 left in the Equitable Trust Company." And there was probably another $50,000 in the offing.

But Marie was neither mentally nor physically able to make immediate use of it. As she wrote to her sister Bronia: "I have suffered so much in my life that I have no more suffering left in me. Only a real catastrophe could affect me now. I've learned what it is to be resigned and I try to find a few small joys in the grayness of daily life . . . Tell yourself you can build houses, plant trees, cultivate flowers, watch them grow and not think of anything else. We haven't much life left ahead of us, [she had thirteen years] so why go on tormenting ourselves?"

She left with her daughters for a much anticipated vacation at L'Arcouest, now so popular among academics that it was known as Sorbonne-by-the-Sea. There her mood brightened and she was delighted to swim in the island-dotted water, proud that she could outdistance Emile Borel and Jean Perrin by using an overarm stroke her daughters had taught her. She pottered in the garden of the rented house, played a word game similar to Scrabble, and began dictating her autobiography to Irène.

Afraid that the French press would misquote her as they had in the past, Marie's contract with the publisher, Macmillan, stipulated that it would not be published in France.

Though she had previously declined the Legion of Honor for herself, she made sure that Meloney got it.

When Marie returned to work in Paris, her daughters stayed on at L'Arcouest, swimming, hiking, and enjoying the antics of a cat that slept in Irène's room. Two days before Irène's twenty-fourth birthday on September 12, her mother wrote to her: "I couldn't think of you more tenderly in these circumstances than I normally do and I can't have a greater wish to kiss you on this day than any other day of our life together. It is why I think with serenity that you will have at L'Arcouest a happier anniversary than you would have in Paris and I'm happy for you without too much regret that we're not together. You know my child that you are for me an excellent friend and that you make my life easier and sweeter. I am infinitely grateful to you. I hope that your year of work ahead can be arranged to give us some satisfaction that's often hard to get . . . I look at our work with more courage when I think of your smile and your always happy face. Let us hope that the difficulties will not be too hard and we'll overcome them at least in part. I kiss you tenderly. I thank Eve for her sweet letter . . . I will write to her on Monday."

Irène replied: "I'm happy that you think I'm good for something because I want so much to make your life a little easier. When you're not with me I feel that something is missing and I shall be very happy to kiss you again before you leave for the Midi."

Having fallen in love with the Mediterranean coast on her previous visit, Marie went to rest there later in the year at the sunny seaside village of Cavalaire. On her return she was surprised to learn that some of the French establishment now regarded her as a national treasure. Baron Henri de Rothschild, for one, had created the independent Curie Foundation to raise funds for the medical use of X-rays, radium, and radon, as well as for research work in the Curie laboratory. But the most remarkable manifestation of her improved public image occurred early in 1922. Then, thirty-five members of Paris's Academy of Medicine broke a 224-year tradition of excluding women, and recommended electing Marie as a member for discovering radium and introducing Curie-therapy as a new medical treatment. Sixty-four more members of the various other academies signed the petition and all those in line for the vacant chair resigned in her favor.

When she was elected on February 7, 1922, the academy's president, M. Chauchard, saluted Marie "as a great scientist, a great-hearted woman . . . a patriot, who, in war and peace, has always done more than her duty . . . You are the first woman of France to enter an academy, but what other woman could have been so worthy?"

The same year, André Broca, a member of the academy, reported the conclusions of a four-year-study into the risks of working with radioactive material. It recommended warning researchers about "the possible dangers" while affirming that "well-known precautions make it possible to avoid them."

In Marie's lab, the only precaution researchers took was to use metal screens to prevent direct contact with the rays, although a visiting Englishman was advised to protect himself by changing "his laboratory coat frequently." However, if radium was the cause, it was having an increasing effect on Marie's eyesight. She now needed a magnifying glass to read, wrote her lecture notes in huge block letters, and placed color-coded signs on her measuring apparatus. Her daughters or a colleague began to take her elbow to guide her across the street, but at the Sorbonne, she still walked up to the rostrum of the lecture hall unassisted to address students whose faces she could not distinguish and to write on the blackboard words she could not make out.

She confided to her doctor sister, Bronia, the details of her condition: "My eyes are very weak now, and probably not much can be done about it. As for my ears, I am plagued by an almost constant, sometimes very intense, humming. I am very worried about it [as] it may interfere with my work—or even make it impossible. Radium may have had something to do with these problems, but we can't be certain of that. So these are my afflictions. Don't talk to anyone about it. I particularly don't want any rumor of it to get around." When she consulted with an oculist to determine if or when he might operate, she used an assumed name, Mme Carré.

A new member of her staff, Marcel Guillot, at first felt pity for the frail woman with an impassive, almost indifferent, expression. But when he revealed his interest in science, her expression "brightened and an extraordinary impression of human availability radiated from this woman, with her gentle voice, who then became capable of the greatest kindness."

She could also be infuriating. There are at least three versions of her enraged chief of staff, Fernand Holweck, a tall, fair-haired physicist from Alsace, finding her office locked and beating on the door as he shouted— according to the different accounts—either "Bitch! Bitch!" "You camel!" or "Pig! Pig!" Why her door was locked and what she had done to infuriate him remains a mystery. Remarkably, she didn't fire him. Perhaps Holweck's outburst was more acceptable in French—or Marie realized he was justified. It was certainly startling in what one lab assistant recalled as the usual atmosphere of a religious convent in which science was the religion and Marie the mother superior.

If some found Marie Curie cold, stubborn, and unhelpful, more had warm, positive memories of her. Lucien Desgranges remembered how each afternoon at four she insisted that he and another youngster go outside for fifteen minutes to breathe fresh air and have a snack, and never complained when they stayed out much longer. Desgranges had his eyes

The only woman to win two Nobel Prizes, Marie Curie was intensely dedicated to her work in the laboratory.

on an apartment two floors above the lab left vacant for a married couple, but as a single man he didn't qualify. However, Marie kept it vacant for two years so that when he did marry he and his wife could move in immediately. The Desgranges' two children were born in the bedroom above Marie's office.

Many lab workers recalled their work with Marie at the Radium Institute as the happiest time of their lives, among them her nephew, Maurice Curie, Jacques's son; and Ellen Gleditsch, a Norwegian, who became a friend. She remembered how Marie's slightly sad face became animated in the lab, when she often smiled, and "even laughed with a fresh, young laugh." To Gleditsch, Marie was a good administrator—Jean Perrin never met anyone better—who knew in exact detail what each student was doing and spent many hours with them. Others thought she was too strict, even harshly autocratic.

She fired those who didn't meet her expectations, even Jacques Danne, Pierre's onetime assistant. Her complaint against him was that while nominally her assistant, he continued to work on his own projects and traded on Pierre's name to promote his outside business interests. Danne was the assistant to whom Pierre referred in his last letter to Gouy, when he wrote that Danne's dream of earning "a lot of money completely turned his head." Danne ran a radium factory, edited a magazine, *Le Radium*, founded his own company, which included a research lab specializing in radioactivity, and died in 1919 from a flu epidemic. But Marie hired many more than she fired, so that, in just three years, the staff grew from seven to twenty-four.

Because of the recent war, the French still hated the Germans. Yet Paul Langevin, now a physics professor at the prestigious Collège de France and an expert on relativity, dared to invite Albert Einstein to lecture in Paris on his astonishing theory. Though a Swiss citizen, Einstein in French eyes was a German, and, even worse, to the many French anti-Semites, he was also a Jew. They launched a violent campaign against Langevin for inviting him to their city, but he did not back down. Einstein accepted, aware of the risk, hoping that his visit would "revive cordial relations between German and French scholars soured by the war."

Langevin and astronomer Charles Noordmann met Einstein at the Belgian border, then all three took the train to Paris. To avoid a possibly dangerous reception committee, the trio emulated Marie Curie's tactic in America, leaving the train on the side away from the platform, crossing the rails, and exiting the Gare du Nord station by a side door. As it happened, there was no violence during his stay and he was generally surrounded by friends.

Marie Curie was among the audience for his lecture at the Collège de France amphitheater on March 31, 1922, which he gave in French and repeated at the Sorbonne. The French press, like almost everyone else, didn't get the theory, but raved about Einstein's sweet smile, noble face, and unforgettable eyes. By this time Langevin had returned to his wife after his controversial friendship with Marie, but he and Marie still remained on good terms, and after Einstein's lecture both went to the Borels' apartment. His mission of reconciliation largely succeeded, but the French Academy decided not to let him lecture to its august group when thirty members threatened to walk out if he walked in.

To prevent such incidents in the future, both Marie and Einstein were among the handful of the world's most eminent scholars invited to join the International Committee on Intellectual Cooperation, an arm of the League of Nations. Its stated purpose was to avoid future conflicts by reuniting intellectuals of different nations isolated by the war. Strangely, Germany was denied membership in the League of Nations itself, and many Germans condemned it as a tool of French and British imperialism. Einstein, being Swiss, accepted the invitation as a representative of German science, but before he could attend, he resigned. He certainly lacked neither moral nor physical courage, but he thought that caution was the better part of valor after nationalist fanatics assassinated his friend Walter Rathenau, a German Jew who was Germany's foreign minister, and he himself received death threats calling him a traitor for joining the league. Einstein told Planck, "I am on the nationalists' list to be assassinated."

He stayed in Berlin, however, attended Rathenau's funeral, wrote an obituary eulogizing him, and preached peace and international reconciliation in the Reichstag. But he said that he had no wish to represent people who wouldn't choose him as their representative and with whom he fundamentally disagreed.

Greatly disappointed, Marie asked Einstein to reconsider, writing: "It is precisely because dangerous and prejudicial currents of opinion do exist that it is necessary to fight them . . . I think that your friend Rathenau, whom I judge to have been an honest man, and whose sad fate I regret, would have encouraged you to make an effort at peaceful intellectual collaboration. Surely you can change your mind. Your friends have kind memories of you."

He explained to his friend Maurice Solovine, "Since the hideous murder of Rathenau, I am being constantly warned . . . Anti-Semitism is very strong." Nevertheless, despite the threats, he agreed to Marie Curie's request to rejoin the Intellectual Cooperation Committee.

A few weeks later, in the fall of 1922, Einstein won the Nobel Prize for physics for discovering the photoelectric effect. But before he could attend the next meeting of the League of Nations, he was enraged by its failure to act when French and Belgian troops occupied the Ruhr, Germany's industrial heartland, claiming the coal and iron there as reparation payments for the war. Demanding that his name be stricken from the list of members on the committee, he told Marie Curie that he knew that she would be justifiably annoyed with him, but he was convinced that the league was a willing tool of power politics.

Marie replied, "I grant you willingly that the League isn't perfect. It has no chance of being so since men are not perfect. But it can improve things . . . It is the first attempt at an international understanding without which civilization is threatened with disappearing." Again, backed up by Lorentz and Eric Drummond, the league's secretary, Marie prevailed, and Einstein promised to support the committee.

Like almost everyone else, Einstein did not know that during the torrid summer of 1923 Marie underwent a cataract operation under the assumed name of Carré, in an effort to hide her failing sight. Complications caused her to stay in the hospital, eyes bandaged, for several days and nights. At the time, Irène was hiking and camping out in the mountains with a new Corsican friend and fellow Sorbonne graduate, Angèle Pompei. So Eve stayed in the hospital, comforting and reading to her mother until she recovered. At best, the operation was only partly successful, because she eventually had to undergo three more.

Soon after her recovery from the operation, Marie traveled to Geneva as part of the League of Nations' International Committee of Intellectual Cooperation. They adopted her suggestion to have "scientific vacation programs in which young scientists, both men and women, from one country, would go to another during the summer." But no government was willing to finance it.

In Paris, on December 26, 1923, the twenty-fifth anniversary of radium's discovery, an enormous crowd flocked to the Sorbonne's amphitheater to honor Marie: military brass, teachers and students from great schools and universities at home and abroad, scientists of many disciplines, politicians, reporters, friends, and relatives. Her sisters, Bronia and Hela, and brother, Joseph, came from Poland, eyes shining with pride. Several men who had played significant roles in her life were on the platform with Marie: the president of France, Alexandre Millerand, who presided, had been one of her lawyers during the Langevin scandal; Marguerite Borel's father, Paul Appell, head of the Sorbonne and now president of the Curie Foundation, who had once tried to fire her from the university and banish her to Poland; Jean Perrin of the Sorbonne's Faculty of Science, who had fought for her to stay; Antoine Béclère, representing the Academy of Medicine, who had encouraged her to pursue her X-ray work in the war; her close friend and collaborator André Debierne; and Fernand Holweck, chief of staff at the Radium Institute, who had once screamed at Marie in frustrated rage.

Now Holweck calmly and efficiently helped Irène to demonstrate several of her parents' early experiments by projecting onto a screen the image of gold leaves rising and falling as, using a sample of radium, they charged, then discharged a gold-leaf electroscope. Debierne read the groundbreaking 1898 report by Pierre Curie, Mme Curie, and G. Bemont, announcing the discovery of radium. President Millerand announced that recognizing what a treasure they had in Marie Curie, the French government had unanimously voted to give her an annual pension of forty thousand francs, which would continue after her death to her daughters.

The Dutch physicist Hendrik Lorentz, representing foreign scientists, spoke of the extremely promising new team of Marie and Irène Curie and said that although Eve might like to emulate her sister, we can't all be physicists.

His wisecrack probably went down well with everyone, even Eve, though she felt that it was condescending of some scientists to assume that theirs was the only profession that mattered. At nineteen, unlike Irène, she had no idea what she wanted to do with her life. Marie never pressured her to follow in Irène's footsteps, but exposure to the company of scientists absorbed in their work may have been an insidious pressure to join them. Almost all her mother's friends were brilliant scientists—Marguerite Borel, the novelist (pen name Camille Marbo), was a rare exception. And it was the family tradition. As well as her mother and sister, her maternal grandfather, uncle Jacques, and cousin Maurice were physicists; her paternal great grandfather, Paul; grandfather, Eugene; cousin Joseph; aunt Bronia; and uncle Casimir were physicians.

When Eve showed musical precocity, Marie had encouraged her with mixed feelings. She bought her a grand piano and hired teachers, then was disturbed by her hours at the keyboard. Marie once confided to Irène her dread of "being cooped up with Eve's piano practicing, if the weather [is] bad in L'Arcouest. We will have to reconcile the scientific work represented by us two with the musical art represented by Evette, which is much easier in good weather than in rain." But Eve never mentioned this problem in her biography of her mother.

Eve's recollection of her mother's public appearances might explain why she had no wish to emulate her: "We have seen Marie Curie in the evening of her life at the mercy of the admiration of crowds, received by presidents, ambassadors and kings in all latitudes. One picture, always the same, dominates the memory of these fetes and processions for me; the bloodless, expressionless, almost indifferent face."

CHAPTER 13

Radium: Miracle Cure or Menace?

1924–1930

In July 1924 Marie took twenty-year-old Eve with her to Geneva for a fourth session of the Committee on Intellectual Cooperation, an arm of the League of Nations, where she was pleased to find her friends Langevin and Einstein again among the group. Writing to Irène, she noted that despite the bad weather, Eve wasn't bored. Perhaps, she added, it was because she saw "a lot of M. Einstein who is very sweet to her." And perhaps because Eve was also planning her debut as a concert pianist.

At the session, Marie suggested awarding international scholarships to students and professors, and donating scientific equipment to the newly independent Hungary and Poland. But as Europe was in the financial doldrums, the response was disappointing. However, she remained one of the most positive, energetic, and conscientious members of the committee.

Einstein had expressed an interest in Irène's work, and Marie urged her to send him her report of the distribution of alpha rays recently published in the *Journal of Physics*.

Marie had remained such close friends with Paul Langevin that even when he asked her to help his mistress, Elie Montel—formerly his student, who later bore him a son, Paul Langevin-Montel—she readily gave her a job at the institute. Langevin had also strongly recommended another of his students, Frédéric Joliot, top of his class at the School of Physics and Chemistry—the technical school where Pierre Curie spent twenty-two years, and where, in an adjoining workshop, he and Marie had discovered radium. Langevin warned Joliot that as he had not been educated at the prestigious Ecole Normale, from which a third of the country's physicists had graduated, his only hope for a distinguished career would be to make a great discovery. The prospect of being Marie's technical assistant overjoyed twenty-four-year-old Joliot, who as a student had briefly worked as a trainee engineer in a Luxembourg steel mill before being called up for military service. He was such a fan of the Curies that when he was eight he had cut their photograph from a magazine, which his artistic sister, Marguerite, had framed. It still graced a wall of his home.

Joliot later recalled his first meeting with this woman he idolized: She was "at her desk, small, with gray hair and very bright eyes. I sat before her in an officer's uniform (at the time I was doing my military service in the anti-gas corps) and I was very nervous." Especially when she interrupted him with: " 'What! you don't have your bachot [bachelor's degree]? If you want to do any teaching, you will need your second bach [master's degree] and your [teaching] license!" Then, to his relief and surprise, she asked: "Can you begin work tomorrow?"

Because he still had three weeks of military service to complete, Marie wrote to his colonel requesting Joliot's immediate release. As he took her letter with him, Irène glimpsed a slim, muscular young man in a blue officer's uniform leaving her mother's office. Next evening she saw him again, face-to-face. Eager to start work, instead of mailing Marie's letter, he had taken it to his colonel and now had the positive reply. Back at the lab, told that Madame Curie had gone home, he went there and rang the bell. Irène answered the door, heard his brief explanation, and, instead of inviting him in, left to fetch her mother. Marie read the letter and told him to report to Cailliet, the technical assistant he was to replace, next morning, December 17, 1924. He would be paid 540 francs (about sixty dollars) a month—half his pay at the steel mill—from a Rothschild grant.

Leading him along its narrow corridors, Cailliet gave him a tour of the Curie Laboratory over the next few days to meet some thirty or so physicists and chemists of various nationalities, many of them young women, each with his or her own small room filled with scientific equipment. André Debierne, Marie's friend and second in command, startled him by asserting that there was nothing more to learn about radioactivity because everything had been discovered. In those days, many physicists agreed with him.

On January 1, 1925, Joliot was handed over to Irène, also Marie's technical assistant. She was hardly more encouraging than Debierne. After an indifferent greeting, she assigned him to what would become an ongoing research task: to study the chemical properties of radioactive elements, especially polonium. Knowing next to nothing about radioactivity,

he followed her instructions carefully—to determine the electrical properties of extremely thin sheets of metal on different supports, such as mica,
quartz, and glass. Then he went beyond Irène's instructions, to conduct
experiments for his doctorate thesis, investigating extremely thin layers of
gold foil that worked as electrodes and simultaneously allowed the passage
of polonium's alpha rays. After an intense study of the gold's preparation
and physical properties, he deposited a gold layer on a support. He then
dissolved the support in acetone, ending up with an unsupported metal
plate a few hundred-thousandths of a millimeter thick—a remarkable
achievement.

As Joliot biographer Biquard explained: "This process was later used
by the British physicist G. P. Thomson in studying the diffraction of electrons [for which Thomson won the 1937 Nobel Prize for physics]. Joliot
did not stake further claims in this direction, but it is only right to recognize that he had performed a true piece of pioneering work in a field
which today has seen great scientific and industrial development."

At first Joliot shared the prevailing view of Irène as cold, aloof, and
spoiled, and thought she deserved her nickname, "the Crown Princess."
But he gradually had a very different take on her. As he still had only an
elementary knowledge of radioactivity and she was an expert, he peppered
her with questions. But as she was often too preoccupied with her own
research to respond immediately, he began waiting for her after work to
walk her home, asking questions all the way. Soon they were also meeting
on weekends to continue their peripatetic conversations through Paris
streets and parks. Then he discovered that this girl (as he called Irène,
though he was three years her junior) was not the "block of ice" others
called her, but, in his words, "an extraordinary person, sensitive and
poetic, and in many things gave me the impression of being the embodiment of what her father had been." Knowing a lot about Pierre Curie
from reading about him, and listening to the talk of teachers who knew
him, Joliot "rediscovered in his daughter the same purity, commonsense
and tranquility." He also found that her cold appearance was misleading:
she was extremely kind, with a passionate nature and a lively sense of
humor. And he had no doubt about her scientific aptitude as he watched
her working quietly at her desk and marveled at her speed, ingenuity, and
dexterity in handling dangerously radioactive polonium.

They had such different personalities that if opposites do attract, they
should have fallen into each others' arms on sight. He was a charming
extrovert; an impetuous and talkative chain-smoker, a cigarette always

dangling from his lips (for which Marie eventually banished him to a lab in the basement). Full of energy and drive, with dark hair and a direct gaze, he seemed always on the move. He hunted, fished, flirted, painted, played soccer (as a goal-scoring inside left), Ping-Pong, and the piano, and was enchanted by Edith Piaf belting out her heartfelt songs. He had the knack of persuading others to adopt his views by reasoned, nonconfrontational argument and was so charismatic that everyone in the lab began to call him Fred, while continuing to address each other with customary formality. Yet being hypersensitive about the opinion of others, he was hurt when cynics quipped that he was an opportunist, courting Irène to advance his career.

Irène couldn't have cared less about her "image" and was frank to the point of bluntness. To her, personal relations and social affairs were simply a nuisance that interfered with her work. Introspective and impatient of small talk, she didn't hunt, fish, paint, or smoke; she had few friends and no musical talent. But she loved poetry, especially Kipling's, and excelled at swimming, skiing, and hiking in the mountains. On long weekend walks together, often through Fontainebleau's forest, the couple discovered how much more they had in common than love of science and France. They were both humanists and pacifists. Two of Joliot's brothers had died young, one as a soldier in the recent World War, and Irène had witnessed its horrors firsthand.

Politically, both sympathized with the underdogs, Irène influenced by her paternal grandfather and Joliot by his mentor, Paul Langevin. Joliot's father had taken part in the workers' rebellion, known as the Commune, in 1871. This first organized uprising of the workers against the capitalist system was also supported by Irène's grandfather. But Joliot felt that his own father had betrayed his class because after becoming a successful businessman and financially secure, he had advised his children not to bother with politics. Instead, Joliot took an active interest in the welfare of the workers. At seventeen he felt more sympathy for Karl Marx's view that "the bourgeois class had grabbed all the benefits of the industrial age, exploiting those who should reap the profits of their own labor" than for his own father's selfish attitude.

Although Joliot's maternal grandfather had a royal connection as Napoleon III's cook, the only servant allowed to be present when the emperor ate, and who conversed with him when they were alone together, his daughter, Joliot's Protestant mother, was a staunch liberal republican, who supported left-of-center representative democratic government and

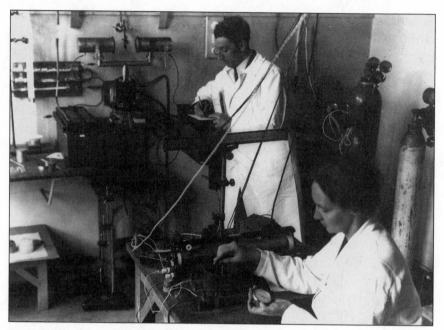

Irène and Frédéric Joliot-Curie worked together at the Radium Institute in the late 1920s, a time when there were many reports that radium could be deadly as well as lifesaving.

was opposed to monarchies and theocracies. Growing up in Alsace with its large German population, she had shocked the neighbors by being friendly with Jewish families. Irène's mother, too, was a liberal republican who hated bigotry and injustice.

Joliot's early days at the lab were shadowed by the premature deaths of Marie's former students, thirty-five-year-old Marcel Demalander and forty-one-year-old Maurice Demenitroux. Demalander had died of severe anemia and Demenitroux of leukemia. The *New York World* gave their obituaries an optimistic spin, noting that although 140 other scientists had died through experimenting with radium, the latest precautions make "the manipulation of radium or the use of X-rays as innocuous to both operator and patient as the pounding of a typewriter. The exploration has cost many lives and untold agonies, but the martyrs would undoubtedly be the first to assert that the gain in knowledge had been worth the price. Both discoveries are now thoroughly established as safe, healing agencies of the utmost value." Of course, this wasn't true.

The death of Demenitroux got more play on the front page of the *New York Times* on January 4, 1925, where he was described as a distinguished radiologist, a collaborator of Pierre Curie and Mme Curie, and a victim of scientific research. "Like Professor Bergonie and several other eminent scientists [Demalander and Dr. Charles Valliant], M. Demenitroux had been resigned for months to death as inevitable, but continued to work to the last. The cause of death was a malady of the blood caused by the action of radium rays. He had been kept alive for many weeks by blood transfusions . . . In Bordeaux an autopsy was performed on the body of Professor Bergonie by his pupils and a group of scientists, in accordance with the wishes of this martyr to science, whose experimentation with X-rays was largely devoted to search for a cure for cancer." Bergonie had forbidden any funeral services, asking only that his body be used to study "the type of affection that is killing or maiming so many experimenters in his branch of science."

Four days later the *Chicago Tribune* reported that Dr. Maximo Menard, director of X-ray at Chicago's Cochin Hospital, was saved from "the same fate and mysterious malady" as Professor Bergonie. After constant exposure to X-rays, Menard "suffered a strange loss of red corpuscles," followed by "enormous growths which necessitated the removal of several of his fingers, and recently he despaired of his life. Dr. Regaud, director of the laboratory of the Radium Institute, however, applied to the . . . region a wax tube containing radium, the cancer growths being cured within a few days, he said. Dr. Regaud admitted that a cure might not be affected in all cases, but his success in Dr. Menard's case gave hope that science was nearing a solution."

Told of the deaths of Demenitroux and Bergonie, Marie Curie ordered an investigation. In the resulting report, a former colleague, I. Jaloustre, said that the men had died after working with a radioactive element, thorium X. Previously Demenitroux had worked with radium for twenty years and the only symptoms he felt—common to other radium workers—were occasional fatigue and aching limbs. But just before his death, he had whispered to a friend, Albert Laborde (who had worked with Pierre Curie), his conviction that recent exposure to radium was the culprit.

Marie believed both victims were partly to blame because they had worked without screens in a windowless, unventilated room. Not that she was unsympathetic: she gave her name to a fund for the widows of the two men—Demenitroux also left a small child—and contributed a thousand francs. In her 1921 book, *Radiology and the War*, Marie had warned that prolonged exposure to X-rays—though painless—could cause gangrene and death to both the operator and the patient.

In 1925, at the request of the French Academy of Medicine, she joined experts Béclère and Regaud on a commission to improve safety measures.

Their report, published in the academy's bulletin, emphasized the danger of working with radioactive material and strongly recommended enclosing it in thick, heavy metal, to protect the workers behind lead screens, ventilating hoods to clear the air, using tongs rather than fingers to handle radioactive material, and periodically testing the researchers' blood for abnormalities. All these measures had ostensibly been in effect in Marie's laboratory for several years, although "she had always scorned the precautions which she so severely imposed on her pupils." The committee also suggested that any place or vehicle in which radioactive material was prepared, manipulated, or transported should be labeled as a health hazard and regulated by the Ministry of Work and Health. But no such precautions had been taken in the United States.

There, a New Jersey dentist, Dr. Theodore Blum, had discovered that several female patients were dangerously radioactive. His first clue was that they all had diseased jawbones that failed to heal after dental work. His second, that they were all employed at an Orange, New Jersey, factory, painting watch dials and military instruments to glow in the dark by using a radium-based paint. His final clue was that to bring their brushes to a point, the women habitually licked the bristles—still containing fragments of the radium-laced paint, a practice known as "tipping."

Blum concluded that having ingested radium, his patients had "been invaded—yes, and pervaded—by radioactivity." The women had absolutely no warning that the luminous radium paint was dangerous. Some even put it on their teeth to surprise their boyfriends after dark with glowing smiles. Americans and Europeans generally thought of it as a "natural" element and a miracle cure-all, sold over the counter in patent medicines, for almost everything from impotence to insanity. Doctors and patients drank radioactive water as a tonic. Women sought to regain their lost youth with radium face creams and relaxed in radium baths. Children ingested radium-laced candies and sodas.

On May 29, 1925, Dr. F. L. Hoffman, a Prudential Insurance statistician, told a meeting of the American Medical Association that "five women had died and ten others have been stricken with a new disease believed to be 'radium necrosis,' because of infection received while painting watch dials with a radium preparation." He suggested that this was a new occupational disease and hoped that stopping the women from licking the paintbrushes would prevent further fatalities.

County medical examiner Harrison Martland launched an independent investigation and confirmed Dr. Blum's view that the radioactivity was pervasive. The moment he held a radioactive counter near a dying thirty-five-year-old dial painter with bleeding gums and inexplicable bruises all over her body, the instrument began to click. And after analyzing her breath, he determined that she had inhaled radon, a gaseous form of radium. While conducting her autopsy, Martland wrapped a sliver of her bone in a piece of dental film. It fogged the film. He believed that radium and mesothorium, an isotope of radium used in the luminous paint, had killed her and a company physicist who died about the same time. Other radioactive dial painters he examined—all young women—were so crippled from bone fractures that they couldn't stand without support, and their jaws were so fragile that they "were in danger of snapping when [they] yawned."

The director of the United States Radium Corporation, the company that had employed the women, William J. A. Bailey, denied that there was any evidence that radium was responsible for their deaths, and cited Marie Curie as a witness for the defense. "No one has worked longer or with greater amounts of radium than has Mme Curie," he said. "For over twenty-five years she has toiled increasingly in her laboratory and today she is not only alive but reported recently to be in excellent health."

In fact, the fragile Marie Curie, with almost constant ringing in her ears and radium-scarred hands, was facing a third cataract operation. Eventually the company conceded that radium might have caused the dial workers' health problems and ordered that the brushes be sterilized before use and that the workers no longer point brushes with their lips. Three families filed lawsuits against the United States Radium Corporation, which were settled out of court for a total of thirteen thousand dollars. When Marie Curie learned of the tragic deaths and afflictions, she also advised the survivors to stop licking their paintbrushes, and to counteract anemia by eating raw calf's liver.

At the same time Marie was getting encouraging reports of radium's healing powers. A baby girl had been brought to the institute in December 1923 with a vivid birthmark on her face and head. After radium had been applied to it over three years—as before-and-after photos showed—it had completely disappeared. There was also good news from Marie's American friend Meloney, who had been keeping the diagnosis of her own suspected malignant tumor to herself. Now she confided to Marie that she had undergone experimental radium treatment. Either the tumor was nonmalignant or the treatment was successful, because she lived for another twenty years. Even before Marie's trip to America, her avant-garde dancer friend, Loie Fuller, had been diagnosed with breast cancer and sought Marie's advice. Should she undergo surgery or radium therapy? Several surgeons had recommended surgery. Only one had suggested radium therapy, which he claimed had an 80 percent chance of success. As always, Marie had asked for Claude Regaud's expert opinion and relayed it to Fuller. Presumably, he advised radium. Encouraged, Fuller had replied, "Dear, dear friend. Once again in your debt." Now, three years later, at sixty-three, she was not only alive but back in Paris still dancing up a storm, competing with the sensational young African American dancer Josephine Baker. (Fuller's last performance was in *Shadow Ballet*, in London in 1927. She died a year later, aged sixty-six, of pneumonia.)

With radium hitting the headlines, it was hardly surprising that the *New York Times* decided to cover Irène's defense of her doctoral thesis on March 30, 1925. A thousand people squeezed into the Sorbonne's amphitheater to hear her present and defend her views. Dressed as simply as her mother for a similar event more than twenty years earlier, Irène had gathered her notes from her Quai de Bethune apartment and walked to the nearby university where—despite the huge crowd—she calmly and confidently spoke of her work on polonium's alpha rays. As Eve recalled, "The examinations for the bachelor's and master's degrees, which had made even our mother in her time feverish and nervous, were for Irène, just like any other days." Her thesis was titled "Research on the Alpha Rays of Polonium: Oscillations of the Trajectory, Initial Velocity and Ionizing Effects." To learn more about the atomic nucleus, she explained, she had bombarded it with polonium, and was fascinated by the way alpha particles—emitted by the radioactive polonium as it disintegrated—slowed down as they passed through matter. Polonium, of course, was the radioactive element her mother had discovered and named after her beloved mother country. Irène had dedicated the thesis "to Mme Curie by her daughter and her pupil." But Marie wasn't there, probably because, as the the *New York Times* suggested, "she wanted all attention to be given to her daughter and to avoid having the meeting turned into a personal tribute to herself." Much of Irène's talk was doubtless over the heads of many in the audience, but when she finished they applauded as if she were a star of the Folies Bergère. So did her examiners.

Marie had arranged a tea and champagne party in the institute's garden to celebrate Irène's success, to which the entire staff was invited. On several tables under the lime trees, developing dishes from the photographic darkroom were filled with cookies. Tea had been brewed in laboratory flasks, the water heated over bunsen burners, and lab beakers were used as teacups. Langevin stopped by for a champagne toast and predicted a bright future for the new doctor.

Less wary of the press than Marie, Irène answered a young woman reporter's questions. No, she did not consider science an unsuitable career for women, and she believed that the scientific ability of men and women was identical. She considered science to be the fundamental interest of her life, but did not preclude the possibility of having a family. She thought radium was less dangerous in the laboratory than in industry because she and her colleagues protected themselves with periodic blood tests. She admitted to having once had a slight radium burn, but said that did no serious damage. Yet according to Curie biographer Robert Reid, Marie had recently told a new young Polish worker who was guiding her steps—because of her failing sight—as she walked home in the dark, "that she did not fully understand radium's effects on the human body."

As if to avoid more probing reporters, Marie whisked Irène away for a tour of Algeria. Soon after, Marie was back in Warsaw to lay the cornerstone of the Marie Sklowdowska–Curie Institute, which her sister Bronia had energetically and successfully promoted. She had persuaded the state, the city, and several Polish institutions to support it, and had distributed thousands of postcards to the public asking them to "Buy a brick" for the institute. At the ceremony, Marie met Stanislav Wojciechowski, cofounder of the Polish Socialist Party—a leader of the struggle for Polish independence—and now the second president of the free Polish republic. He had known Marie thirty-three years earlier when he was in exile in Paris, and recalled the "traveling cushion" that she lent him when he was returning on a secret mission to Russian-controlled Poland. Yes, she replied with a laugh, "I even remember that you forgot to return it to me."

While in Poland, Marie attended a play at the Popular Theatre, where M. Kotarbinsk was starring. He was the touring actor she had a crush on in her teens and, as he was leaving town, had run after at the railroad station with a bunch of flowers. Now he recognized her in the audience and complimented her from the stage.

Irène often went with her mother on these journeys abroad as her scientific partner and caring friend, and when they returned, Eve invariably met them at the railroad station platform, noticing, with an eye for telling details, how her mother always clutched in one hand her big leather handbag stuffed with research papers, several eyeglass cases, presents, and cardboard banquet menus, on the backs of which she intended to scribble math calculations. And in the other hand, a bouquet of flowers, now wilted, which someone gave her on the journey and she felt honor bound to keep until she reached home.

Eve was lonely when they were away, with only a cat for company, and when she had finished practicing on her grand piano and was tired of reading, would press her head against the third-floor apartment window listening to seagulls and counting tugboats as they moved along the Seine.

She had toyed with the idea of being a journalist. A few years earlier, the thought would have horrified Marie, who then, from personal experience, had a low opinion of the press. But that view had been modified by knowing the marvelous embodiment of journalistic integrity, Marie Meloney. So Marie encouraged Eve to follow her dreams. Eve was uncertain, and at times she wished her mother would give her directions—if only to allow her the chance to rebel.

Now, at twenty-one, having no interest in or aptitude for science, she had finally decided to be a professional pianist. And she was naturally concerned with what to wear for her debut. Her interest in fashion puzzled Marie, who would sit on the divan in her daughter's bedroom and comment critically as she dressed for an evening out. As Eve remembered, Marie once exclaimed: "Oh, my poor darling! What *dreadful* heels! No, you'll never make me believe that women were made to walk on stilts . . . And what sort of new style is this, to have the back of the dress cut out? Décolletage in front was bearable, just; but these miles and miles of naked back! First of all, it's indecent; secondly, it makes you run the risk of pleurisy, and thirdly, it's ugly: the third argument ought to move you if the others don't . . . However, apart from this, your dress is pretty. But you wear black too much. Black isn't suited to your age."

Then, as Eve completed her makeup, Marie said: "I have no objection in principle to this daubing and smearing. I know it has always been done. In ancient Egypt the women invented far worse things . . . I can only tell you one thing. I think it's dreadful. To console myself, I'm coming tomorrow morning to kiss you in your bed, before you've had time to put those horrors on yourself. And now, you must run, my dear child. Good night. Ah! By the way, you haven't anything you can give me to read?" Colette and Kipling were among their shared favorites.

Marie's hard-earned advice to Eve about romance had been: "It is unsatisfactory to let all one's interest in life depend on feelings as stormy as the feeling of love." Love as well as radon were certainly in the air in the Radium Institute. Buoyed by getting his bachelor's degree in July 1925, and having fallen in love with Irène, Joliot planned to propose. This extremely handsome lady-killer, as his colleague Bertrand Goldschmidt called him, had also decided that if she didn't say yes, he would remain a bachelor for life. An echo of Pierre Curie.

One account has Marie laughing when Irène told her that she meant to marry "Fred." It was certainly a surprise. Eve recalled that it was "one morning [at breakfast] in 1926 [when] Irène calmly announced to her family her engagement to Frédéric Joliot, the most brilliant and the most high-spirited of the workers at the Institute of Radium. The existence of the household was turned upside down . . . A young man suddenly appeared in the female household where, except for a few familiars, nobody ever penetrated."

Yet soon after, Irène agreed to fulfill her promise to accompany her mother for a several-months-long trip to Brazil—arranged before the engagement—where Marie was to lecture and promote Franco-Brazilian relations. In Rio de Janeiro they swam in the ocean and took a flight in a hydroplane. Each morning, Irène woke early to make Marie's breakfast, carry it on a tray to her bed, and chat with her about such topics as the behavior of polonium on nickel and magnetic deflection, as well as the previous day's adventures and their literary favorites. And of course they also spoke of Irène's forthcoming marriage to Joliot.

Although his handwriting was almost illegible, in writing to Irène he managed to convey that he had passed the second of two exams on the road to his doctorate and to tell her that he loved her. "What makes life interesting in the lab," he wrote, "are the people who animate it. And since your departure I find it empty. I feel very strongly that I am most attached to the laboratory only when you are there. I shall not return with any happiness until you are there. Because what I love and adore in you, ma chérie, is that you do everything possible to create this spirited atmosphere."

In her reply she said that she longed to embrace him, to rub her hands through his hair until it stood on end, and asked whether he was smoking a reasonable or an unreasonable number of cigarettes. "Does such discretion on your part signify that the second hypothesis is the correct one? Try not to smoke like a factory smokestack, speed at a hundred kilometers-an-hour on your motorbike, and do all the other unreasonable things of which you are capable." In handling Joliot's chain-smoking, Irène demonstrated her direct no-nonsense manner: she simply grabbed the cigarette out of his mouth.

On September 12, 1926, Marie and Irène returned to France aboard the SS *Lutetia* and Irene invited Joliot to join her in L'Arcouest, where he explored the fishing possibilities and she handled the paperwork needed for Marie to have a small cottage built there.

L'Arcouest attracted an extraordinary friendly and compatible community of scientists, artists, and politicians under the leadership of Charles Seignobos, known as "Le Capitaine," a short, energetic, slightly humpbacked professor of history, invariably dressed in a white flannel suit with thin black stripes and a tattered straw hat, and who sported a monocle. The door was never locked on his granite house overlooking the bay of Paimpol, and the house was full of paying and nonpaying guests. To Eve Curie, words could not "indicate the charming devotion of which he was the object, nor above all by what characteristics of his nature he had deserved the veneration, tenderness and comradeship which surrounded him. This elderly bachelor had always had all men's friendship, and more wives than any pasha: thirty, forty companions, of ages from two to eighty . . . If you wanted to talk physics there were Jean Perrin, Marie Curie, André Debierne, Victor Auger. Mathematics, integral calculus? Apply to Emile Borel, draped in his bathrobe like a Roman emperor in his toga. Biology, astrophysics? Louis Lapicque or Charles Maurain could answer you. And as for the enchanter, Charles Seignobos, the numerous children of the colony whispered to each other in terror that he 'knew all his history.'" The regulars called themselves "sailors," mocked strangers as "philistines," and discouraged them from joining the insular group. Friends and relatives with no passion for the sea—one day roaring "like a creature outraged," and the next purring "like a gentle pet"—were tolerated, but the butt of endless jokes. The most expert sailors, familiar with the currents of the bay, equally at home aboard ship, rowboat, or swimming in the ocean, were known as "crocodiles." Marie had graduated from "elephant" to "sailor," but never expected to become a "crocodile."

Someone described the group as practicing a sort of snobbish egalitarianism: superficially informal and democratic—but underneath, rank, being part of the establishment, wealth, and influence counted. When Irène first introduced Joliot to them, only Seignobos and Jean Perrin welcomed him wholeheartedly. Marie, who was enjoying a brief vacation at Cavalaire with Eve and Debierne, sensed that he would be regarded as an intruder and tried to soften the impact, writing to Irène that she hoped that Joliot would realize that he was "not obliged to keep company with all the Arcouestian world, if that was not agreeable to him."

Some still regarded his courtship of Irène with suspicion. According to his colleague Bertrand Goldschmidt, who was part of the French scientific establishment, Joliot "had an inferiority complex all his life. Very strange. Probably because he wasn't part of the establishment. Probably because [he chuckled] he'd married the daughter of the boss."

Lew Kowarski, another colleague who was not part of the establishment, believed that "Joliot was a complete outsider in the scientific establishment, which was very closely linked by family ties and so on. He was selected more or less by Irène as her husband—a kind of prince consort to the princess. And the establishment treated him at first with contempt. He had a kind of slightly coarse good looks [and as a member] of the peculiar community which had its summer quarters in Brittany [he was known] essentially as Irène's gigolo. That was supposed to be his defining function. Yet he knew that he was more able than all the people surrounding him who sneered at him, and it left him with a bitterness, which probably you will find no traces of in any literature about Joliot, but about which I can testify firsthand." He never felt that he was truly accepted at L'Arcouest and learned to spend time there on his own terms: sailing and fishing with "a joyous intensity the others did not share. He allowed himself to be engulfed by nature as he had when a boy on expeditions with his father." Not that he was eager to be accepted. With the exception of the Perrins, Seignobos, and his family, Joliot preferred the company and conversations of the local fishermen and farm laborers.

He and Irène were married by the mayor in the 4th arrondissement town hall in Paris on October 9, 1926, with only immediate family members and close friends present. True to their mutual passion, they went straight from lunch with their guests at the Curies' apartment to work at the lab. That night Irène returned home and Joliot slept at his family's Montparnasse house, delaying their honeymoon until the next day, when Marie left for a week of lecturing in Copenhagen, taking Eve with her.

To save her strength, Marie warned Martin Knudsen, her Danish host, that she would only accept dinner invitations from him and Niels Bohr, and to rest as much as possible, she would skip lunches. At one place they stayed, according to biographer Robert Reid, Eve was so determined to protect Marie's health that she "was not beyond removing one uncooperative hostess from her bedroom, and putting her mother in, when it was clearly the best-heated room in the house." Eve, however, doubts that she would have dared to be that rude or that her mother would have approved.

The newlyweds had the Quai de Bethune apartment to themselves for the week while Marie and Eve were in Denmark. But their carefree life was short-lived. Irène soon became pregnant and Joliot had an appendix operation from which he recovered very slowly. In March they briefly rested on the island of Porquerolles, where he indulged his passion for fishing. He had arrived with the wrong kind of bait but was able to buy the right kind locally. Otherwise, as Irène wrote to Marie, in a moment

The Joliot-Curies shortly after their marriage in 1926. He invariably beat her at tennis, which explains his grin. Their successful professional partnership, like that of her parents, would also win them a shared Nobel Prize.

of nervous prostration he would have killed himself or her. She obviously handled his momentary despair with appropriate concern, judging by his letter to his mother in which he wrote that he had an adorable wife.

On their return they moved into a fifth-floor apartment Marie had given them near the Latin Quarter, opposite a children's park and playground. So many scientists who vacationed at L'Arcouest also lived in the building, which Marie partly owned, that it was known as the Sorbonne Beach Annex.

Marie didn't expect the marriage to last, especially as Joliot was three years younger than her daughter. And because under French law he would have control of Irène's property, Marie had insisted on a prenuptial agreement stipulating that Irène would inherit the use of the laboratory's radium. His mother-in-law also humiliated Joliot when VIPs visited the Radium Institute, by either ignoring him or introducing him as "the young man who married Irene." Naturally she missed Irène's loving companionship, even though the couple lunched with her several times a week.

Her attitude to Joliot changed after the birth of Irène and Joliot's daughter, Hélène, on September 19, 1927. Then, like everyone else, she began to call him Fred with a special tenderness, according to Irène. And she confided to her friend Jean Perrin, a recent Nobel Prize winner in physics: "The boy is a skyrocket!" In time, the discussions at lunch between Marie and Joliot were so animated and nonstop that Irène felt she was being excluded and had to demand a chance to join in.

Irène welcomed motherhood, confiding to a friend that if she had not brought a child into the world, "I would never have forgiven myself for having missed such an astonishing experience." Soon after, doctors told her that she had tuberculosis and should rest and never have another child. Instead, she returned to work almost immediately, often with Joliot as her partner.

Although on jointly written pieces in academic journals their names appeared as Irène Curie and Frédéric Joliot, in popular magazines they signed articles as by Irène and Frédéric Joliot-Curie. Joliot's explanation for the hyphenated addition of Curie was his admiration for Irène's parents and his wish to perpetuate the name. (Many continued to call him Joliot and the couple the Joliot-Curies, as does the author.)

Eve now had a car and her own small apartment on the nearby rue Brancion, to entertain her friends, mostly artists, writers, and musicians, but she still slept in the family home.

They generally agreed about politics and Marie left no doubt what she thought of dictators at a time when the likes of Churchill, Edison, Bernard Shaw, and the Archbishop of Canterbury admired them. If a Frenchman praised a dictator, Marie calmly replied: "I have lived under oppression. You have not. You don't understand your own good fortune in living in a free country." Not that she thought France was perfect. She deplored the shortage of good schools and hospitals, the awful living conditions of many poor families, and how women were often treated as second-class citizens. Fortunately, their conversations often turned to lighter subjects, especially when discussing little Hélène's amusing antics and sayings, when Marie would laugh until she cried.

Marie attended the Fifth Solvay Conference in October 1927, when Einstein rejected Bohr's quantum theory as a poor attempt to destroy determinism.

Early in 1928, her American friend Marie Meloney, now editor of the *New York Herald Tribune*'s magazine, homeward bound from an interview in Italy with dictator Benito Mussolini, stopped briefly in Paris, and Marie went to see her. Meloney's husband had recently died of tuberculosis and she feared that she, too, had the disease. Nevertheless, when Marie

Marie Curie among her peers, the world's greatest scientists, at the 1927 Solvay Conference. She is the only woman among twenty-eight men. Among them in the front row are Max Planck (on her right) and Hendrik Lorentz (on her left). Albert Einstein and Paul Langevin were also at the conference.

said that she had to use her own funds to supply the Warsaw Institute with radium, Meloney offered to raise the money to provide the radium as a gift.

But soon after her return to New York, Meloney had disappointing news for Marie: "The Polish radium seems far off. I have not been well and America is in the throes of a terrible political upheaval." (The Teapot Dome scandal involved Albert B. Fall, secretary of the interior, who got a two-hundred-thousand-dollar payoff for secretly leasing U.S. government Teapot Dome oil reserve lands in Wyoming to Harry F. Sinclair of the Mammoth Oil Company. Congress ordered President Harding to cancel the leases and Fall paid a one-hundred-thousand-dollar fine and went to prison for a year.)

In the summer of 1928 Marie began to hear more accounts of radium's devastating effects. A Polish chemist, Sonia Cotelle, a friend of Marie's who had also worked with Irène, had died from radioactive exposure. In America, Walter Lippmann, an editorial writer for the crusading New York *World*, tried to pressure the New Jersey court system into advancing the case of five more "Radium Girls"—all dial painters—dying of radium poisoning, which the U.S. Radium Company was trying to delay. "If ever a case called for prompt adjudication," Lippmann wrote, "it is the case of five crippled women who are fighting for a few miserable dollars to ease their last days on earth."

Frederick Flynn, a Columbia University consultant for U.S. Radium, claimed that the women could survive and that he found no radioactivity in the tests he had made on them. Nor, he said, has a consultant who was present at the examinations. (It was later discovered that the two men were part of a misinformation campaign by the U.S. Radium Corporation. Flynn was not licensed to practice medicine, and the so-called consultant, who also had no medical training, was a vice president of the U.S. Radium Corporation.)

Lippmann responded: "To dispute whether they can live four months or four years while lawyers wrangle over technicalities is to make the case more stupendously horrible than ever. The whole thing becomes a legal nightmare when, in order to obtain justice, five women have to go to court and prove they are dying while lawyers and experts on the other side go to the newspapers to prove they may live somewhat longer."

At the same time, a New Jersey journalist, Florence Pfalzgraph, sought help from Marie Curie: "Twelve women have died and five are dying a most horrible and painful death," she wrote. "In your wonderful work, I wonder if you have discovered anything which might benefit these women?" Marie had previously said, regretfully, that there was no way of destroying radium once it had entered the body. But she was puzzled by the symptoms of the American women. Even during the war, when many French factory workers also used radium to make instruments shine in the dark, no similar symptoms had been reported, perhaps because they had used small sticks with cotton wadding instead of paintbrushes. She again recommended eating liver to counterattack the anemia-like effects of radiation sickness, but said that there was no sure cure for radiation poisoning. A New Jersey newspaper, the *Newark Ledger*, announced that she had "affirmed the doom already sounded by leading medical authorities who have examined the girls," and that on hearing the news "some of the victims were prostrated with grief."

Told of their reaction, Marie responded, "I am not a doctor, so I cannot venture an opinion on whether the New Jersey girls will die. But from the newspaper descriptions of the manner in which they worked, I think it is imperative to change the method of using radium."

Press publicity and public outrage pressured the court system to re-schedule the "Radium Girls" case from September 1928 to early June the same year, with U.S. District Court Judge William Clark as the mediator, even though he was a stockholder in the U.S. Radium Corporation. Days before the trial the five women—too weak even to raise their arms to take the oath—agreed to an out-of-court settlement. The company gave them each ten thousand dollars (rather than the two hundred fifty thousand dollars they had hoped for) with an annuity of six hundred dollars, and agreed to pay all their legal and medical expenses.

Despite the grim news from America, neither Marie, Irène, nor Frédéric seem to have taken extra precautions for themselves, although they got plenty of fresh mountain and sea air on their various vacations, especially at L'Arcouest on the Atlantic coast. The Joliot-Curies were there with their daughter, Hélène, in September 1928, living at the small house Marie had bought in 1926, when Irène wrote to her: "For the past two days the weather has been splendid. Sea very calm and sunny. We fished for shrimps yesterday at l'Ile Verte and Fred gathered lots of them: we ate them like wolves last night." And Joliot added, "We are terribly sorry you can't be here with us because the sun is roasting us all. We water the plants and our work goes on." Writing about life at L'Arcouest, their novelist friend Marguerite Borel indicated that Joliot was becoming more at ease with the group: "Return home at dusk. Quite often with beautiful sunsets. The calm sea makes us use the oars, or sudden storms to don well-worn covers . . . Hair wild, flowing with rain, we sing . . . As night falls, the big petrol lamp at *Taschen* (le Capitaine's house) stands out like a beacon . . . In the house, talk, games, sometimes dancing with the local people: Jean Perrin with the grocer's wife, Irène with the postman. The triumph of le Capitaine is the *bourrée* he does with his Auvergne cook Annette, which we accompany with a patois song, and which the Joliot, Langevin, and Curie children still dance . . . Fred and Irène Joliot-Curie do a *pas de deux.*"

In the spring of the following year, suffering from the rigors of her work, Marie went to L'Arcouest to rest. Before leaving Paris she had cautiously approved an experiment suggested by one of her most brilliant researchers, Russian-born Salomon Rosenblum. He proposed subjecting alpha rays emitted in the decay of radioactive thorium C to the forces of a powerful electromagnet—the first in France—recently constructed by Aimé Cotton at his Bellevue laboratory near Paris. Because Cotton was the husband of Marie's former student Eugénie Fertis, she had no trouble getting permission for Rosenblum to use it. Irène sent her news of the positive result of the first experiment, in which he had analyzed the fine structure of the spectrum of alpha rays given off by decaying thorium, and suggested that Marie should work with Rosenblum.

Marie had a large stockpile of different radioactive elements available for such experiments because, instead of investigating the mysteries of the atomic nucleus, like Rutherford, she had encouraged friends and colleagues to bring her minerals from Norway, Italy, Belgium, Indochina, the United States, and even the North Pole, identified those of use to her, then isolated, purified, and measured the radioactive elements. Some doctors, after depleting the radon from the ampoules Marie had sent them, returned them to her. These "seeds" were a great source of polonium. Though some criticized her for this preoccupation with building up her radioactive supplies, it enabled several of her researchers to make significant breakthroughs. Rosenblum would be the first.

She was so excited by his early results that she told all her chemists to stop what they were doing and to help him, and she joined in the effort. On the day Marie chose for Rosenblum's second experiment with the electromagnet, she woke before dawn to prepare the source of radioactive actinium, so that when he and the other chemists arrived at the lab at 8 A.M. it was ready. She remained at the lab while they all drove the few miles to Bellevue. Chemist Moise Haissinsky, who developed the negative plate, was amazed to see that instead of the expected two lines there were six. Shown the plate, Rosenblum gave a wild dance of joy around the electromagnet. Haissinsky immediately drove back to Paris to get another radioactive source, and called out from Marie's doorway that the spectrum showed six lines. As he recalled, she quickly turned, took off her glasses, gave a smile that lit up her tired face, and said that he must be joking. Then, realizing he meant it, she promised to make a really beautiful radioactive source. Marie didn't break into a dance but later told Irène that Rosenblum was in seventh heaven and that she was delighted with the results.

What had he discovered? According to physics professor George Dracoulis, of Australian National University: "Initially, it was thought that each element would have a distinct energy for [radioactive] decay, but Rosenblum found that groups of alpha-particles with different energies were emitted. He was also the first to observe what became known as alpha-decay fine structure. The alpha-decay process itself and the existence of discrete energy levels in nuclei were important for the development of the quantum theory." It was the first major discovery at the Curie Institute.

Rosenblum had been at the institute almost five years and funds to support him were running out. So Marie appealed to Einstein for help: "I haven't told M. Rosenblum that I was going to speak to you about his situation: he has not asked it of me in any fashion. If I do speak to you, it is only because I know how much your name is used to raise funds for Jewish causes and that I wonder if there might not be means there to help a young Israelite for whom I have a very great respect." Einstein replied on September 6 saying that he had started to get financial help for Rosen-blum because he liked the man and his work very much. (Rosenblum's cousin, Zalman Shazar, would become Israel's third president, 1963–1973.)

Despite radium's bad publicity in the United States, Meloney encour-aged Marie to make a second trip there to raise money for the Polish Insti-tute, which had no radium of its own, stressing that her presence was vital to its success and that she would be protected from an intrusive press. Meloney accepted Marie's proviso that she would do none of the follow-ing: give autographs or interviews, sit for portraits, shake hands (with some exceptions), or attend large formal dinners or receptions — except for a banquet honoring Thomas Edison. She was willing to make only four pub-lic appearances during her stay.

When Marie's upcoming visit was publicized, the fund was again over-subscribed, and the new White House incumbent, Herbert Hoover, agreed to present Marie with a fifty-thousand-dollar check. His wife had been one of the official sponsors of her previous visit.

As Meloney was preoccupied with organizing various events and nei-ther of Marie's daughters could accompany her on this trip, a New Yorker, Mrs. Henry Moses, a member of the Marie Curie Radium Fund Com-mittee in 1921, made a special journey to Paris to accompany her to the United States on the liner *Ile de France*. Its captain was reported to be so concerned for Marie's health that he requested special radio weather reports, prepared to change course to avoid rough seas. Luckily, it was a smooth crossing.

As the *New York Times* reported: "Representatives of three Govern-ments welcomed her, cut the red tape of landing, shielded her from annoyance and treated her as if she were a little old lady made of glass."

At Meloney's Fifth Avenue home Marie remained in strict seclusion, then for the next few days she rested in Meloney's country home in Pawl-ing, New York, delighting in the trees' spectacular fall colors. On the weekend she traveled to Dearborn, Michigan, to celebrate the fiftieth anniversary of Thomas Edison's invention, the incandescent lightbulb. There she was a houseguest of their mutual friend Henry Ford. President Hoover was the keynote speaker at the banquet in Edison's honor, also attended by John D. Rockefeller Jr., George Eastman, and Orville Wright.

Next stop was Schenectady, where she inspected the experimental laboratories of the General Electric Company headed by Owen Young, her shrewd financial adviser, who had already donated a lot of equipment for her institute. She was overwhelmed by the huge enterprise: the mass-production lines, great ranges of newly designed cathode-ray tubes, hundreds of photoelectric measuring devices, and scores of research workers. After staying with the Youngs for two days, Marie dedicated the Hepburn Chemistry Laboratory at St. Lawrence University, Canton, New York, which had a carved figure of her on the building's stone entrance. She rested briefly at Meloney's country home before heading for Washington, arriving at Union Station on November 29. That night she and Meloney dined with the president and his family at the White House. The next day Hoover handed her the fifty-thousand-dollar check.

The following evening she was back in New York at a banquet for the New York City Committee of the American Society for the Control of Cancer. There, looking exhausted, almost as if in a trance, she posed for a formal group photograph along with Meloney.

She told Irène that she was treated like a head of state during one out-of-town trip, when "I came down the service stairs to avoid sixty reporters waiting at the main entrance. Then we made a sensational ride from New York to Long Island, with a policeman on a motorcycle in front of us sounding blasts on his siren and scattering all the vehicles on our road with an energetic movement of one hand or the other; in this way we carried on like a fire-brigade off to a fire. It was all very amusing." When she found that the bedroom doors had neither keys nor keyholes, she complained to Irène: "They come into your room sometimes having knocked, other times not taking the trouble. The maid thinks that she pleases me by moving my things around, displacing them, opening and closing the windows ten times in an hour without consulting me, turning the fire when there's no need. I spend my time keeping her from making me happy according to her personal views. My good friend Mme Meloney has the same tendency, but it's rather touching the way she tries hard not to annoy me."

She stayed at Meloney's home for a week, countering the well-meant movements of Meloney and the maid, then sailed for France with enough money to buy sixty milligrams of radium for the Polish Institute and with gifts of radioactive elements and scientific equipment, and promises of scholarship endowments for her institute.

Marie was extraordinarily lucky in her timing. A few days after President Hoover handed her the check, the worst financial depression of the century shattered the American economy. But the Wall Street crash obviously hadn't hurt Henry Ford too badly. He offered her a gift of one of his cars and Mrs. Moses offered to pay for a chauffeur. She gratefully accepted both and resumed her routine, working long hours in the lab, as well as teaching radioactivity at the Radium Institute every Monday and Wednesday afternoon.

Joliot was also teaching to augment his meager salary, lecturing to large classes at the Ecole d'Electricité Industrielle Charliot. Just when the workload was getting too much for him, he got unexpected relief. His March 1930 doctoral thesis, "On the Electrochemical Properties of Radioactive Elements," was judged to be so outstanding that he was awarded one of the few new government grants for scientists.

Now he could devote himself full time to research. But for this grant, Francis Perrin believed, Joliot would have had to quit research and get a job in industry, where he would have been a brilliant engineer, "but his name would not have become known and honored throughout the world, and France without doubt would not have played a key part in the scientific development which led to the liberation of atomic energy."

In July 1930, Marie went to Geneva for the annual League of Nations Commission on Intellectual Cooperation, anxious to reform the flawed system. When its members conceded that overexpansion largely explained why its goals had not yet been precisely defined, Marie reminded them that she had warned against this, and against spending commission funds to entertain representatives of international organizations. She recommended reducing the staff and redistributing its funds. The others agreed and appointed her to oversee the reorganization. Between meetings Einstein had been working on his unified field theory equations and was often spotted talking with the frail, white-haired Marie.

When cornered by a *New York Times* reporter, she recalled her first impression of Einstein as "the funniest man," always thinking of the same thing, discussing the same problem of relativity, and seeking to talk with any scientist in any possibly related field. At this session, however, he was infuriated by the behavior of most members, because he believed they were behaving as nationalists rather than as scientists. After complaining that they had almost approved the suppression of minorities and refused to take a stand against militarism, he damned the committee as the most ineffectual enterprise with which he had ever been associated. And then he threw in the towel for a second time. Marie was disappointed, of course, but more concerned with family problems. Her sister Bronia was devastated by the recent death of her husband, Casimir, and her brother-in-law,

Mutual admirers—Marie Curie, her eyesight failing (which
explains the stick she carries), and Albert Einstein—walk near
Lake Geneva in 1930, after taking part in a meeting of the League
of Nations Commission on Intellectual Cooperation.

Jacques Curie, was seriously ill. Dropping everything, she hurried to Montpellier to help nurse Jacques and stayed until he had recovered.

That summer of 1930 the Joliot-Curies were again vacationing in
L'Arcouest, where Joliot had built his own boat, a whaler he named *Le
Marsouin*. "We've been here for a week," he wrote to Marie. "The weather
is mixed, but we take advantage of the bright periods to walk. *Le Marsouin*
looks fine with its new sail. Hélène is already beginning to brown. She is
very spoiled and gets on marvelously with Le Capitaine: from each visit
she brings back flowers . . . Le Capitaine is in good form and his company
is always a delight. I am learning many interesting things, told with exceptional youthfulness and originality. He is a good friend whom I like very
much."

Meanwhile, Eve was making her mark in the arts. But after giving
piano recitals in Paris, the French provinces, and Belgium, she realized
that she had started the piano too late to excel at it. She began to write
music reviews in the weekly journal *Candide* under a pseudonym to avoid
trading on the family name. Then she branched out as a film and theater
critic for various Paris magazines. She also began translating into French
an American play, *Spread Eagle*, by George Brooks and Walter Lister,
a political satire that would resonate with today's audiences. The original
version was later described as a clash between commerce and heroism,
and as having the crackling dialogue of *The Front Page* with very contemporary *Wag the Dog* cynicism. It featured a business titan who orchestrates
a U.S. invasion of Mexico. As a Broadway play staged by George Abbott

and produced by Jed Harris at the Martin Beck Theatre in 1927, *Spread Eagle* ran for eighty performances. It was revived and taped in Los Angeles in 1999 by L.A. Theatre Works, starring Ed Asner, Jamey Sheridan, Fred Savage, and Sharon Gless.

During 1930, at sixty-three, Marie had her fourth and final operation for cataracts and while recuperating in Cavalaire wrote to Eve that she was getting used to moving around without glasses, even taking fast walks along mountain trails and never once falling.

While Eve was tackling *Spread Eagle,* Irène and Joliot were trying to solve the mystery of polonium's complex radiation. Fortunately, Marie had the world's largest stock of radioactive sources for both research and medical purposes. Working with polonium was dangerous because it is so toxic, and they had to be extremely careful as they used electrolysis and evaporation to quadruple the amount of very active polonium available for their purpose.

Irène had inherited her father's ability to use ingenious devices, such as the cloud chamber, which enabled her to visualize the trajectories of atomic particles and proved a vital tool in studying nuclear physics. Her laboratory was on the ground floor, but because of Joliot's smoking, Marie had relegated him to the basement. He loved to spend much of his time there, however, because it housed his favorite tool, the cloud chamber, which Irène had taught him to use. Because he wasn't satisfied with it, he brilliantly redesigned the model so that he could photograph tracks of the ionizing particles seventy-six times longer than was possible with Wilson's instrument.

Once when Joliot was demonstrating the cloud chamber to visitors, he said enthusiastically, "In this chamber an infinitely tiny particle reveals its own trajectory, in a succession of drops of condensation. Isn't it the most beautiful phenomenon in the world?" "Yes," Irène replied. "It would be the most beautiful phenomenon in the world, were it not for childbirth." What was also beautiful, Irène's hiking friend Angèle Pompei noticed, was the affectionate atmosphere in which the young couple worked together. "It was a pleasure," Pompei recalled, "to share their happiness in exploiting and enriching the heritage from Pierre and Marie Curie." They were soon to be among the small group of scientists throughout the world determined to solve the puzzle at the heart of the atom.

CHAPTER 14

A Great Discovery — at Last

1931–1934

After Christmas 1930, the Joliot-Curies went skiing in the Swiss resort of Megève with several friends and colleagues, including Pierre Biquard and Salomon Rosenblum. It was fun and therapeutic for Irène, who was encouraged to seek the Alpine air for her uncertain health. In the spring, at a physics conference in Zurich, the couple was intrigued by Walter Bothe's account of his recent discovery. Using polonium to bombard beryllium with alpha particles, the German physicist and his partner, Herbert Becker, had been astonished to find that it gave off enormously powerful rays that penetrated lead two centimeters thick. Bothe thought that they must be an extraordinary kind of gamma ray. Several others at the conference were eager to get started and beat the competition in solving the puzzle, among them the Joliot-Curies. But not Peter Kapitsa, a brilliant and somewhat eccentric Russian researcher at Rutherford's Cavendish Laboratory. He listened attentively, but was in no hurry to identify the new phenomenon. He even delayed his departure to have himself photographed lying in front of a parked car, saying: "I just want to know what I should look like if I were run over."

Having the world's largest supply of polonium with which to experiment, the Joliot-Curies had an advantage over their rivals. Anxious not to lose a drop of the deadly material, which they isolated by electrolysis or evaporation, they sometimes used their mouths to transfer it with a pipette from one container to another. Joliot took even more risks in handling it, so that one of his fingers became radioactive, and he sometimes used it to check that the Geiger counter was working.

In the fall, Marie Curie also met Bothe at a lively nuclear physics conference in Rome organized by Enrico Fermi, when Caltech's Robert Millikan, a 1923 Nobel Prize winner, stated that "cosmic rays consist of

223

high-energy photons and were "the birth cry of atoms" from outer space. And Niels Bohr suggested that the law of conservation of energy might have to be abandoned at the microscopic level. During the conference Marie wrote to Irène that "Bohr insisted a good deal on the impossibility of applying quantum mechanics at this time to the interior of the nucleus." All three ideas—of Fermi, Millikan, and Bohr—were to influence the work of the Joliot-Curies. As Marie put it: "A great discovery does not issue from the scientist's brain ready-made, like Minerva springing fully armed from Jupiter's head; it is the fruit of an accumulation of preliminary work."

The Joliot-Curies employed their own techniques to detect and analyze what occurred when alpha particles collided with the nuclei of atoms. Using the cloud chamber he had designed and built, Joliot could determine the energies of the electrified particles passing through it, and observe the tracks of particle seventy-six times longer than was possible in conventional cloud chambers. So using high-speed cameras he was able to record the normally invisible made visible. That occurred when a sudden decrease of pressure in the cloud chamber caused water droplets to gather along a track of charged particles, the positively charged ions in one direction and negatively charged ions in the other—but only for a fraction of a second, which Joliot recorded with a high-speed camera. His remarkable skill in handling the equipment was soon noticed by a new arrival, twenty-six-year-old Pierre Savel, who on a Saturday afternoon in November 1931 joined Joliot in an empty room of the Radium Institute. Savel had applied for the job as his assistant. After a few general questions, Joliot showed him photos he had just obtained from tracks in the cloud chamber and gave him detailed explanations of how it worked and what the tracks indicated. Savel was overawed and anxious. He felt completely inadequate for the task. But Joliot assured him in a conversation that lasted two hours that he, too, had felt exactly the same way when he started and of the great delight he had since found in the work. Savel got the job and stayed for twenty-seven years.

Soon after Savel appeared for work on Monday morning, a very sensitive Hoffmann electrometer was delivered, a new model with which Joliot was unfamiliar. While they were assembling it, a thread holding a mobile needle broke, and the new suspension required to fix it couldn't be obtained for several weeks. Joliot immediately began to tackle the problem. As Savel recalled, "I admired the dexterity with which he soldered to a platinum thread almost invisible to the naked eye, the mobile needle at one end and the suspension cord at the other." And Joliot succeeded at the first attempt. Even so, it took a month to get the electrometer working.

At the end of that first morning, Irène, obviously pregnant, came down from her ground-floor laboratory and Savel was introduced to her. She wanted to see how things were going and to accompany Joliot to lunch. She also appeared in the evening to go home—a regular occurrence. So was Joliot's reluctance to leave the experiment, and Irène's pleading with him to join her. Often his dinner was a bunch of cherries, which he ate while working far into the night.

He and Irène realized that the Bothe-Becker discovery of powerful, penetrating rays presented a new, enhanced way to investigate the constitution of the atom's nucleus, and that they had a good chance of being the first to discover their nature. As well as access to about two hundred millicuries of polonium, they had first-rate equipment to conduct their research. They were also experts in using an ionization chamber attached to their new Hoffmann electrometer to detect charged elementary particles.

When the couple quickly replicated the Bothe and Becker experiment, they obtained rays that were even more energetic and penetrating. And on December 28, 1931, Irène reported to the French Academy of Sciences their early conclusions that alpha particles from polonium had knocked protons (positively charged hydrogen nuclei) out of the target substances. As the Joliot-Curies' daughter, Hélène, explained: "Their next step was to close the ionization chamber with a very thin aluminum window, hoping this would help them observe a possible secondary radiation, and then to place—instead of an absorber—various thin layers of various substances close to the window and in the path of the radiation."

With thin layers of cellophane or paraffin wax containing hydrogen, they were surprised to find that the electric current in the ionization chamber increased. After several sophisticated tests they were persuaded that the increased current in the ionization chamber was explained by protons being vigorously ejected from hydrogen-bearing substances. On January 18, 1932, they reported their preliminary findings to the Academy of Sciences, headed "The Emission of Protons of High Velocity from Hydrogenous Materials Irradiated with Very Penetrating Gamma Rays." This defied credibility: gamma rays were known to deflect electrons, but protons are 1,836 times heavier than electrons. As author Richard Rhodes wrote, the Joliot-Curies' hypothesis "was as unlikely as if a marble should deflect a wrecking ball." Or a puff of wind destroy a solid house.

In Denmark, physicist Niels Bohr thought the phenomena extremely interesting, but he did not accept the Joliot-Curies' interpretation. In England, at Cambridge University's Cavendish Laboratory, James Chadwick read the report and was also highly skeptical. A physicist by accident, having intended to study mathematics at Manchester University, he had walked into the wrong line at the entrance interviews and found himself being interviewed for the physics course. The questions were so interesting that he decided to read for physics instead of mathematics and became a tireless and talented researcher.

As Ernest Rutherford's assistant director of research at the Cavendish Laboratory, Chadwick hurried to tell him of the French couple's work. Rutherford listened with growing amazement until he finally blurted out: "I don't believe it!" Now it was Chadwick's turn to be amazed. Never having known the great New Zealand physicist to make such an impatient remark, so utterly out of character, he attributed it to the electrifying effect of the report itself. Rutherford agreed with Chadwick that they must believe the observations—as they respected the Joliot-Curies' talent and integrity— but he was convinced that "the explanation was quite another matter."

Rutherford had found that when a narrow beam of alpha particles penetrated a thin sheet of metal, it became a broad band with a blurred boundary, and the thicker the sheet, the more blurred the boundary. He assumed this to represent the scattering of the particles as they encountered atoms in the metal, and that the thicker the sheet, the more atoms the alpha particles would encounter. In 1909, two of Rutherford's assistants conducting a similar experiment, Hans Geiger and his student Ernest Marsden, came to him one day greatly excited. They had been able to get the alpha particles to ricochet backward. "It was quite the most incredible event that has ever happened to me in my life," Rutherford recalled. "It was almost as incredible as if you fired a 15-inch shell at a piece of tissue paper and it all came back and hit you." As author Edward N. da Costa Andrade asked: "How could an atomic force exist large enough to turn right back an atom rushing at a speed of some 10,000 miles a second?—10,000 miles a second, not an hour." Two years later Rutherford had the answer: the atom must consist of a central particle, extremely small compared with the entire atom, and in which most of the atom's mass is concentrated. For the atom as a whole to be neutral, the central particle (nucleus) must be surrounded by an electrified sphere of an opposite electric charge.

Because atoms were inaccessible to ordinary physical and chemical action, it had been Rutherford's idea to explore their makeup by using radium's alpha particles as projectiles. Because most alpha particles he fired at gold foil "went right through the foil, he reasoned that the atom was mainly empty space," with a small, heavy, and positively charged core able to repel and scatter most of the alpha particles fired at it. In his

Bakerian Lecture before the Royal Society in 1920, he had envisioned "the possible existence of an atom of mass 1 [very little] which had a zero nuclear charge able to move freely through matter. Its presence would probably be difficult to detect by the spectroscope. On the other hand, it should enter readily the structure of atoms, and may either unite with the nucleus or be disintegrated by its intense field, resulting possibly in the escape of a charged hydrogen atom or an electron or both." He called it the neutron.

By 1932 most scientists accepted the Rutherford-Bohr conception of the atom as having a tiny nucleus, surrounded at a great distance by orbiting electrons, with empty space in between—not unlike our solar system with the nucleus as the sun and electrons the planets. Or, in Joliot's vivid simile: the atom was like the place de la Concorde, and its nucleus an orange seed.

But nuclear scientists were sure there was more to discover about atomic structure than Bohr and Rutherford envisioned. Chadwick and everyone else at Cavendish knew that there had been many futile attempts at the lab to find Rutherford's neutron (a very tightly bound proton-electron system), but it was still thought to exist. Spurred by the Joliot-Curies' report, Chadwick set to work to replicate their experiments, keeping an open mind, though still very much aware of Rutherford's informed speculations. He relished nuclear research as a kind of sport—contending with nature.

Marie Curie's Radium Institute had the world's biggest source of polonium at its command, but the Cavendish was a close second, thanks to glass tubes of depleted radon provided by the Kelly Hospital in Baltimore, Maryland, and some sent by Lise Meitner from Germany. With this at hand and Rutherford's encouragement and lab equipment, Chadwick started immediately, on Sunday, February 7, 1932. He worked day and night for ten days, snatching an occasional catnap, determined to discover the true nature of the powerful radiation. He had good equipment, including an ionization chamber and a valve amplifier, which worked a recorder registering on photographic paper. Each time a particle entered the chamber, its appearance was photographed and recorded on a moving strip of paper.

To start, he replicated the Joliot-Curies' methods—putting a paraffin wax sheet in the path of the rays—and confirmed their results. Next, instead of using the paraffin wax, he directly bombarded elements, including lithium, beryllium, boron, carbon, and nitrogen, hydrogen, helium, and argon. In every case, the reaction caused about the same number of protons to be vigorously ejected from each element. His most important conclusion was that the mysterious radiation did not consist of gamma rays, but probably of uncharged particles of approximately the same mass as protons. Being uncharged, they would not be repulsed or deflected by the electrical barrier of electrons orbiting the nucleus. And that was how they were able to penetrate lead. He was convinced that the particle was an essential part of all atomic nuclei and proposed calling it the neutron.

To stake his claim for priority, he mailed a brief report of his findings to *Nature* magazine (and sent a full account three months later to the *Proceedings* of the Royal Society). After a celebratory dinner that night with a few friends, Chadwick was cajoled into speaking at a club meeting organized by the charismatic Peter Kapitsa, where he said he was sure that the radiation consisted of neutrons, not gamma rays, and agreed with Rutherford's 1920 prescient definition of a neutron as a proton and an electron bound together. C. P. Snow, who was also at the dinner, called it "One of the shortest accounts ever made of a great discovery." After which Chadwick muttered, "Now I want to be chloroformed and put to bed for a fortnight."

His article for *Nature* contained a devastating attack on the Joliot-Curies' theory, in which he invoked "the basic physical rule that no more energy or momentum can come out of an event than went into it," and continued, "It is evident that we must either relinquish the application of the conservation of energy and momentum in these collisions or adopt another hypothesis about the nature of the radiation. In order to explain the great penetrating power of the radiation we must further assume that the particle has no net charge. We must suppose it [to be] the neutron discussed by Rutherford in his Bakerian Lecture of 1920."

Joliot's Russian assistant, Lew Kowarski, also a physicist, recalled Chadwick's report being discussed at Jean Perrin's home during a regular tea-time get-together of friends, colleagues, and celebrities. Irène, Joliot, and Kowarski were also there when, according to Kowarski, "someone remarked: 'Oh, that Englishman, Chadwick—he has ideas that they are neutral particles of the same weight as protons.' There was general laughter in the room, in which Joliot heartily joined. But Joliot had an extremely sane view of his role (in the discovery of the neutron). There was an initial phenomenon discovered by Bothe and Becker. Then there was the central phenomenon discovered by the Joliots [in which they gave Chadwick the clues to follow]. And there was the final crowning phenomenon discovered by Chadwick."

Almost as exhausted as Chadwick from sleep deprivation because of his own intense work habits, Joliot took a respite at Marie's seashore home in Brittany, while Irène stayed in Paris with their new son, born on March 12, 1932. He was named Pierre after her father.

On April 2, 1932, Joliot referred to Chadwick's "very attractive hypothesis," in a letter to Russian friend Dimitri Skobeltsyn—an alumnus of the Radium Institute and his former colleague—and on April 15 he and Irène offered "solid support for the hypothesis of the existence of neutrons."

Later, reflecting on Chadwick's triumph, Joliot remarked: "Old laboratories with long traditions always have hidden riches. Ideas previously expressed by our teachers, living or dead, taken up a score of times and then forgotten, consciously or unconsciously penetrate the thought of those who work in these old laboratories and, from time to time, they bear fruit that is discovery."

Chadwick had other advantages over both his German and French competitors. The point counter used by Bothe and Becker was almost exclusively sensitive to the gamma rays produced in the reaction; the Joliot-Curies' ionization chamber counter was sensitive to both gamma rays and the protons produced in the reaction. But Chadwick's ionization chamber was almost exclusively sensitive to the protons produced in the reaction. "Gamma rays and protons [charged particles] ionize gases," wrote R. H. Stuewer, "but neutrons [uncharged particles] do not."

Irène did not let motherhood delay her scientific projects for long. Her son was barely a month old when she left Paris to join Joliot at an international scientific station in Switzerland, precariously attached to the side of a mountain, the Jungfaujoch, known as the Top of Europe. There, from April 25 to May 8, 1932, while Joliot's mother took care of their children, they sought to discover the effect of cosmic rays from outer space on atomic nuclei. Joliot wrote to tell his mother that they were having a wonderful time in the dreamlike setting reached by rail through tunnels in the mountains. They worked in bad weather and went skiing in good, and as the only scientists there, when they dined in the nearby hotel they were treated like royalty. Their experiments paid off: they established that there were no neutrons in cosmic rays. Instead, they found that they consisted entirely of charged particles.

Marie and Eve were also abroad, in Spain, where the poet Paul Valéry had asked Marie, on behalf of the League of Nations, to preside at a debate in Madrid titled "The Future of Culture." As well as presiding, she opposed the proposition that creative artists were being stifled by science. Valéry had jokingly called the debate participants—writers and artists from several countries—"Don Quixotes of the mind fighting against the windmills." But Marie took it seriously, giving a spirited defense of her profession:

"I believe that Science has great beauty. A scientist in the laboratory is not a mere technician; he is also a child confronting natural phenomena that impress him as though they were fairy tales. We mustn't let anyone think that all scientific progress has been reduced to mechanisms, machines, gear boxes . . . though these things, too, have their own beauty . . . I also don't think that the spirit of adventure is in danger of disappearing from our world. If I see anything vital around me, it is this very spirit of adventure, which seems ineradicable and is very closely related to curiosity."

It was an exhilarating time for Eve, who spoke with many Spaniards eager to support their newly formed government dedicated to radical reform. She learned that the monarchy had maintained a stranglehold on Spain for fifteen centuries, with one brief intermission. But when, in 1931, the country had voted overwhelmingly for a republican government, their king, Alfonso XIII, first offered to step down in favor of his son. When that was rejected, he had gone into exile to avoid a bloody civil war, taking with him a huge private fortune. "It is very moving," Marie wrote to Irène, "to see what confidence in the future exists among the young and among many of their elders . . . What interests me a lot are conversations with republicans and the enthusiasm they have for revitalizing their country. I hope they succeed!"

During Alfonso's autocratic reign many workers had been desperately poor, while landowners and the Catholic church, which dominated the education system, were enormously rich. The country as a whole was ruled by a semifeudal aristocracy. The new government had given women the vote and equal rights for the first time. Civil marriages were now legal and divorces more easily obtained.

The new regime also "brought the backward country into the 20th century," according to American foreign correspondent William L. Shirer, "and broke the stranglehold of the Catholic church by separating church and state." It instituted land reform, liberalized the medieval penal codes, abolished titles, and made primary secular education compulsory and free. But, as we know, it was doomed.

On her return from Spain, Marie put the final touches to her new, definitive book on radioactivity, went to the laboratory every workday, gave her twice-weekly lectures at the Sorbonne, and demonstrated once again how determined she could be when something dear to her heart was in danger.

Because increasing traffic on the Pierre Curie Street outside her lab was disturbing sensitive instruments, she asked the police chief to solve the problem and kept up the pressure until he changed the traffic pattern.

There was, however, little she could do about the scandals reported mostly in the United States concerning the continued use of radium as a tonic and health cure, but when asked for advice, she warned of the dangers and advised caution. But its promoters continued to do a roaring and deadly trade, particularly William Bailey, a self-styled doctor who had grown rich from his patented radium-laced drink called Radithor. One millionaire customer, Erben Byers, a national amateur golf champion, drank, over the course of a few years, more than a thousand bottles of the toxic drink advertised as a pick-me-up and a cure for almost everything including insanity. He died at fifty-one on March 11, 1932, in New York City's Doctors' Hospital. The once powerful, athletic man was a ninety-two-pound skeleton. Most of his upper and lower jaw and part of his skull had been removed in the vain hope of preventing the splintering and breaking of his bones. An autopsy blamed radium poisoning.

In Chicago, a physician had given several hundred patients weekly injections of ten microcuries every week for a year, and when his victims started to suffer, he destroyed his records and skipped town.

Investigations spurred by press publicity and a public outcry finally encouraged the Federal Trade Commission to shut down the Radithor operation in 1932. Then, wrote Roger M. Macklis, "Public health officials pulled the dangerous materials off store shelves [and] nervous citizens sheepishly came forward to turn in their own radioactive medicines." Among them was Mayor James J. Walker of New York City, who at first refused to give up his radioactive rejuvenator because, he said, "it made him feel so good."

That spring of 1932 at the Cavendish Laboratory, two Englishmen, John Cockcroft and Ernest Walton, directed streams of hydrogen protons, accelerated by high voltages, to produce the first artificial disintegration and transmutation of the element lithium, another giant step in exploring the atom. To interpret this nuclear reaction, they used Einstein's $E=mc^2$ formula (which Bainbridge confirmed experimentally the next year) defining mass and energy as different aspects of the same thing. The Joliot-Curies gave a lecture on the Englishmen's achievements and demonstrated their own experimental techniques before the French Physical Society. Marie, who was in the audience, was impressed and moved by their performance.

Soon after, Marie slipped and fell in the laboratory, breaking her right wrist. She expected to continue working after a few days' rest, but then began to feel weak and feverish, and had dizzy spells that kept her bedridden for several days at a time. She still endured an almost constant ringing in her ears, and her fingers were sore—sometimes suppurating—

from radiation burns. Not knowing when she would be able to return to work, the university appointed Irène temporary director of the Radium Institute.

Ernest Rutherford had not expected Marie to live this long. Ten years previously, in anticipation of her imminent death, he had written her obituary for the *Manchester Guardian*. Learning of her broken wrist, he sent her a letter of sympathy. It took several months before she replied to any correspondents. Among the first was one to Meloney in America, hoping that they could spend a vacation together in Chamonix and asking her to destroy all her letters, because "they are part of me and you know how reserved I am in my feelings." Fortunately for biographers, Meloney only destroyed some. Marie didn't respond to Rutherford for five months, explaining, "I felt so badly that I even did not have the courage to reply earlier."

By July 1932 she felt fit enough to travel to Warsaw for the inauguration of the Marie Sklodowska-Curie Radium Institute, where cancer patients were already being treated with the radium she had been given on her first visit to the United States. On her return, a letter awaited her from the mother of one of her favorite laboratory assistants, François Reymond. Eve had never seen her so overwhelmed as when she learned how Reymond—who told his mother that he had spent the best years of his life in Marie's laboratory—had accidentally drowned while swimming in a river in Ardeche. "What was the good of it, if it had to end like this?" the deeply distressed Marie asked. "Such a beautiful youth, so much grace, nobility, charm, and such remarkable intellectual gifts—all that disappeared because of a wretched swim in cold water."

Distraught and needing a change of scene, she joined Irène, who was resting on doctor's orders in the mountains near Chamonix with a friend, Angèle Pompei. Meanwhile, Joliot held the fort in the lab and at home in Paris. Having virtually acknowledged their defeat and Chadwick's victory in identifying the neutron, he and Irène had started a series of experiments to learn everything they could about the elementary particle. But, as Joliot complained in a letter to Irène, "We have trouble with the electrometer because the thread keeps sticking, due to the blasted Vaseline that you used. That really is a most impressive gaffe, ma chère." In his next letter, he told her how their five-year-old daughter, Hélène, asked about her new brother, "'Tell me, Papa, how much have you paid for the little Pierre?' I replied that it was Irène who had made him. Hélène was not astonished, but she asked if she, too, when she was taller, could also make one . . . I am at the laboratory every day where I am clearing up many things. I have taught Lecoin how to use the directional counter, and

I have been able to regulate the Hoffmann apparatus of Savel's and ours which were making errors." Presumably, he had gotten rid of the Vaseline. He then reassured her that he had also taken care of all the domestic chores.

On Easter 1933, Irène was again in the mountains seeking a health cure, while Joliot stayed at L'Arcouest with their children. A new couple, Marinette and Jo Segal, had recently joined the seaside colony. They had quickly become friends and dined together every Wednesday. One sunny day, Joliot sat on the terrace of Marie's house, a newspaper on his knees as a writing pad, to tell Irène the news.

Joliot's letters hardly give a clue to his character or personality, but Lew Kowarski has provided an informed insider's view of both Irène and Joliot, having, it seems, studied them carefully, as if they were the subjects of a scientific investigation. The illegitimate son of a businessman and an opera singer, he first got to know them as Joliot's assistant and eventually became a notable nuclear physicist. Asked to compare them, he characterized Irène as:

> an exquisite technician who had a profound understanding of what she was doing. Joliot had a more brilliant, more soaring imagination. He was the prince consort whom the princess had selected for her life . . . It shows Irène's taste in men—that she did choose a genius. They complemented each other marvelously. He had an extremely acute aesthetic sense of science. Chadwick's experiments were among the most beautiful I know, and Joliot immediately sensed a kindred soul . . . Joliot had brilliant ideas—very brilliant because totally unexpected. Chadwick very much admired this quality. Joliot always tackled a problem from a completely unexpected angle, with some usually very simple idea which gave an immediate and obvious result. And he was the most ambitious man since Richard Wagner. Wagner, you know, wanted to be Beethoven and Shakespeare and Caesar all rolled into one. [Joliot] believed that science was the great historical force which shapes history. And at a crucial moment the great scientific discovery turns history in a completely new direction; and he wanted to be that man. And in some sense he was that force.

Unquestionably, he and Irène were about to shape history. Soon after she returned from a rest in the Swiss mountains to rejoin Joliot at the Radium Institute, they pursued an intense investigation of neutrons. First they produced them by bombarding beryllium and boron with alpha particles, then sent the neutrons through paraffin wax and other substances. Finally they recorded the arrival of protons ejected by neutrons and electrons in their ionization chamber, and photographed their tracks in Joliot's improved cloud chamber. Each "hit" by alpha particles was converted into electric pulses that were counted electrically.

One result confused them both: a cloud-chamber photograph of an electron's tracks showed it to be "curved the wrong way in a magnetic field." When they published the photograph in a November 1932 review article, they suggested that it represented an electron moving through the magnetic field in an opposite direction from the other electrons, toward, rather than away from, the source of radioactivity. Four months later they realized that Caltech's Carl Anderson had beaten them to the true explanation: the peculiar, oppositely curved track had not been made by an electron, but by Anderson's discovery, the positron, a positively charged electron, an elementary particle with a brief existence. Meeting an electron, mutual annihilation occurred, leaving only energy in the form of gamma rays.

It was evidence that the universe consisted of antimatter as well as matter (predicted by Paul Dirac two years earlier), and it confirmed Einstein's theory that matter could be converted into energy and vice versa. After hurriedly reexamining their cloud-chamber photographs, the Joliot-Curies realized that Anderson was right. For a second time they had been first to make a discovery but had failed to recognize it. And when they repeated their experiments, sure enough, they found two tracks in the cloud-chamber photographs, one of a positron and one of an electron. "On July 10, 1933," wrote physicist Stuewer, "they submitted a paper for publication that included the first ever cloud-chamber photograph of electron-positron pair production."

Joliot's mentor, Paul Langevin, just back in Paris from a trip to China and Russia, spoke enthusiastically of how the Soviet government offered an advanced education to all and funded its scientists generously. In France, by contrast, with a few exceptions, only children of the establishment got a first-rate education and—although students of all classes were admitted to the elite Ecole Polytechnic, for example, on the basis of highly competitive entrance examinations—working-class youngsters had little hope of becoming scientists.

To give them a chance, Langevin, who came from a working-class family, proposed starting a Workers' University, and persuaded Joliot and Jacques Solomon—a physicist, and his future son-in-law—to join him in the enterprise. They began to give lectures several evenings each week in the annex of a Trade Unions Hall. When Joliot taught there, Irène attended his classes, which often had a Marxist orientation.

Langevin, Joliot, and other Western scientists were deceived when they visited the Soviet Union. They were allowed to meet only a selective group of fellow scientists in Stalin's favor who had been given special privileges, and so got a distorted picture of the situation. This is now clear because, as historian Helge Kragh explained, "about 1933, the climate in the Soviet Union was marked by an unhealthy cocktail of xenophobia, suspicion, sycophancy, and fear of the secret police. Whereas Soviet physicists had earlier been active participants in the international physics life and main contributors to German physics journals, they were increasingly forced into isolation. . . . Stalin's victims came from everywhere, and they included physicists. The Russian despot was no more interested in physics than was Hitler, and nobody, scientists or not, could feel secure under the Great Terror."

Hitler had recently come to power in Germany and was already making life impossible for Jews. By April 1933 more than a thousand university teachers, including 313 full professors, had been fired. Albert Einstein had already left Germany to live in the United States after writing to a friend, "I am afraid that the epidemic of hatred and violence is spreading everywhere."

Langevin, his friend and admirer, agreed with him and saw the Soviet Union as the only viable opposition to growing fascist aggression and intolerance. And in the fall of 1933 he and Joliot, who generally shared Langevin's radical, reformist views, went to the Soviet Union with several other western European scientists, including Paul Dirac and Victor Weisskopf, for conferences in Moscow and Leningrad on the atomic nucleus. Irène was not well enough to make the trip.

After Joliot's return in October, Irène and Marie joined him for the less strenuous journey to Belgium for the seventh Solvay Conference. Apart from Marie and the Austrian Lise Meitner, a slight, intense woman, Irène was the only other woman at the conference. (During World War I, hearing that Marie Curie was an X-ray nurse in field hospitals, Meitner had become an X-ray nurse-technician with the Austrian army. Later, in 1917, she and the German radiochemist Otto Hahn had discovered the element protactinium.)

According to reporter Robert Jungk, only the inner circle knew "that between [Irène and Meitner] who played leading roles in the drama of the uranium experiments an increasing personal rivalry had developed, though [it was never] admitted in polite scientific society. Madame Irène Joliot-Curie and Fraulein Lise Meitner were among the greatest experts in

Three Curie family members attended the 1933 Solvay Conference. Irène
sits in the front row, second from the left, with Niels Bohr on her left.
Marie is seated in the center of the front row. Frédéric Joliot stands
in the middle row, second from the left, with Francis Perrin on his right
and Werner Heisenberg on his left. The Joliot-Curies' rival, Lise Meitner,
who challenged the accuracy of their work, sits second from the right.

radium research of their time. No one disputed their pre-eminence. Yet a
contest began between them."

It certainly seemed so, not only at the Solvay Conference, but also judging by Meitner's subsequent behavior. Following the death of Lorentz,
Paul Langevin, now a respected international figure, presided over the
conference on nuclear physics to which forty-one scientists from eleven
countries had been invited. Most turned up, a curious and colorful lot,
among them James Chadwick, Werner Heisenberg, Walter Bothe, Enrico
Fermi, Peter Debye, George Gamow, Rudolf Peierls, Ernest Lawrence,
and Patrick Blackett.

Blackett was a tall, lean former British naval officer, who, after a furious argument with Rutherford, left the Cavendish to teach at Birbeck College in London. Wolfgang Pauli, who had recently predicted the neutrino,
was a Viennese working in Zurich, who, when a bright idea occurred to
him in Munich, had danced for joy in the middle of a crowded street. But
when he faced a tough problem he had told a friend, "I wish I were a
movie comedian or something like that and had never heard anything
about physics." The British Paul Dirac, who had recently predicted the

positron, was a man of so few words that he was reputed to utter an entire sentence only once every light-year. On the other hand, Niels Bohr, a Dane, was a man of many words, but in whatever language he spoke many found him almost incoherent.

No one accepted the invitation to the conference more gleefully than George Gamow, credited with the big bang theory of the expanding universe, and with explaining why some radioactive elements decay in seconds, while others last for thousands of years. He was a "merry and freakish soul from Soviet Russia . . . fond of conjuring tricks and childish games," according to Robert Jungk. His most effective trick was conning party chairman Molotov into letting him attend the Solvay Conference and take his physicist wife, Rho, with him, although she did not participate. Both were on a secret mission. The previous year they had tried to escape from their country by paddling in a collapsible rubber kayak across the Black Sea from the Crimea to Turkey 170 miles away. After paddling for a day and a night, rough seas had driven them back to Russian soil. They intended to take this opportunity while in Belgium to defect, which they did, later emigrating to the United States. Two invited no-shows to the conference were Albert Einstein and Paul Ehrenfest. Einstein was in the United States, which had prompted Langevin's prophetic remark: "It's as important an event as would be the transfer of the Vatican from Rome to the New World. The Pope of Physics has moved and the United States will now become the center of the natural sciences." Paul Ehrenfest, who suffered from depression, had committed suicide.

The Joliot-Curies were flattered by the invitation to join some of the world's leading scientists, and excited by a chance to redeem themselves after having twice failed to interpret their own data. They believed that they had made a new discovery and were eager to discuss it. Speaking for them both at Irène's request, Joliot first explained how they had jointly discovered the neutron and the positron—without knowing it—and displayed cloud-chamber photographs as evidence. Then, referring to their report entitled "Penetrating Radiation from Atoms Bombarded by Alpha Rays," he said that in recent experiments they had bombarded mediumweight elements with alpha rays and observed protons. But when they bombarded lighter elements, especially boron and aluminum, they sometimes saw protons, neutrons, and positrons. They concluded that in certain cases a neutron and a positron could be emitted together in the transmutation, instead of a proton. This indicated, Joliot said, that the proton was a compound, not an elementary particle.

Langevin called on Patrick Blackett to respond. He was not impressed by the French couple's conclusions. Irène countered his comments, but he stuck to his guns, saying that they had probably misinterpreted their results. Then Langevin called on Lise Meitner. She immediately went on the attack, totally refuting the Joliot-Curies' claim to have observed neutrons, saying that they must have seen something else. She did not believe it, she explained, because her similar experiments conducted with a colleague had not produced a single neutron. This also brought into question the validity of their calculation of the mass of the neutron, which differed from both Lawrence's and Chadwick's.

Chadwick reported that his experiments showed the neutron's mass to be low: 1.0067 atomic mass unit (amu). Lawrence said that his figure was much lower: 1.0006 amu. And the Joliot-Curies disagreed with both of them. Their figure was 1.011 amu, making it a much higher mass. Historian Roger H. Stuewer points out that it was important to discover the exact mass of the neutron because it would determine whether it was a compound proton-electron or a new particle.* The following year a twenty-three-year-old refugee from Nazi Germany, Maurice Goldhaber, suggested an experiment to Chadwick, who obtained a sufficiently accurate figure, 1.0080 atomic mass unit, which indicated, to Chadwick's surprise, that the neutron was a subatomic particle.

When Chadwick had the floor at the Solvay Conference, he agreed with Meitner that the Joliot-Curies were mistaken in their interpretation of their recent results. Later in the session Chadwick was under fire himself from Heisenberg. What he thought was an unfair attack ended only when Dirac broke his customary silence to come to Chadwick's rescue. An American, Ernest Lawrence, was also offended by responses to his comments.

---

* "An atomic mass unit (amu) is the physical mass unit defined as precisely 1/16 of the mass of the isotope oxygen-16 and thus is equal to precisely 1.000000 amu, which also equals an energy of 931 MeV (million electron volts) using Einstein's $E=mc^2$. All other isotopic masses then are relative to this mass. . . . (Typical nuclear binding energies, incidentally, are several MeV, while in the hydrogen atom the electron is bound to the nucleus [proton] by about 13 eV, or a million times less energy. So it requires a million times more energy to split up a nucleus than to ionize a hydrogen atom by removing its electron.) . . . As we know today, the mass of the neutron is indeed greater than the sum of the masses of the proton and electron, [and] the excess mass of energy is released, that is, the neutron decays spontaneously into a proton and electron (the mean lifetime for this process is around 10 minutes)." E-mail to author from Professor Roger H. Stuewer, University of Minnesota, November 13, 2003.

At the end of the sometimes acrimonious debate, which was mainly Joliot against the rest—while Marie sat in shocked silence—most agreed with Meitner and questioned the Joliot-Curies' accuracy. The couple had arrived with great expectations and left the conference room depressed and humiliated. Groups of scientists who gathered in the garden outside the building largely ignored them, until Niels Bohr approached and told them that their data was extremely important. That cheered them a little. So did Wolfgang Pauli, who gave them a few words of support. But they both still felt somewhat desperate. Marie was furious with Chadwick for having sided with Meitner, and happened to sit next to him later at lunch. Chadwick, who greatly admired her, greeted her warmly. She briefly responded, then turned away and didn't say another word to him during the entire lunch.

Ironically, the verbal attacks at Solvay were a blessing in disguise, because the work the couple did as a result was responsible for a monumental discovery, which brought them international fame and a shared Nobel Prize.

Although they were confident in their work, just to make absolutely sure, as soon as they returned to Paris they repeated their previous experiments and confirmed their accuracy. Again they produced neutrons. And three weeks after the conference, Meitner made a dramatic about-face, writing to Irène on November 18, 1933, that she had been mistaken in her criticism. After conducting more experiments in Berlin, she now had become "fairly convinced" that the Joliot-Curies' interpretation of the disintegration of aluminum was correct after all, and that the positrons do "actually come out of the nucleus." She was therefore submitting a correction to her remarks in Brussels, which in fact appeared in the conference proceedings. Like many others, Meitner found Irène an enigma. She seemed to her "to be afraid of being regarded as the daughter of her mother rather than as a scientist on her own account. This fear may have influenced her attitude to strangers. She was also entirely indifferent to social conventions. She had a strong inner feeling of self-sufficiency, which might be mistaken for a lack of amiability."

Meitner remained suspicious of Irène's work. A few years after the Solvay Conference she had an assistant, Von Droste, check Irène's report that under radiation the thorium isotope sent out alpha rays. Because the young man introduced a filter to avert particles with a range of under three centimeters, he didn't find any alpha rays. "Once more," as author Jungk pointed out, "Fraulein Meitner believed she had convicted her rival of inaccuracy. And once more she was mistaken."

In December 1933 the Joliot-Curies began a new series of experiments based on their idea that when they bombarded aluminum-foil targets, the appearance of neutrons and positrons rather than of the expected protons depended on the high energy of the alpha particles they used as "ammunition." To test the theory, they gradually made the alpha particles less energetic by moving the polonium, the source of the radiation, progressively farther away from the target. Making them travel greater distances slowed and weakened the effect of the alpha particles when they reached their target. The couple was getting promising results when Marie became ill and was in great pain. X-rays revealed a large stone in her gallbladder—the disease that killed her father. Afraid that an operation would be fatal, she went on a strict diet instead. It worked so well that she was able to witness and appreciate the imminent triumph of her daughter and son-in-law.

When Joliot resumed their experiment, moving the polonium back from its aluminum-foil target, he noticed that at a certain distance, although no neutrons were emitted, positrons kept appearing. Even when he removed the polonium source entirely, positrons continued to make their presence known in the Geiger counter, and Joliot called Irène down to the basement room to witness what seemed quite amazing. Now, as he replicated the experiment, again removing the polonium source of alpha rays, the Geiger counter aimed at the aluminum-foil target still kept giving its familiar crackle for several minutes. He noticed that the number count was decreasing exponentially, which characterized the decay of a radioactive isotope. Had the normally stable aluminum become radioactive, or was the Geiger counter defective? It was a critical question. But the Joliot-Curies couldn't wait to find the answer. It was already six in the evening and they had an important dinner engagement they couldn't escape. So Joliot asked Wolfgang Gentner, the young German physicist spending a year with them, to check if their Geiger counter was functioning properly. Gentner tested it on gamma rays and left a note reporting the results. When Joliot read the note first thing next morning, he felt "a child's joy." The Geiger counter was working well. It meant that he and Irène had chanced across a new astonishing phenomenon: artificial radioactivity. Alone at the time, he later recalled how he "began to run and jump around in that vast basement [as] I thought of the consequences which might follow from the discovery." For a brief moment he had achieved the ancient alchemists' dream, transmutation—changing one chemical element, aluminum, into another, phosphorus, then into silicon.

He hurried to tell Irène, who swore Gentner to secrecy. Then she and Joliot verified the new phenomenon by irradiating boron and magnesium with similar results. They had just finished when one of Marie's assistants, Ladislas Goldstein, using the basement entrance to escape from the rain, happened to walk by. Joliot called him and again demonstrated the phenomenon. A friend of his student days, Pierre Biquard, tells in his biography of Joliot how

> a telephone call made me leave my laboratory in the rue Vauquelin and hurry to the Radium Institute in the rue Pierre Curie, where Frédéric Joliot was waiting for me in a semi-basement room. The apparatus which he wanted to show me consisted of equipment scattered over several tables. Its newness and apparent disorder revealed . . . that here was an experiment set up. In haste, to reproduce as a demonstration a discovery made several hours beforehand with Irene . . . "I irradiate this target with alpha rays from my source," he said. "I remove the source. The crackling ought to stop. But in fact it continues." At that moment, the laboratory door opened behind the experimenter, who was once more overcome with enthusiasm for his discovery and Marie Curie and Paul Langevin came in. The demonstration was performed again with the same precision and simplicity . . . Joliot often reminded me of that moment and spoke of his emotion, his pride and his joy at having been able to offer before the two great scientists, to whom he was bound by so many ties, a fresh example of the vital character and ever-widening horizons of science.

As visible proof of this discovery the Joliot-Curies chemically isolated the new radioactive substances in a race against time, because nitrogen-13 produced when boron was irradiated had a half-life of fourteen minutes; and phosphorus-30, produced when aluminum was irradiated, of only three minutes, fifteen seconds. Joliot was never to forget "the intense expression of joy which seized [Marie] when Irène and I showed her the first artificial radio-element in a small test-tube. I can still see her taking between her fingers, burnt and scarred by radium, the small tube containing the feebly active material. To check what we had told her, she placed it near a Geiger counter to hear the many clicks given off by the rate meter. This was without doubt the last great moment of satisfaction in her life." A few months later, she would be dead.

Jean Perrin communicated the Joliot-Curies' report to the Académie des Sciences on Monday, January 15, 1934, four days after Joliot's first observation, in which they concluded: "For the first time it has been possible to make certain atomic nuclei radioactive using an external source."

It was one of the most important discoveries of the twentieth century—and a triumph for the Joliot-Curies. As Joliot said, "With the neutron we were too late; with the positron we were too late—now we are on time."

"Nobody had ever dared to imagine that nuclei could be found other than in Nature," said their daughter, Hélène, "but the chemical identification of phosphorus produced by bombarding aluminum proved for the first time the reality of artificial transmutations [nuclear reactions]. And with the emission of positrons and not electrons in the decay of phosphorus, the Joliot-Curies also discovered a new type of radioactivity."

The discovery of artificial radioactivity created a worldwide sensation among scientists. Niels Bohr considered that it had opened an "entirely new epoch" in nuclear physics. Rutherford congratulated them "on a fine piece of work which I am sure will ultimately prove of importance . . . In the past I have tried a number of experiments using a sensitive electroscope to detect such effects but without any success." Now he found it comparatively easy, and personally demonstrated artificial radioactivity in a lecture at London's Royal Institution on March 17, 1934.

Max von Laue wrote from Switzerland to Einstein, in Princeton, to tell him about it. In Berkeley, California, Ernest Lawrence was stunned by the news, which he read in *Nature* and *Time* magazine, and spent the weekend of February 24–25 bombarding element after element with deuterons from his cyclotron, finding radioactive isotopes (nuclei of the same atomic number but different atomic weight) everywhere. He then knew for sure that he or someone in his lab could have made the discovery at any time during the past six months. His "standard apology" was that the switch that turned off the cyclotron also turned off their Geiger counter, but his two recent biographers have suggested that "It was not a question of labor-saving switches, but of labor-saving thinking."

Marie received an unexpected letter from Stefan Meyer, director of the Radium Institute in Vienna, who congratulated the Joliot-Curies on their "fundamentally new" and "especially beautiful" discovery. She replied immediately, very touched by his letter. Marie had great affection for Meyer. He had supplied her and Pierre with tons of pitchblende from Joachimsthal uranium mines at the start of their career, and although they were on opposite sides during World War I, through diplomatic channels he had obtained news for Marie of her family in Poland as well as sending them food parcels. The Joliot-Curies accepted his invitation to give a lecture on their discovery in Vienna—which Irène delivered—followed by a reception at the French embassy.

What should have been a great time for Joliot was overshadowed by his encounters with André Debierne. Joliot was apparently on good terms with everyone at the Radium Institute with the exception of this close friend of the Curies, suspecting him, because of Debierne's secretive and introspective nature, of intrigues. And on April 2, 1934, while at L'Arcouest, Joliot wrote to Irène complaining of Debierne's growing hostility. "He is someone I frankly detest," he continued. "Perhaps I will change my mind once again?" Joliot's assistant Bertrand Goldschmidt thought Debierne was "a strange man. The rumor was that he had been Marie Curie's lover." But there is no reliable evidence for the suspected intrigues or for Debierne's rumored romance with Marie Curie.

In Rome, just back from a skiing vacation, physicist Enrico Fermi heard of the Joliot-Curies' discovery and, working with his colleagues, induced radioactivity in dozens of elements using neutrons rather than alpha particles. They were a playful crowd, spending their free time racing small toy boats powered by candles on a nearby goldfish pond. Fermi had found that an effective way to irradiate elements was to reduce the speed of neutrons he had obtained by bombarding beryllium with alpha rays and then passing them through paraffin, which contained a lot of hydrogen. Water also contained plenty of hydrogen, so that when he was working with silver as a target, Fermi suggested testing the effect of water "on silver activity." The nearest body of water being the goldfish pond where they sailed their toy boats, a silver cylinder was dumped into the pond. And it worked. The water greatly increased the silver's radioactivity.

But when he used uranium (number 92 in the periodic table) as the target of the slowed neutron bombardment, he produced strange radioactive substances he couldn't identify. Some colleagues thought that by "capturing" a neutron, a radioactive isotope of uranium had been created, which then decayed into transuranic element number 93. (Transuranic elements are those beyond uranium in the periodic table.)

Instead, Fermi had split the atom's nucleus and inadvertently stumbled across the key to the atomic bomb. His subsequent excuse for failing to recognize his fateful discovery was that he did not know enough chemistry. An assistant had a different explanation: that God, for his own inscrutable ends, had made everyone blind to the phenomenon of atomic fission. But he was not inscrutable to a German chemist, Ida Noddack, who had discovered the element rhenium in 1925. However, no one of consequence, Fermi among them, took her seriously when she wrote in *Applied Chemistry Magazine* in 1934, "It is conceivable that in the bombardment of

Members of the Radium
Institute in the early 1930s
included Irène and Marie,
seated in front, and the
bearded and somewhat
enigmatic André Debierne,
standing far right.

heavy nuclei with neutrons, these nuclei break up into several large fragments." But it was not until 1938, with the Hahn-Strassmann experiment
and its interpretation by Meitner and her nephew, Otto Frisch, that the
scientific world at large accepted nuclear splitting as a fact—and gave
the foursome the credit. (According to historian Steuwer: "This is a contentious issue—Strassmann and Meitner and Frisch were excluded from
the Nobel Prize: see for example Robert Marc Friedman, *The Politics of
Excellence*.")

Hélène Langevin-Joliot believes that "Nodack was not taken seriously
because she made no experiments to confirm her point, she was a woman,
and had recently published a wrong result. She nearly got it right—two
fragments are emitted."

Fermi reported his still puzzling discovery at an international conference in London and Cambridge in October 1934, followed by the Joliot-
Curies, who remarked that the terms *artificial radioactivity* and *induced
radioactivity* were misnomers—convenient but not very appropriate. To
them it was just as natural as ordinary radioactivity, though its impact, as

Joliot had surmised, was and is immense—in engineering, industry, biology, and medicine. Author Manuel Valadares remarked in *The Impact of Science on Society*: "If the magnitude of a discovery is measured by the extent of the new insights into nature it affords and the applications which can be made for the good of mankind, the discovery of artificial radioactivity was a very great discovery indeed."

Joliot knew this, judging by his response when his assistant, Lew Kowarski, told him the names of the Nobel Prize winners for 1934 and he was not among them. "Don't worry," he said. "I will get it next year." And he did, but not until his nearly disastrous attempt to replicate Fermi's work with neutrons. The experiment was set up on a balcony of the Radium Institute looking out on the rue Pierre Curie, and Joliot used liquid air to cool the paraffin. Liquid air mixed with paraffin can cause a big explosion, and it did, sending all the radioactive material into the rue Pierre Curie. As Gentner remembered: "They had used a very special source [of radioactivity] and it was bad. Everything was lost. So we went out into the street with portable Geiger counters to recover the source."

There were even more explosions in Paris streets early in 1934, but this time they were deadly, as forty thousand enraged, mostly right-wing Parisians battled in the place de la Concorde, a mile from the Radium Institute. Serge Stavisky was the proximate cause, having disappeared with a quarter of a billion francs of the public's money in an investment scam. During his sordid career, the Ukrainian émigré son of a dentist had sold wooden refrigerators that didn't work and land that didn't exist—and conned enough suckers to buy a theater, two newspaper companies, and a stable of racehorses. His trial had been postponed nineteen times because, it was reasonably assumed, he was protected by cops and politicians on his payroll. Stavisky was eventually traced to the fashionable French winter resort of Chamonix. As the police stormed his ski chalet, he shot himself. Officially, he had committed suicide, but in fact they had let him bleed to death for an hour, making no effort to save him. Shortly after, the mangled corpse of Albert Prince, a magistrate appointed to investigate the affair, was found on the Paris-Dijon railroad. Although he had been tied up and drugged, the police again called it suicide.

The forty thousand mostly right-wing Parisians holding a protest meeting in the center of the city streets on February 6, 1934—along with Frenchmen of every political stripe—had been incensed not only by the Stavisky scandal but also by the firing of the Paris police chief believed to support their views. Then the angry meeting escalated into a riot. Thousands swarmed across a bridge on the way to the Chamber of Deputies, apparently to drive the left-wing politicians out or even to assassinate them. Overwhelmed, the police opened fire, killing fifteen and wounding more than a thousand. Many of the fighters were members of "veterans' groups and paramilitary leagues . . . not unlike fascist groups elsewhere in Europe," according to historian Joel Colton. Future Socialist prime minister Léon Blum "interpreted the riot as proof that the potential danger of fascism existed in France, and that 'the fascist organizations were strong enough, and skillfully enough led, to divert and exploit to their profit . . . a troubled and aroused opinion.'" Russian journalist Ilya Ehrenburg (later Joliot's friend), living in Paris, believed the rioters were "led by reactionary and monarchist organizations such as Action Française and Croix de Feu, which [wanted to restore the king to the throne and] sympathized with Hitler's anti-Semitism."

Six days after the riot, Paul Langevin and his son, André, marched in a counterdemonstration of 120,000 jointly organized by Communists, Socialists, and workers' unions, their banners announcing "Unity Against the Fascist Peril." Because he feared that if the extreme rightists and fascists came to power they would endanger scientific research, Langevin also joined academic Paul Rivet and philosopher Alain in establishing "the Vigilance Committee of Antifascist Intellectuals." Joliot, who had already learned from Gentner how the Nazis were mistreating Jewish scientists, now realized it was time to make a stand. He joined the committee and became a Socialist. For several evenings he accompanied his friends Biquard and Langevin in turning out antifascist political posters on an antiquated printing press and plastering them throughout Paris.

Marie Curie and her daughters also supported this resistance to fascism. It had taken Marie fifteen years after World War I even to consider having a German at her institute. And the one she had welcomed, Wolfgang Gentner, a Geiger counter expert, remained because he was not a Nazi. Despite her understandable suspicion of Germans, she was no chauvinist. Gentner, in fact, had been astonished to see the international makeup of the institute, which consisted of people from Spain, Portugal, Romania, and Yugoslavia. Out of some thirty scientists at the institute, "certainly ten came from outside France," Gentner recalled. A brother and sister, researchers Moshe and Malka Feldenkrais, came from Palestine, then under British mandate. Moshe had been the first man in Europe to earn a black belt in judo, and several colleagues, including Joliot, Irène, and Bertrand Goldschmidt, rented a gymnasium to take judo lessons from him, during which Goldschmidt was Irène's partner.

As Gentner was from Nazi Germany, Marie was anxious to hear his views on the political situation in his country. And he remembered how, one lunchtime, "she was sitting in the garden waiting for a car, and I sat with her for some time and she asked me, 'Could you explain what is really going on?' From the beginning, she told me that I should work together with Joliot," who was also interested to know what Hitler was up to. Gentner reassured them that Hitler would not last much longer.

CHAPTER 15

Marie Curie's Last Year

1934

M arie spent the winter vacation with Irène, Joliot, and her seven-year-old granddaughter, Hélène, in the French Alps at Notre Dame-de Bellecombe. Although she was expected to rest, she joined them on the skating rink and for walks. One evening she put on her snowshoes and left without a word. When it got dark and she had not returned, they searched the area. No Marie. Irène became extremely worried, despite Joliot's reassurance that her independent, self-reliant mother could take care of herself. Sure enough, Marie returned, delighted with her little adventure and surprised that they had worried. She had gone quite a long way, she told them, to see the sun set over Mont Blanc.

At Easter, when her recently widowed sister, Bronia, came to Paris, they decided to take a trip south to her tiny, bougainvillea-covered villa in Cavalaire. To show Bronia the enchanting French countryside, they went in Marie's small Ford rather than by train, but the scenic route was extremely long, and Marie arrived exhausted and shivering. The house was cold and damp and when a hastily lit fire failed to warm it quickly, Marie uncharacteristically broke down and sobbed in Bronia's arms. She feared that she might develop bronchitis and so be unable to finish an updated edition of her book on radioactivity. According to her daughter Eve, "On the following morning Marie had conquered the spiritual despondency, which was never to recur." After staying five weeks with Marie, Bronia returned to Poland.

But Marie never fully recovered from a feverish cold, though she made the most of the brief, comparatively healthy spells to work at the institute. When weak and dizzy, she stayed home, proofreading her book and completing her plans to move to a new apartment in the city and to have a country home built in Sceaux. "I feel the need of a house with a garden more and more," she wrote to Bronia in May 1934, "and I ardently hope that this will succeed. The price of the building has been brought down to a sum suitable to my means. Therefore it will be possible soon to lay the foundations."

She resisted having a regular doctor on the grounds that doctors bored her and refused to let her pay them for treatment. It was true. No doctor had ever accepted payment from her. Eve confided in Dr. Regaud, in charge of the adjacent Pasteur Pavilion, who got a Professor Boulin to pay her a friendly visit. At first sight of her ravaged face, he said, "You must stay in bed. You must rest."

But of course she didn't. She continued her work at the Radium Institute almost daily, and to drag herself up and down the three stories to and from her apartment. One afternoon late in May she told a colleague at the institute that she was going home because she had a fever. Outside in the garden she called out to a lab mechanic to look after a drooping rose in need of water. And as she got into her waiting car, she told him not to forget. It was the last time he would see her.

Both Eve and Irène realized that Marie was seriously ill when she agreed to be taken to a clinic. But tests there did not explain her illness. Eve then hired four leading Parisian specialists to examine her, but none could diagnose a specific disease. Their guess was that clouded X-ray photos of one lung might indicate the inflammation of old tuberculosis lesions, and they recommended immediate treatment in a sanatorium.

Pierre's brother, Jacques, blamed an inadequate diet for her illness, and wrote urging her to have more than a cup of tea for an evening meal. "You've got an energetic soul, but that isn't enough; it ought to go along with a resistant body in good health. When you are back on your feet you must resolve to follow a more serious and less debilitating regime. Tenderest wishes, and affection."

To Eve's relief and amazement, after several weeks in the clinic, Marie agreed to go into "exile," believing that the noise and polluted air of the city had been preventing a cure, and that fresh air would restore her health. Arrangements were made for Eve to accompany her to the sanatorium and stay with her for several weeks. Marie's brother and sisters from Poland were willing to keep her company through July, when Irène would take over and spend August with her. By then she was expected to be fit enough to return to Paris. One of her fears had not been realized. She had been able to finish and proofread her book, as she told Irène and Joliot when they visited her before her journey.

Eve spent long hours in the radiant spring days with her mother and found her sweet nature almost unbearably poignant in the circumstances: Marie spoke hopefully of her children's future, of the future of the Paris and Warsaw Institutes, and of her confidence that Irène and Joliot would soon get the Nobel Prize.

Eve and a nurse accompanied her on the journey south to Sancellemoz, near Annecy, where she used an assumed name, "Mme Pierre," still anxious to avoid publicity. On arriving at Saint-Gervais she fainted in the arms of Eve and the nurse. When they finally reached the sanatorium and she was examined and X-rayed, Eve was stunned by the news. The awful journey had been unnecessary: nothing was wrong with Marie's lungs.

Professor Roch arrived from Geneva to examine her and reported an extremely high temperature above 104 degrees, assured her that she would not have to face a gallstone operation, and diagnosed extreme pernicious anemia. Then, in confidence, he told Eve that Marie's condition was hopeless. Determined at all costs to protect her mother from the fear that she was dying, she chose not to call the family to the bedside, and, to save her from additional suffering, vetoed any treatment that would only prolong the pain. Eve never forgot the tender care given by Dr. Tobé, the sanatorium director, and Dr. Pierre Lowys, who helped her maintain the illusion that Marie would recover, and promised to ease her last days with painkillers and soporifics.

In her waking moments, Marie complained wistfully, as if to herself, "I can't express myself anymore. I'm absentminded." And later, "The paragraphing of the chapters ought to be done all alike . . . I've been thinking of that publication." Once, staring intently at a cup in which she was stirring tea with a glass rod, she asked: "Was it done with radium or with mesothorium?"

Despite painkillers, Marie suffered terribly. Eve wrote to Meloney that she could not bear to witness her mother's pain and had to leave the room so that she would not see her crying.

On July 2, Irène and Joliot arrived. Next morning, as always, Marie held the thermometer in her shaking hand to check it for herself, the scientist to the end. She smiled joyfully: her temperature had gone down. To Eve it was a premonition of the approaching end, but she kept up the pretence, assuring her mother that it was a good sign.

As Marie glanced through the open window at the sun sparkling on the mountain, she said, "It wasn't the medicine that made me better. It

One of the last photographs of Marie Curie, taken outside the Radium Institute, as she looks at the garden she planted. She had once been briefly tempted to retire to spend her time gardening and writing scientific books.

was the pure air, the altitude." Her last coherent words were to protest with a sigh to the doctor about to give her an injection: "I don't want it. I want to be let alone." After she lost consciousness, either Eve or Dr. Lowys held one of her cold hands. One or the other stayed at her bedside for the next sixteen hours. Irène was too distraught to stay in the room with her mother. Then, at dawn on July 4, 1934, as the sun rose in a clear sky and suffused the room with light, Marie Curie's heart stopped. She was "all in white," Eve would remember, "her white hair laying bare the immense forehead, the face at peace, as grave and valiant as a knight in armor, she was, at this moment, the noblest and most beautiful thing on earth."

The death of sixty-seven-year-old Marie Curie made front-page news throughout the world. The *New York Times*'s headline the next day read "Mme Curie Is Dead: Martyr to Science;" among many columns of text, the article reported: "Mme Marie Curie, whose work alone and with her husband on radium and radiology has been one of the greatest glories of modern science, died at 6 o'clock this morning . . . Her death, which was caused by a form of pernicious anemia, was hastened by what her physicians termed 'a long accumulation of radiation which affected her bones and prevented her from reacting normally to the disease.' . . . Her daughters, Eve, who is a dramatist and pianist of considerable talent, and Mme Joliot, who with her husband was carrying on the family tradition of the radium institute over which her mother presided, were at her bedside when the end came."

Among the many scientists who mourned her death and acclaimed her life was Professor Colt Bloodgood, a cancer expert at Johns Hopkins University Medical School. He said: "Two years ago when I was in Paris attending a scientific meeting of the French Association Against Cancer I brought to Mme Curie a poem from an American actress whose life had been saved by radium. Countless lives are being saved and the ravages of cancer are being controlled by the use of X-ray and radium."

Rutherford, now a lord of the realm, applauded her "brilliance, her scholarship, and lifelong devotion to her work, [which] played a most important part in the origination of an entirely new science," adding that: "Her work will go on. Only recently Mme Curie's daughter, Mme Irene Curie-Joliot, [*sic*] made an important discovery in connection with the transmutation of matter." Nikola Tesla, the eccentric inventor who had produced man-made lightning flashes and discovered the rotating magnetic field, said that "she leaves among her contemporaries an impression akin to that of a rare, ethereal phenomenon. By sheer force of mind she managed to sustain her frail body through years of concentrated effort." William Coolidge, director of the General Electric Research Laboratories, and designer of the million-volt X-ray tube in use at New York's Memorial Hospital, recalled that when he visited Marie in Paris the previous October, "and she learned that in coming from Russia, I had just passed through her beloved Poland, her eagerness to hear about it was touching . . . She has placed in the hands of the medical profession a powerful tool for the relief of suffering and the prolongation of life."

In Paris, Prince Louis de Broglie called her role "in science, to which she had devoted her life, primordial in that field," and questioned whether her work was responsible for her death: "It may only be stated that throughout her life she accepted serious risks which her researches involved and there is no doubt that she exposed herself to dangers which could easily have a weakening influence on her health. There are two sorts of rays to which she might have been exposed, those known as alpha particles, which result in burns, and the gamma rays, which are even more penetrating and which have a direct action upon the globules of the blood." (In 1995 *Nature* magazine reported that X-rays, not radium, might have killed Marie Curie.)

Interviewed on vacation at Watch Hill, Rhode Island, Albert Einstein spoke of her ingenuity, extraordinary energy, and unusually independent character, and of her "standing up wholeheartedly for justice and for progress in politics and in social matters." He gave a more considered view of her at a memorial service in New York on November 23, 1935. Then he spoke of their "twenty years of sublime and unclouded friendship . . . Her strength, her purity of will, her austerity toward herself, her objectivity, her incorruptible judgment—all these were of the kind seldom found in a single individual . . . The greatest scientific deed of her life—proving the existence of radioactive elements and isolating them—owes its accomplishment not merely to bold intuition but to a devotion and tenacity in execution under the most extreme hardships imaginable, such as the history of experimental science has not often witnessed. If but a small part of Mme Curie's strength of character and devotion were alive in Europe's intellectuals, Europe would face a brighter future." Another remark by Einstein when she was alive, and still frequently quoted, was that "Marie Curie is, of all celebrated beings, the only one whom fame has not corrupted." The same, of course, could be said of Einstein.

In her introduction to her moving and eloquent biography of her mother, Eve Curie wrote: "I have not related a single anecdote of which I am not sure. I have not deformed a single essential phrase or so much as invented the color of a dress. The facts are as stated; the quoted words were actually pronounced. My mother was thirty-seven years old when I was born. When I was big enough to know her well, she was already an aging woman who had passed the summit of renown. And yet it is the celebrated scientist who is strangest to me—probably because the idea that she was a 'celebrated scientist' did not occupy the mind of Marie Curie. It seems to me, rather, that I have always lived near the poor student, haunted by dreams . . . And to this young girl Marie Curie still bore a resemblance on the day of her death. A hard and long and dazzling career had not succeeded in making her greater or less, in sanctifying or debasing her. She was on that last day just as gentle, stubborn, timid and curious about all things as in the days of her obscure beginnings. It was impossible to inflict on her, without sacrilege, the pompous obsequies which governments give their great men. In a country graveyard, among summer flowers, she had the simplest and quietest burial, as if the life just ended had been like that of a thousand others."

As Marie would have wished, there were no officials, priests, prayers, or politicians at her funeral; just her family, friends, and loving coworkers— among them Langevin, Regaud, the Perrins, and the Borels. One wreath was from the president of the Polish republic. She was buried at the cemetery in Sceaux above Pierre's coffin. As her sister Bronia and brother, Joseph, threw earth from Poland into the open grave, they were watched at a distance by uninvited reporters who had climbed over a wall to watch the burial and refused Joliot's request for them to move away.

CHAPTER 16

Nobel Prizes, Spanish Civil War, and Fission

1934–1939

N ewcomer Bertrand Goldschmidt was pasting labels on flasks in the chemical stockroom shortly after Marie's death when André Debierne told him to sort out her documents and personal papers. As someone said to him, "You are the one who knew her least, so it will be least painful for you." As he read her correspondence, he noted that she had unsuccessfully proposed Paul Langevin and Pierre Weiss for the Nobel Prize in physics for their work on magnetism. But what most struck him was her perseverance and rejection of celebrity.

Despite Joliot's suspicion of him, Debierne, a sixty-year-old bachelor, had been appointed director of the laboratory and Irène became his deputy and chief of research projects. Debierne was very close to the Curie family, having worked with them for most of his career. He was Eve's godfather and had spent many vacations with them. Though modest and introspective, he had a fierce temper that became very evident—his face turned purple—when Irène or Joliot occasionally enraged him. He was also extremely absentminded, shaking hands with newcomer Goldschmidt several times a day, as if meeting him for the first time. He once came into the room where Goldschmidt was working and after a brief conversation, as he went out, turned off the light, leaving the young chemist in the dark.

Another of Goldschmidt's memorable moments was when he first glimpsed thirty-year-old Eve Curie and was bowled over by her beauty and elegance. He was so smitten that fifty years later he remembered exactly how she entered the institute—through "the little chemistry room where

I worked, appearing at the glass door facing the garden." She was then romantically linked to a popular playwright, Henry Bernstein, who called her one of the three most beautiful women in Paris.

During Goldschmidt's early days at the institute, he was surprised by the almost affectionate manner in which Joliot gave him useful advice on his future career. Joliot stressed that it was vitally important to be popular with colleagues and revealed his own unexpected vulnerability by confiding, "I am hated." This puzzled Goldschmidt at first, because everyone seemed to like Joliot, especially such great friends and mentors as Langevin and Perrin.

Eventually Goldschmidt understood the problem: Joliot felt that he was "an intruder in this liberal and closed university mileu of the Curies, where the diploma from the Ecole Normale and often a family connection were the best passport." If not hated, he at least aroused scorn in some colleagues for both attending the wrong schools and marrying up. He aroused jealousy in others because despite such "drawbacks," he was unquestionably a genius. Whatever the cause, Goldschmidt believed that Joliot "needed to be surrounded by colleagues and friends who were greatly attached to him," and that his detractors were the cause of his enduring resentment.

He was particularly hurt by those who suspected his motives for marrying Irène. "Why do they claim that I don't love my wife and that I have married her just for the sake of my career?" he once asked a colleague. "I do love my wife very much." Another time, he was overheard saying, "No I have not yet been unfaithful to my wife, but if I am it will not affect our marriage."

Whenever they were apart they exchanged teasing, affectionate letters. When he was out of town, he wrote to her that he missed her despite her terrible bossiness. And when she was away, she regretted having too much room for her things. She even regretted, she wrote, that she didn't have to make his bed, something she never liked doing.

A reporter described Joliot at the time—giving an open lecture at the Sorbonnne on artificial radioactivity—as "elegant, discreet, fluent, and dominating." In the lecture, he predicted that "Chemistry would produce a variety of unheard-of products, while medicine would make marvelous advances." As author Spencer R. Weart comments: "Joliot held forth the same scientific utopia that his seniors preached" (especially his late father-in-law, Pierre Curie). Whether or not Joliot had an inferiority complex, as Goldschmidt suggests, his feelings of exclusion may have spurred him to greater effort. About his work he was enormously confident. And justifiably so when, as he had expected, he and Irène shared the 1935 Nobel Prize in chemistry for their synthesis of new radioactive elements. Among those who had nominated them were Paul Langevin and Jean Perrin.

Forewarned of the award, Irène had persuaded Joliot to hide from the press by reminding him how reporters had invaded her parents' home and written disparaging reports in the same circumstance. So when the prize was officially announced, they both dodged the press by going out to shop in the local Bon Marché, where they bought a plastic tablecloth for their new home at Sceaux, just outside Paris near where the Curie family had lived. With the prize money of about forty-one thousand dollars they planned to buy the house outright.

They felt no need to hide in Sweden, where, Joliot recalled, the ceremonies took place "in an atmosphere of cordiality." And Irène was able to correct the misapprehesion that she had merely been Joliot's assistant. Nothing, it seems, had changed since her mother's day.

At the Nobel celebrations they listened to their English "rival" James Chadwick speak about the neutron, for which he got the physics prize. It was an unusually short, off-the-cuff speech, because he had not been advised that a talk was expected from him. (He acknowledged later that he had been helped in his work by the observations of the Joliot-Curies.) The well-prepared French team was then announced.

Irène spoke first, responding to the false press coverage that implied that she had merely played a secondary role: "These experiments were carried out by Monsieur Joliot and myself working together, and the way we have divided up the lecture is merely for convenience." Joliot backed her up, speaking of "our experiments," which had enabled them to add fifty new radioactive elements to the thirty naturally radioactive ones presently on Earth. During the speech he glanced at his wife and, in an aside that moved the audience, said, "It was certainly a satisfaction for our late lamented teacher, Marie Curie, to have seen the list of radioactive elements that she had the honor to inaugurate together with Pierre Curie so extended." He continued with a vivid picture of the atomic world: "The several hundred different types of atoms which constitute our planet should not be considered as having been created once and for all time. We observe them because they have survived. Other less stable ones have disappeared. It is probably some of these 'vanished' atoms which have been re-created in the laboratory. Hitherto, it has only been possible to obtain atoms which have a relatively short life, extending from a fraction of a second to several months. In order to create an appreciable quantity of an element with a much longer life, it would be necessary to have at one's

Almost a family tradition—
Irène and Frédéric Joliot-Curie
(at right) receive their Nobel
Prize for chemistry from the
king of Norway (center) in
1935. They had discovered
artificial radioactivity and
shared the prize for their
synthesis of new radioactive
elements.

disposal an extremely intense source of nuclear radiation. Is there any hope of realizing this new dream?"

In his Nobel lecture thirty-two years previously, Pierre Curie had warned that "in criminal hands radium could become dangerous." Joliot gave an even more cautionary prognostication, virtually predicting the atomic bomb:

> If we look back at the past and consider the progress made by science at an ever increasing pace, we may feel entitled to believe that researchers, building up or breaking down elements at will, will be able to bring about nuclear reactions of an explosive nature—veritable chain reactions [and] one can imagine the enormous release of useful energy which will take place. But, alas, if all the elements on our planet are contaminated, we can only look forward with apprehension to the consequences of the unleashing of such a cataclysm. Astronomers sometimes observe how a star of mediocre brilliance . . . suddenly increases in size and becomes very bright and visible without the aid of instruments—this is the apparition of a supernova. It may be that this sudden inflammation of the star is caused by these explosive chain reactions—a process which researchers will no doubt try to bring about, while taking, let us hope, the necessary precautions.

The one sour note was when Hans Spemann—a German embryologist and that year's Nobel Prize winner in medicine or physiology—ended his lecture with a Nazi salute, another premonition of the awful shape of things to come.

Irène lived up to her reputation for being allergic to public receptions when the king of Sweden asked Joliot where she was. He found her away from the crowd reading a book in a quiet corner.

While in Stockholm, Chadwick and his wife stayed in the same hotel as the French couple and all four had a friendly lunch. Chadwick had been impressed by the "panache" with which Joliot had delivered his Nobel speech and in an interview years later said that he was fond of Joliot, who "would have been a very good actor. Irène was much more reserved. Indeed it was difficult to know her properly. She might have said the same thing about me. But on the whole we got along well." She had surprised him once when she was a lunch guest at his Cambridge home, and, "to the consternation of our domestic," she broke up her bread and put some pieces in her mouth, and threw the rest over her shoulder. He assumed it was a nervous habit.

Meanwhile, her sister, Eve, had decided to write a biography of their mother, approaching the task with great trepidation, because she didn't feel up to it. But she was motivated by the fear that another writer would beat her to it and not get it right or even do a hatchet job.

Eve now interrupted this work, succumbing to a request to write an article about her elusive celebrity sister—another labor of love.

In the piece, Eve revealed that she had never been able to make her sister angry, never heard her say anything nasty, and was sure that she had never lied. As a child Eve found her big sister's behavior incomprehensible: Irène took no interest in clothes or makeup, and, given a box of candy she would put it away in a cupboard, take it out later, and eat just one candy, then replace the box and forget it. Whereas Eve would have eaten the lot at a sitting.

The schoolgirl Irène, according to Eve, was "unsociable, slow moving, hard to approach," and "lacked the dash of the brilliant pupils, [but] she had something better; knowledge once acquired was fixed firmly in her well-ordered mind." As for money and possessions, Eve wrote, "I have seen her accumulate in her savings bank sums which seemed enormous to me, but which she never spent—simply because she never wanted anything." As an adult, although Irène hated city life she made the best of it by never agreeing to meet anyone or do anything that bored her. On the other hand, she loved sports and the outdoors so much that "even when

Eve Curie in the mid-1930s, when
she wrote a biography of her mother,
Madame Curie, a labor of love and
an international best seller that was
later made into a Hollywood movie.
Eve was considered one of the most
beautiful women in Paris, as well
as a talented writer.

she has been working hardest has found time to ski, to canoe, swim, and
climb mountains." That was why "she has a house both in suburban Paris
and in Brittany so that she can work all year-round in a healthy atmosphere and lead a simple family life."

Back from their triumphant visit to Sweden, the Joliot-Curies resumed
their work at the Radium Institute. There, according to Bertrand Goldschmidt, now Joliot's assistant, the laboratory continued to be "dominated
by the Joliots . . . They inspired and often directed most of the research
projects under way. The fame of the Radium Institute attracted young scientists from the world over, in particular from central Europe. Among the
most brilliant, there arrived at the end of 1935 Bruno Pontecorvo, an Italian of my age [early twenties], full of charm and very popular, and Hans
von Halban, a few years older, an ambitious and self-assured Austrian.
[There were] an exceptionally large number of young women who were
attracted to the prestige of Mme Curie, a symbol of the successful struggle
for the emancipation of women . . . Among the foreigners some were
financially supported by their governments; others were political refugees
and were dependent on stipends granted by French organizations."

Because of Jean Perrin's bright idea, Irène briefly left her laboratory
to join the government of Socialist Léon Blum, the first Jewish French
premier. He had adopted his friend Perrin's suggestion to create a new government department for scientific research, and to make Irène its under-

secretary. To almost everyone's surprise, she accepted. This was the first time a woman had been appointed to a high government office in France. Although it meant frequently attending meetings—which she hated—she took the job, as she explained to the Curie family's American friend Marie Meloney: "as a sacrifice for the feminist cause in France." She chose Joliot's friend and eventual biographer Pierre Biquard to join her staff, the only one perhaps to understand and appreciate her. The press certainly didn't and soon attacked her "for her dry manner and devastating frankness, and mistakenly labeled her incredible naiveté and artlessness as haughtiness." She also confirmed Eve's account of her meticulous honesty. When a secretary brought her a form letter to sign, declining an invitation to some function, which ended, "I regret I cannot attend," she refused to sign it. Why? Because Irène didn't regret it. And she wouldn't sign the letter until the "regret" phrase was removed. She understood the government job to be a brief appointment—to make a point—and after two months was replaced by Jean Perrin and eagerly returned to her laboratory.

Eve, too, had recently written to Meloney to say that although she had just completed a biography of her mother there was still so much she didn't know about Marie's life. This was understandable. Although Eve had done extensive research in Poland and had great help from both Marie and Pierre's friends and family, much personal correspondence had been destroyed. Consequently, a frank, firsthand account of her great friendship with Paul Langevin is missing from the book, and the savagery of her critics downplayed.

But Eve succeeded in her goal, as defined in the book's introduction: "I hope that the reader will constantly feel, across the movement of one existence, what in Marie Curie was even more rare than her work or her life; the immovable structure of a character; the stubborn effort of an intelligence; the free immolation of a being that could give all and take nothing . . . and above all the quality of a soul in which neither fame nor adversity could change the exceptional purity." Albert Einstein, who invariably spoke his mind and could be sharply critical of Marie, essentially agreed.

Vincent Sheean, an American writer and reporter based in Europe, translated Eve's original French version into English, and the biography was published simultaneously in England, France, Italy, Spain, and the United States. It was an instant and enduring best seller, destined to be converted into a popular movie. Aldous Huxley wrote the screenplay—at least the first version—when the Swedish actress Greta Garbo was slated for the role of Marie. Instead, the Irish American Greer Garson played the part, and the Canadian Walter Pidgeon appeared as Pierre, in a script credited to Paul Osborne and Paul H. Rameau. Altogether eighteen writers had a hand in it.

One of them, Salka Viertel, who traveled to Paris to do research for the script, wrote to the film's director, Sidney Franklin, that "Irene Joliot-Curie dislikes, or rather, is very much hurt by the idea that the life of her mother should be shown in a motion picture. Confidentially, I found out from other people in Paris, that Eve never told anybody that she had sold her book to the movies. Irene and her husband have great influence and are very much respected here in France. As she is not certain what our picture will be like, even if the intentions of my collaborators are the best, she refuses any cooperation, since she would thereby lose the right to protest. . . . And, dear Sidney, when she refuses it is as if the Rock of Gibraltar were to refuse."

Released in 1943 during World War II, *Madame Curie* received seven Academy Award nominations. The book and film inspired many women to enter the scientific field and impressed multitudes. After seventy years the book is still in print and the film is available on tape. There have been several subsequent film and television versions of Marie's life.

Irène was portrayed in Eve's biography of their mother as an endearing and uncompromising personality with precarious health. When she became ill, her doctor invariably advised rest in the country. Now when she became alarmingly thin without apparent cause, her doctor once again advised her to rest. But she was eager to accompany Joliot to Moscow in the fall, where he was to give the inaugural address at the Mendeleev conference. Their discovery of artificial radioactivity had revived an interest in the pioneering work of the Russian chemist Dmitry Mendeleev. He had classified the known chemical elements into groups according to their atomic numbers, leaving gaps for elements still to be discovered. Irène's doctor convinced her that if she didn't rest she would not be fit enough to make the trip to Moscow. So she set off for the mountains with her longtime friend Angèle, while Joliot left with the two children to spend the summer vacation at L'Arcouest. From there he wrote to his wife, encouraging her to gain weight, because he wanted "to have a beautiful Irène with me" in Russia. He suggested that on her return from the mountains, and before they went to Russia, she should first join him in Brittany and then buy smart, warm clothes in Paris for the trip. She was glad, she replied, to learn that he was getting a good rest, "probably by going out at 4 A.M. to check the fishing nets and going to bed at midnight after having danced, not to mention having played tennis in between." And she asked

The new generation: the Joliot-Curies with their daughter, Hélène, and son, Pierre, in 1936. Both children became scientists.

him to take care on his motorcycle and boat "so I shall find you in one piece, [and not to] smoke too much if you want to be my beloved *chéri*."

The mountain air restored Irène's health, and she and Joliot went to Russia in the fall of 1936, where they were the guests of honor at a USSR Academy of Science banquet. At the subsequent Mendeleev conference, where he again broached the subject of a hypothetical experiment in which chain reactions might result in a devastating explosion, he posed a provocative question. Would any of them, he asked his audience of scientists—including Lise Meitner—if they hit on the right process, try the experiment? Joliot answered his own question, obviously with himself in mind: he believed that the curious researcher with a love of adventure would certainly try it. On their way back to Paris, the couple visited Irène's relatives in Poland and toured several Polish laboratories.

They felt compelled to become more politically active when Spanish refugees began pouring into France to escape from the civil war that had erupted that summer. General Francisco Franco, while stationed in Spanish Morocco, had led an armed revolt against his democratically elected government, which quickly spread to the Spanish mainland. Hitler had then responded to Franco's urgent request for help with bombers, pilots, tanks, and technicians. Italy's Benito Mussolini sent planes, munitions, and some seventy thousand troops. The Soviet Union was the only country to support the republicans with soldiers and munitions. Although thousands of volunteers from Britain, France, and the United States—the latter as members of the Abraham Lincoln Division—fought on the republican side, their countries remained neutral.

To writer George Orwell it was "in essence a class war. If it had been won [by republicans], the cause of the common people everywhere would have been strengthened." Kingsley Martin, editor of the liberal British journal *New Statesman*, agreed: "It was the hope of liberation from ancient tyranny that inspired resistance to Franco. The medieval church and aristocracy had always crushed any signs of democracy in Spain . . . The issue was whether Spain must for ever remain a backward, uneducated, impoverished land under the autocratic rule of the priests and army."

Chicago News reporter Edgar Ansel Mowrer challenged the French premier Léon Blum to justify his stance of neutrality. "The Germans in Spain . . . and the Italians are waging the next European war by proxy," said Mowrer. "If they win, there will be no holding them." They argued for half an hour until Blum explained why, although a Socialist and in sympathy with the embattled Spanish government, he wouldn't help them: "My political position is not strong enough at home to allow me both to realize my domestic reforms and to intervene in favor of the Spanish Republicans. I have decided to carry out my reforms. And that's that."

Captured German documents later revealed that Hitler's intention was to prolong the civil war, hoping to keep the Western democracies and Italy at loggerheads (over Italy's invasion of Abyssinia) and draw Mussolini toward him. "A hundred percent victory for Franco [is] not desirable from the German point of view," Hitler said in a confidential talk with generals and his foreign minister. "Rather we are interested in a continuance of the war and in keeping the tension in the Mediterranean." Mowrer proved to be right: Nazi Germany and fascist Italy used the bloody Spanish battleground as a rehearsal for World War II. And Blum's neutrality didn't help him: he was out of office the following year.

Disgusted with their passive government, the Popular Front, a coalition of Socialists and Communists, the Joliot-Curies supported groups helping Spanish refugees and urging the democracies to ensure the survival of a fellow democracy. Although they were seen at a French Communist party meeting to encourage more funds for scientific research, Kowarski denies that this indicated Joliot's switch to the party. "Probably it will surprise most of Joliot's biographers," Kowarski said in a 1967 interview, "but at the time he was violently anti-Communist. He told me many times, 'Communists are Jesuits; they have no sincerity. They are a clique of power-grabbers.' I remember many discussions when he would be expressing his sympathy for this or that figure on the non-Communist left. I would tell him, 'Yes, but this man looks to me very ambitious and unscrupulous. Be careful.' There were a lot of these little groups in France . . . which considered themselves very leftist and which were in fact budding fascists. Fascism always comes from the left, always. Mussolini was an orthodox Socialist in the beginning. Hitler was one of the first members of the German Workers' Party . . . Joseph McCarthy came from the left . . . In America the populist movement of Wisconsin and Minnesota was sort of half-Socialist, half Fascist, in some of its leanings. Joliot was a very non-ideological person really. He had, in a way, a very naïve, warm and generous idea about the good that was in the people."

In 1936 Irène and Joliot no longer worked together at the Radium Institute. A year after sharing a Nobel Prize, they broke up permanently as a team, largely because of their mutual friend Paul Langevin. He had again played a vital role in Joliot's life, by recommending him for the chair of inorganic chemistry at the prestigious four-hundred-year-old Collège de France, the nation's source and symbol of advanced learning. It focused on research, gave no degrees, and provided free lectures open to the public by world-class scientists. But there was a problem: in a drive to economize, the chair of inorganic chemistry had been eliminated and the only vacant seat was in the Sanskrit language. The vote then by members of the Collège became whether to fill the chair in Sanskrit or to replace it with a new chair for Joliot in nuclear chemistry. It was a close call; he just scraped through by one vote.

The appointment assured Joliot that he had reached the pinnacle of his career. It included a full professorship, a first-rate laboratory and staff of his choice, and potentially generous government funding. Russian-born Lew Kowarski, who went with him as an assistant, gave other motives for Joliot leaving the Radium Institute and his productive partnership with Irène. "Joliot," he explained,

was intensely French; and although in the French scientific Establishment he was a complete outsider, resting only on the basis of his genius—which for any Establishment is a very flimsy basis. But, he's been universally recognized; a Nobel Prize [winner], which already in those days was a very rare thing in France; a world celebrity rather more so than in France; and on his way up to something quite dizzy. For a man of that size and of that sort of ambition, it was normal to aspire not just to be a professor at the Sorbonne but a professor in the Collège de France. Which was at that time—and I think still is [1969]—the most prestigious chair an academic can have in France. So he moved in. He had very vast ideas. He considered himself the discoverer, and therefore probably the most important person in his own eyes, of artificial radioactivity. He thinks of using isotopes in biology, in engineering. He also was full of all sorts of humanitarian ideas, which in France meant that he was less xenophobic than the others. He brought two outstanding young men with him to his new laboratory. One was Pontecorvo, an Italian [who defected to the Soviet Union in 1950] and the other was Halban. As for myself, I came into that crowd mostly as his personal secretary. [Joliot] knew I had some kind of queerly inventive mind, although he realized that it was dormant, but he thought it might come in handy later on. It turned out he was right. So I had this dual capacity, but primarily in the capacity of his personal secretary.

Jean Perrin, now a powerful influence in Léon Blum's government, had promised Joliot "some four million francs, to build new laboratories," writes Spencer Weart. "Joliot could not have won the money through family friendship or scientific accomplishment alone. Like Perrin, he was now moving on his own in high social and even aristocratic circles, lionized for the Nobel Prize and appreciated for his personal charm. And like Perrin, Joliot was beginning to show an extraordinary ability to deal with the various men who controlled funds. One government official recalled that when he went to visit laboratories, most scientists were irritated or reminded him that they had been his teachers at the university. Joliot alone welcomed the stranger enthusiastically, explained lucidly what was being done in his laboratory, and revealed an affable but obstinate will to get the means necessary for his research."

Working a short walk from each other, Irène and Joliot frequently met during the day to advise each other and to discuss their latest experiments, plans, and problems. But of course it was not the same as when they were a team.

Irène had found a new teammate, Paul Savitch, a young Yugoslavian, and kept the same rigorous routine as before. At 8 A.M. she arrived at her sparsely furnished office—a table and one chair, with a pile of Geiger counters in one corner and a cot Savitch had installed in the other, and on which her doctor had told Irène to rest between experiments. Yet every Sunday, despite many preoccupations, including her duties as an associate Sorbonne professor, she still made lunch, usually stew, for some twenty family members, friends, and colleagues. And in the evenings her guests included Geiger-counter expert Wolfgang Gentner and his charming

Swiss wife. He proved very useful as an interpreter if there were German- or English-speaking visitors—as Joliot only spoke French. "Normally in France at this time you were never invited by people to their homes," Gentner recalled. "They invited you to a restaurant. But the Joliots were different in this way." Their discussions were more political than scientific during the fall of 1938, when Adolf Hitler threatened to annex part of Czechoslovakia. France was treaty-bound to protect it from aggression, but instead capitulated to Hitler's demands.

Incensed by France's policy of appeasing the dictators, the Joliot-Curies and Jean Perrin did more than talk, sending an open letter to French premier Edouard Daladier, which read in part: "Our external interests are being entrusted to very weak men. We demand that no concession be made to the Italian and German demands."

Across the Channel, Winston Churchill also deplored his own peace-at-any-price government, telling the press on September 21, 1938: "The partition of Czechoslovakia under pressure from England and France [through the Munich Agreement] amounts to the complete surrender of the Western Democracies to the Nazi threat of force. Such a collapse will bring peace or security neither to England nor to France. On the contrary, it will place these two nations in an ever-weaker and more dangerous situation . . . The belief that security can be obtained by throwing a small state to the wolves is a fatal delusion. The war potential of Germany will increase in a short time more rapidly than it will be possible for France and Great Britain to complete the measures necessary for their defense."

To protest France's craven policy toward Hitler and Benito Mussolini, his partner in crime, Joliot and Langevin formed part of a delegation that French president Albert Lebrun agreed to meet. The first speakers were highly emotional, and Lebrun listened to them patiently without interrupting. But when it was Joliot's turn, he spoke with calm deliberation and touched a nerve. "Has not the minister for foreign affairs shown more than compliance?" he asked. "Are we not faced with a complicity verging on treason?" At the word *treason*, Lebrun leaped to his feet, saying that he would not allow his minister to be insulted, and angrily dismissed the delegation.

Soon after, Joliot gave a lecture at the Sorbonne on the medical uses of artificially radioactive substances. Lebrun was in the audience and afterward took him aside, congratulated him on his talk, and then confided: "I was extremely fierce the other day. In the presence of so many people I could not have acted otherwise. But you were right!"

Because Communists were the only members of the French Chamber of Deputies to protest the Munich Agreement, and the Socialists had lost their credibility as a force to resist the fascist dictators, Joliot, Langevin, and other progressive intellectuals increasingly supported the Communist Party.

The tense international situation seemed to have affected Debierne's behavior at the institute. Although titular head of the laboratory, he had become increasingly isolated, and at such times Irène took over. There were still occasions when he exerted his authority, such as when he decided to appoint Bertrand Goldschmidt to replace the departing Marcel Guillot. Irène made it clear that she opposed the appointment and confronted Debierne with a list of all those with more seniority or merit who should get the job. To which he replied, "You are right, I agree with you, but Goldschmidt possesses a quality that all the others do not have." Adding, to Irène's astonishment, "He did not work with your mother. Now get out of here!" (Ten years later, in 1948, Irène told Goldschmidt of this disconcerting conversation with Debierne.)

If Irène told Joliot of this confrontation at the time, it gave him reason for disliking Debierne even more. But now he was happily away from his influence, preparing to build the first cyclotron at the Collège de France. With its many millions of electron volts, it would give Joliot an enhanced means of bombarding the nuclei of atoms to produce more transmutations and artificial radioactivity. To house the cyclotron (an apparatus that gives high energy to particles through the combined action of a homogeneous magnetic field and an oscillating electrostatic field), Joliot supervised excavation for a thirty-foot-deep cellar in the Collège and sent an assistant to the United States to find out from Ernest Lawrence (coinventor of the machine) how to install and operate it. Lawrence was already building his fourth machine at the Berkeley, California, campus.

Meanwhile, with her new partner, Savitch, Irène had been trying to identify an isotope they had recently found and called "R-3-5" because of its half-life of 3.5 hours. As it had highly penetrating beta rays and a comparatively long survival, the French team reported that it should be reasonably easy to measure and eventually identify.

But when Meitner and Otto Hahn failed to find any hint of R-3-5 in their similar experiments, they concluded that it did not exist. Meitner was so convinced that Irène was mistaken that she wrote to warn her that unless she publicly retracted her findings, she, Meitner, would have to publish a criticism of her work. Instead, Irène and Savitch continued to reproduce the isotope and to try to identify it. They thought that it might be lanthanum, number 57 on the Mendeleev periodic table, or actinium (discovered by Debierne in 1899), or even a new transuranic element higher than uranium on the periodic table. At home, Irène and Joliot discussed the problem exhaustively, and when in 1938 Joliot attended the Tenth International Congress of Chemistry in Rome, he brought it up with Otto Hahn. Joliot defended Irène's results, but Hahn, considered the greatest radiochemist of his time, insisted that neither he nor Meitner had ever seen anything like R-3-5, and faulted Irène for using what he called her mother's antiquated methods.

Later Hahn ridiculed Irène's claim to have found a new radioactive element, by playing on the Curie name and calling her "discovery" a "curioism." Though otherwise on friendly terms with the French couple, Hahn was heard to say of Irène: "This damned woman. Now I will have to go home and waste six months proving that she was wrong!" (It was hardly wasted. Through Irène's provocation he came upon nuclear fission.)

In the May 1, 1938, issue of *Comptes Rendus*, Irène and Savitch published a less confident report on their contested work, though still concluding "that this substance cannot be anything except a transuranic element, possessing very different properties from those of other known transuranics." They did concede, however, that their hypothesis raised "great difficulties for its interpretation." Hahn's angry response was to ask Joliot to stop Irène and Savitch from publicly refuting his and Meitner's results. Otherwise, he said, he, too, would be reluctantly forced to contradict them in print. Irène showed Hahn's letter to Savitch and asked for his reaction. "We should continue working on it," he said, and let Hahn "do what he wants." She agreed.

Lise Meitner was now more concerned with saving her life than with disproving Irène's theories. Although her parents were Christian converts and she had been raised as a Protestant, the Nazis regarded her as a Jew. Realizing that there was literally no future for her in Germany, she tried to leave, but was refused a passport—and felt trapped. Several German and foreign colleagues knew of her plight and joined a secret effort to save her. Bohr tried to find her work in Sweden, and another friend offered her refuge in Switzerland if she could use some subterfuge to cross the border without a passport. Finally, when she was desperate, Dirk Coster, a Dutch physicist who had helped several German Jewish refugees to escape, offered to escort her to Holland with a cover story that she was merely going for a brief vacation with his family. She grasped at what seemed her last chance.

Somehow Kurt Hess, a professor of organic chemistry and a fanatical Nazi who lived in an adjoining apartment, heard of the plan and wrote to warn the Nazi authorities that Meitner was about to flee the country. (She declined to testify against him after the war.) Fortunately, someone delayed his letter and probably saved her life. Otto Hahn, who had worked with her for thirty years, was one of the international team helping her to escape. Others were Dutch physicist Peter Debye, director of Berlin's Kaiser Wilhelm Institute for Physics, and Dutch physicist A. D. Focker, who arranged for a Dutch border guard and a customs official to let Meitner enter their country without a passport—if she could reach the border. Exactly why the Dutch officials offered to help isn't clear.

Before her escape attempt she spent the night at Otto Hahn's home with Hahn and her Austrian friend Paul Rosbaud, a science editor and apparently fearless anti-Nazi. There they agreed on a coded telegram to inform them if she had made it safely across the border. (During World War II, the charismatic and erudite Rosbaud, under the code name The Griffin, became known as Winston Churchill's most valuable spy in Europe. He informed the Allies of the work by Nazi scientists on rocket propulsion and atomic weapons.)

Hahn recalled that the danger for Meitner "consisted in the SS's repeated passport control of trains crossing the frontier. People trying to leave Germany were always being arrested and brought back. We were shaking with fear whether she would get through or not." Hahn insisted that she take an antique diamond ring, an heirloom from his mother, hoping that if she managed to escape she could survive on the proceeds. Otherwise, she only carried two small suitcases of summer clothes and a small amount of cash as evidence for her cover story that she was bound for a brief vacation.

Next day, July 13, 1938, as Rosbaud drove Meitner to the railroad station, she panicked and pleaded with him to turn back. But he kept going. Dirk Coster was already on the train, and he greeted her so casually that she was able to control her terror. When they approached the Dutch border, fearful that her diamond ring would arouse suspicion, she again became agitated. Coster calmed her by pocketing the ring. No SS or Gestapo men interrogated either of them on the train, and at the border, as promised, the Dutch officials let her through without a passport. Coster then sent Hahn a telegram: "The baby has arrived. All is well." Keeping up the pretence, Hahn responded: "Heartiest congratulations . . . What will be the little daughter's name?" Among many other congratulatory telegrams to Coster was Wolfgang Pauli's: "You have made yourself as famous for the abduction of Lise Meitner as for [discovering] hafnium." (Coster and George de Hevesy had discovered this new element, number 72, in 1922.)

After a few days in Holland, Meitner flew to Copenhagen, Denmark, where she became reacquainted with her nephew Otto Frisch—also a refugee physicist—who was working with Niels Bohr. Bohr warmly welcomed her, and after a few days' rest at the Carlsberg House of Honor she was on her way to a permanent home in Sweden.

Her French rivals, unaware of her flight from Germany, finally concluded in a paper published in September 1938 that the chemical element they had produced resembled lanthanum, a known element midway in the periodic table. But they were dramatically wrong. And even though the ambiguous discovery was discussed in several seminars attended by researchers from the Curie Laboratory and the Collège de France—some of the brightest minds in the country—none foresaw the puzzle's revolutionary solution.

Otto Hahn was equally baffled. As he wrote to Meitner on December 21, 1938, in trying to refute Irène's recent work he and Fritz Strassmann had obtained results that were "physically absurd." After bombarding uranium with neutrons, they had expected to create a heavier element. Instead they ended up with a much lighter element. Hahn urged Meitner to help him find a way out of his dilemma: in fact, they had inadvertently discovered how to unlock the atom's energy, but didn't yet know it. They did suggest, very tentatively, that "it was possible to consider that the uranium nucleus had split in two under the actions of the neutrons." Meitner immediately replied: "Your radium results are very amazing. A process that works with slow neutrons and leads to barium! . . . To me for the time being the hypothesis of such an extensive burst seems very difficult to accept, but we have experienced so many surprises in nuclear physics that one cannot say without hesitation about anything: 'It's impossible.'"

As Meitner was spending the Christmas holidays with her nephew Otto Frisch, she showed him Hahn's SOS letter. He suggested that Hahn had simply made a mistake. "Hahn is too good a chemist," she replied. "I am sure his result is correct. But what on earth does it mean? How can one get a nucleus of barium from one of uranium?" Frisch wanted to talk about his own plans to design and build a large magnet to study the magnetic behavior of neutrons. But as they walked together in the snow—he on skis, hoping to ski later, she on foot—Meitner managed to divert him into discussing Hahn's weird results. And he became fascinated.

After a while they stopped to rest on a tree trunk and began to scribble mathematical calculations on scraps of paper. "Out of their calculations and discussion," according to science writer Margaret Gowing, "the two physicists evolved an explanation of the phenomenon in terms of Bohr's

. . . model of the nucleus . . . Their idea was that the arrival of a neutron in a uranium nucleus set up violent internal motions in the latter and caused it to split into two more-or-less equal fragments. These fragments would each have roughly half the mass and half the nuclear charge of the uranium atom and would therefore be atoms of elements in the middle of the periodic table."

As Frisch later explained: "Fortunately Lise Meitner remembered how to compute the masses of nuclei from the so-called packing fraction formula, and in that way she worked out that the two nuclei formed by the division of a uranium nucleus would be lighter than the original uranium nucleus by about one-fifth the mass of a proton. Now, whenever mass disappears energy is created, according to Einstein's formula $E=mc^2$, and one-fifth of a proton mass was just equivalent to 200 MeV [MeV represents a million electron volts; 200 MeV is equal to the energy of an electron accelerated in a machine producing 200 million volts.] So here was the source for that energy; it all fitted!"

What helped was that Meitner had never forgotten hearing Albert Einstein lecture in 1909 on his special theory of relativity, when he asserted that mass and energy were interchangeable, expressed as $E=mc^2$, in which energy was equal to the mass of a substance times the speed of light squared.

On his return to Copenhagen, Frisch decided to put their suppositions to an experimental test. So on Friday, January 13, 1939, he began work in the basement laboratory of Bohr's Institute, using an ionization chamber, and continued through the night. By 6 A.M. he had confirmed their hypothesis: Hahn and Strassmann had, in fact, split the atom's nucleus. Then he went to bed, only to be awakened an hour later by a mailman with a telegram. It was wonderful news: his father had been released from a concentration camp. (His father and his mother, then living in Austria, eventually moved to Sweden, where they shared an apartment with Lise Meitner.) Just to make sure, Frisch repeated his experiment later that day, and an Irish American biologist, William Arnold, came down to the basement to watch. Frisch asked Arnold what microbiologists called it when one bacterium divided into two. "Binary fission," he replied. "Could it be called simply fission?" Frisch asked. "Sure," said Arnold. And that is how nuclear fission got its name.

Meanwhile, having completed the paper tentatively suggesting that he and Strassmann might have split the uranium nucleus—not yet aware of Frisch's experimental confirmation—Hahn telephoned Paul Rosbaud with the news. "Paul was electrified," Hahn remembered. "He went to fetch the paper and immediately called Fritz Suffert, the editor of the Springer scientific publication *Naturwissenshaften*, and got him to pull one of the articles already being typeset for the next issue [January 8] to make room for the Hahn-Strassmann paper."

Ten days later the journal arrived at Joliot's office and Kowarski handed it to him. "Joliot probably had his first glimpse of the article in my presence," Kowarski recalled, "and it was, of course, a bombshell. Immediately, everything was understood about the strange findings of Irène and Savitch . . . For the next few days nobody talked about anything else," especially when an account of the Frisch experiment verifying fission was published.

At home, eleven-year-old Hélène Joliot-Curie heard either her father or her mother say, " 'Maybe if we had worked together, we would have discovered fission!' But," Hélène later explained, "from 1935 on, my father had focused on building accelerators."

Kowarski heard a more high-octane exchange between the couple, during which Irène, who always spoke her mind, said, "Oh what assholes we've been!" She "bitterly reproached Joliot for not having been working with her at that time. And she was right," according to Kowarski. "He probably would have been more daring in his interpretation of the results instead of saying these are lighter elements. He would say . . . 'It might be that. If it is that, then it can be proved this and that way.' And he would have done it." (In a January 8, 1939, letter to Meitner, Frisch wrote: "George de Hevesey . . . said that Irène Curie had told him already last fall that she found very light elements from uranium, but she obviously did not trust herself to publish it. Well, she already has the Nobel Prize, she can be satisfied.")

After several days alone and incommunicado in his office, on the morning of January 26, 1939, Joliot appeared at the Radium Institute and seemed very excited. Without explaining why, he asked Irène and Savitch to be at his Collège de France laboratory at exactly 3 P.M. When they arrived—Kowarski and Joliot's other assistant, Pavel Savel, were also there—Joliot told them of his ideas on how to split the uranium atom in two. "Then he designed his experiment," Kowarski recalled. "One of the most elegant experiments I know of in the history of science, and which he performed before our eyes in less than half an hour. So here it was. Fission was proved as physical reality."

His paper on the experiment was presented to the Academy of Sciences on January 30, 1939. But Joliot was unaware that Frisch had already observed and reported fission about two weeks before at the Bohr Institute in Copenhagen, and had mentioned it to his friend George Placzek. He in turn, says Kowarski, "brought this exciting piece of gossip to Halban. But neither Placzek or Halban said a word about it to Joliot, and they considered it quite natural. 'Well, this is not yet published. It will be published in a few days. If we spread this gossip, it's unfair to Hahn and Strassmann.'" Kowarski believed that unconsciously they considered themselves, with Hahn and Strassmann—but not Joliot—part of the inner circle, and "so, according to their lights, they were quite correct. According to Joliot's lights, their conduct was monstrous, because they had a red-hot piece of scientific information, and they were in Joliot's lab, and they deliberately held it from [him]. So Joliot was rudely reminded again that there was this Central European enchanted circle of which he was not part."

Despite Halban's "monstrous" behavior, Joliot retained him as one of his team, along with Kowarski, and the rivalry between Kowarski, the Russian giant, and Halban, the more sophisticated and dynamic Austrian, now naturalized Frenchmen, served to energize their work together.

Goldschmidt recalled that "when Kowarski arrived in the lab he used to sort of walk on your feet and we called him Gawkgoolock—a White Russian who murdered the president of the republic. And he was always obsessed with the intelligentsia and high society—because he didn't belong to high society." Still, Kowarski had hidden talent and had quickly graduated from being Joliot's secretary to become a valuable and equal member of his research team.

In February 1939, when a European war seemed inevitable, American physicist P. W. Bridgman announced his intention to prevent colleagues from totalitarian countries from having access to his laboratory and expected other scientists to follow his lead. He explained why in *Science*: "A citizen of such a state is no longer a free individual, but may be compelled to engage in any activity whatever to advance the purposes of that state. . . . Cessation of scientific intercourse with totalitarian states serves the double purpose of making more difficult the issues of scientific information by these states and of giving the individual opportunity to express abhorrence of their practices."

Joliot had resisted the idea when physicist Leo Szilard, an unemployed Hungarian refugee in the United States, raised the alarm, writing to him on February 2, 1939: "When Hahn's paper reached this country about a fortnight ago, a few of us at once got interested in the question whether neutrons are liberated in the disintegration of uranium. Obviously, if more than one neutron were liberated, a sort of chain reaction would be possible. In certain circumstances this might lead to the construction of bombs which would be extremely dangerous in general and particularly in the hands of certain governments." Joliot did not respond to the letter. He, Halban, and Kowarski were about to undertake an experiment that would make them the first to discover how to create a chain reaction. It proved successful, and they were so determined to have credit for it that on March 8 Kowarski took their account for publication in the British magazine *Nature* to Le Bourget airport, an hour from Paris, to send it by airmail. *Nature* printed such features more quickly than other scientific journals. "Why not secure priority?" Kowarski said years later. "Hell, as I always say, it's not vanity—it's bread and butter."

When Szilard realized that Joliot was ignoring his letter, he had gained the support of several British and American physicists, who agreed to keep sensitive information about the fission of uranium from a potential enemy—especially Nazi Germany. One of them, refugee physicist Victor Weisskopf, sent Halban a telegram emphasizing the seriousness of the situation. Halban was handed it while he was in the bath and told that it was unusually long—170 words. After finishing his bath, he took the telegram outlining Szilard's fears to Joliot, who replied that Szilard's proposal, though reasonable, had arrived too late. He also pointed out that *Science Service* had already informed the press about Richard Roberts's work as early as February. (Roberts had stated that the discovery of fission "brings back the possibility of atomic power.") But the account of Richard Roberts's work at the Carnegie Institution had been in very general terms.

Joliot had not taken the appeal seriously in the first place partly because he thought that Szilard was a maverick, acting on his own. And he was confused by Szilard's telegram because it had arrived on April Fools' Day, making him doubt its seriousness. Halban even thought it was an April Fool's joke. Furthermore, "So important a matter," writes author Jungk, "in the opinion of the formally minded French, should have been broached by the American Academy of Science instead of being raised by a few 'individualists,' and 'outsiders.'" But in the words of one of the French team, they were not concerned with any enemy using the information. Instead, "we knew in advance that our discovery would be hailed in the press as a victory for French research and in those days we needed publicity at any cost, if we were to obtain more generous support for our future work from the government."

Not that any of the trio were eager to help the Nazis, especially Halban and Kowarski, who were part Jewish. Although they all anticipated an imminent war with Nazi Germany, they considered a nuclear bomb to be a remote possibility at best, and still supported the free exchange of basic research between scientists. Joliot believed that the information would leak out whether published or not and that by stifling it they would be allowing Hitler to destroy another freedom.

Joliot might also have thought that the idea of a secrecy pact had been abandoned when he got a letter from Fermi, also in the United States—a refugee from Mussolini's fascist Italy—without a word about secrecy. In fact, Fermi had proclaimed himself a rival, writing on February 4, 1939: "I am presently engaged, like, I think, every nuclear physics laboratory in trying to understand what goes on in the disintegration of uranium." What Fermi did not reveal was that when I. I. Rabi, a fellow physicist at Columbia University, urged him to keep his fission research secret because it might produce superbombs, he had replied, "Nuts!" Both Rabi and Szilard had then asked Fermi to explain his derisive response. "Well," he said, "there is the remote possibility that neutrons may be emitted in the fission of uranium and then of course perhaps a chain reaction can be made." Asked what he meant by "a remote possibility," he said, "Well, ten percent." "Ten percent is not a remote possibility," Rabi countered, "if it seems that we may die from it. If I have pneumonia and the doctor tells me that there is a remote possibility that I might die, and it's ten percent, I get excited about it." Fermi declined to share their excitement.

In Paris the Joliot team spent fourteen-hour days on experiments, followed by frantic discussions on how to release nuclear energy through a chain reaction, which Joliot had predicted as feasible in his 1935 Nobel Prize speech. Any success, they agreed, would be attributed to the team and not to any one of them, and they welcomed a brilliant theoretical physicist, Francis Perrin, Jean's son, to join them in the quest. Less flamboyant than his father, he was a good friend of Joliot's and a pacifist. A diving accident had slightly shortened his nose—and he had a distinctive Vandyke beard.

Biographer Rosalynd Pflaum pictured the four men gathered in the dark, paneled Collège de France library on a cool spring day talking about what seemed like the futuristic scientific fantasies of H. G. Wells or Jules Verne. Kowarski recalled them seriously contemplating altering the face of the map and perhaps diverting the Mediterranean Sea into the Sahara desert, because Joliot's goal was not only to make the first chain reaction and unleashing of atomic energy possible, but to use it for the good of mankind. And especially for France.

With this in mind, early in May they secretly took out three patents: for making and regulating a nuclear chain reaction; and for creating a potential nuclear bomb. Following the high-minded Curie tradition, Joliot decided that all patent rights would belong to a government agency, the Centre Nationale de la Recherche Scientifique (CNRS), which were eventually transferred to the French Atomic Energy Commissariat (CEA).

On April 22, 1939, *Nature* published their report, which indicated that it would be possible to start a chain reaction—because, when a neutron split a uranium nucleus, two neutrons were usually released. This in turn could split into another uranium nucleus, and if this reaction was controlled, it could provide a tremendous energy source. Joliot hoped this energy source might eventually free man from painful and laborious work forever, which also had been Pierre Curie's dream.

The following month Francis Perrin gave a rough estimate of the least amount of fissile material needed in a medium containing uranium (known as the critical mass) to produce a nuclear chain reaction.

A few weeks earlier, Paul Harteck, a German physicist, and his assistant had warned the German War Office that in their opinion, "the newest development in nuclear physics will probably make it possible to produce an explosive many orders of magnitude more powerful than the conventional ones . . . The country which first makes use of it has an unsurpassable advantage over others." His warning spurred a secret meeting in Berlin on April 29, 1939, when the Nazi government agreed to start a nuclear research program, to stockpile radium from the Joachimsthal mines in Czechoslovakia, now under its control, and to ban uranium exports.

Across the Atlantic, on that same day, in Washington, D.C., according to a *New York Times* reporter:

> Tempers and temperatures increased visibly today among members of the American Physical Society . . . over the probability of some scientist blowing up a sizable portion of the earth with a tiny bit of uranium, the element which produces radium. Dr. Niels Bohr of Copenhagen [recently informed by Otto Frisch of his successful experiment], a colleague of Dr. Albert Einstein at the Institute for Advanced Study, Princeton, N.J., declared that bombardment of a small amount of the pure Isotope U235 of uranium with slow neutron particles of atoms would start a "chain reaction" or atomic explosion sufficiently great to blow up a laboratory and the surrounding country for many miles. However, many physicists believed that it would be difficult, if not impossible, to separate isotope 235 from the more abundant isotope 238. The isotope 235 is only 1 percent of the uranium element . . . Other physicists pointed out that [it] would be almost prohibitively expensive and the yield of isotope 235 would be infinitesimally small." Nevertheless they agreed that if

the process of separation worked, then "the creation of a nuclear explosion which would wreck as large an area as New York City would be comparatively easy. A single neutron particle striking the nucleus of a uranium atom . . . would be sufficient to set off a chain reaction of millions of other atoms."

Bohr's telegram congratulating Otto Hahn on his "wonderful discovery" found Hahn in an angry mood over a *Nature* article that seemed to denigrate his work. The article implied that the Curie-Savitch team had identified the 3.5-hour substance as lanthanum and that he had merely verified this finding. He wrote to Meitner complaining about it. She in turn was exasperated by Hahn because in his writings and lectures he never mentioned her vital contributions to his work. This may explain why she unexpectedly supported the French team, replying to Hahn: "Feather is not quite fair to you, but you once again are not quite fair to Curie-Savitch . . . In one of their *Comptes Rendus* articles they emphasized strongly that their 3.5-hour substance had very remarkable chemical properties and emphasized the similarity to lanthanum. The fact that they tried to place it among the transuranes doesn't change their experimental findings. And these findings led you to begin your experiments. And again you have not stated that clearly . . . [Irène] Curie obviously saw that something remarkable was going on even if she did not think of fission. In November 1938, Hevesy heard her say in a lecture that the entire periodic system arises from U + n bombardment . . . If I may give you some advice, I think you should not get involved in discussions of priority . . . The English don't like that sort of thing."

At the time the English were less concerned with priority than with cornering the market in uranium as possible weapon material, which General Leslie Groves revealed in his book *Now It Can Be Told.* As director of the Manhattan Project overseeing the development of the atomic bomb in World War II, he was privy to inside information.

Among his revelations is an account of a May 1939 meeting in England between Edgar Sengier, a Frenchman and president of the Union Minière; Lord Stonehaven, a fellow director of the Belgian company; and Sir Henry Tizard, director of the British Imperial College of Science and technology. Tizard asked Sengier to give the British government an option to buy all the uranium ore from his mine in the Belgian Congo. Sengier refused, but as he was leaving, "Sir Henry took him by the arm and said most impressively: 'Be careful, and never forget that you have in your hands something which may mean catastrophe for your country and mine if the material were to fall in the hands of a possible enemy.' The remark, coming as it did from a renowned scientist, made a lasting impression on

Sengier." And it also explains his extraordinary decision a few days later, when he returned to Europe and agreed to meet Joliot, Francis Perrin, and Halban. They told him that "their work could eventually lead to an experimental bomb which might be tested in the Sahara."

Sengier then came to a gentlemen's agreement—with nothing signed—that the Union Minière would supply Joliot's laboratory with five tons of uranium oxide, the first five thousand kilograms of which arrived on June 1, 1939.

The following month the Associated Press reported that Professor Joliot was "trying to find a way to make a two-dollar pound of uranium produce enough energy as was obtained by burning $10,000 worth of coal . . . It has been found that when uranium is bombarded by neutrons the difficulty is to get the neutrons to make enough hits. That has been the insurmountable trouble in all previous attempts to unlock atomic power. But the uranium may offer a way to dodge the trouble. For it has shown indications of having its atoms act like a bunch of firecrackers. Set off one cracker and the others follow by what is known as a chain reaction. Uranium atoms will do the firecracker trick under certain restrictions."

Author Thomas Powers reports that when Otto Hahn was convinced by the Joliot-Curies' work in Paris on secondary neutrons that an atomic bomb was possible, he discussed the subject with Carl Friedrich von Weizsacker. The prospect "depressed Hahn so severely that he contemplated suicide. In a discussion among friends at the Kaiser Wilhelm Gesellschaft it was proposed that German scientists make bombs impossible by dumping existing uranium stocks into the sea—a notion, never serious, dismissed after someone pointed out that new uranium was readily available from the mines of Joachimsthal."

By midsummer of 1939 World War II seemed inevitable. Spain had fallen to Franco, Mussolini had invaded Albania, and Hitler, having seized all of Czechoslovakia, was threatening Poland. To Winston Churchill's great relief, Britain anticipated Hitler's intentions, abandoned its policy of appeasement, and unilaterally guaranteed Poland's security. So did France.

In July 1939 refugee physicists Leo Szilard and Eugene Wigner visited fellow refugee Albert Einstein at his vacation cabin in Peconic, Long Island, and told him of the looming danger of an atomic weapon in the hands of the Nazis. Soon after "Einstein signed a letter to President Franklin Roosevelt stating that it was highly likely . . . that explosive bombs of unimaginable power could be constructed out of uranium . . . whose chief source was the Belgian Congo . . . It seemed necessary to take precautions to keep stocks out of the hands of political enemies." With it was a note from Szilard saying that the French work was probably the most advanced. Roosevelt then created a committee to study the possibility of using uranium as a weapon.

On August 5, 1939, briefed by his science adviser, Frederick Lindemann, Churchill wrote to Kingsley Wood, the British secretary of state for air: "Some weeks ago one of the Sunday papers splashed the story of the immense amount of energy which might be released from uranium by the recently discovered chain of processes which take place when this particular type of atom is split by neutrons. At first sight this might portend the appearance of a new explosive of devastating power."

Churchill went on to discount the possibility of this happening for many years. But because a future enemy might attempt to scare Britain into surrender by threatening to destroy London with a terrible new secret explosive, he asked the minister to assure the public that "only a minor constituent of uranium is effective in these processes [which would take many years], that the chain process can take place only if the uranium is concentrated in a large mass, [and that] as soon as the energy develops, it will explode with a mild detonation before any really violent effects can be produced." (A problem, of course, that would be overcome.) He added that "only a small amount of uranium in the territories of what used to be Czechoslovakia is under the control of Berlin. For all these reasons the fear that this new discovery has provided the Nazis with some sinister, secret explosive with which to destroy their enemies is clearly without foundation. Dark hints will no doubt be dropped and terrifying whispers will be assiduously circulated, but it is to be hoped that nobody will be taken in by them."

In his *Gathering Storm* Churchill notes the accuracy of his forecast, adding: "Nor was it the Germans who found the path. Indeed they followed the wrong trail, and had actually abandoned the search for the atomic bomb in favour of rockets or pilotless airplanes at the moment when President Roosevelt and I were taking the decisions and reaching the memorable agreements . . . for the large-scale manufacture of atomic bombs."

Nine days after he wrote that warning letter to the British secretary of state for air, Germany and the Soviet Union signed a nonaggression pact, which was immediately supported by the French Communist Party. Shortly before, Irène had written to Meloney that Communism was the hope of the future. Bitterly disillusioned by this alliance with the Nazis, she, Joliot, Jean Perrin, Langevin, and other members of the Union of French Intellectuals signed a manifesto condemning the agreement. It was published in *Le Temps*. The Socialist former French premiere, Léon Blum, who for years had been exposing the subservience of French Communists to Russia, and appealing to their leaders to break the "alliance with Moscow," now declared: "The curtain has been lifted. The Soviets are accomplices of Hitler. The Soviets, the only proletarian state of the world, the one that has boasted of having 'constructive socialism,' has become the bloody accomplice of the most monstrous iniquity."

His successor, Premier Edouard Daladier of the Radical Party, banned two Communist daily newspapers, *L'Humanité* and *Ce Soir*, and outlawed the French Communist Party. Its leader, Maurice Thorez, briefly drafted into the army, deserted and escaped to the Soviet Union under Stalin's protection, where he sat out World War II.

Germany's invasion of Poland—the trigger for World War II—began on September 1, 1939. In two days German planes wiped out the Polish air force parked on airfields. Amazingly, the Poles were still using cavalry. So it was hardly a surprise when the overwhelmingly superior German army of fifty-six divisions, nine armored, and Russia's massive army won the war in a month. Poland, in Churchill's words, "fell into the merciless grip of those who sought not only conquest but enslavement, and indeed extinction for vast numbers."

Both Irène and Eve were specially horrified by the German attack on Poland because it endangered their close relatives. And when the Soviet Union's invasion on Poland's eastern front trapped them, it brought into question the Joliot-Curies' growing sympathy for the Communist system. Their children, Hélène and Pierre, were still on vacation at L'Arcouest, where Irène wrote to her twelve-year-old daughter, much as her mother had written to her at the start of World War I: "What is happening is sad, . . . and we may be separated for some time . . . I have seen children being evacuated. Pinned on their clothes were large cards with their destinations printed on them. They looked like small packages waiting to be mailed. We are organizing the laboratories to work for National Defense." She advised her to study her music and do her gymnastics every day and to try to help the farmers in the fields. "Naturally, if you help, you must do it very seriously and not quit as soon as you have had enough. I embrace you, my beloved little girl. P.S. Make your little brother [Pierre] go into the ocean while you watch."

Joliot was drafted as an artillery captain and appointed director of Group I Scientific Research by Raoul Dautry, the intelligent and quick-thinking new minister of armaments, admired for having effectively modernized the French railroad system. When the rest of Joliot's team was drafted into the army, Dautry allowed them to remain with Joliot on special assignment at Ivry. (Except for Perrin, who joined the army.) Now their work was top secret, and there was no question of publication. But with posterity in mind they found a way to establish their claim to being the first to have discovered how to create a nuclear chain reaction using uranium. They sent their dated account in a sealed envelope to the Academy of Science, where it was not opened and read until long after the war.

Then it impressed Patrick Blackett, a British future Nobel physicist (1948), who wrote that, "Unfortunately France was to be submerged for four years by occupation, darkness, and betrayal. Defeat separated the members of the Collège de France team, but for a further two years Halban and Kowarski were to continue in Britain [and Canada] the work they had started with Joliot in execution of his direct instructions and under his recognized authority . . . Had the war not intervened, the world's first self-sustaining chain-reaction would have been achieved in France." And Leo Szilard, who helped Enrico Fermi to achieve the first controlled fission reaction at the University of Chicago in 1942, conceded that "if his work had not been interrupted [Joliot] might have beaten us to it."

The Soviet Union's lame excuse for its attack on Finland in December 1939 was to strengthen its borders, but the "crime" as Léon Blum saw it was proof that Stalin was motivated solely by Russia's interests and not, as he claimed, by concern for the international proletariat.

Joliot absorbed himself in organizing several laboratories for the war effort, hoping, he told his mother, that by working he could forget the stupidity of man. Irène, also ready and willing to do her part, remained at the Radium Institute, while Eve, preparing for a tour of the United States to promote her biography of Marie, wondered how she could help her country while abroad and on her return.

Irène wrote to Marie Meloney in the United States: "We very much hope that the U.S. will abrogate the neutrality act. This law is both unjust and is against the interests of the U.S. for, if there is a fascist victory, it is clear how fascism would establish itself, first in South American countries and then moving to the North. If the U.S. does not help the democracies, at least by selling arms, it will be a crime against our common civilization."

CHAPTER 17

France Defeated

1940

What the British dubbed "the phony war," the French "la drole de guerre," the odd or funny war, and the Germans "sitzkrieg," the sitting war, lasted for months, as enemy forces faced each other on the Western Front. Without firing a shot, the French army did advance toward the Germans' defensive Siegfried Line and occupied a few undefended frontier villages, but then, trained and equipped only for a defensive action, they failed to attack. Six weeks later they retreated to their own Maginot Line. Farmers took the hint and continued to plow their fields between the two inert armies. Bombers on both sides remained grounded, the British Royal Air force persuaded apparently by French Premier Daladier's plea for them not to bomb German targets, as it might trigger reprisals against France's "indispensable war industries." However, they did drop a few explosives on German naval bases. There were also battles at sea in which during the first week alone the Germans sank eleven British ships and the British destroyed two U-boats. But for various reasons, after conquering Poland, Hitler postponed his land and air attack in the west until the spring of 1940.

Despite grim reports of the sea battles, Eve Curie risked an Atlantic crossing to New York. She arrived on Wednesday, January 18, 1940, aboard the Italian liner *Vulcania* for a lecture tour in English on "Science and a Woman." It was both to promote her biography of her mother and to win support for the endangered democracies. The thirty-city tour had been postponed because of her work as director of women's wartime activities for the French Ministry of Information. Soon after arriving in Manhattan, she made an unannounced visit to Mayor LaGuardia at City Hall, looking chic in a simple black silk dress with hat to match. She later told a reporter that "France is proud to have your sympathy, but there is a feeling that America is needed in this conflict."

The next morning Eve gave a lecture in the Town Hall on "French Women and the War," in which she complained that French women had no political rights. At midday, she was guest of honor at a Hotel Astor luncheon given by Town Hall trustees to discuss "The Arts and America." It was attended by some fifteen hundred people, among them actor Paul Robeson and authors Dorothy Thompson and Maurice Hindus.

Without mentioning Hitler, Stalin, or Mussolini by name, she said that: "The most terrible condemnation of regimes of oppression which today rule several countries of Europe is the sudden, the total disappearance of their art. This does not only come from the fact that many artists of these countries are persecuted or exiled. Some of them are not persecuted, not exiled. Some have been given full powers to create, by order of the dictator of the moment, a totalitarian art which would leave the world breathless. And yet their creations amount to nothing. Having been ordered to speak, artists have nothing to say. [On the other hand] liberalism, by allowing the artists to admire freely the treasures of the past, to be nourished by them, provokes renovation, reaction, invention. To defend those spiritual values, France has been obliged to enter a war."

Eleanor Roosevelt invited her for dinner and to stay the night at the White House on February 2, 1940, and mentioned in her column next day that "The President was very glad to see her again . . . I looked at this slender, dark, very chic and charming woman, who does not look as though she were made for hard work, and yet can come over to this country and spend two months on the road. She looks her best on all occasions, meets people, I am sure, with the thought in her mind that she is not only making friends for herself, but for her country and that, therefore, she must try to meet as many people as possible to draw out their questions and their points of view and, if possible, leave them with a friendlier feeling toward her nation than they had before."

Eve was still on her lecture tour in February when Joliot, in Paris, accepted an invitation to become an honorary member of the Committee to Aid Polish-Jewish Refugees. That same month the French Military Intelligence (the Deuxième Bureau) warned Raoul Dautry, minister of armament, that the Germans were trying to buy two tons of heavy water from the world's sole producer in Norway, but refused to say why they wanted it. The wary Norwegians, suspecting they might want it for biological warfare, had delayed their response. Soon after, Joliot called on

Eve Curie after escaping from France during World War II, pictured here in New York City with Eleanor Roosevelt, 1941.

Dautry and asked for permission to buy heavy water as a vital moderator in his ongoing nuclear research. He backed up his request with a five-page report that gave his latest research results and stated that heavy water was needed to control a potential chain reaction. Now Dautry realized why the Germans were so anxious to get it: they, too, must be working on nuclear experiments, doubtless for military purposes. Joliot agreed, and as a German invasion of Norway seemed imminent, they decided to act fast.

Jacques Allier, a lieutenant in the French Intelligence with good Norwegian contacts, volunteered to beat the Germans to it and buy all the available heavy water. With Premier Daladier's approval, he was given a letter of credit for thirty-six million French francs (half a million Norwegian crowns) to clinch the deal, and secret service agents to protect him and the heavy water on the mission. Before Allier left, Joliot handed him a tube of cadmium and advised him to pour a little of it into the heavy water if it was in danger of being captured, to make it unusable.

The day after the team left for the mission on February 28, 1940, the French intercepted a German secret cable telling their agents in Norway to arrest Allier, but they lost track of him. The previous French ambassador to Norway had suspected Axel Aubert, the manager of the Norwegian heavy-water plant, Norsk Hydro, of being pro-Nazi. But Allier had such a different impression that he explained Joliot's intended use of the heavy water. To play it safe, he offered to leave half for the Germans. His instincts were right. Far from being pro-Nazi, Aubert sympathized with the democracies and not only offered to lend Allier the entire stockpile of heavy water, but refused any payment until after the war. He even offered to give France priority for all future heavy-water production. As they shook hands on the deal, Aubert said that if France lost the war he was likely to be shot, but it was an honor to take the risk. Allier, in turn, promised that if nuclear power transformed the world's economy after the war, the Norwegian company would be additionally recompensed. (Obviously the Germans never suspected Aubert's role in helping the French, because when soon after they invaded and occupied Norway, he was not even arrested. He died of natural causes in 1943. The French paid for the heavy water after the war.)

By midnight on March 9, 1940, 185 kilograms of heavy water had been poured into twenty-six aluminum canisters secretly made by Oslo craftsmen in their own homes. Allier and his team—Jean Mossé, a Sorbonne professor; Knall-Demars, a counterespionage agent; and Jean Muller, an army officer—then drove the load in trucks for ninety miles over icy, mountainous roads to Oslo. There, as author Per F. Dahl reports, "it was off-loaded and stored in a house belonging to the French Embassy, amid considerable nervousness, for good reasons: a pavilion next door belonged to the Abwehr, German Military Intelligence, and remained brightly lit all night." The next day, Allier and Mossé arrived early at nearby Fornebu airport and, under assumed names, first booked seats on a plane to Holland and then on another going to Scotland. When they returned later that day they found, as was standard practice, that two Junkers-52 planes were parked on the tarmac side by side, and the one for Perth, Scotland, its propellers turning, was about to take off. As they were walking from the terminal, making a great show of heading for the plane to Holland, Knall-Demars arrived at the airport in a cab with thirteen canisters of heavy water, now in suitcases.

"Because he made a fuss, his cab was allowed to drive onto the tarmac, and stopped between the two aircraft out of sight of the terminal building," says Dahl. "The canisters were quickly manhandled onto the Scottish plane, Allier and Mossé changed direction and climbed aboard, and Knall-Demarts headed back to the gate. The plane for Holland took off soon after theirs. The subterfuge had worked, because it was forced by Luftwaffe fighters to land in Hamburg, where a search by police and security agents uncovered its cargo of crushed Norwegian granite, but no team members or heavy water. The plane for Scotland was also chased by a

German fighter, but Allier explained to the pilot of his plane that he and his companion were French officers in civilian dress on a mission of great importance for the Allied cause. The pilot understood, headed into a dense fog, and diverted the flight from Perth to Montrose in Scotland. The two Frenchmen spent the night in an Edinburgh hotel; and the next day were joined by Knall-Demars and agent Muller, bringing the remaining 13 canisters from Norway on a second plane. All four caught the train for London with their precious cargo stashed overhead."

Although Britain was at war, no customs officer had questioned them or searched their luggage when they arrived from Norway by plane. And no British official expressed the slightest interest in them or their suitcases as they traveled by train from Scotland to the French mission in London, or at the Channel port where they boarded a ferry to France. (After the war a thrilling documentary film based on the heavy-water adventure appeared, in which Joliot played himself.)

Apparently, although it is still officially secret, according to author Michael Smith, their success in getting the canisters away from the Germans and their unquestioned journey through Britain was due to the help of Captain Frank Foley of the British Secret Service [MI6]. He has been compared with Oskar Schindler and Raoul Wallenberg for his role in helping at least ten thousand Jews escape the Holocaust. As cover for his intelligence work, he was appointed British passport control officer in Berlin just before the war, when he even went into concentration camps to give Jews false papers and passports allowing them to emigrate. In August 1939, a month before the war broke out, Foley was posted to Oslo, where he is believed to have played his part in making sure that the Frenchmen, as allies, got away with the heavy water and had no trouble transporting it through Britain. He died in 1958.

By mid-March 1940, to Dautry's and Joliot's relief, virtually the world's total supply of heavy water was stored near Joliot's laboratory in a cellar of the Collège de France. According to Dautry, the French government wanted Joliot to use it to produce a nuclear bomb and began negotiations to rent land in the Sahara desert to test it. But Joliot, Halban, and Kowarski were committed to building an experimental nuclear power plant for industrial use.

Germany ended the standoff or "phony war" on April 9 by invading Norway and Denmark. The same day *New York Times's* front-page banner headline read: "Germans Occupy Denmark, Attack Oslo; Norway Then Joins War Against Hitler," Eve Curie, who was still on tour in the United States, addressed a meeting of the American Booksellers Association in

New York. Speaking for France, she said: "We discovered that peace at any price is no peace at all. We discovered that life at any price has no value whatever; that life is nothing without privileges, pride, rights, and the joys that make it worth living . . . And we also discovered that there is something more hideous, more atrocious than war or than death; and that is to live in fear . . . Let's face it: however old-fashioned and out of date and devalued the word is, we like the way of living provided by democracy."

The Germans attacked Holland and Belgium on May 10, 1940, claiming to be protecting their neutrality, and that same day Winston Churchill took over from Neville Chamberlain as Britain's prime minister. Holland collapsed after five days of fighting, and traitors almost kidnapped its Queen Wilhelmina, who broadcast a warning to her people, "Do not trust your best friend." She and Dutch government officials escaped to England on British destroyers.

On May 14, screaming German Stuka dive bombers, followed by history's most devastating army of tanks and motorized troops, attacked the Allied armies defending Belgium. The sitzkrieg (sitting war) was over and the blitzkrieg (lightning war) had begun with a vengeance. In one day the rapidly advancing Germans destroyed seventy French tanks and shot down forty of seventy-one RAF bombers vainly trying to slow their advance.

When, on May 16, Paris itself was threatened, War Minister Dautry ordered Joliot to hide the heavy water from the approaching enemy. He in turn gave the urgent task to his friend Henri Moureu, his deputy director at the Collège de France. As Moureu recalled, Joliot called him to his office and said, "The front at Sedan has been broken by the Germans. Dautry just phoned. The heavy water must be put straightaway in secret somewhere in the center of France. I give you the job. Absolute secrecy. You have a free hand." That night, armed only with a pistol, Moureu loaded the laboratory's Peugeot truck with the twenty-six containers and headed south with Delattre, an eighteen-year-old lab assistant.

The same day, Churchill flew from London to Paris to assess the situation and was "dumbfounded" when General Gamelin, commander in chief of the Allied armies, told him that the French army no longer had any troops in reserve to defend Paris. "It was unheard of," Churchill wrote later, "that a great army, when attacked held no troops in reserve. I admit that this was one of the greatest surprises of my life." In fact, French soldiers held in reserve had already joined the battle against the overwhelming enemy forces.

Moureu reached Clermont-Ferrand on May 17, stored his secret load of heavy water known as "Product Z" in vaults of the Banque de France, and hurried back to Paris. Three days later, the combined Allied armies— Belgian, French, and British—were trapped fifteen miles from the English Channel. The manager of the Banque de France feared that he could no longer protect the mysterious deposit, so the cans of heavy water were transferred to an empty cell in the nearby women's prison at Riom. (French leaders whom the Germans blamed for declaring war on Germany would eventually be imprisoned there.)

During the winter Field Marshal Alanbrooke, as leader of the British forces in France, had evacuated eight hundred thousand civilians to save them from the anticipated terror and destruction the Luftwaffe's planes would be spreading along French and Belgian highways. This had cleared the roads for his troops. But now he noticed to his despair that the refugees were all crowding back into the evacuated area. As he noted in his diary: "They were all haggard-looking, and many women were in the last stages of exhaustion . . . with their feet tied up with string and brown paper where their shoes had given out; they were covered with mud from throwing themselves into ditches every time a plane flew over. There were old men trundling their old wives in wheelbarrows, women pushing prams piled high with all their belongings . . . small children worn out with traveling but hugging their dolls . . . and all their faces distorted by fear, a heartbreaking and desperate sight."

Alanbrooke began his diary for May 23: "Nothing but a miracle can save the BEF [British Expeditionary Force] now," and ended, "It is a fortnight since the German advance started and the success they have achieved is nothing short of phenomenal. There is no doubt that they are most wonderful soldiers." Five days later, Belgium's King Leopold III defied the unanimous advice of his government and surrendered. Most of his government then left for England.

The German advance against the remaining Allied forces seemed unstoppable. Yet within days, inexplicably and irrationally, Hitler went from being beside himself with joy at his military successes to fearing that his luck wouldn't hold. He became cautious, and instead of ordering his Stuka bombers and tanks to demolish the remaining resistance in France, he told them to hold their fire.

Churchill took advantage of the brief lull to launch "Operation Dynamo," a desperate attempt to rescue soldiers trapped by the German onslaught near the French port of Dunkirk. When word of the situation spread throughout Britain, hundreds of civilian volunteers in small boats, tugs, trawlers, lifeboats, fishing boats, drifters, rowing boats, and even the London Fire Brigade's fire-float joined cruisers and destroyers in the rescue effort. French, Belgian, and Dutch ships also joined them.

Now Hitler regained his confidence and unleashed his Luftwaffe to bomb and machine-gun soldiers on the ten-mile stretch of beach, and to sink the rescue armada. His soldiers made it to within a mile and a half of the seashore, held back by a rear guard of thirty thousand French soldiers, who fought fiercely until they ran out of ammunition. Despite the efforts of Spitfires to protect the rescuers, the Germans sank hundreds of vessels. The British had hoped at best to bring back 45,000 men, but by June 4, 1940, an astonishing 338,226 British, French, and Belgian soldiers had been saved from the Nazi onslaught. There were also some women, children, and pets among them. The London fire-float had made three journeys and saved over six hundred men. A steam yacht, HMS *Grive*, commanded by sixty-seven-year-old the Honorable Lionel Lambart, who came out of retirement, rescued two thousand.

As Paris was expected to fall any day, Lew Kowarski and several young soldiers loaded Geiger counters and other research equipment into army trucks and drove south to Clermont-Ferrand in south-central France, where Halban, who had gone ahead, had already set up a makeshift lab in a rented villa. He and Kowarski were able to continue their experiments by using running water from the kitchen and bathroom, and simple equipment erected by army engineers. Before joining them, Joliot and Moureu burned confidential records of their nuclear experiments. (The effort was futile, because Germans later captured copies of Joliot's top-secret correspondence with Dautry, the minister of armaments, in an abandoned railroad car.)

On June 10 Italy declared war on France and Britain, confirming Churchill's prediction in a cable to Roosevelt twenty-five days previously that Mussolini would join the war to collect his share of the "loot of civilization." The same day the French government began a brief move from Paris to Tours in west-central France, to which Churchill flew for another meeting. Brigadier W. H. A. Bishop, who was present when Churchill returned to London, eventually told Eve Curie what happened. Churchill had "announced to his dismayed ministers that France was on the verge of asking Hitler for his terms. The prime minister had painted the situation in the grimmest possible colors. He had reviewed the desperate military outlook, the desperate political outlook. Coming to his conclusion, he had said, in a low, firm voice: 'We are now facing Germany completely isolated. We are alone.' Then there was a dead silence that Bishop never forgot, as Churchill lifted his head, looked defiantly at his ministers, and said: 'I find it rather inspiring.'" So did President Franklin Roosevelt. And although he responded to Premier Reynaud's plea for help only with words of "utmost sympathy," he was already aiding the British. Under a lend-lease agreement, he had sent the British fifty old U.S. destroyers in return for ninety-nine-year leases on several bases in the West Indies, and followed up with shipments of rifles, ammunition, and artillery.

During World War I, Premier Georges Clemenceau had warned the Germans that he and fellow Frenchmen would fight to the finish — in Paris, on the Loire, on the Garonne, and in the Pyrenees. And if defeated in the mountains, they would continue the fight at sea. But he would never sue for peace. Twenty-two years later, facing the sons of the same enemy, Churchill went even further with his rallying cry: "We shall go on to the end, we shall fight in France, we shall fight in the seas and oceans . . . we shall fight on the beaches, we shall fight on the landing grounds, we shall fight in the fields and in the streets, we shall fight in the hills, we shall never surrender." And if the worst happened, Churchill told *Chicago Daily News* reporter Edgar Ansel Mowrer, he would send the British fleet and air force to Canada to continue the fight from there.

Joliot and Irène were among the last to leave the Collège de France, on June 10, just two days before the Germans entered the city. The couple loaded a Peugeot 402 with lab equipment and Marie Curie's precious gram of radium, and drove south to Clermont-Ferrand, passing black clouds of smoke billowing from burning oil refineries along the Seine. Henri Moureu followed in a Peugeot 303. When they arrived, Irène was so exhausted that without a word, she lay down on the floor of the villa and fell asleep.

The group continued their experiments until June 16, when Joliot and Moureu were taking a brief walk in the sunshine and Allier drove up to warn them that because France was on the verge of defeat, they and the heavy water were in danger of capture. Joliot then gave Halban and Kowarski official approval to take the heavy water from the nearby prison to England for the use of the Allies. But as Halban recalled, "The Governor of the prison, probably already in fear of the new masters, refused to release the deposited articles. Dautry's special commissioner had to threaten him with a drawn revolver before he would give them up."

Although the future seemed anyone's guess, during a conversation with Halban and Kowarski, Joliot made an extremely accurate forecast. According to Kowarski, he said: "Germany will overrun the whole of

France, but will only occupy territories which they consider necessary. Eventually there will be an uprising in the non-occupied part, and the Germans will occupy the whole of France. From the occupied coast the Germans will prepare an airborne attack on England. They will try to knock out England by air raids but will fail. So the sea-borne attack will not take place and England for a while will resist alone, but then both the United States and Russia will enter the war. And Germany, after a number of years, will be defeated."

After this last conversation with Joliot on June 16, Halban and Kowarski drove off next day at dawn, heading due west for Bordeaux. Halban had his wife and one-year-old daughter beside him in the front seat, having stacked the heavy-water canisters in the back. As Kowarski had not learned to drive, a lab assistant was at the wheel of a large station wagon, with Kowarski's wife and young daughter alongside the driver. Twenty canisters of heavy water were in the back under several blankets on which Kowarski rested uncomfortably as the driver made sharp turns along bumpy, hilly country roads crowded with scared and exhausted refugees. They arrived at Bordeaux near midnight and found the provisional office of the Ministry of Armament in a requisitioned schoolroom. There, Dautry's assistant, Jean Bichelonne, tore a sheet from a child's copybook and wrote, recalled Kowarski,

> that we are ordered to go to England on Lord Suffolk's commandeered ship [and] put ourselves, our materials, and our records at the disposal of the British authorities. And to observe absolute secrecy. It later made difficult our situation with De Gaulle and his Free France. De Gaulle was not "British authorities" and communicating with De Gaulle would mean an infringement of the "absolute secrecy." And so we stayed apart from Free France during our whole stay in England. I might add that a few years later, Bichelonne distinguished himself by organizing the transfer of French labor to Germany and after the war he was tried as a notorious collaborator and shot. The midnight scene left quite an imprint on my memory . . . The last gasp of belligerent France quite naively and touchingly put its faith in these two departing magicians and that obviously meant that we were not just refugees leaving the country. We were carriers of a mission, we had been entrusted with something important. [Nevertheless] Halban and I were left to fend for ourselves as best we could. I found in the hold of the ship a heap of coal, collapsed on it, and fell asleep. In the morning things got organized. There was a captain of the ship, but Lord Suffolk was obviously in charge—a very picturesque personality looking like an unkempt pirate . . . the twentieth earl in a line which was considerably older than the house of Windsor. He was

dressed in rags, with a very picturesque beard [and] walking around the ship with two secretaries, one blond and one brunette.

Bombs had exploded near the ship that night but Kowarski slept through the bombing. The next morning the ship was moved to another part of the Bordeaux harbor.

Joliot was still with Irène, who had recently suffered a second attack of tuberculosis, for which she had first been diagnosed at the end of the 1920s. After hiding the gram of radium, he left her in good hands to recuperate in a sanatorium at nearby Clairvivre, before joining the earl of Suffolk, who was still on the Bordeaux seafront continuing to organize the evacuation.

Stripped to the waist, which revealed his extensive tattoos, Suffolk was armed with two revolvers he called "Oscar" and "Genevieve," and shod in hunting boots. He was giving orders and directions with an imperious wave of a loaded hunting crop, while cracking jokes in fluent French with a strong English accent. His instructions, he had told Kowarski, were to rescue everyone and everything of value from the clutches of the rapidly approaching Nazis. And he had been remarkably successful, having collected some fifty scientists and fifteen million dollars' worth of industrial diamonds. Joliot was certainly somebody of value. Suffolk knew him and his work as a fellow member of the Anglo-French Society of Scientists, which was established to develop scientific cooperation between the two countries. British members included J. D. Bernal, P. M. S. Blackett, and Sir Solly Zuckerman, who were known in England as the Encyclopedists because they apparently knew everything about everything. On first sighting Joliot, Suffolk grabbed him by the arm and insisted, "You are coming to England with me at once. Don't worry about your wife and two children. I will be responsible for seeing them tomorrow, and for taking them . . . across the [English] Channel. Everything has been arranged for Halban and Kowarski, who at this moment should be on board the *Broompark* [a British collier he had commandeered] with the heavy water."

Because of the intense bombing, Suffolk gave the ship only an even chance of reaching England, so he had stored all the heavy-water canisters and industrial diamonds on a raft. If the ship sank, the raft would float free, but he had given orders to destroy it and its cargo with explosives if it was in danger of falling into enemy hands. Despite Suffolk's offer, Joliot decided to stay in France. Goldschmidt believed it was because Joliot had a poor grasp of English and feared he would not be sufficiently respected in England and consequently would be deprived of the facilities he needed for his work. British science writer J. G. Crowther, who knew the Curie family, thought that Irène had persuaded him to stay. She had contempt for the Nazis, he said, felt they would not dare harm a Curie, and was "willing to put up with them until they became a nuisance." Their daughter, Hélène, thought Joliot was influenced by stories he had heard as a child of the long German occupation of Alsace after 1870, and that he expected history to repeat itself with the Germans occupying France for a long time. And, despite Suffolk's offer to get his family out of the country, Joliot didn't want to risk leaving them behind.

His friend and biographer, Pierre Biquard, agreed with Hélène, and quoted as evidence a stilted conversation between Joliot and Moureu, in which something may have been lost in translation. In it Joliot says: "Should I accept Lord Suffolk's offer? The work must go on here." Moureu replies, "That's what I think. For you the position is not an easy one. To some extent you are a standard-bearer." And concludes with Joliot's: "I definitely ought to stay."

He had a last chance to go when the ship's departure was delayed. As Kowarski recalled, Suffolk's crew was too drunk to sail immediately: "There was seasickness and there were twenty-five women aboard. Suffolk was pouring them champagne. 'This is the perfect remedy,' he said. The ship stayed in harbor for a day, where we were bombed. [And a ship alongside was sunk by a mine, though all the passengers and crew were rescued and transferred to other ships in the convoy.] After the crew sobered up, the trip took thirty-six hours. At the end of it I found myself, not speaking a word of English, sitting on a beautiful June day in the garden of a dentist of Russian extraction in the Finchley Road."

The heavy water was first stored in London's Wormwood Scrubs prison and then moved to Windsor Castle, where, somewhat inappropriately, the castle's librarian was put in charge of it.

Under Churchill's orders, Field Marshal Alanbrooke returned to France from England to command some 150,000 British and Canadian troops still there—hoping to bolster the French army and sustain the French government. But in Alanbrooke's view, although "there were plenty of Frenchmen ready to die for their country, their leaders had completely failed to prepare and organize them to resist the blitzkrieg. What had formerly been the finest army in Europe was now, for all practical purposes, a herd of sheep in process of being rounded up by wolves."

On June 12, 1940, Premier Reynaud warned his cabinet: "You take Hitler for another Wilhelm I, the old gentleman who seized Alsace-Lorraine from us, and that was all there was to it. But Hitler is Genghis Khan."

As Reynaud wanted to fight on alongside the British and most of his cabinet did not, the eighty-four-year-old Marshal Henri-Philippe Pétain took over the armistice negotiations.

The frail, white-haired hero of World War I was once again entrusted with his country's destiny. On June 17 in a radio broadcast he ordered the French forces to stop fighting. Moments later, according to Alanbrooke, one of his French liaison officers "burst into my room, and collapsed in a chair shaken from head to foot with sobs of tears. When he had sufficiently composed he repeated to me the news of Pétain's broadcast . . . It was a strange situation . . . Here I was in command of a force sent to their assistance in their final struggle. And when the end came, they never even had the decency to inform me officially that the French forces had ceased fighting. They just abandoned the British forces in France to their fate and left them to extricate themselves as best they could in the face of an unopposed victorious German Army."

However, in almost a repeat of the miracle of Dunkirk, Alanbrooke evacuated from Cherbourg and St. Malo some 150,000 British troops, 47,000 Allied troops, and 300 heavy guns. All arrived safely in England. But German bombers sank the liner *Lancastria* loaded with servicemen, as well as women and children, as they tried to escape from the port of Saint-Nazaire in Brittany. The death toll reached an estimated nine thousand. It was Britain's worst World War II maritime disaster, and to protect public morale, Churchill forbade publication of news of the tragedy in Britain. However, the *New York Times* broke the story some weeks later.

On June 15, 1940, Verdun fell to the Nazis in one day of fighting. By vivid contrast, in 1916 French troops defending the same city, which Churchill had called "the anvil upon which French manhood was to be hammered to death," had held out for ten months with the loss of some 160,000 men.

After only six weeks of fighting, on June 22, 1940, France agreed to sign an armistice with Hitler. To emphasize the humiliation, the ceremony took place in the same railroad coach at Rethondes in the Forest of Compiègne in which Germany had surrendered to France and her allies in World War I. A telephone in the railroad coach allowed French negotiators to discuss the terms with Pétain's cabinet. Before he signed, Pétain asked for permission to make a statement. A German interpreter, Dr. Schmidt, in a German army communications van nearby hidden behind a clump of trees, had tapped the line and was recording the ongoing conversations. Listening in, an enterprising American reporter, William L. Shirer, heard Pétain say in French, which he later translated into English: "I declare that the French government has ordered me to sign these terms of armistice . . . Forced by the fate of arms to cease the struggle in which we were engaged on the side of the Allies, France sees imposed on her very hard conditions. France has the right to expect in the future negotiations that Germany show a spirit which will permit the two great neighboring countries to live and work in peace."

The conditions were brutal. The agreement divided France into two zones. The occupied zone, three-fifths of the country, would be directly controlled by the Nazis. It included Paris, the rest of northern France, and the entire Atlantic coast. And France was to pay the cost of keeping German troops there. The rest, unoccupied France in the south, would be governed by a French government at Vichy headed by Pétain and his deputy, Pierre Laval, a power-hungry pro-Nazi politician. The French army would shrink to one hundred thousand men, who were to act as policemen by maintaining domestic order. All anti-Nazi German refugees in France and her territories were to be arrested and handed over to the Nazis. All French nationals captured fighting on the side of another country against Germany would be immediately shot. Reynaud, who had resigned on June 16, was arrested and imprisoned for the rest of the war.

Hitler entered Paris in the early morning two days later, as the German swastika flew from the Eiffel Tower, and watched his triumphant troops parade under the Arc de Triomphe.

Unlike her sister and brother-in-law, thirty-five-year-old Eve Curie decided to escape to England. Having recently returned to Paris from her American lecture tour in late April, she and her friend, playwright Henry Bernstein—whose anti-Nazi drama, *Elvire*, was still running in Paris— joined some 1,300 other refugees aboard a small British ship, *Madura*, which normally carried 180 passengers. They were bombarded in the Bordeaux harbor but escaped unharmed and saw one German bomber shot down.

Also on board were Pierre Cot, the former French air minister; Marcel-Henri Jasper, former Belgian cabinet minister; André Garner of the *Exchange Telegraph*; and Baron Robert de Rothschild of the French banking family. After sleeping three nights in a deck chair, she and the other refugees disembarked at Falmouth, a Cornish seaside resort, on June 20, 1940, and took the train to London.

Joliot seemed reconciled to his decision to stay, judging by the letter he sent his mother and sisters on July 14, 1940: his two children were safe and well at L'Arcouest, Irène's health was improving with medical treatment, and, after a brief visit to Vichy, the capital of the new Nazi-approved French government headed by General Pétain, he was awaiting instructions. He continued cautiously, as if expecting the Gestapo to see the letter: "The Germans are behaving very correctly . . . Generally we must wait and remain patient without causing any ill will . . . We hope to be in Paris this winter."

He made it by August, but alone, having left Irène in the sanatorium and their children in Brittany. As the German army had requisitioned the Joliot family home at Antony, he stayed at the Hôpital Curie near the Radium Institute.

Joliot was one of the many Parisians who returned to the city shaken by their country's lightning defeat—after only six weeks of resistance—and surprised to find themselves alive in a city hardly touched by the war. He was told that German soldiers, with physicist Walther Bothe as their guide, had already sealed and searched his laboratory, taken note of the almost-completed cyclotron in the basement—there were no cyclotrons in Germany—and hunted for uranium, heavy water, and Joliot's notes without success.

What he didn't know was that due to some bureaucratic snafu, copies of his research notes had been left in an abandoned railroad car—where the Germans found them.

Joliot wrote to Irène on August 9 in an upbeat mood: all was calm in Paris, which, millions having left, was free of heavy traffic and awful gasoline smells, and so had become a more agreeable city. Debierne had returned from L'Arcouest with good news of the children. Joliot hoped Irène was taking her rest cure seriously and advised her not to take excessively long walks because "I wish to find my wife in perfect health again, so that we can work together this winter . . . All goes well at the Radium Institute."

A few days after Joliot returned to his laboratory in September 1940, he was surprised by the arrival of German general Erich Schumann—a physicist, descendant of the composer, and himself a composer of military marches—now director of science affairs in the German army. And even more surprised to find that Schumann's interpreter was Wolfgang Gentner, the expert on Geiger counters who had worked with Joliot a few years earlier, and whom he knew to be an anti-Nazi. The general called the lab workers together and, instead of delivering the expected threats or warnings, paid tribute to Joliot's genius. The realists, of course, knew that this was the kind of buttering up the occupying forces employed to disarm them. Afterward the general questioned Joliot in his office, with Gentner—who was fluent in French—still interpreting.

Interviewed after the war, Gentner gave this account of the event:

They asked Joliot about heavy water and uranium, [and said] that he should tell them exactly where the heavy water is . . . And he told the truth. This was the strange thing. He told them he brought the heavy water to Bordeaux and that probably the water was on the boat to Great Britain. But they didn't believe him. And when we went out, I let the people go out first, and then stayed a little back and I said to Joliot, "I have to see you alone. I have the evenings free. Couldn't we meet in a café on the Boulevard St. Michel?" So I went back to the hotel and said, "I have to see some friends to see the night life of Paris." When I saw Joliot that evening in the café, he was very distressed to see me and I was also a little. [It was a] difficult situation. And I told him that they [Gentner's fellow-German scientists] were interested in the cyclotron and we could use it perhaps for research. And I asked him what he would say if I should come to Paris [from Walter Bothe's laboratory]. Joliot told me that he would be interested . . . to have a friend [with whom] he could discuss the situation.

According to his friend and biographer Biquard, who presumably heard it from Joliot, he did not tell the Germans the truth about the heavy water. In Biquard's more detailed version, Gentner, as General Schumann's translator, asked Joliot: "What happened to the heavy water and the uranium?"

"The heavy water was put on to an English ship at Bordeaux," Joliot replied.

"What is the name of the ship?"

Joliot named two possible ships, knowing that both had been sunk.

"And the uranium?"

"Withdrawn by the Ministry of Armaments to an unknown destination."

In fact, the uranium had been hidden near Toulouse. As for the heavy water, whether he told Schumann the truth or tried to deceive him was immaterial. He knew that the heavy water had either reached Britain or been sunk—and in either case the Germans couldn't get their hands on it.

Out of Joliot's hearing, the general told Gentner that everything had probably been sent to North Africa and they should send a mission to find it. As the visitors were leaving, Gentner whispered to Joliot to meet him secretly that evening. They met in the back room of a students' café on the Boulevard Saint-Michel at six, when Gentner told Joliot that several German scientists, himself included, were scheduled to move into the Collège de France, but he would only do so with Joliot's approval. Joliot, who regarded Gentner as a friend with democratic sympathies, asked him to stay. When Gentner warned him that the Germans planned to seize the twenty-seven-ton cyclotron and take it to Germany, Joliot made an interesting offer: to let them use it where it was, but only if they in turn granted several critical concessions.

The Germans hoped that by treating prominent individuals like Joliot with consideration they would become collaborators. So they agreed to his strict provisos: he would remain in charge of the laboratory, where only basic research, and no war work, would take place. Finally, he would accept five German researchers in his laboratory under Gentner's direction, but he must be kept fully informed of their activities. Joliot even received a written agreement to that effect.

Afterward he confided to a young Japanese woman student, Toshiko Yuasa, that his main concern was what his friends in England and America would think of his decisions. And with this in mind, to ensure that they were not working on military projects, each night after the German researchers had left the premises Joliot secretly checked their rooms.

Fortunately for Joliot, the German instructed to keep his eye on him turned out to be Gentner, a loyal friend and anti-Nazi. And it belies the superefficient reputation of the Gestapo that they didn't catch on until much later.

We have Joliot's own account of how he felt about the situation in a formerly top-secret letter he wrote to Bichelonne in 1943: "In June 1940 the laboratories which I direct were seized . . . as [a] prize of war . . . Gen. [Erich] Schumann, Chief of Research Service of the [German] Army [told me]: 'The activities of the laboratories since October 1939 were completely devoted to research in the interest of National Defense. In this, the research concerning radium was particularly outstanding. The German Military Services possess the documents, found in the train from La Charité, proving this activity.' Schumann [then] informed me . . . that he would give the order to lift the seizure on condition that the activity of the Laboratories which I direct will be devoted only to pure research and that three German research workers, disinterested men of science, frequent the Laboratory. In any case, work furthering the war would not be undertaken, either by the French or the Germans . . . I waited until the occupation authorities entered into relation with the French Government [Vichy] and it is only after an accord with both parties that I have resumed direction of the laboratory . . . Representatives of the German services . . . know that I will refuse any participation in scientific effort of the German war."

Then Joliot turned to his future plans: "I believe that it would be practically impossible and moreover scarcely opportune to resume our old experiments and I would not want it. It is in the field of pure research and in creating the greatest number of research workers that I believe I am most useful. As for the situation of the French State with regard to realization by foreigners of a generating apparatus for Uranium energy, I call your attention to the fact that since 1939 my associates and I have taken out the most important patents through the National Center of Scientific Research, state department, etc."

Did Joliot do research for war weapons or not? Author Spencer Weart explains: "Certainly Joliot's lab, like every lab in France, from the start of the war was supposed to work exclusively on matters of value to the national defense, under the direction of the military. The creation of a new source of industrial power, especially one that might be useful in warships and the like, was considered to fall under this heading. After all, they thought the war might well last quite a few years, time enough for a nuclear-powered something to play a military role. And even a new source of purely industrial power was important . . . coal played a role in the grand strategy of the First World War, and control of oil fields was at the very center of the second." But Joliot did not continue this work when the Germans were occupying Paris.

In his book *France Under the Germans: Collaboration and Compromise*, Phillipe Burrin revealed that "the workroom [at Joliot's laboratory] and a number of technicians, but not research assistants, were made available to the Germans. Each of them received [his] own workbench and they were not permitted access to the rest of the laboratory except with permission from Joliot who, for his part, retained the right to move about as he pleased and could thus keep his eye on everything that was going on. However clearly defined, the situation remained a delicate one and rumours of 'collaboration' were soon rife."

While Joliot and his family spent peaceful nights in their homes, across the Channel Eve Curie was sharing the nightly ordeal of Londoners, as German bombers began their massive attacks. They started on September 7, 1940, when hundreds of bombers protected by hundreds of fighters set the city ablaze. Then, in a daylight attack on September 15, two hundred bombers protected by six hundred fighters headed for London. This was the start of Hitler's all-out air attack before his planned invasion of Britain by seaborne troops, to be known as Operation Sea Lion. RAF fighters stopped most of the planes before they reached London, shooting down thirty-four bombers and twenty-two fighters with a loss of twenty-six Spitfires. The RAF then routed a second attack by an even stronger bomber formation.

It was a turning point in the war. Needing to achieve air supremacy for his invasion of Britain, Hitler called it off. But he continued the devastating nightly bombing of London and other cities.

Diana Cooper, wife of the former British ambassador in Paris, wrote in her diary for September 30: "Last night [in London] we dined with a lot of French—Eve Curie, Monsieur Palewski, airman and politician, all violent de Gaulleites. The guns, bombs, orchestra and jabber deafen and bewilder . . . While the Huns are turning London's heavens into hell, they are not doing much harm to our factories for war-production . . . Eve Curie told me that she had been on a tour of provincial ARP [air raid] shelters with Lady Reading. All the little children of five have Mickey Mouse gas-masks."

By contrast, the Paris to which Irène and the children arrived at the end of September was peaceful. And after their house at Antony was returned to them, she resumed her work whenever her uncertain health allowed.

The following month Joliot attended a secret meeting with Jean Wyart, Professor Eugène Aubel, and physicist Jacques Solomon, Langevin's son-in-law, to discuss how to keep French intellectual life alive under German occupation. They agreed to recruit a group of like-minded students and professors from the Faculty of Sciences to form the nucleus of the Universitè Libre.

In early November 1940, the Gestapo ransacked the office of Joliot's sixty-eight-year-old friend and mentor Paul Langevin, then arrested him. Going through Langevin's desk, the agent in charge, Professor Bohmelburg, a historian in civilian life, occasionally threw a letter to the floor as he shouted angrily, "Another Jew!" But on finding one from Einstein, he put it in his pocket. When Langevin asked why he was being arrested, he was told: "For activities against National Socialism. In particular, you have sought to prevent Germany from getting rid of the Jews, and you have been for our way of life as dangerous as the Encyclopaedists were for the Monarchy."

The Gestapo agents drove Langevin to La Santé Jail, where they removed his fountain pen, shoelaces, and belt, and locked him in a cell with petty criminals. It took Joliot and Langevin's family three days before they discovered where he was, and they were given a different reason for his arrest—antifascist activity, especially when in Spain. Offers of asylum came from Switzerland, the United States, and the Soviet Union, which the Germans rejected.

To protest Langevin's arrest, young Communists stood in front of the Collège de France on the morning of November 8, handing out pamphlets calling for a demonstration that evening when Langevin, still imprisoned, had been scheduled to give his first lecture of the semester. The Germans countered by locking the doors to the lecture amphitheater.

When the time for the lecture approached, students crowded outside the college doors guarded by German soldiers, wondering what would happen next. What happened next was Joliot. Shortly before the lecture was due to start, he appeared, striding through the crowd of students. He brushed past the guards without a word, took a key from his pocket, and unlocked the doors. By the time he reached the podium, most of the seats were taken and an overflow crowd had gathered outside to hear him. His voice breaking with emotion, Joliot risked prison or worse by announcing that he was closing his laboratory and suspending his classes until Langevin, "the glory and pride of France," was freed from jail.

On November 10 Langevin's children visited him and spoke of Joliot's protest. They took back a letter from him to Joliot: "I have learned today of your attitude towards what has happened to me, something still incomprehensible, and I want to thank you with great affection."

On November 11, a day of remembrance for those who died fighting Germans in World War I, Joliot joined a large peaceful demonstration of students supporting Langevin at the Sorbonne's war memorial. But nearby, at the Arc de Triomphe, when students sang "La Marseillaise" they were attacked by Nazi supporters in the crowd. German troops intervened and ten students were killed.

Gentner happened to be in Heidelberg when Joliot had announced he was closing his laboratory, and he persuaded the Gestapo that not having access to the cyclotron would hinder the German war effort against the British—even though it was not being used for military purposes. It was not until December, after thirty-eight days in jail, that Langevin was let out and told that he would be taken to the small provincial town of Troyes, over a hundred miles southeast of Paris, which had no scientific institutions. There he would be kept under house arrest. Before he left, the Gestapo officer in charge allowed him to return to his home at 10 rue Vauquelin to have dinner and spend the night there. His family phoned close friends with the news and many joined him that evening to celebrate his one night of freedom. All were happy he was out of jail, but worried about his future. The next morning, after he had packed some clothes, he was driven to Troyes.

In a book about his father, André Langevin wrote, "They thought they were isolating him from his friends. They were wrong. He became the symbol of intellectual resistance." At Troyes he was kept under house arrest in an apartment owned by a Jew, Jean Blum, who had escaped to the "free south" zone of France. Blum wrote to Langevin that he was proud to have such a distinguished man in his home and to take whatever he wanted—if there was anything left.

While in Troyes, Langevin met Mme Margaret Flavien, a warm-hearted woman and political activist who had been his student at Sèvres in 1932. Because food was scarce, she occasionally left gifts of butter and eggs outside his apartment door. Joliot often visited Langevin, but some thought he should have done more to help his friend and mentor, who was forbidden to leave Troyes under any circumstances. Author Philippe Burrin, an expert on the German occupation of France, comments: "It is worth noting that Joliot's justification for his [briefly] stopping work was the criticism of his colleagues and it should be added that he never made Langevin's liberation a condition of his own resumption of work, but limited himself to asking that [Langevin's] lot be alleviated." Burrin concedes that this was still "courageous behavior, for not all the consequences were predictable. Clearly he [Joliot] continued to believe that the best policy was to hold on and endure, even if it meant having to put up with a most unpleasant situation."

In fact, Joliot had already joined the Resistance. Hélène Langevin-Joliot adds: "I don't know of anybody who did more or tried to do more than my father did for Langevin. He made sure that Langevin was safe in Troyes."

Joliot's normal workday now involved not only lecturing, supervising researchers in his laboratory, and the ongoing construction of the cyclotron, but devoting some time to medical research. This included using radioactive tracers to study the biological and chemical processes of the thyroid gland, and collaborating with Dr. Antoine Lacassagne, director of the Pasteur Laboratory of the Radium Institute, to induce cancer of the liver in a rabbit by irradiating it with neutrons. But he was also secretly meeting with a dozen or so members of a Resistance Committee. They got together at different locations, including the studio of his artist sister, Marguerite. Irène obviously knew what he was up to, because he often left home unusually early and arrived home very late at night—which even a heavy workload would not explain. But she never asked him why. Nor did she ask him to introduce her to the occasional Resistance Committee member who visited their home.

At the laboratory, Wolfgang Genter proved an invaluable ally and established his anti-Nazi credentials by risking his life to warn Joliot whenever he or any of the French staff were under Gestapo surveillance.

CHAPTER 18

Joliot Keeps the Gestapo Guessing—Eve Curie Tours the Battlefronts

1941–1942

When New York–born Anglo-Irish fascist William Joyce (nicknamed Lord Haw-Haw), an unsuccessful actor, was broadcasting Nazi propaganda from Germany to several million avid British listeners—most thought him a joke—Eve Curie was broadcasting anti-Nazi propaganda from London to her compatriots in France. After the war Joyce was executed as a traitor.

Eve stayed in the English capital for six months, enduring the worst of the nightly bombing attacks to continue her radio talks and to visit Polish air crews at airfields in the London area as well as her cousin, Wladyslaw Sklodowski, stationed with the Polish Brigade in Scotland. Then she left for America in January 1941 aboard the liner *Excambion*—but not to escape the bombing. She had agreed to give a lecture tour throughout the United States and Canada to promote the cause of freedom to an even larger audience.

Her support for the British blockade of supplies to France prompted a Vichy spokesman to complain that her attitude would be excusable if she had stayed in France to share the deprivations of the French, "but [as] she left . . . to escape the consequences of the blockade her stand takes very little account of French suffering. Mlle Curie, who has . . . never suffered hunger and cold, demands that for the success of the British cause French women and children should suffer cold and hunger. Every French woman who loses her child for the lack of vitamins during the war will have accounts to ask of those who are conducting this campaign in America."

Eve shot back: "The deep suffering of France is inflicted not by our people, not by the British, but by the Germans who are looting food from a country previously self-supporting, who have 2 million soldiers living on our soil . . . Having lived in London for the past six months, I feel sure the British have reasonable and humane views on this question and that they will take every decision that can help the French people . . . which will not conflict with the conduct of this war or [postpone] a victory, which is the only hope of the French nation. As soon as my contract [with a lecture agent] in America is fulfilled I intend to go back to London [to] help the British by all means in my power to fight for victory which will be not only theirs, but ours too."

In mid-February, Eleanor Roosevelt invited Eve to the White House and after her visit wrote to a friend, Joseph P. Lash, "I've wished for you and Trude [Lash's wife] tonight, for Eve Curie is here, a gallant and tragic person, and Harry Hopkins [FDR's adviser on Britain] is really interesting. I'll tell you more when I see you." Mrs. Roosevelt told a little more in her newspaper column "My Day" for February 18, 1941: "Mlle Curie has been in the Middle West, and shortly she will start on a long lecture trip which will take her all the way to the West Coast. She has lived in England ever since she left France and I think there must be moments when our whole mentality in this country must seem like an unreal dream to her. There is no use denying that seeing the bombs drop, even if they do not hit you, puts a different prospective [*sic*] on life."

Angry opposition to Eve's views came from a group of isolationists known as the America First Committee. Its most influential members were Colonel Robert McCormick, owner of the *Chicago Tribune*, and aviator Charles Lindbergh, a national icon, who considered the German Luftwaffe all but irresistible and had written Britain off as a lost cause. Where the isolationists had a committee and newspaper publisher on their side, Eve had newspaper columnist Eleanor Roosevelt and her husband, the president of the United States. She also had a fervent, patriotic group supporting her in the Free French Relief Committee. Before addressing its members in New York after her return from the West Coast on April 21, she was introduced as a woman who, after a miraculous escape from the Nazis, had not been deterred from fighting Hitler by fear of the consequences to herself or her relatives still in France. In her speech, Eve compared France to a wounded, shell-shocked soldier taken prisoner who still hoped for freedom.

She blamed wishful thinking and pacifism for France's defeat and believed that if Germany offered Britain a negotiated peace, British women would say, "'No, thank you; we don't want a Hitler peace; we want a real peace—which means victory.' Great Britain can resist the bombing; she can resist the threat of invasion, but to win the war . . . she needs the help of all of us, and she needs warships, planes and tanks, and she needs them at once."

If Britain was defeated, she warned, France's last hope of liberty would be lost, and the United States would be in great danger without an ally or friend in a hostile world. And she appealed to both the United States and Britain to stand by France for the sake of peace and civilization.

As Eve continued on the lecture tour, the Vichy government accused her, her friend playwright, Henry Bernstein, and twenty-seven others of harming the French state and revoked their French nationality and asked the U.S. government to expel them. Eve had already "received with pride" her American citizenship papers, sent to her soon after Roosevelt and his wife let it be known that she had been their guest in the White House. The Vichy decision was no surprise to Bernstein. As he explained: "Since 1934 I have violently attacked Hitler and Nazism many times in my articles and my plays. [And when Pétain took charge] I realized that my country was being turned over to the conqueror. I went first to England and then to this country, convinced that my chief duty was to defend the real France against the men who have betrayed it." But he said he would continue to wear his Legion of Honor medal because it was given to him by President Georges Clemenceau for his World War I service as a French air force pilot in Macedonia. He, too, was allowed to stay in the United States.

A *New York Times* editorialist wholeheartedly supported Curie and Bernstein: "The French government which Hitler destroyed ten months ago was confused and weak, but it had a welcome and a home for free and creative spirits. It would not have disowned Eve Curie, distinguished daughter of distinguished parents. We do not know whether Vichy's recent action in revoking the citizenship . . . was voluntary or whether it was ordered by Berlin. In either case it was Nazi or Fascist, not French. The true France continues to exist. If it no longer has a vote or voice on the soil of France it can speak on free soil. We are the gainers that Mlle Curie and others have found freedom here."

Eve knew through American friends still living in France that many Frenchmen had left France and volunteered for de Gaulle's Free French forces to continue the fight from abroad. A million and a half were still prisoners of war. Many scientists and intellectuals and their families had escaped to Britain or the United States.

Yet except for Joliot's secret early morning and late-night resistance meetings, his and Irène's routine was little changed. They continued their scientific work. She still kept open house for friends on Sundays and Joliot played tennis, often with Leprince Linguet, loudly and triumphantly announcing his winning scores. The shortage of gasoline pleased him because the Paris air was fresher, and he enjoyed riding his bicycle everywhere instead of using his car, which he'd left in the south.

When the collaborationist paper *Paris-Soir* attacked Joliot as "the great protector of Jews," especially academicians, those looking for Machiavellian motivations suggested this was a planted item to ease the pressure on Joliot from accusations that he was collaborating with the Nazis. Unfortunately, he seemed to confirm the rumor by giving an interview to the pro-Nazi *Les Nouveau Temps* in February 1941. In it he excoriated the country's former leaders, often graduates of the elite Ecole Polytechnique, as "the grand abettors of our industrial bankruptcy and our deficiency in war materials."

He was right about the war materials. Some French soldiers couldn't continue fighting simply because they ran out of ammunition. In the interview, Joliot suggested that French scientists like himself, passionately attached to their country, must have the moral courage to draw the lesson from defeat. One of his remedies for a better country was to end all class privileges and obstacles to a scientific career, from which he had suffered. This had always been his strongly held opinion.

According to his daughter, Hélène, Joliot realized that the interview had been a mistake, and soon after turned down a request for an interview about Franco-German intellectual cooperation from Georges Paulet of *Le Petit Parisien*. He also vetoed a German proposal to film Irène working in the Curie Laboratory, pointing out that no Germans worked there. He stressed that even at the Collège de France, where Germans did work by orders of the German High Command and the French government, he would not allow any filming to take place.

His lack of cooperation might explain why, on Sunday, June 29, 1941, while the Joliot-Curies were having breakfast at home, two men in plainclothes arrived, charged Joliot with encouraging university students to resist the occupation, and drove off with him in an unmarked car. Gentner had left his phone number with Joliot for such an emergency, and he had given it to Irène. She called Gentner at his hotel but was unable to tell him who had ordered the arrest. As it was a Sunday, most government offices were closed, but he promised to try to help and would stay in his room to be available if she had any fresh news. She then phoned her friend Angèle Pompei, who came to stay with her and share her ordeal of waiting.

Meanwhile, Joliot had been driven to police headquarters on the Ile de la Cité and was left in the waiting room, under guard. Another detainee introduced himself as Maurice Bataillon. Joliot knew of him as a fellow member of the Committee of Antifascist Vigilance, and during their brief conversation they decided that they had been brought in for questioning because of their membership in this group. Many members of anti-Nazi organizations, including the head of the Committee of Antifascist Vigilance, had recently been rounded up after the French police had given the Germans lists of Communists and their alleged sympathizers. Joliot's calm demeanor impressed Bataillon, and he was surprised by the assurance with which he said that "the German physicists working at his side would intervene in his favor. It was clearly inconceivable to Joliot that the camaraderie of the laboratory would not show itself [regardless of nationality] on such an occasion. Remember, that there was still a minimum of peace in that war: an illusory peace. The machine to fill the concentration camps was not yet on the prowl."

After a brief, amicable conversation with a police inspector, they were driven by bus to Gestapo headquarters in the rue de Saussaies. Joliot was told to get out and the car continued on, taking Bataillon to Romainville. (He survived the war.) At Gestapo headquarters an agent accused Joliot of being an influential member of the Communist Party, registered in the Third International (the international organization of Communist parties). Joliot truthfully denied the charge, but was kept at Gestapo headquarters until late that night. By then, Gentner had made the right contacts and the Gestapo agent was told, by phone, that antagonizing Joliot would jeopardize the secret work Germans were doing at the Collège de France. The agent immediately released him, even offering to drive him home—an offer that would have been dangerous to accept. Knowing that if spotted as a passenger in an official Nazi car it would brand him for sure as a collaborator, he made his own way back by public transport—to Irène's immense relief.

When, on June 22, 1941, Hitler's forces launched their no-atrocities-barred attack on the Soviet Union, the still illegal French Communist Party—supporting the Nazi-Soviet nonaggression pact—were now ordered by Moscow to become wholehearted supporters of Britain. Its leaders then circulated an appeal throughout France for the creation of a National Front Committee to fight the occupying Germans and Vichy supporters by all means including force. Although Joliot was a former Socialist—he had left the party because he disagreed with its nonintervention policy during the Spanish Civil War—and though not yet a Communist, he was secretly named president of its national committee. Among its other members were novelist, poet, and playwright François Mauriac (a future Nobel Prize winner) and General Paul Dassault.

About this time, Joliot had another chance to escape from France with his family. The American ambassador to France, Admiral William Leahy, had already helped Jean Perrin and Pierre Auger to reach the United States, and, perhaps hearing of Joliot's arrest, he now approached him with the same offer. But Joliot declined, saying that he felt he should remain in Paris near colleagues who were unable to leave France.

Eve, now back in London, and Meloney in New York were also trying to help the Joliot-Curies to leave France. Irène's reason for staying, despite the Gestapo fright, was not unlike her husband's—to continue their research work, to prevent the dispersal of scientists from French laboratories, and to protect the radioelements vital for their work. If they found they were no longer useful, then they would try to leave the country.

Anxious to recover the radium, gold, platinum, and other metals Joliot had hidden in Clairvivre—and needed for research—Irène talked the authorities into letting her cross the border into Vichy France. Joliot couldn't accompany her, as he had been refused a permit to leave occupied France, so two lab technicians went along instead. Shortly after she and her escorts had returned with the vital material in mid-June 1941, Irène's chronic illness recurred, and Gentner and his Swiss wife got permission for her to stay at a sanatorium in the Swiss mountains. While there, she worked on a history of the radioelements, and gained a much-needed five pounds.

By the fall of 1941 the Nazis in France were justifying their revolting reputation by executing a Frenchman, Henri Gautherot, and a Polish Jew, Samuel Tyszelman, for "helping the enemy." Their crime? Taking part in a Communist demonstration. A few days later, two members of the Organisation Spéciale, a militant arm of the French Communist Party, knifed and beat to death a German officer as he was emerging from a brothel, leaving a note on his body: "Ten Nazi officers will pay for every patriot killed!" More patriots began to strike back at their enemy. Pierre Georges (cover name Colonel Fabien), a wounded twenty-two-year-old veteran of the International Brigades in Spain, firebombed a factory in Vitry that made parts for German U-boats. Shortly after, on the morning of August 21, 1941, he joined three companions waiting outside a Montmartre Métro station, where he shot to death Alphonse Moser, a German naval officer.

All four escaped in the rush-hour crowd. On September 3, Acher Semhaya, a Jewish Communist from North Africa, shot and wounded a German NCO near the Hotel Terminus, and an unknown man wounded a German captain in the Boulevard Strasbourg. As Maurice Goldsmith noted, "Collaboration, terror and repression were on the increase. The 'Great Hunt' for communists, Jews, resistants, parachutists from London intensified. Arrests, tortures, executions and deaths were the common-place . . . In September 1941 all Jews had their radio sets confiscated. On October 3, six of the seven synagogues in Paris were dynamited. On Octo-ber 12, the Legion of French Volunteers took an oath of loyalty to Hitler. Collaborators and informers were everywhere," and throughout France resistants were being betrayed and destroyed.

Because Joliot remained untouched after that first brief arrest by the Gestapo, and Germans worked alongside him at the Collège de France, but none at the Pasteur Institute or other equally famous institutions, rumors intensified that he was collaborating. Eugénie Cotton, a family friend, quickly came to his defense: "My husband, Aimé Cotton, arrested twice by the Gestapo, has retained full confidence in this great patriot." Yet apart from his secret meetings with fellow patriots, for which he at least risked prison, life was only slightly more uncomfortable for Joliot than before the war. He was forbidden to travel to L'Arcouest on the Atlantic coast (the children were back in Paris) and refused a permit for a motor scooter, which consumed little gasoline and would have saved him one and a half hours a day traveling between Paris and his second lab at Ivry. Even to replace his worn bicycle tires, he had to swear on oath that his present ones were useless and this was his first request for new ones.

Life was becoming even more challenging for Eve Curie, the only member of the immediate family to have left France. As her contribution to the war effort, she was preparing to return to the war zones to give the American and British public, as well as expatriate French and Polish com-munities, vivid, eyewitness accounts of life on the various battlefronts — the first woman to undertake such a hazardous enterprise.

Thanks to President Roosevelt, under the lend-lease program the United States had been sending airplanes, munitions, tools, and food to foreign countries whose defense was judged vital to America's safety. And Eve got a seat on one of the first lend-lease transatlantic flights in a huge Clipper seaplane — the start of an often perilous journey of more than forty thousand miles that would take her to the fighting in North Africa, Lebanon, Syria, Palestine, Iraq, Iran, the Soviet Union, Burma, China, and India.

The *Herald Tribune* Syndicate in New York, *Allied Newspapers* in London, and a book publisher had agreed to finance her journey. The newspapers would print her ongoing feature stories and Doubleday would publish a full-length account, appropriately titled *Journey Among Warriors*.

Arriving at LaGuardia Airport before dawn early in November 1941, inoculated against typhoid, smallpox, cholera, and yellow fever, Eve was told by an airline official that her flight had to be kept secret, but not why. So to hide from the press that was expected to cover the takeoff, Eve entered the empty plane before anyone else had arrived with her two canvas bags, portable typewriter, and Anglo-French dictionary, took a seat, and waited — out of sight.

The rising sun was shining through a mist when the aircrew — eleven men in black — and forty passengers, all men, appeared on the gangway. She had been told that her forty fellow passengers were pilots, mechanics, and engineers hired by Pan American Airways to build and operate a new airline running from the Gold Coast to Khartoum. A group of news cameramen took flash photos of them before they entered the plane to illustrate news reports of the historical departure. None knew that they were missing the biggest news of all: a woman was among them for this experimental trip.

The seaplane rose in a chilly mist and landed five hours later on the sea near Bermuda, where they all lunched at the air base. Then the plane headed for Puerto Rico. As some men slept or played cards, one confided to her that most on board were not mechanics or engineers, but U.S. army pilots on six months' leave, who planned to ferry lend-lease material to Khartoum via Brazil, as well as war planes to the British in the Middle East. Although President Roosevelt had approved the scheme, it had to be done secretly because America was officially neutral.

Eve spent the night ashore in Belém, Brazil, where the seaplane had landed guided by floodlights that made the water glitter. She skipped sleep to write all night in her hotel room, despite the piercing voice of a woman singing in the nightclub under her window. After crossing the South Atlantic, as the plane approached West Africa on the evening of November 13, 1941, passengers were sprayed with an antimosquito flit before they disembarked so they'd be insect-free when they went ashore in Bathurst, British Gambia. There the group lunched with Governor Sir Wilfrid T. Southorn, and afterward two Free French representatives took Eve for a ride around town to see military camps, the mud huts of the local population, and, in the distance, the Vichy-controlled Cape Djinnak. After enjoying a four-course meal provided by the Frenchmen, which included wine confiscated from a Vichy ship seized by the British, she boarded the plane at one in the morning, which landed in Lagos, Nigeria, at four that afternoon.

Eve left the seaplane for a BOAC Lockheed Lodestar for the next leg of her trans-Africa journey, across Free-French Chad to Khartoum, Sudan's capital. There the governor, Sir Hubert Huddleston, and his wife invited her to stay at their white palace guarded by soldiers in British and Egyptian uniforms, and she enjoyed her first full night of sleep in a real bed since she left New York. All other times she had worked through the night.

At dawn on November 21 she traveled in a Sunderland BOAC flying boat for hours over the desert and landed on the Nile at Wadi Halfa. While having breakfast and listening to the radio at a nearby hotel, she heard that advancing British troops were only ten miles from their goal—Tobruk.

Eve's plane then took her over the pyramids to Cairo, giving her a critical bird's-eye view of "a huge beige-and-white city, with a few beautiful buildings sunk in an ocean of cheapness." A Free French officer who was waiting at the airport drove her to the home of her friends Michael Wright, secretary at the British Embassy in Cairo and his wife, Esther. She had first met the couple before the war when he had worked at the British Embassy in Paris.

Eve was well educated, well informed, and well read; she spoke French, Polish, and English, and if she didn't know the language, she used interpreters. She sought information from everyone willing to talk, from men at the top, troops at the front, and people in the street, often taking detailed notes when possible. Then she would spend several hours at her portable typewriter. If her English was a little shaky, she grabbed her dictionary. Some contacts were influential personal friends, such as the Roosevelts, who enthusiastically supported her mission and gave her letters of introduction to others who had information she wanted.

Being an attractive, articulate, and charming woman known to many as her famous mother's biographer, during her first few days in Cairo she got inside, detailed information from Air Marshal A. W. Tedder, head of the RAF Middle East Command; Alexander C. Kirk, the American ambassador to Egypt; Sir Walter Monckton, director general of the British Ministry of Information; and the Right Honorable Oliver Lyttelton, a member of Churchill's cabinet permanently located in the Middle East.

They told her that five days before she arrived, British Commandos had tried to kill or capture the brilliant German general Erwin Rommel, "the Desert Fox." Led by Colonel Geoffrey Keyes, son of a World War I hero, about fifty Commandos in black uniforms, their faces and hands darkened with burned cork, "had been landed from a submarine onto enemy territory, with the mission of depriving the German Afrika Korps of its dynamic leader." After hiding in sand dunes at night and checking the lay of the land in daylight, on the third night they made a surprise attack on Rommel's house. Using automatic guns and grenades, they killed or wounded German staff officers in every room. But they couldn't find Rommel—because he had taken a rare trip out of the country for a birth-day party in Italy. The sudden bad weather made it impossible for a sub-marine to rescue the raid's survivors, so they were forced to find their way back to their lines through the desert, "hoping to escape the German patrols and to be rescued by British columns. Out of the fifty raiders, only two [Lieutenant Colonel Bob Leacock and an NCO] were ultimately to find their way back [having wandered together in the desert for forty-one days, living on iron rations]." Keyes, shot to death in the attack, was awarded a posthumous Victoria Cross.

When Eve appeared on the scene, General Sir Claude Auchinleck had just appointed General Sir Alan Cunningham to command the Eighth Army. Attacking in a rainstorm, he had quickly surrounded Rommel's advanced forces. However, the official British communiqué had called the outcome "confused." As Eve explained in her report: "The word meant exactly what it said . . . It meant soldiers, tanks, guns, trucks, losing their way and finding it again on this flat terrain where nothing was easier than to get lost. . . . It meant entire battles of tanks moving at full speed on the sand, like ships in battle action on the ocean. Sometimes Auchinleck's and Rommel's mechanized formations met and clashed in terrific fights. Sometimes they did not meet at all. They lost sight of each other and gained ground separately, in different regions of the empty map." Or what British soldiers called, "miles and miles and bloody miles of damn all." Eve's British friend Harold Nicolson, a member of Parliament, took a more jaundiced view of the situation, noting in his diary for December 1: "When we get on both sides of an enemy, that enemy is described as 'sur-rounded,' but when the enemy get on both sides of us, we are told that we have driven 'a wedge' between his two armies."

On his return from the birthday party in Italy, Rommel counter-attacked with massive eighteen-ton Mark 14/41 tanks, which destroyed many of the less formidable lend-lease American twelve-ton M3 tanks used by the British. But the fight went on.

Before dining as Lyttleton's guest, Eve made a few quick phone calls. She was told that Major Randolph Churchill (Winston's son), then in charge of the Middle East Army Bureau of Propaganda and Censorship, was leaving for the desert fighting front at dawn the next day, November 23, a Sunday—and that he was more than willing to take her with him, if only to shock the brass hats who thought it was no place for a woman. Long before dawn she was at Cairo Airport and then flew with Churchill in a Lockheed Lodestar, landing in the early afternoon at a runway near the Libyan border and the frontlines.

A lean, handsome officer greeted her and Churchill in a tent at Fort Maddalena—battle headquarters—and Eve was delighted to recognize Colonel Philip Astley, formerly married to film actress Madeleine Carroll. Before the war she had met them socially in Paris. Now she and Astley watched together as Blenheim bombers took off with their Hurricane and Tomahawk fighter escorts. The planes were to attack columns of German and Italian troops and tanks at Sidi Omar, some twenty-two miles to the north, and to the south near the besieged British military base at Tobruk.

As she watched, Eve thought: "There are so many planes in the sky— all Allied planes, all *our* planes. This is not like the empty sky of France during our defeat. This is like the English during the Battle of Britain that Britain won."

Randolph Churchill persuaded Eve and American writer Quentin Reynolds, representing *Collier's* magazine, to interview pilots from Britain, Australia, Rhodesia, and France for a BBC broadcast. But the highlight of Eve's day was at sunset, when she watched a Free French squadron of Blenheim bombers, each bearing the Cross of Lorraine, return with a British squadron from a successful raid.

Dinner was served in Colonel Astley's tent—the only one with light. Blackout precautions were enforced in all the other tents. The meal consisted of bully beef (canned meat), a canned vegetable, and a little rice pudding with marmalade. Fellow diners included Frenchman André Glarner, of the *Exchange Telegraph*, whom Eve had met when they were both aboard the British cargo ship *Madura* escaping from France, and later during the London Blitz.

That night, as the only woman around, she was given special sleeping quarters—the backseat of a military car with an inflatable rubber mattress. Despite her protests, Randolph Churchill insisted that she use as a blanket the sheepskin coat that he had bought in a Jerusalem bazaar. "Around me," she recalled, "British soldiers crawled into little trenches dug in the sand, to shelter themselves against the incredible cold of the night. To the right of my car about ten soldiers camped in a truck. To the left there were two tiny individual tents, so short and small that I could see the feet of the offi-

Eve, as a member of the Free French Forces, speaks with
pilots in the Libyan desert during her daring tour of the world's
battlefronts. Her vivid account, which included interviews with
world leaders, was published in a book, *Journey Among Warriors*,
in 1943.

cers who slept there sticking out at the end." She woke at dawn the next
morning from a dream that someone was knocking violently at her door: it
was dozens of planes taking off for a raid.

She quickly learned of the shortage of water in the desert when she
was handed a cup of water—and told that it was her ration for the day.
After using the same cupful to clean her teeth, then wash her hands and
face, she was intending to save it for future needs, when an English soldier
asked politely: "'Please . . . may I have your water?'—which made me
reluctantly part with the remaining liquid. The soapy contents of my cup
were carefully pooled in a basin with water from other cups and used to
wash handkerchiefs and military socks."

Eager to see more action, she accepted a lift from an RAF press officer
heading north into Libya to visit a reconnaissance squadron. As Quentin
Reynolds saw it, "The desert was a correspondent's paradise. We could go

wherever we wished. We could go on night patrols far in advance of the front. We could talk to prisoners freely . . . When we wrote a story, all we had to do was toss it to Randolph Churchill or Philip Astley, and we knew that it was as good as in New York [by plane from Cairo]." After an hour of driving through the desert en route to the reconnaissance squadron, Eve spotted a truck convoy of German and Italian prisoners. The trucks had stopped to let them stretch their legs, and Eve went to speak to some of the Germans. However, they "were sulking and speaking to no one." She had better luck with the Italians. Some were even smiling and talked about their families and how they hated the war and longed for a drink of water. When Eve asked one why he was barefoot, he replied with a laugh: "I ran so fast when the British offensive started that I just left my shoes behind." She eventually got a twenty-four-year-old German pilot from Cologne to talk. He began by naming the French towns he had gone through as a conqueror, then added, "You believe the British will win, but I believe the Germans will win." When she said she was French, he asked severely: "May I ask what Marshal Pétain would think of a Frenchwoman being here with the British? He would not be too pleased, I suppose!" She explained that many French people, like herself, believed the war would not be over until they had defeated the Germans.

During the recent battle General Cunningham had been reluctant to press home the attack. According to Reynolds, "Cunningham was driving at Tobruk, and was well on his way to taking the battered old city. But then he slowed down. He kept worrying about his railhead some sixty miles away, and he diverted part of his attacking forces to the East to protect it. That is like stopping to tie your shoelace when you're fighting Joe Louis" (a world heavyweight boxing champion). A fellow general thought the problem was more personal, that Cunningham "seemed on the verge of a nervous breakdown." Auchinleck returned to Cairo to discuss the problem with Oliver Lyttelton, who agreed that Major-General Ritchie should replace Cunningham, a decision endorsed by Winston Churchill. Though why Auchinleck hadn't taken over command himself was puzzling. Rommel's attempt to rescue his trapped or "surrounded" forces, as Eve would soon learn, ultimately failed, and the corridor leading to Tobruk, a threatened British military base in Libya, was secured—for the moment, prompting a British commander to telegraph to Auchinleck, "Tobruk is as relieved as I am."

Cecil Beaton, an official RAF war photographer (later to design the costumes for the movie *My Fair Lady*) apparently never met Eve, but he got the lowdown on her from an information officer while they were chatting about women journalists in the Middle East. As Beaton recorded in his diary: "Eve Curie was by far the most popular, and she was a beautiful, smiling woman until she transformed herself into a journalist; then her mouth became contorted and turned down at the corners, her eyes popped, and she barked, 'How many aeroplanes are passing through here a week? I must have hard facts for the great American public.' [Another] one who is known as WOV [World's Oldest Virgin] boasted that she [herself] acquired most of her information in bed. Least loved of all was Clare Boothe [Luce] . . . She was full of machine-made epigrams, and did not ingratiate herself further by calling the fighter pilots 'flying fairies.'"

When the two men chatted about her, Eve was already long gone and bedridden with malaria, in the Cairo home of the Michael Wrights. There, Wright woke her at seven in the morning on December 8, 1941, by knocking on her door and shouting: "Japan has attacked Hawaii. The Americans have suffered great losses."

The Japanese sneak attack on Pearl Harbor on December 7 destroyed half the U.S. Navy, killed 2,330 servicemen, and brought the country into the war against Japan and her allies, Germany and Italy. The response of the American friends who came to see Eve was upbeat. They said it was a hard blow, but they needed it. Now they would wake up. Soon after, the Japanese attacked Hong Kong, Siam (Thailand), Malaya, the Philippines, and Burma. More battle fronts for Eve's itinerary.

By mid-December Eve was fit enough to board an Egyptian airline plane for Beirut, Lebanon. From there she was driven to Syria to celebrate a recent Allied victory. Hitler's Middle East battle plan had been to hold on to Syria—which had been mandated French territory since the end of World War I. But the leader of Free French volunteers, General Georges Catroux, a former governor of Indo-China, supported by Free French, Australian, Indian, and British troops, had recently frustrated Hitler's plan by defeating the entrenched Vichy French defenders. Eve spent from morning to night talking with Free French soldiers, "almost drunk with happiness to have found again the France in which I believed." The defenders had put up a ferocious fight, General Catroux told her, especially against their own countrymen. Obviously distressed at having had to attack fellow Frenchmen, he had resolved to give no medals or promotions to any of the fighters. "None of the men would want a reward for fighting other Frenchmen," he said. Later, as she walked through a military graveyard on the outskirts of Damascus, Eve noticed that the men from both armies were buried in the same cemetery side by side and "each cross bore the simple words, 'Mort Pour La France.'"

General Catroux didn't tell her, apparently, that a group of Jewish volunteers from Palestine led by Moshe Dayan had joined the Australians in spearheading the successful attack on the Vichy French, during which Dayan—a future leader of the Israeli army and minister of defense of Israel—lost his left eye. In fact, after Syria, Eve was on her way to Palestine, where Dayan was recovering from his injury.

The genial General Catroux lent Eve his car and two aides-de-camp to drive her to Jerusalem, where she was a houseguest of Sir Harold Mac-Michael, the British high commissioner for Palestine, and his wife. From Government House Eve had a superb view of Jerusalem, which she saw up close but at lightning speed during a tour of the city, taking in the Mount of Olives, the new Hebrew University, and the Dead Sea. Next day she stayed at the King David Hotel, which was crowded with British army officers. After a night fighting a feverish cold, she took a plane crossing the Trans-Jordan desert and Iraq to Habbaniya, the largest British air base in the Middle East. She hoped eventually to reach Russia through Iran, but there were problems ahead. She was bumped off one plane to Iran and replaced by the Polish vice-consul in Istanbul, who had to meet General Sikorksi, leader of Poland's government in exile.

Instead of waiting for the next plane, she made the sixty-five-mile trip to Baghdad, Iraq, by car. In Baghdad she typed out her latest impressions in a BOAC rest house smelling of burned paraffin, and met three artillery officers—a Scot, a South African, and an Englishman—serving in an Indian regiment. A young Assyrian left her speechless when he insisted that the United Nations must create a free Assyrian state after the war. "I could not help assuming," she wrote, "that it had died twenty-five centuries ago, after the great days of Nineveh, and I remained speechless, entirely incapable of picturing to myself what Assyria's *Lebensraum* ought to be. It was the lot of our generation to witness the extraordinary phenomenon: the oldest countries in the world: Egypt, Persia [Iran], India, China, and others—gradually waking up from their sleep or from their decadence and claiming their freedom from the younger powers."

During what seemed an endless wait for permission to visit the Russian front and then, when she got that, more waiting for a plane to take her there, Eve asked for an interview with the new twenty-two-year-old Shah of Iran and was surprised when it was immediately granted. She met him, a thin, tall "boy" in military uniform in a dull office, and was pleased that he spoke French like a Frenchman but disappointed that he often left his sentences unfinished as if approaching dangerous ground and afraid to continue. He did explain that he had joined an alliance with the British and Russians—their tanks and troops were in the city—"to avoid for Iran the fate of the countries doomed by Hitler." (He seemed no more confident two years later when Harrison Salisbury, reporting for the United Press, saw him as "a nervous youngster, wondering whether the British, the Russians and the Americans would let him keep the Peacock Throne or dump him as they had his terrifying father.")

Eve took off for a cold and bumpy flight to Moscow reading a booklet, *Brush Up Your Russian—Conversations of Real Use*, then gave it up to take in the white peaks of the sixteen-thousand-foot Elburz Mountains and then the calm, blue Caspian Sea, which gradually changed into a solid gray and white plate. The plane stopped en route at Kuybyshev, where she stayed the first night in the dormitory of a school taken over by the British Embassy, and next in the Grand Hotel, where all the women residents shared the same cold bathroom.

She spent most of her time with an interpreter interviewing factory workers and wounded Russian soldiers. On Sunday, January 11, 1942, she visited an almond-green Orthodox church, at first surprised to find it crowded, and again surprised to see not one young person among the fervent worshipers. Far from indicating a religious revival in Russia, she wrote, "the old and destitute, the ignorant, the superstitious, the humble, the irremediably crushed—had in fact strikingly confirmed to me that, on the whole, the young Russian generations had parted with Christianity, that they had converted to a new faith that left room for no other worship." An Orthodox priest gave her a succinct explanation for the situation: "There have been two opposite propagandas in the Soviet Union," he said. "One for God and one against Him. Obviously, the most successful of the two has not been ours."

When Eve arrived in Moscow the fighting front was only eighty miles away and she immediately asked to be allowed to go there. The Soviet government supplied her with an interpreter-handler, Liuba Mieston, an army lieutenant whose husband, a lieutenant-colonel, was at the front. Liuba would stay with her night and day. They were both put up at the huge Moskva Hotel close to Red Square, which was usually forbidden to foreigners. After checking in, Eve dressed for a walk around town in thirty-two-below-zero weather, putting on three pairs of woolen stockings and two pairs of socks, two sweaters, two pairs of gloves, two coats, and sheepskin-lined overshoes. And she still shivered.

There was less bomb damage than she had seen in London during the Blitz, but from the sight of women lined up for hours in the deadly cold to get the measly food rations and accounts of atrocities on the population by

Nazi troops, it was clear they were enduring much greater hardship. Through Liuba, Eve spoke with workers, shopkeepers, waiters, intellectuals, and soldiers. All said that though many had fled from the city, they were comforted by the news that Stalin was staying put. Yet they were not willing to say what they thought of the Soviet government. She concluded that "Russian suspicion of foreigners is immense, but Russian hospitality is overwhelming, and the two are not in the least contradictory: one can give food and retain secrets."

The short, plump, ebullient handler and Eve soon became friends, visiting Russian officials at party headquarters in provincial towns, public buildings, and laboratories, where snacks of cakes and caviar invariably appeared. Eve also dined at the Hotel National with the head of the British Military Mission, General Mason MacFarlane. He later conceded that she had been allowed to see more of the Red Army in the field than he or any of his staff had.

On January 14, 1942, Colonel Boltin, a Russian with a perpetual smile, drove the two women close to the battlefront in a Russian-built limousine. Snow fell steadily as they passed many antitank barriers; columns of marching soldiers; battle-scarred cars and trucks, armored cars, and machine guns rigged on small sleighs—all painted white. On their return to Moscow, Liuba Mieston sang a love song about the city.

But Eve wasn't satisfied with the trip. She wanted to get closer to the front, and on January 15 she persuaded Colonel Boltin to drive to the village of Mikhailovka, retaken from the Nazis just two days previously. On the way they passed burned buildings, shell craters, and abandoned trucks, tanks, and guns. And wounded, bandaged Russian soldiers trudging through the snow toward the army hospital. Artillery fire grew louder as they reached a spot retaken two days previously.

Many hundreds of dead Germans lay in the snow, among dead horses and scattered equipment. Boltin warned Eve not to touch any of the corpses, because many were mined. She still risked walking in what might have been a minefield to inspect a German tank and three of its dead crew. She noticed that "their uniforms, stiffened by frozen blood, told the whole story of Germany's fight against the Russian winter. These uniforms were of thin woolen material, hardly warm enough to protect a man quartered in occupied France, the boots were of black leather. They were tight boots—the very thing that makes the cold unbearable. From what I could see, the underwear was thin, too." She was not moved by the sight of the dead men, "after seeing the burned houses in the villages, and the gallows where peasants had been hanged."

Refusing to take Eve any closer to the front, Boltin drove her instead to the headquarters of the commander of the area, the tall, tough, and energetic Major General A. Vlasov. He was asleep when they arrived, but soon joined them and enthusiastically shared the news that one of the fifty prisoners taken that day was a Hans Hitler, who claimed to be Hitler's nephew, but it was not confirmed. True to form the general invited them to a supper of hors d'oeuvres, sausages, salted cucumbers, cakes, hot tea, and vodka—a feast even the richest civilian in Moscow could only dream about. During the meal, the general described his week's work: beating back three German divisions and the sixth tank division under General Heinz Guderian (commander of the first panzer group to reach the outskirts of Moscow in 1941) and leaving fifteen hundred enemy corpses on the frozen battlefield.

No starry-eyed visitor, Eve rarely hesitated to say what was on her mind. As a patriot she despised French, British, and American workers who had "been blind enough to follow the suicidal order" from the Soviet government at the start of World War II to slow down production and agitate for peace at any price. Why? Because, according to the Comintern, it was a war between imperialists. She remembered this while chatting with the manager and four engineers of a tank factory she had just toured. She had asked them, somewhat diplomatically: "Don't you regret, in the light of present events, having so dreadfully underestimated Germany's strength when the war broke out in 1939, and having gone to so much trouble to weaken France and England, who, 'imperialistic' as they may have been, were nevertheless fighting your potential enemy, Hitler? I'm wondering why you made the superfluous move of slowing down the work in our war plants in the West . . . Germany was ultimately to attack you—you knew it—and France and Britain were fighting Germany. Why undermine our effort, even if you wanted to remain neutral?" The response was a dead silence, during which Liuba, having delivered the message, gave Eve an odd, disapproving look. Eventually the manager said that he and his managers did not know what Communist parties in foreign countries had decided to do when the war started, and neither endorsed nor disavowed their actions. Eve smiled and changed the subject, but she speculated that what he meant to say was, "What kind of people were they anyway [French and British Communists], not to work overtime . . . for the defense of their country in danger?"

Before the war, Eve had known such Communists in France, England, and America who were willing to stab their own country in the back. "Today," she wrote, "when heroic French Communists, engaged in the underground struggle against the oppressors, were caught by the Nazis and sent to the firing squad, it was not the 'Internationale' that they were singing but the 'Marseillaise'—and their last cry, before falling under the German bullets, was: 'Vive la France!'"

On January 18, Eve joined Leo Tolstoy's grandniece, Sophia Andre-yevna Tolstoy, Professor Minz of the Moscow Academy of Sciences, and his young female secretary in a trip to the novelist's estate. Of course, Eve's handler went along, too. They were driven in a dilapidated limousine by a disgruntled old chauffeur who stopped several times to let them get out and run on the frozen road to bring their freezing feet back to life. Sophia Tolstoy, in charge of all five Tolstoy museums in Russia, spoke English and French fluently and, to Eve, "like many well-born Russian women, had a real peasant's face, round and a little stout, with strong cheekbones and clear eyes." Within a mile of the estate, the chauffeur refused to go any farther, claiming that the car would get stuck in the snow. And he resisted all their arguments.

As they walked toward the estate, a group of peasants approached. One stared at Eve and began shouting fiercely at her. Liuba also looked at Eve and she, too, began shouting. Then everyone joined in. Eve's nose had become as white as the snow: a sign that it had a touch of frostbite. So she followed Liuba's instructions, rubbing it vigorously with wool and snow until it hurt and became red. The warnings came in time. Eve saved her nose.

They were greeted at the Tolstoy house by the curator and his wife. Most of Tolstoy's books, documents, pictures, and furniture had been evacuated to Siberia. What was left had been assembled in a small room: a few pieces of furniture, picture frames, and two grand pianos. Eve went to a ground-floor room where Tolstoy had written *Anna Karenina*, and which Nazi officers had used as a mess hall for the forty-five days of their occupation, then to a charming low-ceilinged study where he had worked on *War and Peace*. She was shocked by the sight of the upstairs bedrooms and small library, where straw had been stuffed into the windows to replace the broken glass, and there were large holes in the floors where the retreating Nazis had tried to burn the place to the ground.

On their return to Moscow the limousine got stuck on a slope, and children skating nearby came to their rescue with pieces of wood from a forest, which they stuck under the wheels, then helped to push until the car was free. Driving though the night, shivering though buried under sheepskin coats and blankets, Eve and Sophia discussed people they worshipped. For Sophia it was Tolstoy, for Eve, her mother. Oddly enough, although Marie Curie and Tolstoy were so different in character, tastes, beliefs, and their approach to life, in some things they were strikingly alike. Both felt somehow personally guilty for social inequalities that most contemporaries took for granted or ignored. Tolstoy had taught the Russian illiterates on his estate. Marie had started a secret school for children in a Polish village. Both had great respect for manual workers. He was ashamed to be rich, and tried to get rid of his money. She, after experiencing poverty, had avoided being rich, by declining to patent discoveries that could have made her a fortune.

Eve judged her mother the more successful of the two in living up to her principles. Marie had died without wealth. Tolstoy's wife and children kept part of the riches he was trying to give away, and some of which still clung to him. Eve contended that "his moving efforts had never really made of him 'a common man.'"

Back in Moscow, Eve and Liuba were moved into the historic Metropol Hotel, now ready for an influx of foreign correspondents and Russian army officers. Before World War I the Metropol had been "the rendezvous of the city's millionaires and their most expensive ladies." After the revolution it became the House of Soviets No. 2, where the Soviet Executive Committee met and "approved the execution of the Czar and his family."

Early on January 23 a cheerful young chauffeur drove Eve and her handler in a little Russian-built Ford with a chronic cough (the twenty-two-below-zero temperature didn't help). Forty miles west of Moscow they passed Nova Osakova, the limit of the German advance, then reached Mozhaisk, which the Russian counterattack had liberated just three days earlier. Eve was astonished at the sight of disabled guns, tanks, and crashed airplanes, Russian and German, all mixed together in the snow. "The whole thing looked like a giant amusement park where everything had suddenly gone wrong . . . and where the various cars with crazy shapes, driven by foolish people, had been thrown in every direction . . . A huge German tank majestically dominated the scene, lost in a field of snow like a motionless battleship in a white ocean."

A young girl in the street who had been sobbing told Eve that before the Germans retreated they had locked two hundred Russian prisoners of war and local civilians in the Cathedral of Holy Trinity, then blew it up. To confirm her story Eve had the chauffeur take them to the headquarters of Lieutenant General Leonid Govorov, an assured and energetic man. He confirmed the atrocity story, saying that the fascists' ways were tragically monotonous in their ruthlessness.

So were the Communists' ways. Eve did not know it, but the previous year under Stalin's orders some forty-five hundred Polish prisoners had been massacred by the NKVD in Katyn forest. In civilian life they were doctors, lawyers, businessmen, scientists, writers, and journalists. The intent was to create a weak postwar Poland by destroying its non-Communist intelligentsia and potential leaders. The Russians blamed the Nazis for the massacre, but in 1992 the Russian government gave Polish president Lech Walesa previously secret evidence that Stalin had ordered the killings.

Eve accepted the general's offer to let her interview German war prisoners, and three ragged and exhausted men were brought into the room: a middle-aged corporal who before the war had played the tuba in a provincial orchestra; a bearded man of about thirty; and a fair-haired boy whose head was bandaged. As Eve moved to approach them, a Russian soldier held her back to protect her from contact with the lice-ridden men.

The corporal showed her his blistered fingers, thin uniform, and worn shoes and said that they were forced to retreat because they weren't equipped for such cold weather. The other two nodded agreement. When she asked if Hitler had been right to attack Poland and start a world war, he said he thought invading Poland was a good idea because it succeeded, and repeated the propaganda line that Germany didn't start a world war. The French and British did. They had no business helping the Poles. If they hadn't interfered there would have been no world war. However, all three agreed that from what they knew now, Hitler had been wrong to attack Russia.

On January 26, Eve and her handler flew from Moscow in brilliant sunshine, landed at Kuybyshev, and waited for the next plane to Teheran. She made good use of the time, visiting the Chinese ambassador, Shao Li-tse, who gave her letters of introduction to Chinese officials in Burma and China. In the nearby Polish embassy she learned that more than a million Poles were still in Russian prison camps, labor camps, and jails.

A British Embassy car took her to the airport, where she sadly said good-bye to her handler friend, Lieutenant Mieston, and took a flight to Teheran. In Teheran she felt warm for the first time in weeks and gave up hoping for a plane seat to continue her journey, taking instead the Trans-Iranian Railway, and then a flying boat across northern India. When she had asked an English diplomat if he thought she had a chance to reach Singapore, he replied drily, "'Not unless you are a Jap.' The maddening thing," Eve wrote, "was that he was right."

Libya, Syria, Palestine, Iran, Russia, and Singapore were not the only battlegrounds. In France there was growing resistance to the Nazis. Paul Langevin was still under house arrest, and another Curie family friend, Emile Borel, after being arrested for the third time, had been sent to prison for six months, suspected of anti-Nazi activities. Far worse was the atrocious fate of Fernand Holweck, an assistant professor at the Radium Institute. As a leader of a resistance group, he had been helping downed RAF crews to escape across the Spanish border, until a police agent posing as an Englishman penetrated the group, and betrayed Holweck and seventy members of his group to the Gestapo. They had arrested Holweck on December 11 as he was entering the Radium Institute, tortured him to death, and then sent his clothes, covered with blood and feces, to his family.

The news sent shock waves through the scientific community but did not deter Joliot, or Henri Moureu, his Collège de France colleague, recently appointed director of the Paris police department's Municipal Laboratory. After investigating acts of sabotage, the police gave Moureu any unexploded devices they found to examine, identify, and finally destroy. But instead of destroying the explosives and detonators, after completing the official reports, Moureu handed the material to Joliot for the Resistance.

CHAPTER 19

Joliot Becomes a Communist—Eve Curie Interviews Nehru, Gandhi, and Jinnah

1941–1943

D uring the harsh winter of 1941–1942 in Paris, the food shortage forced some to eat cat meat, despite a warning that cats ate rats that were full of bacteria fatal to humans. Joliot and his family were never that desperate, although to satisfy his chain-smoking addiction, an assistant brought him cigarettes reconstituted from butts he'd picked up in the street. The cold weather and general deprivations lowered their resistance, and Joliot was the only one of his family not to fall seriously ill. Pierre, nine, had mumps and rubella, and fourteen-year-old Hélène had rubella. Irène, herself suffering from bronchitis, cared for them in bedrooms where the temperature once dropped to one degree below freezing.

Suspecting Gentner's sympathies, the Nazis ordered him to leave Paris and return to Heidelberg. Fortunately he was replaced by a man he had recommended, Wolfgang Riezler, who proved equally accommodating. In April 1942, when Irène's health grew worse, Joliot again turned to Gentner, who somehow had retained his influence, and got permission for her to recuperate in the Swiss Alps.

According to Hélène, her father "had an agreement that no researches related to the war would be conducted at his lab and that he, as director, would have access to all parts of the lab, including those where the German physicists were working. It happened that one evening, my father found one of the German physicists apparently working on a radio emitter clearly of the German army type. He was very angry, but after looking more carefully at the apparatus and hearing the explanations, he understood that the apparatus was being dismantled so that some pieces could be used to complete the Radio Frequency of the cyclotron."

Joliot reduced the risk of being caught at his clandestine work by meeting fellow members of the National Front Committee at different locales: the Museum of Natural History, a dentist's waiting room, the Palais-Royal, and various little cafés. To cover their tracks, Joliot gave a talk in the Collège de France amphitheater to an audience of Germans and leading Vichyites, while Ligonnière, a fellow member of the National Front Committee, cultivated an outspoken Hitler-admirer, a buxom blonde from Lorraine, and made a pretense of being her friend.

Meanwhile, Eve Curie had arrived in Rangoon, Burma's capital, as British soldiers were making a hasty retreat from the advancing Japanese. Singapore had fallen on February 15, 1942, the exact day Japanese diplomats had predicted it would be captured when she was in Russia several weeks previously. Eve got to work immediately in her hotel room, pounding at her typewriter from noon until 4 A.M. and only stopping when a British officer on the floor above yelled in a fury that she was ruining his sleep. Early that day she took her copy to the censor at the Public Relations Office. With typical British understatement, the colonel in charge said that he would be greatly relieved if she left town that afternoon.

At ten o'clock she met Sir Reginald Dorman-Smith, Burma's governor, who remarked that he couldn't make a move without his servants noticing, and if he moved a suitcase from one room to another the rumor would quickly spread that he was leaving town. Eve noted his "handsome, artificial smile in support of his statement that Rangoon would hold out," and felt like telling His Excellency, "Why do you take all that trouble? I am French. I *know* what a defeat looks like." On what would be her last day in Rangoon, the governor gave her the use of his limousine and his aide-de-camp, Lieutenant Bettersby, as her escort. Two banks about to close for good within hours refused to change her American dollars into the rupees she needed to pay her hotel bill. Bettersby suggested the American Consulate, where an official persuaded the local National City Bank to exchange a hundred dollars.

Before boarding the train that night she witnessed "how a large town stricken by fear can go to pieces, just as an individual can have a nervous breakdown." Shops open half an hour earlier were now barricaded, clothes she had given to be washed at the hotel had not been returned, because the washer had disappeared. The restaurant where she had planned to join other American correspondents was locking its doors as she arrived. She was lucky to find a place to get a plate of curried rice at Pegu railroad station. There, a lean young American in canvas slacks, open shirt, and dirty sweater told her he was a fighter pilot and hadn't been able to get on the train. She agreed to squeeze him into her compartment.

The slow, dusty train headed for Mandalay was packed with Burmese, Europeans, Indians, and Chinese, many in uniform, escaping from the approaching enemy. A British contingent reinforced by Chinese troops under Chiang Kai-shek's unofficial "adviser," the American general "Vinegar Joe" Stilwell, would not be able to hold them off much longer.

According to historian Barbara Tuchman, Stilwell was trying "desperately to organize transport and food for the retreat before it collapsed in chaos. The Chinese general who was Chiang's personal liaison officer could not be found because . . . he was elsewhere engaged in organizing the retreat to China of a Rolls-Royce, which he had delightedly acquired from the British Governor-General in trade for two jeeps."

Three young English soldiers in Eve's compartment had been walking through Burma for four days carrying heavy equipment. One, with a Yorkshire accent, complained to her: "Everything was against us in this campaign. First we had the wrong equipment; no tommy guns, no planes overhead, very little artillery. The climate, the jungle, the animals, the inhabitants, were foreign to us, hostile to us. As for malaria, it is a worse enemy than the Japanese." Of the eleven hundred men in his unit, four hundred had been stricken. The disgruntled pilot in the dirty sweater told Eve that he was from New York State and had joined a group of volunteers known as the Flying Tigers, who had been sent from Rangoon "to fight this suicidal war." (Under their formidable organizer, Claire Chennault, they morphed into the U.S. Fourteenth Air Force.) Having shot down three Japanese planes, he had been given an extra fifteen hundred dollars on top of his monthly six hundred dollars.

"My idea of fighting," he said, "is each for himself and no orders. Above all, no inspections. Inspections are the hellish part of military life. They must have been busy with an inspection the day we got our licking at Pearl Harbor." (They weren't.)

At Mandalay, Eve changed trains and left for Lashio farther north. The American pilot went along, too, and as the train climbed slowly through the hills he steadily helped himself to apples from her paper bag, until there were none left. She spent a miserable night shivering with cold and fatigue, vainly trying to get warm by wrapping herself in her camel's-hair coat. Although the train arrived at Lashio at dawn, thirty hours late, a government official was waiting for her at the station with a car. After dropping off the pilot at a hostel, she reached the official's house, took a bath, and had breakfast with her host, who was eager to hear the latest news from the south.

Eve waited for three days at Lashio for a plane to China, sadly aware that within a few weeks this terminal station of the Burmese railway would be in Japanese hands—along with most of Burma.

Landing in China's Chungking airport was a strange experience: the runway was a sandbar paved with stone in the middle of the Yangtze River, and available only in winter and spring, before Tibet's melting snows flooded the entire place. After leaving the plane she reached the city itself by a footbridge.

The Chinese had been fighting the Japanese since the summer of 1937. A year later the Japanese armies had occupied most of northern China and were still in control when Japanese planes attacked Pearl Harbor on December 7, 1941. When Eve arrived early in 1942, both the United States and Britain were allies of the Chinese. The Americans had sent a military mission to China and promised to create a modern Chinese air force and to arm thirty army divisions. But not yet. The strategy of both the United States and Britain was to defeat Germany first.

Eve met the well-educated and charismatic Communist leader Chou En-lai at a candlelit dinner of good food and wine arranged by his wife. He had put aside political differences to cooperate with the Nationalist anti-Communist leader Chiang Kai-shek in order to fight the Japanese. He told Eve that China's problem was to hold out until the Western powers could attack Japan. Chou En-lai had captivated *Time* magazine's Theodore White by his charming personality and easy manner. He leapt to his feet when Eve asked him which war songs were most popular among the Chinese guerrillas, saying that he'd ask his boys to sing for her, then roused four teenage soldiers who had been resting outside and brought them in. At his command, they sang four lively war songs, bowed shyly, and left.

Eve found the beautiful Madame Sun Yat-sen living in an unexpectedly simple home. She was one of three powerful Soong sisters, the youngest of whom had married Chiang Kai-shek. Madame Sun praised the fighting spirit of the guerrillas, hoped America would help them soon, and stressed that liberal ideas would never die in China. Strangely, this passionate advocate of left-wing ideas reminded Eve of her mother, the detached scientist who had never engaged in party politics. What they had in common, she realized, as well as simplicity and integrity was "The student's look. A way, also, of being entirely inconspicuous and yet unforgettable. The shyness of every gesture. A carefully concealed but easily wounded sensitiveness. And then the voice: soft, exquisite, speaking in undertone." Eve also met her sister, Madame H. H. Kung, wife of the finance minister, at an elegant and intimate dinner where the company included T. F. Tsiang, the former ambassador to Moscow, now the Chinese government's director of political affairs.

On March 10, 1942, Eve arrived at the "banal" European-style villa of the third and youngest Soong sister, Chiang Kai-shek's extremely attractive second wife, who struck her as "slim, smart, as neat as a Cartier jewel." Educated at Wellesley in the United States, she spoke flawless American English and "there was something American, too, about her mixture of efficiency, cleverness, and charm. What she said was always intelligent, strikingly worded, and sometimes very moving." Eve's fellow correspondent, Theodore H. White, largely disagreed with this impression. He had been exposed to Madame Chiang for much longer and regarded her as "a beautiful, tart, and brittle woman, more American than Chinese, and mistress of every level of the American language from the verses of the hymnal [she had converted the generalissimo to the Methodist brand of Christianity] to the most sophisticated bitchery. Madame Chiang, always stunning in her silk gowns, could be as coy and kittenish as a college coed, or as commanding and petty as a dormitory house mother. She swished briskly into any room like a queen, and could bustle even sitting down. She was interpreter on many occasions for her husband and Stilwell, and when matters snarled, would take them into her own hands." Eve never met Chiang Kai-shek himself, the leader of the Chinese national government, but she was unlikely to have matched tell-it-like-it-is Stilwell's searing assessment of him. The American general gave Chiang Kai-shek the demeaning code-name *Peanut* and dismissed him as "an ignorant, illiterate, superstitious, peasant son of a bitch." Eve expressed a much more benign view of all she met on her brief visit, and was convinced of their determination, whatever their politics, to defeat the Japanese invaders.

Yet "perhaps the most aggressive-spirited enemy of Japan" she encountered there was an American, Colonel Claire Chennault. She squeezed in an interview with him when her plane from Chungking to Calcutta, India, landed to refuel at Kumming, a U.S. airbase in China. As they spoke in his nearby office, its walls covered in maps and charts, the face of this former acrobatic pilot struck Eve as being that of a buccaneer or sailor who had spent his life at sea. "But no," she wrote, "that face, that strong, sturdy body simply belonged to an aviation-crazy American, whose wife and eight children awaited him in his hometown of Waterproof, Louisiana. He spoke slowly, in a low, intense voice, and he listened carefully when I spoke: his deafness was a real handicap to him. He hardly moved at all— but in his black, sparkling eyes, there was enough willpower and enthusiasm to lift the world. What was spellbinding about him was his entire concentration on his task . . . to attack Japan." He believed that air power could destroy Japan and was reputed never to take shelter during an air raid. Instead, he watched the Japanese plane formations as they came over, "as a football coach studies film of a team he expects soon to meet in the field." And it paid off. In the first six months of 1942, his less than eighty Flying Tigers in their Curtiss P-40 pursuit planes destroyed 286 Japanese planes.

From China, Eve continued on the long flight to Calcutta, India. She was arriving at a critical time in the nation's history, with Japanese troops already on its northern borders and its political future in the balance. Eve planned to meet the leading contenders for political power in India: Nehru, Gandhi, and Jinnah. All wanted freedom from British rule.

Gandhi's strategy to gain independence was to launch a civil-disobedience campaign in 1940 in which leading advocates for Indian independence agreed to participate in turn. Nehru, the first, was arrested by the British and sentenced to four years in prison. He was released after over a year, with other Congress prisoners, three days before Pearl Harbor. Now with India threatened by the Japanese onslaught, Winston Churchill sent Stafford Cripps, a Labor member of his war cabinet and personal friend of Nehru's, to persuade the Indians to join the war effort.

Though India was directly menaced by the Japanese army, Eve saw little evidence of any Indian prepared to defend the country. On the contrary, Calcutta seemed "like a fat, weak animal, fascinated by the vicious snake of war and rendered powerless by it [and from which] a good many of its inhabitants had fled," spurred by the news that the Japanese were heading for Bengal. Walking in the streets—almost dizzy from the humidity and sun's glare—she was surprised at the lethargy and indifference of everyone. They even ignored an air raid warning. She could always take refuge from the heat and humidity as a guest at the palatial residence of the governor of Bengal, Sir John Herbert, and his wife, Lady Mary. In Chungking she had shared a bathtub with fifteen other foreign correspondents. In Calcutta she had two rooms and a bathroom all to herself. Breakfast in bed, and a car and chauffeur, were always available. One ring of a bell, and a barefoot, turbaned servant appeared to bring her tea, clean her shoes, press her evening dress, take handwritten notes to people in the palace dozens of rooms away, and bring back their replies.

Sir Guthrie Russell, in charge of munitions production in India, told Eve that she could inspect any war factory, and she chose one that employed seventy-three hundred Indians and seven hundred Englishmen, the most highly skilled among the Indians using micrometers accurate to the eight-millionth of an inch.

A balanced reporter, Eve found reason to damn and praise the British for their treatment of Indians, writing: "The old woman who sewed leather soles in the Calcutta slums was not concerned with India's fight for independence, she was not even aware that India was ruled by England, and the words 'Germany' or 'Japan' meant strictly nothing to her. Her problem was that she worked too much and did not eat enough. And the fault of the British toward her and her kind was not that Britain ruled India: it was that Britain . . . by refraining from offering drastic material improvements to the needy Indians, from checking unemployment, from blasting illiteracy, from developing both agriculture and industry in order to raise India's standard of living and to make her self-sufficient . . . should have done much too little for India as a whole in the last two hundred years."

On the other hand, Eve conceded that Britain's achievements in a country of 390 million people included the efficient railway system — the fourth largest in the world — an increase of twenty-one million irrigated acres in the past fifty years, the building of canals, which reduced widespread famine, the creation of the large, modern cities and factories, and the establishment of a centralized regime of law and order, as well as "the maintenance of peace on Indian soil. It remained, however, that the sinister specters of poverty, malnutrition, disease, obscurantism — plus those of superstition and religious fanaticism — were still keeping watch over India . . . Even in Calcutta, the second largest city in the British Empire, with a population of one and a half million people, one could sense within a few minutes that India was medieval . . . The old woman whom I had seen sewing leather soles in her mud shed was no more ready to be a citizen of a free India . . . than of any other political setup. Nobody had prepared her or her children to become citizens of any land in the world."

Still, Eve gave Europeans and Indians alike a lively argument when they said there was no difference between Hitler and the king of England, and little difference, if any, between British rule and totalitarian conquest by the Japanese or the Germans.

"Whenever I heard such irresponsible statements," she wrote, "the picture of my crucified country, tortured by barbarians, had come to my mind, in a violent contrast with what I saw with my own eyes in India." Then she pointed out, for example, that books advocating nationalism and the overthrow of the British regime were available with British approval in Indian bookstores. In the evenings Eve felt ashamed of her unglamorous Western dress when she dined among Indian women in their beautiful colored saris, and noted somewhat wryly that while the men spoke quietly to each other in Bengali or Hindustani, the women always spoke to her in English about her mother, Marie, never failing to mention her youth spent in Poland under foreign domination.

In India she found that the Hindus especially were more interested in their quarrels with the British than in winning the war. As author Byron Farwell reports, "Some actually conspired with the Nazis and with the Japanese army. Gandhi, now a national figure, whose call for [a strike] resulted in increasingly bloody riots, [also] called upon the British people to submit peacefully to the Nazis and Fascists. Jawaharlal Nehru, usually more level-headed, once remarked that the Japanese would be no worse than the British."

Eve had arranged to meet Nehru at Allahabad railroad station in mid-March 1942, then drive with him to his home, where she hoped to interview him. When he got off the train, alone, he seemed to her like a handsome fairy-tale prince, "with a romantic face; also a witty one." She was amazed to see that one of India's most famous national leaders traveled without a bodyguard, and that the other disembarking travelers virtually ignored him. He wasn't entirely fan free, however. When they arrived by car at his large, white villa, alive with family, guests, small children, and servants, a few students were waiting outside for his autograph.

A leading member of the Indian Congress party, Nehru professed advanced modern views, in contrast to one of his rivals, Mahatma Gandhi. He did support Gandhi's policy of nonviolence to achieve their freedom from British rule. However, Gandhi appeared to have no doubt about who or what he was, while Nehru saw himself as "a queer mixture of East and West, out of place everywhere, at home nowhere."

At a not very tasty lunch of curry with about a dozen others, Eve focused her attention on Nehru, whom she knew to be a "Brahman of Kashmir—a blue blood of India—who, as the only son of prosperous parents, had been brought up by an English governess and an Irish tutor, [then on to] Harrow and Trinity College, Cambridge. Here was a modern thinker of a purely Western variety. A Marxist socialist, an atheist who had, amazingly enough, grown into one of the most popular mass leaders of a medieval and deeply religious India. Just as Madame Chiang Kai-shek was a Chinese nationalist modeled by America, Nehru was an Indian nationalist modeled by Britain, 'Made in Britain.'"

The conversation turned to American lecture tours, and although she knew he would be a hit, Eve teased him by saying that he would have no success as a public speaker in the United States. He stared at her, slightly shocked, and asked: "Why?" "Well, there's your accent," she said. "The Americans just could not understand an Indian as English as *that*." He laughed along with everyone else. But, as Eve noted, "It was extraordinary to hear Nehru use his refined, almost affected kind of English to describe the years he had spent in English jails. [Nine years in all.] But then again, as a conclusion to a strongly motivated attack on British imperialism, he was always ready to say lightly, in his best Cambridge manner: 'Individually, of course, I rather like the English.'" Eve thought his attitude was like that of a woman in an arranged marriage who seeks a divorce for mental cruelty from a husband with whom she intends to remain friends. Nehru amused her by the way he sometimes began an anecdote and forgot the point, when he would laugh at himself and say, "However," and go back to the start of the story. She thought that he and France's ex-Premier Léon Blum had a lot in common, as courageous, sincere, generous, efficient socialists, with "glittering minds," although Nehru disapproved of Blum's policy of nonintervention during the Spanish Civil War.

After tea, instead of attending a political conference, as she had expected, the group was entertained by a Punjabi who blew through his fingers to make bird imitations.

While in Calcutta, Eve also met General Sir Archibald Wavell, the British commander in chief in Southeast Asia, who invited her to stay in his house in New Delhi when she told him she hoped to interview Sir Stafford Cripps in India's capital city. A Socialist member of Churchill's War Cabinet, Cripps had the formidable mission of unifying Indians in defense of their country against an anticipated Japanese invasion by assuring them independence was within their grasp. His meetings with members of the Indian National Congress and their rivals, the Muslim League, began on March 22, 1942, a month after Japanese troops captured Singapore, Malaya, and most of Burma, and were a threatening presence near the Indian border. Implicit in Cripps's mission was a British guarantee to hand over the country to the Indians. When and to which Indians were the critical questions.

In New Delhi, Eve lunched with the "quiet, shy and very pleasant" Viceroy Linlithgow and Lady Linlithgow in "the impressive palace of fifty-four rooms—plus the offices, halls, ballrooms, dining rooms, libraries, and the like," guarded by Sikh troopers and cared for by barefoot servants in red and white uniforms. She wondered, if Cripps did succeed, who would replace the Linlithgows: "Should I come back there one day to see a half-naked Gandhi sipping his daily ration of goat milk? To whom would we curtsy then? Would the delightful Cambridge-educated Nehru be there, swimming in the pool, playing tennis, or holding joint audiences with his ferocious opponent of the Moslem League, Mr. Jinnah?"

At Cripps's press conferences in the Secretariat offices, Eve was stupefied when she learned that the British governed 390 million Indians with 1,185 civil servants, 597 of them Indian, and only 588 of them British—a third of the personnel needed to run New York City's Waldorf Astoria. The country's peacetime army was 60,000 British and 150,000 Indians led by British officers. Eve speculated that had the 390 million decided at any time during the past two hundred years to forcibly evict the British—588 civil servants, 60,000 soldiers, and 65,000 civilians—the British would have been utterly helpless against them. It hadn't happened, she concluded, because "the great majority of the illiterate, semi-starved peasants who lived in the 700,000 Indian villages took absolutely no interest in the British-Indian feud . . . No doubt, Gandhi, Nehru, Jinnah had millions and millions of followers in the villages as well as the towns . . . Yet the largest political party in India, the Congress party, claimed a paying membership of four and a half million—out of 390 million . . . There were two Indias: a huge one, obsessed by her mystical dreams and indifferent to the world—and a smaller one, roused against her rulers."

Though Wavell was a man of very few words, by sitting near him daily at lunch and dinner Eve learned that he was a historian and a poetry lover, and spoke Russian fluently. He had been there several times, once saw the Soviet forces at maneuvers, and greatly admired the Red Army.

Wavell was commander in chief in India as well as a defense member of the viceroy's council. During the Cripps negotiations a bitter feud had developed between the British and the Indian nationalist leaders, who wanted one of their own countrymen to replace Wavell on the council. He never breathed a word of this to Eve, but she and everyone in the house knew that while the Japanese were approaching the Bengal border, Wavell, on whom the security of India depended, also had to fight to keep his job in Delhi.

Though the political situation in India was dynamite and Wavell was in the thick of it, Eve sensed that he was mostly worrying about his troops fighting the Japanese in the Burmese jungle and wondering how soon the enemy would reach Calcutta.

On March 27, 1942, she dined on the terrace of Wavell's house with two RAF officers among the guests: Air Marshal Peirse and the maharajah of Bilcaner. The latter was the first and only prince she met in India, though she'd seen many of them before the war at the Ritz in Paris. A great supporter of the British, he looked to Eve like a "great jungle feline grown a little fat in semi-captivity." Someone told her that he had been an autocratic ruler of his state since the age of seven and had several palaces "and quite a few invisible wives."

During her stay in the country she had found that being French was a great advantage, as she was received with equal friendliness in British and Indian circles.

At dinner she excused herself briefly, and with a letter of introduction from Nehru to Gandhi in her hand, she telephoned the home of the most powerful Indian proponent of nonviolent opposition to British rule. Gandhi's secretary, Pyarelal Nayar, answered and responded to her request for an appointment by asking if she could walk. When she said yes, she was told that Gandhi would take his daily walk with her at seven tomorrow morning.

Even though Gandhi was worshiped by millions as a saint for his leadership of the nonviolent resistance to British rule, Winston Churchill, his chief opponent, regarded him as a fake and asserted that he and all he stood for must be crushed. In a secret telegram to Churchill, Linlithgow had called Gandhi "the world's most successful humbug." What he stood for was astounding: the belief that nations and peoples should commit mass suicide rather than take arms against an attacking enemy. He had advised the Ethiopians not to resist Mussolini's invading army, but to let themselves be slaughtered. Before World War II, he had deplored Hitler's atrocious and ferocious treatment of the Jews and agreed that a war against Hitler would be justified in the name of humanity. Yet he was against such a war.

In anticipating that Hitler might launch a massacre of the Jews, he suggested that "if the Jewish mind could be prepared for voluntary sacrifice, even the massacre I have imagined could be turned into a day of thanksgiving and joy that Jehovah had wrought deliverance of the race even at the hands of the tyrant. For to the God-fearing death has no terror. It is a joyful sleep to be followed by a waking that would be all the more refreshing for the long sleep." Gandhi also advised the Jews to pray for Hitler.

During the war he advised the British "to invite Hitler and Mussolini to take what they want of the countries you call your possession," and during the Blitz, urged them to let the Germans "take possession of your beautiful island with its many beautiful buildings. You will give all this, but neither your minds nor your souls."

At seventy-two, Gandhi was a frail, bald little vegetarian weighing 109 pounds, with no front teeth, absolutely convinced of the rightness of his cause. Married since he was thirteen—his wife, Kasturba, an illiterate girl who was a stranger to him, was also thirteen at the time—and the father of two sons, Gandhi had ended sexual relations at thirty-six, believing that "the conquest of lust is the highest endeavor of a man or woman's existence." He believed that sex should be performed only to procreate. But his main concern was to free India from British control, which Churchill feared would reduce Great Britain to the status of a minor power.

As a voracious reader privy to information from the major players, Eve Curie knew of Gandhi's reputation and controversial views and was prepared to engage him in a respectful but probing interview. On the agreed morning she was driven to Gandhi's residence and led into a bright room overlooking a garden, where the half-naked Gandhi was sitting on the only piece of furniture, a mattress, while a young woman disciple sat at his feet. Shy at first, Eve soon warmed to him. He was friendly, witty, and extremely charming . . . The walk was postponed. After finishing most of his breakfast of sliced oranges and mangoes, this strict vegetarian was ready for the interview. She sat on the floor near him. As she felt it inappropriate to take notes during their conversation, she was pleased to see that his secretary, Pyarelal Nayar, was writing down everything they said; later she would make use of his verbatim account for her news reports and her contracted book.

It turned out to be a lively argument for and against peaceful resistance. Eve told Gandhi that she felt she was representing the views of the average citizen of Europe's conquered nations, who believed that if Hitler won the war he would inflict on India the same fate now endured by the Poles and the French.

Here are the highlights of the two-hour Gandhi-Curie dialogue on war, non-violent resistance, and Indian independence:

GANDHI: I am against all wars, against the use of force. I believe in non-violence. I would like to think that India will be, through her non-violence, a messenger of peace to the whole world. What we have achieved in the past twenty years shows that immense results could be obtained if the principle of non-violence were generally practiced by all our people.

CURIE: You might find it tougher opposing by non-violence Japanese or German divisions than undermining British rule.

GANDHI: (Nodding agreement.) It is, however, the same fight. It will be hard. But this is the hour to live up to our faith. We are working for posterity. I wouldn't encourage our people to fight with arms. I would tell the masses: Do not fight and do not surrender in your souls. If the Japanese rule succeeded the British, it is then the Japanese rule that, in turn, we would fight with non-violence.

CURIE: The fight will be tougher.

GANDHI: It will bring out the best that is in us.

CURIE: But how can you hope to *win* battles over such ruthless enemies by non-violence alone? In your struggle against Britain, you had a fair chance because the British did not fight you "violently"? After thirty years of campaigning, here you are, in good health, exerting a formidable power, publishing a paper freely, and allowed to have your books sold all over India. Here you are, *alive*, on British-controlled Indian soil. Do you think the Japanese would allow patriots to *live*?

GANDHI: In a non-violent struggle, there are two alternatives. Either the enemy comes to terms with you—then you have won without spilling blood—or the enemy annihilates you. This last solution is no worse than what a war brings about anyway.

Eve noted that when Britain faced Germany alone in 1940, Gandhi had advised the British to let the Nazis invade their country and to fight them "nonviolently." He had also expressed his regret that the United States had entered the war, thus abandoning her role as a peacemaker.

CURIE: Some of my own people, the French, *had* given up resisting the Germans by force. Losing heart they sought an armistice with Hitler. Can't you see that, for us, the difference is too subtle between a "non-violent" attitude and certain forms of defeatism, of disloyalty? After the catastrophe that has crushed our country, after so much misery and shame has been inflicted upon us, the French patriots have, today, a profound repulsion for anything resembling a refusal to fight the enemy.

GANDHI: I understand. I do. But now, I will tell you a story. There was a Pathan, in the Northwest of India, who was famous for his bravery. I converted him to non-violence. Now, he says: "It was at the time I fought that I was a coward. When I had only a rifle, I was afraid of the man who had a machine gun. When I had only a machine gun, I was afraid of the man who had a cannon. But since I have understood how useless the slaughter is altogether, I am never afraid." This ex-warrior has found the secret of true courage.

CURIE: But your Pathan lives under the British—not the Nazis—not Hitler. Let's come back to the French. We who are outside France, on free soil, cannot let them *wait* in captivity. If they wait too long, they will die. They will die of hunger. All our families will die of hunger. So will our prisoners in Germany.

GANDHI: They will not die. If they unanimously opposed to the conqueror with non-violent resistance, the Germans would have to come to terms with them *before* they died. I don't blame you for wanting to liberate France, just as I want to see India free. But it is a sign of too great impatience to think that any country can really be liberated by the use of guns. In order to beat the Japanese—you must become stronger than they are—therefore worse than they are. Then what have you won? Nothing.

CURIE: So victory has no importance?

GANDHI: No. In the sense that *you* mean, it has no importance.

CURIE: What would you do if an Indian puppet leader such as Subhas Chandra Bose attempted to come to India as the head of a pro-Japanese "army of liberation" and aroused the country against the Allies in the name of Indian independence?

GANDHI: The only thing such men can do to me is kill me. I will die. If they don't kill me, I will oppose them until my last breath with non-violence.

Eve realized that they would never agree on the subject.

It was now a quarter past eight and time for Gandhi's morning walk in the well-kept garden, during which they resumed their discussion. Gandhi carried a long bamboo cane and frequently leaned on the shoulder of a woman disciple. Eve walked on the other side of him, and his secretary and a few others followed. She had come to the conclusion that for security reasons Gandhi must have no role in the government of India during the war, because the Allies could not win the war through pacifism. To bring up fresh ammunition for her argument, she thought of her mother as one of the most peace-loving people she had known, with a horror of violence. Yet during World War I, Marie Curie had worked and struggled with her country of adoption to win the battle. She mentioned this to Gandhi, then, apparently baffled by his conviction that he was always right—even when irrational—she asked him:

CURIE: Are you not very proud—very conceited?

GANDHI: Yes. Sometimes I do think that I have more pride than the people whom I accuse of being proud. (He smiled.) The hopeful thing is that I am aware of my pride. So I can try to reform. Only on the last day of my life will we know whether I succeeded.

Eve said that she would submit her version of the interview for his approval. When she did so a few days later, he returned it to her without a word changed.

After the war and the death of Hitler, Gandhi said, "Hitler killed five million Jews. It is the greatest crime of our time. But the Jews should have . . . thrown themselves into the sea from cliffs . . . It would have aroused the world and the people of Germany . . . As it is they succumbed anyway in their millions."

One of Eve's many surprises had been to find a photograph of Winston Churchill—the great opponent of Indian independence—on display in the library of Gandhi's home, Birla House.

On Sunday, March 19, 1942, Eve Curie interviewed Gandhi's other great political rival, Mohammed Ali Jinnah, president of India's Muslim League, a rigid, scrupulously honest, and brilliant lawyer with a superiority complex. Although nominally a Muslim, he drank alcohol, ate pork, rarely entered a mosque, and knew fewer verses of the Koran than did Gandhi. Yet ninety million of India's Muslims regarded him as their leader. He scornfully dismissed Nehru as "a Peter Pan who should have been a professor, not a politician," and Gandhi as "a cunning fox" whose teachings were for "the ignorant and the illiterate."

As he strode around the library of his home, the tall, lean Jinnah looked to Eve like a handsome actor with his ascetic face, burning black eyes, and hair of several shades of gray. The interview quickly turned into a brilliant defense of his case: he, like Nehru and Gandhi, was a British-trained attorney.

He believed that although Muslims and Hindus lived in the same villages throughout India and spoke roughly the same language, they never had and never would have anything in common. "How can you ever dream of Hindu-Moslem unity?" he asked. "We have no intermarriages . . . The Moslems believe in an equalitarian society, whereas the Hindus maintain the iniquitous system of castes and leave heartlessly fifty million Untouchables to their tragic fate, at the bottom of the social ladder. [Gandhi called them "God's Children" and said he would free them from their humiliating status when India was independent.] They consider cows sacred. We Moslems think it is nonsense: we want to kill cows and eat them. No Hindu will take food from a Moslem. No orthodox Hindu will even touch Hindu food if the shadow of a Moslem or the shadow of a Hindu of a lower caste has polluted the bowl. Indeed, when you look into the problem, you see that there are only two links between the Moslems and the Hindus: British rule—and the common desire to get rid of it." Eve saw the irony in the situation: it was, in her opinion, the British attempt to introduce a measure of democracy to India that had made the Muslim problem in India increasingly acute, not so much their alleged "divide and rule" policy. As soon as the British had introduced representative government in 1909, the Muslims had agitated for separate electorates. The struggle for power had become more bitter between the Muslims and Hindus in 1935 when thirty-six million Indians were given the right to vote. "The grim prospect," Eve wrote, "was that the more 'democracy' would be given to a united India, the more trouble the Moslem minority would make: any democratic regime implied the potential consent of the minority to accept the decisions arrived at by the greatest number. This consent did not exist among the Moslem League followers, who considered themselves as another *nation*, apart from Hindus."

Eve attended Stafford Cripps's press conference on March 29, 1942, in which he offered Indians self-government at the earliest possible moment after the war, a government entirely free to stay within the British Commonwealth or leave it. When asked if the Indian Union could join any contiguous party, Cripps replied that there was nothing to prevent it, just as Canada could join the United States tomorrow if it wanted to. Eve noted that not one Indian, Hindu, or Muslim in the room expressed approval of the plan, and heard an Englishman standing behind her mutter that now that the Indians had got what they always clamored for, they never seemed more disgruntled. As Eve saw it, they did not realize they were being offered their freedom, because "they were feverishly wondering what advantages the political party opposite to theirs was apt to get from the English scheme, while watching for invisible traps which they suspected Britain had introduced into the wording of the document."

Her mission over, her immensely interesting and revealing 501-page book *Journey Among Warriors* was ready for her publisher, partly based on the features she had written for the *New York Herald Tribune* and *Allied Newspapers*. Eve flew back to the United States by roughly the same route she had taken to reach the Far East—a journey of 40,828 miles. Eleanor Roosevelt again invited her to the White House, writing in her column on May 25, 1942, "It is always a joy to have Mlle Curie here and it was extremely interesting to glean from her some of the impressions of the various countries she has visited on her extraordinary trip. She has a map on which she has traced her journeys, and someone at lunch yesterday, on looking over it, remarked, 'She has outdistanced you many times.'

Mlle Curie certainly has both in mileage and in the variety and interest of her travels. One looks at this chic, well-groomed, delicate French woman and marvels at the calm with which she must have faced many dangerous moments, and one is proud of women!"

The following month Mrs. Roosevelt introduced Eve at Manhattan Center to a crowd of over four thousand at an event sponsored by the French weekly *Pour la Victoire*. For an hour and a half, she discussed her journeys to the world's battlefronts. As Mrs. Roosevelt remarked in her column for June 17, 1942: "There were light touches here and there in the address, but on the whole the factual presentation of these travels made a deep impression on me. They showed a power of observation and analysis of situations and people, which must have been based on a calmness and self-possession even in moments of danger. As a woman, I am always proud when women acquit themselves so well in any job which they are allowed to undertake."

Three months later Gandhi was arrested by the British. Because of wartime censorship, Eve and most everyone else outside the country did not know why. But according to author Byron Farwell, Gandhi's campaign, "Quit India," and his mantra, "Do or die," was anything but a call for peaceful resistance. At a time when the Japanese had almost captured Burma and the British were in mortal battle with a ruthless enemy, Gandhi had approved the destruction of railroads, stations, bridges, and other ways and means of communication. His followers, joined by thugs and bandits, then blew up trains carrying food and supplies for the desperate British army in Burma, "attacked post offices, tore out telegraph lines, and cut great swaths of terror in which arson, murder and sabotage flourished. Two young Canadian Air Force officers who were caught by a mob at a railway station in Bihar were, quite literally, torn to pieces [and several policemen were burned alive]. Police did not always suffice and troops had to be used in some sixty incidents. 'This is open rebellion,' Gandhi proclaimed jubilantly. Ultimately fifty-seven battalions of infantry had to be diverted from the war for internal security duties."

This, of course, was passive resistance gone awry, not what Gandhi had professed to Eve Curie. The British arrested him on August 9, 1942, and imprisoned him in the Aga Khan's dilapidated palace in Poona, guarded by armed police and ringed by barbed wire, where he was allowed to have relatives and friends stay with him.

Had she known what was happening in France that summer and what happened in India soon after she left, Eve would have had a more compelling argument to use against Gandhi's promotion of nonviolent resistance.

For example: The Germans had arrested Jacques Solomon and three colleagues for their nonviolent resistance—producing an underground newspaper, *L'Université Libre*, with a print run of four thousand, and for creating a National Committee of Writers as part of the National Front. On May 23, 1942, they were taken to La Santé prison. The next day, Solomon's mother and his wife, Paul Langevin's daughter, Hélène, were also arrested and imprisoned. Before he was shot on the evening of May 30, Solomon was allowed to say good-bye to his wife. He was moaning because he had been tortured, and he said to her, "I cannot take you in my arms because I can no longer move them." His three colleagues, Politzer, Decour, and Dudach, were also tortured and shot. (Their paper continued production with others in charge.)

Next morning Joliot arrived at his laboratory looking greatly distressed and told a Japanese colleague, T. Yuasa, that the university had been closed the previous evening because several scientists, including Solomon, had been executed.

A month later two of Langevin's grandsons—sixteen-year-old Michel Langevin and his cousin Bernard—were sent to prison for three months for distributing subversive material. (Michel Langevin eventually married Hélène, the daughter of Irène and Frédéric Joliot.)

Several months later, Hélène Solomon and her mother-in-law were being transported in a cattle car with 230 other French women from La Santé prison to Auschwitz.

As the train moved through Troyes, Hélène wrote a note to her father, screwed it up into a ball, and pushed it through an airhole in the cattle car onto the station platform. Shortly after, Langevin was walking along a road in Troyes on his way home when a man on a bicycle, visibly moved, stopped and asked him if he was Paul Langevin. When he said yes, the man handed him a crumbled piece of paper and rode off shouting, "Don't tell anyone you saw me." In the brief note Hélène Solomon said that she was being deported to a concentration camp. She survived the ordeal of Auschwitz and was freed when the Soviet Army liberated the horrific camp at the end of the war. But her mother-in-law died there.

The brutal treatment of the Solomon family and their colleagues—all Communists—spurred Joliot to express his sympathy by becoming one of them: secretly joining the outlawed French Communist Party. This decision would have an enormous effect on his life. The Communists he knew had proved to be among the most reliable in their resistance to the German occupation. And British Intelligence agreed, advising Allied soldiers and airmen trying to escape to seek the help of Communist workers or

Catholic priests as the only groups to be trusted. He explained to Pierre Villon, an architect and the Communist chief of the National Front, that he had joined the party because he was a patriot and if they were caught he didn't want to be treated any better than Villon himself.

According to author Weart, "Like many others in France, after joining the Resistance Joliot had begun to appreciate the party's skill and patriotic zeal." Irène, though too independent-minded to belong to any party, sympathized with many of its goals and principles, among them women's rights. Kowarski believed that by joining the Communist party, Joliot's "resistance status was affirmed at a time when it was still very unpopular and unhealthy. I never had any doubts of his moral courage, so I didn't need this as proof."

Starting on June 7, 1942, the Nazis required all Jews over the age of six to buy three yellow stars from the local police office. (The purchase was deducted from their clothing coupons.) The star had to be worn over the heart. The intent was to both identify and humiliate. Soon eighty-three thousand Parisians were wearing the yellow star. There were occasional reports of a sympathetic backlash. For example, Jews were not allowed to join queues, but when a frail old woman with a yellow star stood hesitating near a food queue, several in line signaled for her to join them. When she did, she was rapidly passed from one to another until she was at the head of the queue and bought a cabbage. Nobody protested and a nearby policeman turned his head. A German officer, Ernst Junger, noted in his diary how he saw the yellow star for the first time in the rue Royale "worn by three young girls who passed close by me, arms linked. I was immediately ashamed to be in uniform."

And Janet Tessier du Cross recalled: "It was not until he was close upon us that I saw the man. He was little and elderly . . . I doubt whether I would have noticed him at all if it had not been for the sinister distinguishing mark on his left breast with *Juif* printed across it. I stopped dead in my tracks, stunned. He passed us by without looking at us, but it was a full minute before I recovered the use of my legs. In all my life I have never felt so deeply humiliated." Writer Ian Ousby believes that the imposition of the yellow star "was the first anti-Semitic measure of the Occupation to provoke a spontaneous protest, however scattered."

Forty cases of young non-Jews wearing the yellow star were reported to the SS. Other sympathizers wore yellow flowers or handkerchiefs, or yellow paper with *Goy* or their Christian names on them. Some non-Jewish Paris students sported *Juif* badges, claiming that the word was an acronym for

"Jeunesse Universitaire Intellectuelle Francaise." Jews were not required to wear yellow stars in the Vichy zone, but their identity cards were stamped *Juif* or *Juive*.

The bitter fall of 1942 and wartime deprivations (the mortality rate in Paris was 40 percent higher than in the years 1932–1939) made Irène so ill that Joliot again got permission for her to go to Switzerland to recover. After an examination at a Zurich hospital, she was sent on to a Swiss sanatorium at Leysin, from where she wrote to her family, through Gentner.

At Christmas Joliot wrote to her, "We were all here, as usual, with a very small Christmas tree. The pleasure of receiving presents, as you can imagine, was mixed with sadness. It is the first time since our marriage that we have not been together for the holiday . . . Both Hélène and I were feeling down in the dumps, but we tried not to show it. I long to hold you in my arms and sleep with you until the end of the world." Hélène explains that, "'Sleep with you until the end of the world' is from a traditional song. The L'Arcouest group and especially my parents loved singing 'On the Castle Steps,' which ends like that." Joliot also mentioned that he was staying at home two days a week working with Pierre to improve his grades.

By November 1942 the Germans had occupied all of France, except for the southern coast, which they gave as a sop to the Italians. That same month, on the Russian front, Hitler sacrificed an army in a futile attempt to capture Stalingrad. On February 2, 1943, eleven German generals and 330,000 troops surrendered. It was the first sign that the Germans were not invincible and the start of a massive Russian counteroffensive. As Hitler now found it necessary to draft industrial workers into the depleted German army, he persuaded Laval, who had replaced Pétain as the head of the French government, to provide 150,000 French workers between sixteen and sixty for German industry. The French Resistance produced false papers for one hundred thousand Frenchmen to avoid being deported, some of whom joined the Resistance. Joliot played his part, with Professor Léon Denivelle, by creating a dummy company, the Society for the Study of Applications of Artificial Radioelements (Sedars), financed by French capitalists, which purported to find nonscientific uses for the cyclotron. Then Joliot was able to save some technicians from being sent to Germany by giving them work certificates identifying them as Sedars's employees.

Putting the squeeze on a potential financial contributor to Sedars, a banker brother of a Vichy official, Joliot used tough tactics. "I do not share your opinions," he told him. "You are a capitalist and I am a technician. I know your capitalist system and I reject it. You cannot contradict me when I speak of board meetings at which members go in and out and give orders to their brokers, as a result of information they have just received. I do not know what will happen to you after the defeat of Germany. Perhaps you will be shot. Nevertheless, we ought to be able to examine together the best condition for insuring that the country makes effective use in industry of scientific and technical progress." Apparently, either the threat of being shot or the appeal to his patriotism worked. Maybe both.

Joliot, of course, was not aware of the top-secret work at Chicago University Stadium where, on December 2, 1942, under Enrico Fermi's direction, the first atomic pile went critical, signaling the birth pangs of the atomic bomb. And confirming what Joliot and his team had reported in 1939: a self-sustaining chain reaction was possible and was capable of releasing an enormous amount of energy.

Although still absorbed in his scientific work, at least once a month Joliot attended National Front meetings with Pierre Villon. At those meetings, Joliot had many onerous duties. He met secret emissaries from London, issued public statements for various underground newspapers, and discussed with Villon how they could unify the various resistance groups under the leadership of the exiled General de Gaulle. He relayed to resistance groups informers' tips about anticipated police raids, and informed the Allies of the damage inflicted in recent air raids. According to Villon, when a suspected traitor was brought before the National Front Committee, it was Joliot's decision whether or not to execute him. Joliot's daughter, Hélène, doubts that traitors were brought before the committee. Maybe, she writes, her father was asked for his advice in certain cases.

In April 1943, Joliot was asked by a nurse to help her patient escape from the heavily guarded prison section of the Rothschild hospital. M. Gonzière, a member of the Resistance, had been arrested by the French police and so severely tortured that he needed hospital treatment. Knowing that he faced more torture and possibly execution, his nurse, Mlle C. Heyman, planned for his escape. She asked Joliot to provide a false passport, and he sent it to her within forty-eight hours. Then, on the morning of May 1, 1945, while the nurse and two patients distracted the attention of policemen guarding the hospital room, M. Gomzière escaped through a hatchway for dirty clothes.

Irène returned home days later, after six months in a Swiss sanatorium, especially pleased that Joliot had just been elected on the first round to the Academy of Science, taking the place of the late Edouard Branly.

Many years earlier Branly had defeated her mother for the seat. Although still exiled in Troyes, Langevin had been Joliot's sponsor.

The fighting was going well for the Allies: several victories in Tunisia signaled the beginning of the end for the Germans in North Africa. Even Hitler conceded that the Tunisian situation was hopeless. On July 10, when the Allies invaded Sicily, Hitler responded by declaring, "Sicily must be made into a Stalingrad. We must hold out until winter, when new secret weapons will be ready for use against England" (probably flying bombs). Mussolini pleaded for German reinforcements to defend Sicily, which Hitler promised but didn't provide.

By August 17, after thirty-seven days of fighting, Sicily fell to the Allies—General Patton's Seventh Army and Montgomery's Eighth Army, together with French and Canadian troops. Mussolini was imprisoned on the island of Ponza, and the king of Italy took over command of what was left of the Italian armed forces. Italian General Badoglio then formed a new cabinet to consider switching sides, which they did, declaring war on Germany on October 13.

General de Gaulle had moved his headquarters from London to Algeria, and from there on October 30, 1943, he paid tribute to those who had died fighting for a free France, mentioning "Politzer who had been shot by the enemy, and Holweck who was tortured to death." Among the many thinkers and scientists still fighting, he named Henry Bernstein, Eve Curie, and Jean Perrin.

German cities were being battered day and night by British and American planes, an intense air offensive that caused massive destruction. On December 7, the Nazi propaganda chief, Joseph Goebbels, noted in his diary: "The English are waging war in Italy very effectively. [A hundred miles south of Rome.] They are making the cleverest use of every advantage. Their most striking advantage is their superiority in the air."

Things were looking up for the French, too. Although in the summer, Jean Moulin, a leader of the Resistance working for de Gaulle, had died of a heart attack after being interrogated under torture by the notorious Klaus Barbie, the *maquis* (the military branch of the Resistance), eleven days after Italy's surrender on September 8, 1943, freed Corsica.

For two years Halban and Kowarski had been advising the British that if nuclear energy was to be used as a power source, it would be valuable to contact Joliot. Toward the end of 1943, de Gaulle's emissary, Colonel Henri Navarre, working in the intelligence arm of the Resistance, had dinner with Joliot in a Paris restaurant in the place Saint-André-des-Arts. Navarre gave him an overview of the advances in nuclear research and suggested ways that Joliot could be secretly sent to London for talks with the experts. Joliot agreed to go, but did not hear from Navarre again. (Ten years later, as a general, Navarre led the French forces fighting in Vietnam.)

Eve Curie's journey among warriors had made her even more devoted to the Allies' cause—convinced that the war was a fight for freedom. The spectacular review of her book by W. L. White filled the front page of the *New York Times Book Review* and spilled over to page 20. White praised her "vivid personal portraits . . . powerful, vivid, honest, and deeply moving portrait of Russia . . . keen interest in the fate of Russia's former Polish captives," and pointed out that in her writing about India, Eve Curie's "qualities of warmth and shrewd detachment combine to give us her most valuable and unforgettable picture." The reviewer concluded that "never before has the whole panorama of the world at war been so honestly, so skillfully and so beautifully presented. [It is] an achievement of brilliant writing and shrewd observation which has not been surpassed by any other reporter."

The MGM movie of Eve's biography, *Madame Curie*, with Greer Garson as Marie and Walter Pidgeon as Pierre, was released to great acclaim and nominated for seven Academy Awards. It won none, losing to *Casablanca* and *The Song of Bernadette*. The book was far superior to the film.

On December 24, 1943, foreshadowing the long-awaited second front against Germany, General Dwight Eisenhower was appointed supreme commander of European invasion forces. By then Eve Curie was back in London in the khaki uniform of a private with the Cross of Lorraine on her collar, identifying her as a member of General de Gaulle's Fighting French Women's Corps—the Voluntaires Françaises. After three weeks of basic training in a British camp she returned to London and applied for a driver's job. Interviewed by Marjorie Avery for the *New York Times Magazine*, she said: "When the time comes for us to go back to France we will go with great humility, almost asking the pardon of those who have remained. We have eaten while they starved. We have been warm while they shivered. We have been free to act while they have kept their courage high under domination and military occupation."

CHAPTER 20

The Battle for Paris

1944

Parisians were eagerly anticipating the arrival of Allied invasion forces during the early months of 1944, rumors of which were discussed with growing excitement and some trepidation. Life had reached a new low: the taking and execution of hostages was escalating, Jews were being deported east in ever greater numbers, more curfews were enforced, there was no coal to heat the freezing homes, food was scarce, and clothes had disappeared from the stores.

Members of the Paris Resistance—some six hundred volunteers in various political and professional groups—were preparing to fight for their city. They had already decided on the fate of known collaborators and sent them, as a hint of things to come, miniature coffins.

Afraid that during the anticipated invasion the Nazis would use Langevin as a hostage, Joliot, Henri Moureu, and Professor Deniville arranged for his escape, giving him false papers and armed protection—a team of four Resistance sharpshooters. According to Russian physicist Peter Kapitsa, an auto accident was faked and Langevin "was bandaged and carried in the men's arms over the mountains." He made it to safety in neutral Switzerland. Kapitsa had previously offered Langevin refuge in Russia, but when an anti-Semitic movement had been launched "at the University of Paris, Langevin headed the fight against it; and so long as this movement remained undefeated, he felt he had no right to leave Paris." When he finally decided to leave, it was too late.

Joliot began to fear for his own safety when he was again arrested, questioned, and released. Expecting that the next move would be to imprison him, Joliot warned his family that they should join Langevin in Switzerland while he went underground in Paris, working with the Resistance.

Irène agreed to go, but wanted, if possible, seventeen-year-old Hélène, about to graduate from high school, to complete her baccalaureate exams. Fortunately, Professor Denivelle knew of a school, the Academy of Besançon, where she could take the exam while living nearby, and as soon as she had completed the exam they could make their escape.

They left their home in Antony just before the end of May, spending two days en route in Montbélard, where they were heavily bombed. They moved on to the village of Le Russey, near the Swiss border. Denivelle's father, Marcel Swandler, also a member of the Resistance, had found them a hotel there. When Irène was not taking short walks, she studied. It wasn't long before everyone at the hotel knew who she was, because she was doing math calculations all the time and using papers and books marked "Radium Institute." To Hélène, "the small village seemed to exist in an unreal time, without war. There were no newspapers, no radio [apparently], and no German soldiers."

The same team of sharpshooting partisans who had helped Langevin escorted Irène and her children to the Swiss border in a small truck, except for the last few miles, when the trio walked with knapsacks on their backs, as if they were hiking in the Jura mountains. There were no Germans on border patrol. By extraordinary good luck it was June 6, D-Day, when the Allies had landed on the Normandy beaches, causing temporary confusion among the German frontier guards. Swiss patrols were controlling the border, and to Irène and Hélène their uniforms and helmets were so similar to those of the Germans that they had some uncomfortable moments.

Although their entry into Switzerland had been negotiated by Denivelle's agents and Swiss secret agents, something went wrong, and after they crossed the border they were taken to Porrentruy castle, which housed other illegal immigrants and escaped prisoners of war, as well some of the Swiss guards defending the border.

They stayed at the castle for three days in a huge room large enough for thirty people. The only furniture was two boards covered with clean straw. Hélène spent much of the time looking through a large sunny window at the soldiers marching in the castle yards. Her twelve-year-old brother, Pierre, was allowed to play outside with local boys but only when escorted by a friendly armed Swiss soldier, who often smiled at the ridiculous situation. Irène continued with her calculations, using a nuclear data table compiled by two German physicists, J. Mattauch and S. Flugge, and published in Berlin in 1942.

A Swiss investigator who asked the two women to identify themselves and explain why they had crossed the border seemed suspicious. He apparently then contacted the prefect of the district, Colonel Victor Henri, who looked in and recognized Irène—a Nobel Prize winner—sitting on straw and reading her nuclear data tables. He had already done his best to improve the conditions of many of the immigrants, and insisted that the three of them move in with him and his family, despite the protests of other officials. Later the trio moved to Lausanne. During their three months' stay in Switzerland they were delighted to meet Paul Langevin again.

All this time, of course, they worried about Joliot's safety.

After several colleagues had been arrested, he had gone underground in Paris, using a false name, Jean-Pierre Gaumont, and posing as an electrical engineer from Lyon. He had rented a neat, clean apartment with a surprisingly comfortable bed in the dreary working-class district of Belleville northeast of the city. Joliot was especially touched when his amiable landlady, who also worked in a paper mill, brought him a basket of cherries from her garden, and he noted in his diary: "Once again I recognized the friendly and generous gesture of those who work 10 hours a day, gestures which they can still make after 10 hours of often exhausting and enervating work."

When he failed to appear at the Collège de France for a few days, the administrator, Edmond Faral, took Joliot's assistant, Pavel Savel, into his confidence and told him that Joliot had escaped to Switzerland. In fact Joliot happened to be sleeping at Savel's apartment that night, and they both laughed over Faral's confidential information.

Later, Joliot told a friend that since his arrival in Belleville he had been playing hide-and-seek, adding, "You know how I like hunting." Although, of course, Joliot was the hunted, not the hunter, as he roamed the city on his bicycle, meeting other members of the Resistance on the banks of the Seine near Notre-Dame, taking a fishing rod with him to mingle inconspicuously with other Parisians fishing for their dinner. Small teams from chemistry, physics, and biology labs were collecting various kind of explosives to use in the coming battle for Paris, and Joliot handed them notes and diagrams describing how to make grenades and antitank mines.

On July 31, 1944, when the Allied armies were just over a hundred miles from Paris, de Gaulle had his headquarters in Algeria. From there he ordered twenty-nine-year-old General Jacques Chaban-Delmas to take charge of the Resistance forces in Paris and to await his word on when to begin the uprising. However, Chaban-Delmas knew that the Communists were the de facto leaders of the Paris Resistance. The overall head of the Paris Resistance, Colonel Henri Tanguy, a peacetime metal worker, was a

Communist. So were many if not most of its members, and Communists dominated the labor unions and the underground press. As they were more than likely to frustrate de Gaulle's plan and to lay claim to the freed city, Chaban-Delmas hurried to England to urge General Eisenhower to be the first to seize Paris to prevent the Communists from beating them to it. But, as Eisenhower told de Gaulle's emissary, whether Communists or Gaullists controlled the city was not his immediate concern. In fact he planned to surround and then bypass the city and drive full speed for the heart of Germany. Disappointed, knowing that whoever controlled Paris would have virtual command of the whole country, the young general returned to the city determined to make it de Gaulle's, traveling the final miles through German lines on a bicycle.

Chaban-Delmas estimated that the Paris Resistance, about 600 before D-Day, now numbered some 15,000 mostly untrained volunteers with 2,000 light weapons, and that they faced 20,000 heavily armed, well-trained German soldiers, able to call on reinforcements. A Communist youth group tried to augment the Resistance fire power by having attractive young women entice German soldiers into alleys, where they were mugged and their weapons stolen. These youngsters were countered by an agent provocateur who promised to lead thirty-five young resistants to a cache of weapons. But when they arrived at the meeting place, they were arrested and handed over to the Gestapo, which tortured and executed them.

On August 19, 1944, with the battle cries, "A chacun son Boche!" and "Tous aux barricades!" Colonel Henri Tanguy announced the start of the liberation. Barricades began to appear, mostly in working-class neighborhoods, and the French tricolor flew from several public buildings, including police headquarters, to which Joliot, who had come out of hiding, headed from his nearby Collège de France.

He had already arranged with police contacts his role in the uprising. So, as planned, he carried two heavy suitcases with bomb-making material into a side entrance of the immense police headquarters on the Ile de la Cité and went to his friend Henri Moureu's laboratory. Expecting an attack any moment, he recruited two others to join him in the cellar, where they grabbed bottles of champagne from the private cache left by the recently deposed Vichy-appointed police chief, and began to turn them into homemade bombs. Meanwhile the new police chief, Charles Luizet, appointed by de Gaulle and secretly parachuted into the south of France, had made his way to Paris and was ensconced in his office overhead.

Stripped to the waist and sweating profusely in the hot and humid cellar, the three men continued to pop the corks of champagne bottles and pour the contents onto the floor—and over their shoes. They refilled the empty bottles with a mix of sulfuric acid and gasoline, wrapped them in paper soaked in potassium chlorate, and handed the now lethal Molotov cocktails to a relay team of policemen, who rushed them to the Resistance fighters waiting at the windows on the upper floors.

Author Robert Jungk points out the irony of "the man who had discovered some of the most important of the necessary pre-conditions for construction of the atom bomb using the most primitive form of bomb imaginable in defense of the barricades."

At midafternoon three enemy tanks—two Panthers and a Renault—crept menacingly toward police headquarters. One fired a shell that shattered the building's main iron gate and sent a young lawyer, Edgar Pisani, flying right across a room, burying him in a thick blanket of dust and plaster.

The police responded with their Molotov cocktails, and a German tank crew member, Willi Linke, watched in dismay as he "saw one of Joliot-Curie's deadly bottles go wavering through the air and plop into the imprudently open turret of the tank beside him 'like a basketball in a basket.' A great burst of yellow flame shot out of the turret. In seconds the whole tank was a mass of flames. Inside his own tank, Linke could hear the jubilant cries of policemen in the Prefecture ringing over his head. Furious, Linke ordered another shell into his own 88 [gun] and sent it smashing against the Prefecture."

The defenders inside police headquarters had only sandbags to protect them, and, apart from the rapidly diminishing supply of Molotov cocktails, were lightly armed with pistols, World War I rifles, and a few slow-action machine guns. They began to panic, and at first a few, and then a flood, headed for safety—the internal subway station with a underground passage leading to the Seine's Left Bank. Police Sergeant Fournet, leader of one of the two Resistance networks in the Paris Police Department, rushed to the head of the stairs, drew his revolver, and threatened to shoot the first man who tried to pass him. "Our only chance of survival," he shouted, "is to win!" Stunned and ashamed, the men halted. And returned to their posts.

Late that afternoon when the police were almost out of ammunition and tanks were moving in the street outside like earthbound vultures, the Swedish consul, Raoul Nordling, arranged a brief truce with the Nazi general von Choltitz for both sides to bury their dead. That same day General de Gaulle had secretly arrived in France.

Under cover of darkness, armed with a German revolver, Joliot returned to the Collège de France, where he directed the manufacture of more homemade bombs, as he did at two other laboratories. Which were then delivered to police headquarters.

When the fierce and sometimes savage fighting was resumed, the Swedish consul general, Raoul Nordling, devised what should have earned him a Nobel peace prize. The Germans had mined the city ready to destroy it, on Hitler's order, if they were forced to retreat. Nordling was anxious to save lives on both sides and to prevent the city itself from being blown up and set ablaze. Realizing that defeat was inevitable, the German commander was prepared to defy Hitler's order to save a city he loved. So, with the German's tacit approval, Nordling contacted the American general Omar Bradley and invited him to enter Paris as rapidly as possible so that the Germans could surrender to Americans rather than to the presumably less lenient French Resistance. According to the *New York Times* foreign correspondent C. L. Sulzberger, "Bradley, [with Eisenhower's approval] thoughtfully taking French national pride into consideration, ordered the French 2nd Armored Division, under Major Jacques General Leclerc to move in, followed by an American division."

That is one account of the situation. Hélène Langevin-Joliot provides a different version: "During the truce, Von Choltitz called for help from a Panzer division, and Rol-Tanguy sent Commandant Cocteau-Gallois with permission to cross the front lines and join General Patton. The liberation had freed a large part of the town, but without heavy armament the French could not expel the Germans from a critical building where they had concentrated their forces. Finally, the mission was successful. Patton sent Cocteau to General Bradley, who referred to Eisenhower, who decided to send the Leclerc Division."

As the Second French Armored Division raced from the south to the rescue of their compatriots in Paris, with war correspondents Robert Cromie and Ernest Hemingway close on their heels, Cromie recalled that "there was some shooting near us and I asked Hemingway about it, and he said, 'That's the Germans keeping their cards in the musicians' union. They're retreating, but they want to fire a few shots before they go.'" He was right. And General Choltitz made it official on August 25, 1944, when, instead of destroying the city, the mild, stocky little man, father of two young daughters, surrendered and handed Paris back to the French.

Choltitz was in a prisoner-of-war camp until 1947, when he returned to Germany. In his 1951 book *Brennt Paris?* he explained that he had defied Hitler's order to reduce Paris to ruins because he believed that the führer had gone mad. Then Hitler had ordered General Hans Speidel to rain destruction on Paris with hundreds of V-bombs, as well as to blow up the

Madeleine, the Opéra, Notre-Dame, the Tuileries, the Arc de Triomphe, and the Eiffel Tower "so its ruins will block the access to the bridges which will already have been blown up." Fortunately, Speidel, Rommel's chief of staff, a doctor of philosophy, had other things on his mind—getting up the nerve to assassinate the führer.

A wildly cheering crowd, some tearful with joy, greeted General Charles de Gaulle as he marched along the Champs Élysées in a victory parade, with his provisional government and prominent members of the Resistance, Joliot among them. The Conservative de Gaulle had outfoxed the Communists: the Allies recognized his French Committee of Liberation as the de facto French government, and in November 1945 he became the provisional head of the country.

The new Gaullist police chief, Charles Luizet, did not seem reassured by the cries of delight from Parisians in the streets. At dinner on a balcony of police headquarters, soon after the city's liberation, he warned an influential American friend, Brigadier General Julius Holmes, that although Paris was no longer threatened by the Germans or Vichyites, it was in terrible danger from the Communists. If they defied a de Gaulle government, there was a good chance that they'd win. "He asked Holmes to get arms for the police and gendarmes. Forty-eight hours later, a convoy drove directly up to the Prefecture. Inside were 8,000 carbines, submachine guns, ammunition and a few bazookas for good measure."

Close behind the first five French tanks to enter Paris was a jeep-load of Americans on an intelligence mission—known as the Alsos mission—under the orders of General Leslie Groves, director of the Manhattan Project to develop the atomic bomb. He feared that the Germans, helped by Joliot, might be close to producing their own bomb. "I always had a deep suspicion of Joliot and was sure that he was very evasive about his work with the Germans," he wrote some twenty years later, surprisingly ignorant of Joliot's early work with the Resistance. "To me he was typical of many French collaborators who collaborated fully until they realized that the Germans could not win and then in the main became quite pro-Communist."

The American team, headed by Lieutenant Colonel Boris Pash, was assigned to discover if Grove's fears were justified.

At five in the afternoon, after returning sniper fire from the belfry of a church, Pash found Joliot in his office at the Collège de France. He introduced himself as the commander of American troops in that sector intending to take over the place as his command post. Joliot welcomed him, saying he would be pleased for American troops to occupy the building, "because I am afraid for my life. I shall be grateful if you will give me protection" (from the Germans, presumably). Pash assigned Private Nat Leonard, a former schoolteacher fluent in French, to guard Joliot, who in turn agreed not to go anywhere without Leonard and not to leave the building. Pash explained that according to army regulations he had to take Joliot into technical custody. To which Joliot replied: "For the past several years I have been free to come and go. But I am sure I did not enjoy it as much as I shall enjoy being in jail in my own office."

Pash began by discussing Joliot's experience under the Nazis, "feeling him out with regard to his work during that time." When, shortly afterward, Joliot overheard Pash talking of London, he expressed a wish to go there to see old friends and for his safety. He had fallen into Pash's trap. "What he did not know," Pash wrote in his *Alsos Mission*, "was that we already had a flight set up to take him to London as soon as he could be maneuvered into requesting such a trip. 'Matter of fact,' said Pash, 'I was about to fly two officers to London. But in view of your desire, and because it would relieve one of worrying about you for the next few days, I would be pleased to have you replace one of the officers—provided you will not tell anyone about the flight.' I heard later that Joliot-Curie told in London that it had all been a trick, [and] questioned my gentlemanly qualities. Towards the end of the war, after receiving reports of the terms he had used to express his lack of esteem for me, I marveled at the rapidity with which Europeans pick up some of the saltier GI expressions."

But at that first meeting in Paris, everyone was in a party mood, and the Alsos group having brought champagne and their K rations with them, they celebrated the liberation of Paris at an al fresco party, joined by several attractive French women, at what to Joliot seemed like a banquet.

Three days later, on August 28, Samuel Goudsmit, scientific head of Alsos, both of whose parents had been gassed in a concentration camp, began to interrogate Joliot. He had previously interviewed Francis Perrin about Joliot in New York City. Goudsmit, a normally cheerful, warmhearted theoretical physicist, was unusually equipped for the task—his hobby being criminal investigation. Joliot's first few answers convinced Goudsmit of his integrity.

Part of Goudsmit's secret report to Groves reads: "'J' [Joliot] insists that no war work or any related to TA [Tube Alloys, the code words for the atomic bomb] was done by Germans visiting his laboratory. Gentner was definitely anti-Nazi and so were Maurer and Retzler. They gave warning to French acquaintances who were being investigated by the Gestapo. They were friendly and talkative and would certainly have dropped clues about German TA work if they had known about it. A hostile visitor was Bothe. 'J' had the impression that he knew a lot."

During the second Joliot interview Goudsmit obtained the names of the soldiers and scientists who had visited Joliot's lab, names of the several anti-Nazi Germans working there, and Joliot's opinion that most of the Germans came to Paris to hide or rest because they did little work and no war work of any kind. As for the cyclotron in his laboratory, he said that it had produced radio phosphorus for biological experiments. And he mentioned his visit to a mysterious site at Watten that he believed was connected with the production of a very unstable chemical product used in V-bombs currently causing death and destruction in Britain.

Despite Joliot's being officially under arrest, between Goudsmit's interviews he had joined other Communists at a meeting of the party's Central Committee at party headquarters, 44 rue Le Pelletier, called by Thorez's deputy, Jacques Duclos, largely to see who had survived the war. A photo of their hero, Stalin, was on one wall.

After Goudsmit had interviewed Joliot, Major Horace K. Calvert, an American intelligence officer, took Joliot to London, where scientists and military men questioned him on September 5 and 7. Among them was fellow Nobel Prize–winning physicist James Chadwick.

They informed General Groves that Joliot had been appointed director of scientific research under the Ministry of Health in the provisional French government and that "he has very strong political views and frankly declared that he is 'a communist,' which we believe to mean that he is a socialist." (They don't explain why they didn't take his word for it.) They reported Joliot's strong belief that no serious work was being done in Germany to produce a bomb or to use nuclear energy as an energy source, and his declaration that he would refuse to undertake work which might be of use to the enemy.

Joliot told them, according to a top-secret Department of Energy report, that he hoped the research being done in America on nuclear energy would be shared "between all the countries whose nationals had contributed to it. [This included the three Frenchmen, Halban, Kowarski, and Goldschmidt.] He expressed his opinion that the T. A. [Tube Alloys] project was not likely now to be of interest in the war, but that it was of great importance from a post-war point of view [as an energy source]. He asked whether there were any arrangements between Governments on this matter and where France would come in. He instanced the case of work during the last war on ultra-sound waves which had been largely done by

French scientists, reported to the Americans and followed up by them under conditions which made it impossible for the French, after the war, to get any useful patents." When Joliot asked his questioners about the progress of nuclear research in America, Chadwick "explained that, however much he might wish to tell Joliot all he knew, he could not do so as the information which he had belonged to the American Government and he was not free to disclose it."

While in London, Joliot went to the center for French scientists in de Gaulle's headquarters and had an emotional reunion with Pierre Auger and Francis Perrin. From them and others he began to get some idea of the massive Manhattan Project under way in Britain and America to produce an atomic bomb.

Goudsmit's positive view of Joliot did not satisfy the suspicious Groves. Despite the report calling him a Socialist, Groves rightly believed he was a Communist and decided "that nothing that might be of interest to the Russians should ever be allowed to fall into French hands." He thought Joliot was evasive about his contacts and, unlike Goudsmit, placed little faith in his statements.

Like Groves, some Frenchmen were also convinced that Joliot had been a Nazi collaborator. Reporter Robert Jungk puts the ambiguous situation in perspective: "He was regarded as a traitor for having handed over his laboratory intact to the Germans in 1940. But in reality this apparent capitulation merely served to camouflage the scientist's extremely active participation in the French resistance movement. After the departure of Wolfgang Gentner the laboratory became an arsenal for the Paris *maquis*, although—or perhaps even because—other buildings in the group comprising the Collège de France were used as offices by the German Military Government. Joliot's quarters were never searched, for the simple reason that no one dreamed the scientist capable of such mad audacity."

Joliot's daughter, Hélène, does not believe that "many Frenchmen were convinced that my father had been a Nazi. At the time he accepted the presence of German physicists in his lab, his position was surely misinterpreted by many . . . if a few people remained suspicious in the following years, [his guilt] was completely out of the discussion at the time of the Liberation."

In September 1944 Irène received exceptional authorization to leave Switzerland and return to Paris. The relaxed life in Switzerland and her treatment in a Swiss sanitarium and stay at Leysin in 1943 had so improved her health that she was able to return to her research at the Curie laboratory. Two weeks after Irène left Switzerland, her daughter, Hélène, persuaded the new French consul in Geneva to allow her and her brother to return to Paris without all the necessary official papers. They spent the night behind the battlefront south of Alsace and arrived at their home in Antony the next day, to their father's delight and amazement.

With General de Gaulle's approval, Joliot had worked quickly to restore France to its prewar scientific prominence, sending groups into Germany behind the rapidly advancing Allied forces to bring back whatever they could find of scientific value. They returned with invaluable scientific information, and retrieved 250 tons of laboratory equipment.

Soon after his return to France, Bertrand Goldschmidt noticed that Joliot was repeatedly boosting "the fraternity and close relations in the [Communist] Party, like a man who had at last found a family." The somewhat conservative Goldschmidt wondered if Joliot was trying to convince himself that he had done the right thing.

To General Groves the Communists were a serious threat, and he was more than uneasy about the British attitude to the situation. Sir John Anderson, political head of the British Atomic Enterprise, had authorized Halban to visit Joliot in Paris and to talk in general terms about the progress of research on the atomic bomb. Anderson had warned Churchill that if they were not careful and did not cooperate with the French scientists, they might drive France "straight into the arms of Russia . . . Account must also be taken of the personality of Joliot," Anderson continued. "He is a very eminent nuclear physicist and a man of high principles. He played a leading part in the resistance movement in France and is now in charge of the French Scientific Organization. He has been known to describe himself as a Communist, but his commitment is of the intellectual variety and he is first and foremost a patriotic Frenchman."

With his jaundiced view of the French, Groves feared that Halban would take the opportunity to discuss such top secrets as the ability of nuclear reactors to produce fissionable plutonium. And that this critical information would be leaked to the Russians. So, as a precaution, Groves had microphones secretly installed in the room where Joliot and Halban were expected to meet. To his dismay, the two met at a spot where the microphones couldn't pick up their conversation.

Had he been able to listen in, he would have heard Joliot telling Halban of his exploits in the Resistance, and Halban explaining how impossible it was at that time for France to be accepted as a partner in the atomic project with the British and Americans. Because, among other things, they feared it would be leaked to the Russians. The Frenchmen also discussed the patents they had secured on behalf of France in certain aspects of the nuclear process.

Joliot was astonished when Halban told him of the gigantic secret effort in America to produce an atomic bomb, of the 150,000 people working in factories covering several acres, which was costing even more than it did to build the Panama Canal—over a billion dollars. As for the British, he said that their work was on a much smaller scale, and the United States had authorized them to continue it in Canada, where Halban, Kowarski, Goldschmidt, and Auger, after a brief stay in Britain, had been employed.

Joliot gathered that the work was very advanced, though it still might take years, and the almost certain success would revolutionize the world's economy. His main concern was that France should eventually share in the benefits of nuclear energy for peacetime use.

After his first meeting with Halban, as France's newly appointed and powerful director of scientific research, Joliot insisted that the British keep their agreement to share their knowledge of the Manhattan Project. That same day, November 24, 1944, General de Gaulle, having been briefed by Joliot on the progress of the American atomic bomb, was in Moscow for his first official visit to the Soviet Union.

CHAPTER 21

Joliot's Fight for Peace and Communism

1945–1950

J oliot confirmed that he was an active and dedicated Communist when, as the president of the National Front, he appeared at a three-day conference in late January 1945. It was rotten weather, but almost a thousand members turned up. Sharing the platform with him were fellow Communists Laurent Casanova, Pierre Villon, Henri Wallon, General Paul Dassault, and Paul Langevin, as well as some important non-Communist members. Many of the speeches were moving accounts of the Resistance, in which Communists played a major role. The high spot of the meeting was when a delegation offered Joliot the flag of the First Company of the Dordogne Battalion, every one of whom had died crying, "Vive la France! Death to the invader!" inspiring the crowd to stand and sing "La Marseillaise."

Despite his increasing political involvement, he was not neglecting his work. As historian Alexander Werth saw it, under Joliot French science began "its greatest expansion and reform of institutions since the Revolution and Napoleon." His visits to the Soviet Union in the 1930s and again in 1945 had impressed him by the way its central government generously funded and honored its scientists, and made sure that important work was sustained and duplication avoided. He intended to emulate the Russians.

Joliot's overriding goal was to restore France to its former greatness. To achieve that, he intended to assign scientific priorities and "to pressure scientists to maintain a flow of ideas from pure research into industrial applications." His proposals came with a dire warning that unless his views were adopted and French scientists given the support and prestige they deserved, France would "sooner or later become a colony."

The response from de Gaulle's government was encouraging. When the country's finance minister and its budget director called in Joliot to discuss the annual budget for his National Center for Scientific Research, Joliot was going to ask for a 200 percent increase. The budget director was sitting near the finance minister "with scissors in hand," while Joliot briefly explained why this whopping increase was justified. To the budget director's horror, the finance minister simply said "Granted." Joliot later remarked: "If the person you are trying to convince understands that you are ready to quit your position, your demand is taken seriously."

In Orléans one March evening in 1945, Joliot spoke in favor of international cooperation and the nationalization of industry. He stressed the importance of science and technology to win the war, and his hope for France's renaissance. He still had a lot more to say, when all the city's lights went out. He continued his speech in the darkness for more than an hour and held his audience. But the electrical failure perhaps was the most telling argument for his thesis.

At 3:35 P.M. on April 12, 1945, sixty-three-year-old President Franklin Roosevelt died of a cerebral hemorrhage, and his successor, Harry Truman, who surprisingly had been kept out of the loop, was briefed on the imminent existence of the atomic bomb. At 3:30 P.M. on May 1, with the Soviet army approaching his underground bunker in Berlin, the desperate and despairing Adolf Hitler put a gun in his mouth and committed suicide. A week later, after five years, eight months, and six days of war, representatives of his monstrous creation, Nazi Germany, surrendered to the Allies. General de Lattre de Tassigny, for whom Eve Curie had worked as personal assistant, was France's representative at the signing of the German capitulation.

Three weeks later, tens of thousands of Parisians paraded for seven hours to honor both the Communists and the Resistance for their part in the victory. Among the leaders of the march was Paul Langevin's daughter, Hélène Solomon, recently freed from the Auschwitz concentration camp.

Germans were clearing the mine fields that surrounded the Joliots' summer home at L'Arcouest when they visited it for the first time since the occupation. The family was still there on August 6, 1945, when they heard that a single bomb dropped by the B-29 super fortress *Enola Gay*, carrying a few kilograms of uranium 235, had demolished the Japanese city of Hiroshima, killing an estimated two hundred thousand. The Soviet Union declared war on Japan on August 8, and the next day the plane *Grand Artiste* dropped a plutonium bomb on the port of Nagasaki, killing about one hundred forty thousand. The two devastating attacks forced Japan to surrender on August 14, 1945.

Advocates of the atomic bomb claim that it saved many lives by preventing the need for an Allied invasion of Japan, which, if undertaken, was calculated to cost a million casualties. And, of course, had the bomb been available and used at the start of World War II, it would have saved millions of lives.

Both Joliot-Curies, however, thought that the use of atomic fission was a betrayal of both science and mankind. Until then they had always believed science to be a positive factor in human progress. Since the atomic bomb was partly the result of their own pioneering work, they felt partly to blame. Joliot tried to assuage his sense of guilt by writing in an article published in *L'Humanité* on August 10: "The immense reserves of energy contained in the uranium devices can [also] be liberated slowly enough to be used practically for the benefit of mankind. I am personally convinced that atomic energy will be of inestimable services to mankind in peacetime."

De Gaulle quickly responded, asking Joliot and Raoul Dautry to give him a plan for an atomic energy program. Irène, Pierre Auger, and Francis Perrin joined the team and soon had something to show the French leader. He accepted their ideas with alacrity and with his signature established the Commissariat (Ministry) of Atomic Energy (CEA) on October 18, 1945. Perhaps its charter was intentionally ambiguous, directing the CEA, as it was known, to find uses for atomic energy in various scientific fields, in industry, and in national defense. The last item was important to de Gaulle, who wanted France to have its own atomic bombs. Yet he had also accepted Joliot's policy statement that the research would be entirely for peaceful purposes.

Joliot was not bothered by this contradiction, believing that for years to come France would have neither the money nor the manpower to produce atomic bombs, and if and when it did have both, he expected international agreements to effectively ban the bomb.

Pierre Auger recalled the first meetings of the CEA commission: "We were like members of a club planning the ascent of Mt. Everest or a trip around the world in a sailboat. Proposals which were very audacious for that era could be made and discussed without having their wings clipped by protocol of budget. [We were] all united by a common desire for rapid changes in the lives of the masses and their hopes for state Science."

General Groves still feared that when the French scientists who had worked on a heavy-water reactor in Canada returned to France, they would leak secrets to Joliot and that he in turn would slip them to the Russians. Groves once said that although French Communists claimed they were not connected to the Russian Communist Party, they "go to Moscow all the time." He had a point, according to Goldschmidt, who believed that French Communists regarded the Russian Communist Party as the Mother Church. To ease the situation, Goldschmidt, who was not a Communist, met Groves in Washington, D.C., and the Americans and British came to an extremely odd agreement as follows. The Frenchmen Bertrand Goldschmidt, Jules Guéron, and Lew Kowarski, who had worked on the bomb-related research in Canada, must not divulge any nuclear secrets they possessed, but they could gradually reveal as much of their own research as the French needed to produce nuclear energy. They were also forbidden to take any relevant documents with them. But of course they couldn't be prevented from taking what was in their minds. This as good as gave Kowarski carte blanche, as he had a phenomenal memory. But he had no need to make use of it. Because, when he asked John Cockcroft, representing the British authorities, if his own handwritten notes were considered documents, Cockcroft said they weren't and that he could take them with him. In fact, they contained an enormous amount of top-secret information. And all three men had a lot of nuclear know-how.

Groves was in luck. None of them were Communists or Communist sympathizers, and all three were men of their word. Nothing apparently was leaked through them to the Russians.

Eve Curie was already back in Paris. After her war work, she had begun to work as codirector of a center-right newspaper. Foreign correspondent William Shirer soon contacted her and noted in his diary for October 1945: "To lunch at a little bistro in Le Vallois with Eve and Philippe [Barrés]—each of them the child of famous parents—after they put *Paris Presse*, their afternoon newspaper to bed. I had seen a good deal of them during the war."

When Goldschmidt returned to Paris and called in at the Radium Institute, Debierne welcomed him back affectionately, but the reunion with Irène was rather difficult, because he had to question her about a recent fatal accident at the Curie Laboratory, and she was still mourning the victim, Sonia Cotelle. A Polish physicist and one of the most popular and talented members of the lab, Cotelle was heating a strong polonium deposit when the glass container cracked and she inhaled a fatal dose of polonium. Irène was resting in the Alps at the time and Joliot had written to her about it, explaining that he had ordered Sonia to stop working when he saw that she was losing hair. Irène wrote back that she must rest and commented, "I performed the same procedure many times and it never happened to me!" However, Sonia Cotelle had been irradiated more than others at the Radium Institute when, many times, she handled strong radioactive sources.

Chadwick, on behalf of General Groves, had asked Goldschmidt to investigate the accident because the information might be helpful in case of a similar accident in a U.S. factory. Goldschmidt was sworn to secrecy, so he couldn't explain to Irène why he was questioning her. Still very upset, she told him it was none of his business, and he learned nothing more about it.

Joliot, on the other hand, was very friendly and began to address Goldschmidt, as he recalled, "by the familiar *tu*. Didn't ask me any indiscreet questions . . . He spoke to me at length about his life and that of his laboratory under the Occupation, of his research on the use of radio-scopes in biology, of his membership in the Communist party after the murders of Holweck and Solomon, of the warm welcome he received in the party, of his role in the Resistance as president of the National Front [a Communist-dominated organization], of his going into hiding during the two months preceding the liberation, and finally of his laboratory's role in making explosives and Molotov cocktails for the last fighting in Paris."

Joliot also had an emotional reunion with Kowarski and Guéron. Because of their invaluable experience and information, he immediately enlisted them, as well as Goldschmidt, into his CEA group.

Irène was the main speaker in London at a March 1946 meeting for International Women's Day, and when Debierne died later that year she formally replaced him as the Curie Laboratory's director, with twelve colleagues and sixty researchers under her control. Soon after she had been made a full professor at the Sorbonne, she applied for membership in the Academy of Sciences. But like her mother, she was rejected. She took it in good spirit, saying that at least they were consistent.

Meanwhile in the United States, General Groves, worried about losing the nuclear weapons monopoly, asked a DuPont engineer how long it would take "our pals the British" and "the Frogs" to have a nuclear reactor. The engineer estimated it would take the British a couple of years, and the Russians, with great effort, four to five years. As for the French, he thought that technically they had very fine minds, individually, but because it was "impossible ever get two Frenchmen to agree," it would take "them damn near eternity." He was slightly off.

He had hardly reckoned with Joliot, who had been formally inducted into the French Academy of Sciences on November 17, 1945. His friend and mentor, Paul Langevin, had presented him with the ceremonial sword.

Paul Langevin (far left), hands Joliot his academician's sword at the Sorbonne as Irène watches, November 17, 1945.

Langevin died the following year, and at his funeral, Joliot, deeply moved, recalled that it was Langevin who got him a job with Mme Curie and so determined his destiny.

At the end of 1946, Joliot had 215 CEA employes, most of them working in the dilapidated old fort of Châtillon, outside which collaborators had recently been executed, and inside which hundreds of tons of explosives were still in storage. Kowarski had noticed blood from prisoners who had just been shot when they first inspected the place. It was there that Joliot aimed to establish a nuclear center and eventually to build a number of giant reactors to provide nuclear energy for most of France. The nuclear center at Châtillon and even the center at Saclay were still preliminary steps on the way to a one-hundred-megawatt reactor that would produce energy by the end of the 1950s.

Joliot's administrative offices for the CEA were in the confiscated home of collaborator Louis Renault, the auto manufacturer, and two luxury apartments overlooking a garden at 41 avenue Foch. He was able to get five tons of heavy water from the Norwegians, keeping to their wartime agreement, but had a problem in finding uranium. Although he had some that he had hidden from the Nazis, he needed much more. And the Americans and British with their worldwide monopoly were unlikely to share any with him. Irène came to the rescue. With her expertise on mineralogy and geology, she persuaded Louis Barrabé and Jean Orcel to organize a crash course in the Museum of Natural History's mineralogy laboratory. Eager to continue their adventurous outdoor life, scores of former members of the Resistance turned up. Irène's role was to teach them about radioactivity. Early in 1947 Joliot had three hundred potential uranium prospectors at his disposal. By year's end a hundred were already on the hunt.

For the more advanced stage of bringing nuclear energy to France at large, Joliot and Dautry bought a large agricultural site at Saclay near Versailles, where Irène, emulating her mother, had five thousand trees planted to beautify the place. Afraid of having a nuclear plant in their neighborhood, local farmers protested, circulated petitions, and stopped construction for several months. So Joliot met them in a Saclay schoolroom, sketched the plans on a blackboard, and, as always, comfortable among working people, by his charm and powers of persuasion won them over, returning home "exhausted but exhilarated by his rapport with the villagers."

In June 1947, Joliot and Augur crossed the Atlantic as delegates to the United Nations Atomic Energy Committee at Lake Success in the United States, to study the feasibility of international control of nuclear energy. Alexander Parodi, the French ambassador, described Joliot's CEA as "entirely directed towards peace, and towards activities whose essential object is the welfare of mankind." And added: "Our wish is that the nations of the world take the same attitude as speedily as possible."

Fascinated by Manhattan's intense nightlife, Joliot told an American radio audience on July 8 that the brilliant cinema signs, the shops' dazzling lights, "and the sight of all the things we want and have not got, remind me of the Paris boulevards at Christmas when I was a child. It seems to me that it is Christmas every day in New York and that I am amongst big children."

At the United Nations, America's Bernard Baruch and Russia's Andrei Gromyko presented conflicting views for the international control of atomic energy, and Joliot feared that it would be impossible to reconcile them. The Americans were suspicious of Joliot, yet Baruch tried to persuade him to remain in America. "It is madness to try to do atomic energy in France," he said. "A pile—two piles—you'll never get them in the state your country is in. Your industry is not capable of providing what you need. You'd do better to stay in the United States."

"What can you offer me here?" Joliot asked with a smile.

"Laboratories, a team of colleagues, and a handsome salary." Baruch named a large sum.

"I should require ten times that," Joliot said, playing him along.

"Oh, come now, you're exaggerating."

"Why? How much do you make a year yourself?"

Joliot surely knew that Baruch was a multimillionaire.

From the United States, Joliot flew to London, where representatives from fourteen governments established a World Federation of Scientific Workers and named him its president. He was willing to accept this additional responsibility because he wholeheartedly agreed with its goals: to encourage scientists everywhere to oppose secrecy in basic research and to support the movement to outlaw atomic warfare.

Goldschmidt believed that "he was thrilled to feel himself in harmony with an enthusiastic crowd, convinced in the justice of their cause. When returning from Poland, where his name had appeared on posters alongside those of Marx, Engels, Lenin, and Stalin, he had declared: 'Once one has known this, one cannot do without it.'"

The first project in giving France nuclear energy was named ZOE by Kowarski—from the initials of Zero—the power of the pile was very small—Oxide, and Eau Lourde (heavy water).

In the French national elections of November 1947, the Communists emerged as the leading party, getting 30 percent of the votes and sending over 180 members into the National Assembly. Aboard the U.S. presidential yacht in the Potomac a week later, Truman; Britain's prime minister, Clement Atlee; and the Canadian Mackenzie King reacted to the Communists' triumph in France by agreeing to continue to keep nuclear secrets from the French. And the U.S. House Committee on Un-American Activities expressed their fear of homegrown Communists by accusing ten Hollywood screenwriters, believed to be Communists, of writing propaganda for foreign ideologies.

During this time, Irène had accepted an invitation from the American Joint Antifascist Refugee Committee to tour the United States in the spring of 1948 to raise funds for Spanish refugees from Franco's fascist Spain. To her dismay, when her plane landed at LaGuardia Airport, because the U.S. attorney general considered her host committee a subversive organization, she was refused entry. Bertrand Goldschmidt, adviser to the French U.N. delegation in New York, had gone to the airport to meet Irène, but he was forbidden to talk to her. He was reduced to signaling to her through a glass partition, and she returned his signals with a grin. That evening she was driven to Ellis Island—the destination for undesirable aliens.

Goldschmidt contacted the French embassy in Washington and she was released the next morning, when she told a press conference that it had not been the friendliest of receptions "but that Ellis Island was very adequate, that she had spent an excellent night in a room in which three young women were already asleep, had some good coffee, and was able to profit from the moment of calm to darn her stockings." She also said that she had not been surprised by her detention, because "I am here to aid the antifascists. This is not always as favorably considered as aiding the Nazis. Americans look with much more favor on fascism than communism . . . Americans think fascism has more respect for money."

At dinner with Goldschmidt that evening she expressed her outrage that nothing had been done to help the Spanish republican refugees who had opposed Franco, but former Nazis were treated favorably. They also discussed Ellis Island, changes taking place at the Commissariat of Atomic Energy, and the recent *Kinsey Report on the Sexual Behavior of the Human Male*. The next morning she left for Princeton to chat with Einstein.

Unlike in New York, during her subsequent tour of the West Coast, Chicago, Boston, and Philadelphia, she felt no hostility. *Time* magazine, however, asserted that she deserved worse than a night on Ellis Island and that all Communists in a democracy were potential spies and traitors. The French, regardless of political orientation, were largely incensed by her treatment.

In August 1948 Irène went to a conference of "Intellectuals for Peace" in Wroclaw (formerly Breslau), Poland. The purpose was to debate "in freedom and friendship" the hopes for a cultural rapprochement for intellectuals and artists on the two sides of what had become known as the Iron Curtain. Julian Huxley, director-general of UNESCO and brother of Aldous, was there in a private capacity, together with Pablo Picasso, historian A. J. P. Taylor, Martha Gellhorn, and the *New Statesman*'s editor Kingsley Martin. Picasso was characterized by a right-wing Paris paper as "that old clown who has produced the Marxist dove which befouls all the walls of our beautiful but, alas, defenseless Paris."

Huxley recalled how,

The communist block displayed its real intentions, which were simply to denigrate Western culture. Fadeyev's opening speech set the tone: "If hyenas could type, and jackals use fountain pens, they would write such things as the so-called poetry of T. S. Eliot and Auden." This and other similar utterances were wildly applauded by the communist crowd . . . The Congress gave a frightening display of the power of doctrinaire opinion in a cultural confrontation. Stampar [a Yugoslavian politician] told me that he was there "by order" of the Kremlin to toe the Party Line . . . Picasso was more daring. As a member of the Party, he had been "ordered" to paint in the way the Soviet authorities wanted. He just replied, "Merde!" [and continued as before].

He also sketched Joliot's portrait.

Writer Ilya Ehrenburg, a spokesman for Soviet interests among European intellectuals, and later Joliot's friend, warned his audience that "the culture of various European nations is threatened by a dangerous barbarian invasion . . . This barbarianism can teem with refrigerators and adult romances, automobiles and stereo-films, laboratories and psychological novels, but all of it remains barbarianism . . . They are screaming as if they are afraid of our tanks. But in fact they are afraid of our tractors, our saucepans, our future." (He later admitted privately to William Shirer, but apparently never told Joliot or Irène, that life in Soviet Russia was "terrible.")

After Jean-Paul Sartre was maligned, together with Albert Camus, because he called for an investigation of Soviet concentration camps, Irène was also about to leave in protest. But the organizer of the congress, Jerzy Borejsza, quickly telephoned Joliot, and he persuaded her to stay.

In November 1948, the Joliot-Curies' daughter, twenty-year-old Hélène, married her college classmate Michel Langevin, bringing the two families even closer together. Michel was Paul Langevin's grandson. Both were training to be scientists. At her wedding, Hélène was amused to see her aunt, Eve Curie, a codirector of a slightly right-wing newspaper *Paris Presse*, together with Georges Cogniot, the director of the Communist paper *L'Humanité*.

Because miners were on strike in the area at the time and suffering great hardships, the Joliot-Curies had taken the daughters of two strikers into their home while the strike lasted. The girls, aged nine and five, attended the wedding at Antony, together with Maurice Thorez, head of the French Communist Party. Irène was hospitalized the next day for a double mastoiditis operation she had postponed until after her daughter's wedding, not having realized that her life was at risk. She was saved by injections of the recently discovered antibiotic streptomycin. While recuperating, she sent for a student, Henriette Faraggi, to discuss a new way to record nuclear particle tracks on special thick emulsion plates produced in Britain.

Even an anti-Communist critic was charmed by Joliot in those days, describing him as "a fast-talking, delicately jointed individual whose thin lips, hollow cheeks and sharp bony nose give his face a somewhat ascetic look. He may examine you, for an instant, head cocked, much like a curious blackbird. But the tautness quickly gives way to a smile of warmth, his major tool in making friends and influencing people. Men like, women adore, Joliot."

The adoration reached its climax on December 15, 1948, when, at 6:30 A.M., he and Kowarski appeared at the old fort of Châtillon to start the first French atomic pile—hoping, if it worked, to break the monopoly of the Americans and British. It worked.

France was on its way to having its own nuclear energy and eventually the bomb. A centrist newspaper, *L'Aube*, applauded it as both a French and a peaceful achievement, "which strengthens our role in the defense of civilization."

However, the British *Observer* was astonished that "at the moment when measures of security against Communists are reinforced in England and in America, the High Commissioner of French Atomic Energy should be Professor Joliot-Curie." The London *Economist* was equally perturbed and advised the French to do something about it. So did Donald MacLean, an undersecretary at the British Embassy in Washington, D.C., and one of the strongest advocates for Joliot's dismissal. Strangely, MacLean turned out to be an undercover Communist who later defected to the Soviet Union.

Joliot's response to reporters' questions at a meeting of the Anglo-American Press Association in Paris on January 5, 1949, was characterized by Bertrand Goldschmidt as "a poignant episode in the complex drama of Joliot's downfall." He tried to convince the group that he was first and foremost a French patriot. "Let me speak frankly," he said. "Suppose tomorrow one of my assistants or I make a discovery essential to the introduction of atomic arms. [The critics] suggest it would be our duty—willingly accepted—to pass on every detail of such a discovery to the Moscow government. In so doing, it seems to me, we would intentionally commit the crime of treason."

A rebuttal that infuriated Joliot came eighteen days later at a Paris meeting to honor the twenty-fifth anniversary of Lenin's death. Jacques Duclos, secretary of the French Communist Party, contradicted Joliot: "A communist does not consider the U.S.S.R. a foreign country . . . Every progressive man has two lands, his own and the Soviet Union, the great land of socialism." As Joliot's daughter points out, "It is worthwhile to notice that the sentence by Duclos is directly inspired by the following one: 'Every man has two lands, his own and France.' A sentence pronounced by the well-known poet Heinrich Heine in the mid-nineteenth century, referring to the role of the French Revolution."

Shortly afterward, Joliot's friend Laurent Casanova, a Resistance leader who had approved of Joliot's decision not to leave for England in 1940 and had welcomed him into the Communist Party two years later, called on Joliot at the Collège de France. Goldschmidt, who had an appointment with Joliot, was kept waiting for over three hours while the two men talked. When Joliot emerged, Goldschmidt remembered, "he was pale with fatigue and nervous exhaustion and could not hide the torment through which he was going . . . He remained in the party, probably because he did not have the courage to face the attacks and slander his political comrades of the Resistance and the postwar period would have heaped on him had he left. He had always needed to feel loved and admired. These comrades resolved to keep him on by catering to his vanity and demanding his pledge of loyalty in return. The process that ended in his departure from the CEA had begun."

Joliot continued to show his dual loyalties soon after, when Victor Kravchenko, a Russian defector to the West, published his account of Stalin's reign of terror in *I Chose Freedom*. In it he revealed the purge trials, the famines organized in Ukraine that killed millions, and the mass deportations to the gulag prison camps that killed millions more. A French Communist paper, *Lettres Françaises*, ridiculed the book as fiction, and Kravchenko sued for libel. He provided a group of witnesses to testify that Russia was hell, and the paper's witnesses countered that it was heaven. Joliot testified on March 7, 1949, when he defended "the Moscow show trials of the 1930s," and stated that Kravchenko's book "gave a wrong picture of education in Russia. Contrary to what the book said I found that every effort is being made in Russia to educate the people, in all possible fields." Irène also testified that she had visited the USSR and that the brutal Soviet gulags as described in the book did not exist. Yet one of the witnesses, Alex Weissberg, had given vivid testimony of his own imprisonment in a gulag.

Irene's daughter, Héléne, later explained that "she was *really* convinced it wasn't true. She hadn't seen. She hadn't understood. Both my parents were really convinced that Kravchenko was lying. Unfortunately, he was not lying about the gulag and other important facts. It is true that important efforts were being made in Russia for education, even if education was badly deformed on 'political' questions. The promotion of Lysenko was a disaster for biological researchers. My father was successful in stopping approaches of a similar type, even if less serious, concerning physics." Kravchenko won the case.

Communists were turned out of the French government in 1947 and became a strong opposition. The Communist vote in 1948, despite a brutal Communist takeover of Czechoslovakia that year, came close to 40 percent, and the American press hinted at a possible military intervention in France. But by 1949 it was becoming evident that France would remain an ally of the Western powers. "In that polarized atmosphere," Kowarski recalled, "Joliot and most of the people immediately around him were either Communists or fellow-travelers . . . At first he had hopes that he would win me over to France, to his conception of France. But then he realized that I was completely bewitched by the English. He considered Goldschmidt— a brilliant scientist and manager and married to a Rothschild—as a representative of the enemy capitalist class and therefore not to be trusted. So the atmosphere was not very conductive to discussion of common goals."

On December 5, 1949, Goldschmidt, Guéron, and Kowarski had a showdown with Joliot, who was rarely available for consultation because of his increasing world travel and involvement in politics. And when he did appear he was irritable, complaining that Goldschmidt had deliberately extracted the first milligram of plutonium in his absence; that Kowarski did not respect him and was making his life impossible; and that he did not trust Guéron's experimental results on the uranium-ore treatment and was having the Curie lab check them out.

Guéron stormed out of the room, announcing his resignation as he went. After a long silence, Joliot said: "I think I overdid it." The other two agreed. "I think I should apologize to him." They nodded agreement. They had to tell him where Guéron's office was. That evening they had a peacemaking dinner together at Joliot's favorite restaurant, Roger la Grenouille in the Latin Quarter. Over spaghetti Joliot agreed to be available every Wednesday afternoon, and they promised not to criticize his political activities.

Goldschmidt believed that "the leaders of the Communist party seemed decided on pushing him toward his downfall: they had probably concluded that he would be more useful to them as a martyr for his opinions." During the few months following "the spaghetti compromise," Goldschmidt "was under the spell of Joliot's charm and impressed by his dynamism and his comprehension of human problems, other than political ones. In spite of his nervous tension, he was now interested in nearly all aspects of the life of the CEA which, in large part, owed its existence to him and from which he was soon to be separated."

Kowarski observed that "all through 1949 Joliot was making anti-government speeches which were mounting in tone, and after one he said: 'Why don't they dismiss me?' Joliot was one of the heads of an organism which had definite government functions, including defense. When he became the leader of people who went about the country and Europe pro-claiming, 'If the government orders us to make weapons, we will say no,' he was no longer a suitable person to be in charge of an establishment which . . . had to make weapons."

Few Frenchmen in authority or knowing the facts doubted Joliot's patriotism, but the American general Groves did, saying that he still dis-trusted Joliot and that "my recent experience with Joliot has convinced me that nothing that might be of interest to the Russians should ever be allowed to fall into French hands."

Although the U.S. State Department was particularly wary of Joliot, the CIA believed that half the members of the French Commissariat for Atomic Energy were Communist sympathizers, listing only Goldschmidt and Guéron as politically reliable. Catering to French sensibilities, writes author Weart, "The Americans, however, wanted to avoid any appearance of directly pressuring France to remove Joliot. Seeing the CEA as a nest of Communists with or without him, the State Department simply did what-ever it could to impede the CEA's progress. As the official in Washington responsible for such matters remarked, 'Joliot-Curie's presence [as high commissioner] made it easier to say no to any French request for coopera-tion in the atomic field.' But the Americans in common with [the French Prime Minister Georges] Bidault's government, were finding it harder and harder to tolerate the Communists."

In response to the Soviet Union's test explosion of an atomic bomb at the start of 1950, President Truman ordered the building of a hydrogen bomb that would be a thousand times more devastating than the atomic bomb. He made the decision despite the unanimous disapproval of the American Atomic Energy's scientific consultant committee headed by Robert Oppenheimer, and a don't-do-it letter from Einstein. A few days later British nuclear scientist Klaus Fuchs, who had worked at Los Alamos, was arrested and eventually confessed to being a Communist spy who had given British and U.S. atomic-research secrets to the Soviet government. He was sentenced to fourteen years in prison.

In mid-March 1950 when Joliot arrived in Stockholm at the first meeting of Partisans for Peace, he was asked to leave the hotel where he had stayed fifteen years previously when he and Irène had been given their Nobel Prizes. The management did not approve of "Reds." Ilya

Ehrenburg, the Russian writer, there for the same meeting, met him in the street. Joliot was carrying his suitcase, having been refused a room in several hotels, which Ehrenburg thought ludicrous rather than tragic. Joliot finally found someone to accommodate him. In stark contrast to his previous visit, the Swedish press ignored him, although at the meeting he suggested what would become well known as the Swedish Appeal, in which he advocated the total abolition of nuclear weapons—the start of a worldwide peace movement. Ehrenburg returned with him to France and celebrated Joliot's fiftieth birthday with him at Antony on March 18, 1950.

The Joliot-Curies spent Easter in a chalet they had recently built at Courchevel, and Joliot went from there to a mass meeting of the French Communist Party in the "Red" working-class suburb of Gennevilliers. There he declared that progressive and Communist scientists were serving France and all humanity by refusing to use their science for a war against the Soviet Union.

On April 16, 1950, *La Presse* suggested Goldschmidt or Kowarski as Joliot's possible replacements, adding that being Jews, their names and origins might be an obstacle. *France Tireur* had a cartoon showing Fort Châtillon and ZOE surrounded by French people saying, "It seems that the Russians have taken the [atomic] pile."

At the time the Joliots were in India attending a scientific congress sponsored by Indian Prime Minister Nehru, greeted by adoring crowds wherever they went. Joliot got a very different reception on his return to Paris. On April 26, 1950, Kowarski, Goldschmidt, and Guéron were at their weekly meeting with him in his office when their prime minister, Georges Bidault, phoned and asked Joliot to meet him at the nearby Hôtel Matignon. He left, obviously upset, saying that it would be either a strong reprimand or a dismissal.

According to biographer Biquard, as Joliot arrived in Bidault's office the prime minister said, "Before taking any action against you, the administrative rules oblige me to show you your dossier. Here it is." He indicated a cardboard folder with the name High Commissioner for Atomic Energy on the cover. Inside was one item: "the decree giving his appointment. And that was all! But lying beside the dossier on the Minister's desk were a mass of newspaper clippings. [Many, of course, charging that he was a security risk.] Obviously distressed, the minister said that he regretted having to take such a decision, and realized that it meant losing Joliot's friendship."

Kowarski, Goldschmidt, and Guéron were still waiting in his office when Joliot returned after forty minutes, pale and dejected. He told them that Bidault, a fellow fighter in the Resistance, had reluctantly fired him, and asked them to keep it a secret because it would not become public for two days, after a meeting of the Council of Ministers.

A dinner had been planned that evening for Joliot and a group of friends and colleagues. Goldschmidt had managed to have his house-guest, one of Joliot's favorite former students, Bruno Pontecorvo, invited. And Goldschmidt never forgot how "at the end of the meal Joliot, under extreme stress, made an interminable three-hour-long speech, a sort of confused testament on anything that passed through his head; in particular, a long digression on the Roman civilization. Faithful to my promise, I did not explain to Pontecorvo why the guest of honor was so tense. Pontecorvo remarked contemptuously: 'A good Communist does not behave like this.' He knew whereof he spoke." (Italian scientist Pontecorvo later defected to the Soviet Union.)

Joliot's dismissal was the major front-page story in the *New York Times* of April 29, 1950, headlined "French Remove Joliot-Curie As Chief for Atomic Energy: Communist Head of Science Commission Dismissed by Premier Bidault." In the text, Michael Clark reported that "The Communist organ L'Humanité, in an editorial headed 'A Step Towards War,' declares that 'American warmongers gave the order and Bidault obeyed.' The moderate and conservative press is unanimous in expressing satisfaction."

The news story was continued on page thirty-two. On that same page was a two-paragraph account reading: "Senator Joseph McCarthy, Republican of Wisconsin, began a short Arizona vacation today with [a] promise he will continue to use 'bare knuckles' in his exposure of Communists in the State Department."

Bidault explained to the National Assembly that he had dismissed Joliot not only as a Communist who was embarrassing the government, but because he was both refusing to build weapons and supporting workers who were on strike or sabotaging arms shipments intended for French troops fighting the Viet Minh in Indochina. A strong majority of the assembly approved the government's position, which only the Communists opposed.

"They could have forgiven me any error, any crime," Joliot told his friend and biographer Pierre Biquard, "but not that of being a Communist. I was born into a middle-class family. I received a good education. I have been successful. I am comfortably off. In their eyes I have no excuse and the ostracism I am subjected to has no other origin than this."

Biquard, himself a fellow traveler, remarked that, "Joliot's family background, despite its relative prosperity, had predisposed him to be very liberal and generous in his attitudes."

When, on May 5, a dispirited Joliot entered the lecture room at the Collège de France to give his weekly lecture, he was applauded as everyone sang "La Marseillaise." "His desk was piled high with flowers," reported biographer Goldsmith. "He was choking with emotion as he began to talk on nuclear reactions caused by charged particles. . . . He also stressed the necessity for scientific research with purely peaceful objectives, and that scientific institutions should not be centers of propaganda for any but scientific objects, always open to research by competent men, whatever their political opinions."

The other positive event in those days for both Joliot-Curies was the birth of their granddaughter, Hélène's first child, Françoise, on May 21, 1950.

Joliot was soon absorbed in writing his opposition to the possibility of American scientists building a hydrogen bomb, published in *The Bulletin of the Atomic Scientists* in June 1950. He proposed that the first government to "use the atomic weapon against any country whatsoever," no matter how righteous the cause, "should be treated as a war criminal." Calling the atomic weapon "the weapon of terror and of mass extermination of populations," Joliot suggested establishing "a rigorous international control to assure the application of this measure of prohibition."

The bulletin responded that Joliot, France's "leading experimental physicist," was known as a Communist and was recently fired "from his post as French Atomic Energy Commissioner because of his declaration that progressive scientists will not work on weapons which could be used against the Soviet Union." The bulletin also pointed out that Joliot's primary purpose was to represent

> the Soviet Union as the true protagonist among nations of the abolition of atomic weapons, and America as a militaristic power . . . It is the American government at whom the threat of being branded as "war criminals" is unmistakably directed . . . [His] three proposals hark back to the statements made by Molotov, Vishinsky, and Gromyko in the United Nations. We cannot help recalling here that these professions of a desire for atomic disarmament have accompanied the refusal of the Soviet Union to agree to an atomic energy control plan which, in the opinion of the Western nations, backed by a formidable array of technical and scientific experts, was the only one under consideration, adequate to achieve the very aims proclaimed by the Soviet leaders.

The bulletin concluded with an attack on Joliot's partisan stance:

> When Professor Joliot-Curie addresses sympathetic writers, actors and movie stars in "peace congresses," he may assume that they do not know where the matter of atomic energy control stands, and are ready to believe that the

principal obstacle on the way to its establishment is the refusal of the American Government to renounce atomic weapons; but he cannot assume such lack of information when he speaks to American scientists. They are the ones who initiated the discussion of atomic energy control five years ago and have followed, with bated breath, the fate of this, their brainchild, in the endless discussion of the UNAEC [United Nations Atomic Energy Commission]. They have seen with dismay how the unanimous conclusion of experts that control is technically possible, has been brought to naught by the intrusion into the subsequent negotiations of power-politics and ideological conflicts — and, principally, by the Soviet Union's isolationism and distrust of the outside world.

Therefore, we do not expect Professor Joliot-Curie to find many American scientists eager to sign the proposal petition to the U.N., however wholeheartedly they agree with all its three points. But if [he] will use his reputation as one of the great atomic scientists of our time, and his access to both sides in the controversy, to help in seeking a universally acceptable solution of the one of his three points [control] which has caused the present deadlock in the U.N. Atomic Energy Commission, he will find scientists in this country wishing him success, and eager to cooperate.

Of course Joliot was still admired by his students and people opposed to nuclear weapons — the "peaceniks," as their critics called them. He still held his chair at the Collège de France and remained director at the laboratory for nuclear synthesis at Ivry.

But, instead of returning to research work, he became increasingly involved in the world peace movement, despite the belief of many in the West that it was a cynical Russian ploy to get the democracies to disarm while it built its own stockpile of atomic weapons.

Joliot Launches Peace Offensive and Charges the United States with Using Germ Warfare in Korea

1950–1958

J oliot was deeply depressed after his sudden loss of power and prestige, especially by the reaction of old friends. Many seemed to avoid shaking hands with him, and former colleagues kept their distance as if they feared contamination. People once eager to greet him crossed the street to avoid him, or took the stairs rather than share the same elevator. He was no longer welcome at the scientific establishments he had largely created—Châtillon and Saclay. Even the Communist Party showed signs that it had lost interest in him.

For most of the rest of his life Joliot spent almost all his energy in a feverish round of conferences and rallies, as president of the World Peace Council and of the World Federation of Scientific Workers, never without a bottle of bicarbonate of soda at hand. Irène also played an active part in the peace campaign, with and without Joliot. At a Paris meeting of thirty thousand women celebrating International Women's Day in March 1951, she denounced the arms race and France's ongoing war in Vietnam— before the United States became involved in the conflict.

Both Irène and Joliot were bitter at first when their friend Francis Perrin took over Joliot's post as high commissioner of the CEA, although Joliot conceded that with Perrin in charge it would save the CEA from too much government interference. But he had less influence than Joliot had enjoyed. The French government, rather than scientists, now determined its direction and the future uses of nuclear fission.

There were signs that the Communists were taking a renewed interest in Joliot. In the summer of 1951 he and Irène went to Moscow, where, in the Kremlin's Great Hall, Joliot was given the Stalin Peace Prize—the first of the ten awarded on that occasion. Their friend Eugénie Cotton also got one, along with Soong Ching Ling, Sun Yat-sen's widow. Afterward the Joliot-Curies and Cotton had a vacation in the Russian countryside, living in a dacha at the state's expense. During their stay Joliot visited writer Ilya Ehrenburg in his country cottage in nearby New Jerusalem, where Joliot seemed to his Russian friend to be in the best of spirits, joking, reminiscing, and once blowing into the chimney with all his might until he got an old samovar going for a cup of tea.

Ehrenburg joined the trio when they traveled to Helsinki, Finland, in a special state railroad coach for a meeting of the World Peace Council. During one of the less gripping speeches at this event, Ehrenburg, who sat next to Joliot, was so taken with his whispered words that he jotted them down: "'Physicists are like poets,'" Joliot said. "'They make discoveries in their youth. It's a matter of inspiration. Fermi created his theory of the beta-decomposition of radio-active atoms when he was thirty-three. Rutherford showed his genius at thirty-two. Broglie and Pauli made their important discoveries at thirty-one, Dirac at twenty-six. And do you know how old Einstein was when he formulated his special Theory of Relativity? Twenty-six.'"

"Joliot's eyes sparkled merrily," Ehrenburg writes in his memoirs, "then he grew grave: 'We must listen to what this chap's saying.'"

He also went with Ehrenburg to Leningrad's Hermitage, where, after looking at landscape paintings by Sisley, Monet, and Pissarro, Joliot said, "I feel as if I've spent the summer in the country." During the journey, while waiting for a plane delayed by fog at the Prague airport, Joliot asked Ehrenburg, "Do you ever think about death?" Then he went on: "I seldom think about death, but when I do, I think about it steadily and without dodging the issue. The thought that he will cease to exist is unacceptable to a man. It is not physical fear, but something deeper, the rejection of non-existence, of a void. The idea of a life beyond the grave must have arisen from this feeling, and so long as science was in its infancy people comforted themselves with that sort of illusory hope. But knowledge exacts fortitude. The absence of life after death doesn't mean a negation of continuity. In the first place there's the physical continuity between the generations decreed by nature. And then there's work, creativity, love—the things that remain after the man himself, his name and even his bones have vanished."

On June 25, 1950, encouraged by the Soviet Union, fifty thousand troops from the Communist Democratic People's Republic of Korea attacked the pro-West South Korean republic. Although North Korea and the Soviet Union claimed that the south had invaded the north, few in the West believed them. The United Nations, with the United States providing the most men, money, and munitions, came to the aid of the south; and in the late fall, 180,000 Chinese troops poured across the Chinese border to reinforce the embattled North Korean army.

In March 1952, when a North Korean offensive had stalled, Kuo-Mo-Jo, a poet and playwright and the president of the Chinese Academy of Sciences, spoke in Oslo, Norway, at a meeting of the World Peace Council, of which he was vice president, accusing U.S. troops of waging germ warfare in Korea. In his detailed report he claimed that the Americans had disseminated large quantities of germ-laden insects and other poisonous objects over cities and communication lines in Korea. He also claimed that in March 1951, Brigadier General Crawford F. Sams, then chief of the Public Health and Welfare Section of Ridgeway's headquarters in Tokyo, led landing craft no. 1091 of the U.S. naval forces to make a secret landing at Wonsan harbor, Korea. Aboard this craft, he said, "captured Chinese from the small island within the harbor were then subjected to plague tests." Kuo-Mo-Jo added: "The Chinese people fully support the appeal of Joliot-Curie—demanding the prohibition of bacteriological weapons, chemical weapons and other weapons of mass destruction which was passed at the Warsaw Peace Conference in 1950."

Reluctant to comment at first, Joliot had been impressed by a telegram from Kuo-Mo-Jo informing him of the charge and of the confirming report by Chinese physicist San Tsiang Tsien, Joliot's former student at the Radium Institute and at the Collège de France. It was only then that he had launched a protest against the Americans.

Warren Austin, the U.S. delegate to the United Nations, wrote to Joliot on April 3, 1952, accusing him of "prostituting science" for launching an appeal for an independent inquiry into the charge that Americans were using bacteriological weapons in Korea. Joliot replied: "You charge me with prostituting science because I speak against the criminal use of the discoveries of the great Pasteur and because I am calling to public opinion to prevent the pursuit of bacteriological war. For me, those who prostitute science are those who have inaugurated the atomic era by destroying

200 thousand civilians in Hiroshima and Nagasaki." He mentioned that only Japan and the United States had refused to sign an international agreement in 1925 outlawing bacteriological weapons, and added: "It is not because the Koreans and Chinese had chosen to set up a regime different from that of your country, and because their skin is not white, that it is legal to wish to exterminate them in mass with napalm or bacteria . . . It is because I know all that science can bring to the world that I shall continue my efforts to serve the happiness of men, whether they be white, black or yellow, and not to wipe them out in the name of some divine mission."

In an open letter to Joliot in the *Saturday Evening Post*, headed, "How Did the Communists Take Over One of France's Greatest Scientists?" Bruce Bliven wrote:

> To every scientist a matter of overwhelming importance is the absolute devotion of science to truth. Yet for about twenty years an important segment of the world's population — that behind the Iron Curtain — has tended increasingly to deny the validity of this principle. In the communist countries, scientists themselves willingly or under compulsion have repudiated their own doctrine. You have connived at their actions . . . You have condoned unscientific claims made by the Russians, claims rejected everywhere else in the world where men possess knowledge and freedom. The Russians say that good cultivation of any organism, animal or vegetable, will produce good hereditary strains [Lysenko]. They claim that when a plant is grafted upon another plant, the heredity of the host takes on some of the hereditary characteristics of the scion. Scientists of the free world insist that these claims contravene scientific laws and reject them all. How does it happen that a man like yourself has gone over to condoning this mess of rubbishy voodoo?"

Bliven believed that at first Joliot's impulses were humanitarian, and that his "study of the intricate mysteries of physics" predisposed him to accept the "strange and novel systems intended for the fields of which you knew nothing."

Professor Sidney Hook, chairman of the graduate school of the New York University graduate school's Division of Philosophy, was incensed when Joliot claimed to have personally investigated the charge that the United States had used germ warfare in Korea and to have confirmed that the allegation was true. Hook, as chairman of the American Committee for Cultural Freedom, asked several American Nobel scientists to sign a letter asking Joliot to join them in an objective scientific investigation of the charge, or withdraw his accusation. All but Albert Einstein signed. Einstein replied that none of the signers of the letters had ever before collectively protested the military abuses of science and so had no right to express moral indignation over Joliot's action. Although he did say that he was disappointed by Joliot's "insincere attitude."

When Hook told Einstein that he was disappointed by his reply, Einstein conceded that Joliot had obviously made an assertion, the accuracy of which he could not be sure of, and that it was a disgraceful thing for a scientist to do. But he thought that giving the subject publicity would do more harm than good.

Hook disagreed, writing back: "Just as neither Christian love nor Trappist silence could have deflected Hitler, so they will fail with Stalin . . . And having studied Stalin's mind for twenty-five years, I am convinced that the only thing that will prevent him for giving the signal for war is an adequate defense system in the West and knowledge of the *truth* about the West among the peoples of the Soviet Union." To that Einstein replied that he would welcome an objective investigation of Joliot's charges. But he thought it was inappropriate to be indignant over the situation when the United States had not forsworn the first use of bacteriological weapons.

Joliot never undertook an objective investigation, having accepted the reports of the Russians, Chinese, and North Koreans as the truth, though he did later ask for an independent and competent committee to investigate the facts.

What are the facts?

In Bertrand Russell's "Ten Commandments for a Liberal," the first commandment is: "Do not feel absolutely certain of anything." That uncertainty applies to the validity of Joliot's charge even today. The best and most reliable evidence is that the Americans did not use germ warfare in the Korean War.

An Associated Press report in 1998 stated that the Soviet Union and China "fabricated a campaign . . . to persuade the world that the United States used germ and chemical warfare in the Korean War. New documentary evidence from Moscow's still secret archives suggests that the charge was instigated by Chinese field advisers to the North Koreans. With many Koreans dying of cholera, the Chinese advisers decided U.S. chemical and biological warfare must have been the cause. To make the charge stick, the communists . . . infected Northern Koreans awaiting execution with plague and cholera so their bodies could be shown to outside investigators."

While Joliot was increasingly establishing his Communist credentials and sympathies, his sister-in-law, Eve Curie, was demonstrating her devotion to the democratic West. Having left her editing job in Paris, since 1952 she had been on the international staff of the first secretary general

Irène with Bertrand Russell, in Stockholm, 1950. Both were strong peace advocates.

of the North Atlantic Treaty Organization (NATO), General Ismay, serving as his special adviser. NATO was a military alliance between the United States and the Western democracies, a military counterweight to a Soviet presence in Europe, with atomic weapons as part of their armory. Winston Churchill considered NATO "the only chance of peace in our time." (De Gaulle pulled France out of the treaty in 1964.)

Joliot's worldwide campaign to ban weapons of mass destruction and his disapproval of NATO did not cause a rift in the Curie family. He regarded non-Communists and NATO supporters like Eve not as the enemy, but as the opposition; and, he hoped, open to a change of heart.

On a typical day at his Antony home in the early 1950s, Joliot is to be found at his desk in his favorite black-and-white-check jacket, chain smoking while reading what catches his eye in the latest *Physical Review*. A tray on his right is filled with newspapers, brochures, and pamphlets. Another holds letters waiting for replies, and a third, scientific magazines in English and Russian, the latter translated by his secretary, Roger Mayer. Beside the overfilled ashtray is a slide rule. Behind him on the wall is a montage of photographs. His friend and biographer Biquard remembers them as of "his wife, his children, Langevin, Lenin, a meeting hall, his colleagues by the atomic pile at Châtillon, the scene of a demonstration at Oradour-sur-Glane, a picture taken in a cloud chamber." His secretary is completing a task in the dining room behind him. Joliot resumes work on his next speech, filling a page, then cutting out everything except two sentences. He starts again. When he has finished the speech—invariably about the peace movement—he calls in two colleagues, who discuss with him possible improvements. He is eager for their opinions and urges them to act as devil's advocates. From time to time he looks enviously through the French windows on his right to see his son, Pierre, playing tennis with friends and Irène taking care of their garden. He still makes time to play with their grandchildren—Hélène has recently had a second child, Yves.

At midday, Irène appears to say that lunch is ready and Joliot protests: "You have an absolute genius for interrupting a discussion just when everything is about to become clear!" She leaves, only to return every few minutes until, with a smile, Joliot calls a halt and invites his colleagues to join them for lunch.

After playing tennis, the Joliot-Curies' son, Pierre, has returned to work on his doctoral thesis on photosynthesis. He joins the group for lunch, when he picks flaws in his father's ideas on how to make direct use of the sun's energy. Irène, unable to break into the fiery, nonstop conversation, is reminded of the mealtimes with her mother and husband.

Joliot will deliver the carefully and laboriously crafted speech he has written that day over the next few months at protest meetings and conferences in Poland, Finland, Austria, Hungary, Italy, Czechoslovakia, and the Soviet Union. He was banned from Britain and never made it to China, although he was invited there.

Surprisingly, despite Joliot's dismissal, Communist influence in the French nuclear energy program remained strong. When Steve Dedijer, head of the Yugoslav atomic energy commission, visited France in the spring of 1954, he estimated that at least 60 percent of those in the business were Communists. Dedijer told *New York Times* correspondent C. L. Sulzberger that he made this estimate "based on such clues as pictures of Joliot-Curie, Picasso doves, etc., he saw in the various offices and laboratories," adding, "I'm a Communist; I ought to know."

Hélène Langevin-Joliot believes 10 percent would be closer to the truth, adding that, "Maybe a Yugoslavian visitor imagined that you must have strong communist convictions to dare to have a picture of Joliot-Curie or a dove in the office."

In October 1954 Irène was off to Warsaw to observe the twentieth anniversary of her mother's death at an inauguration of a Curie Museum in the house where Marie was born. She returned to join Joliot at the Sorbonne's amphitheater Richelieu to be honored for their discovery of artificial radio-activity. The affair, presided over by the minister of education, was packed with high-ranking government officials.

Yet when Irène made a final attempt, true to her feminist convictions, to become a member of the all-male Academy of Sciences, she was again turned down. She took her rejection by the misogynist old fogies with amused tolerance. As a sop, perhaps, the Academy awarded both her and Joliot the prestigious Lavoisier Gold Medal.

By this time, supporters of the "Stockholm Appeal" inaugurated by Joliot—which demanded the banning of atomic weapons, a rigorous international control to implement the ban, and the condemnation as a war criminal of any country that used atomic weapons—had collected five hundred million signatures.

Joliot was delighted to hear that the controversial British philosopher Bertrand Russell shared his views. In a December 1954 BBC broadcast titled "Man's Peril," Russell had warned that the world faced nuclear destruction if it could not forget its quarrels and outlaw atomic weapons. Joliot wrote to Russell on January 31, 1955, suggesting that prominent scientists make a joint statement along the same lines. Russell agreed, with the proviso that "the signatories should have no common political complexion and that their declaration should strenuously abstain from any blame to either side for past mistakes or what were thought as such. We all have our prejudices in favour of one side or the other, but in view of the common peril it seems to me that men capable of scientific detachment ought to be able to achieve an intellectual neutrality, however little they may be neutral emotionally. If such a declaration as I have in mind is to be effective, the signatories should represent all shades of opinion so that, collectively, they could not be regarded as leaning towards either side."

After a further exchange of letters, they agreed to meet in Paris on April 20, 1955. Russell had good news: he intended to tell Joliot that several scientists from both the East and the West, Albert Einstein among them, had expressed a sympathetic interest in the idea. And Russell had followed up by sending a statement to them for their signatures. But while Russell was in flight from Rome to Paris to meet Joliot, the pilot announced that Einstein had died. Russell was shattered by the news and the apparent loss of an important supporter. However, when he arrived at his Paris hotel there was a letter for him from Einstein agreeing to sign—perhaps the last he ever wrote.

When soon afterward Russell met Joliot for the first time, he told him: "I am an anti-Communist and it is precisely because you are a Communist that I am anxious to work with you." As an anti-Communist, Russell had taken a lot of trouble with the manifesto to avoid offending Communists, because it was critical to get the cooperation of both sides.

Joliot welcomed Russell's statement except for one phrase: "It is feared that if many bombs are used there will be universal death — sudden only for a fortunate minority, but for the majority a slow torture of disease and disintegration." "To die is *not* fortunate," Joliot exclaimed. "Perhaps he was right," Russell remarked later. "Irony, taken internationally, is tricky." And he agreed to delete it.

Russell returned to England and awaited responses from Chinese and Russian scientists. Russell never heard from China, and three of the Russians, though commending the plan, declined to sign. Niels Bohr surprisingly also refused to sign. So did Otto Hahn, but his explanation was that he was working on a similar statement to be signed only by scientists from the West. But Max Born signed, and Linus Pauling volunteered his signature, which Russell gladly accepted.

Joliot, however, was not yet completely satisfied with what became known as the Einstein-Russell Declaration. Because he had already hired London's Caxton Hall in July 1955 for a conference during which the manifesto and the names of the signatories would be read, Russell begged Joliot to hurry to London to discuss his objections. Instead, because Joliot was bedridden with influenza, he sent his friend Biquard to represent him. Biquard arrived at 11:30 P.M. Sometime after midnight they agreed that as it was too late to change the manifesto, Joliot's reservations would be printed in a footnote and included in the reading of the text at next morning's conference.

Joliot's reservations in the footnote were: "Limitations of national sovereignty should be agreed to by all, and be in the interest of all." And, "Governments should renounce war as a means of settling differences between states." This was to avoid condemning "movements seeking to fight injustice within a nation, or wars of independence fought by subject peoples."

That same July, the United Nations held an Atoms-for-Peace Conference at Geneva, Switzerland, and although scientists from around the world, including many French scientists were there, the Joliot-Curies were not. The British exhibition on display named the Joliot-Curies and credited their important contributions, but the French exhibition even omitted their names. When a reporter asked why they weren't at the conference, Francis Perrin replied: "The French Government did not consider their participation to be necessary." Neither did the French delegates: when various scientists had requested a lecture from Joliot, they vetoed the idea by a majority vote.

But Joliot still had his influential champions. Soon after, when Otto Hahn visited the new French reactor at Marcoule, he saw that his portrait was on exhibition in the conference room but not Joliot's. Hahn told his host to add Joliot's portrait or to remove his.

Bertrand Goldschmidt partly explains the situation: "Joliot wasn't a scientist anymore. From 1946 on he was a politician. He was in the hands of the communists and couldn't get out. By the mid-1950s he and Irène were out of the picture and he was quite tired. He had hepatitis which lasted quite long."

Late in 1955 Joliot was hospitalized in a small private ward at the gloomy Saint-Antoine hospital in Paris. Doctor Jacques Caroli, who ran the place, was unable to say what was wrong with him but put him on a strict diet. Ever the scientist, Joliot began a self-diagnosis and taking notes. Bored with nothing to do, he studied mathematics and made pencil sketches. When he had finally recovered—but from what no one yet knew, although hepatitis was suspected—Joliot handed the doctor his notes suggesting improved methods of diagnosis and treatment. Having become his friend, the doctor accepted it in the right spirit, along with a present of one of Joliot's pencil sketches.

While recuperating at home he took up painting simple landscapes—the view from his window, trees, his courtyard, the wall of a house—and welcomed visitors and workers from his laboratory at the Collège de France. Having been asked to be an expert witness in a notorious poisoning case, he had a small lab set up in his home, with a darkroom for photographs and a workshop with a lathe and drill. He also began to test condensed milk of various dates to see if it had been polluted by radioactive fallout. He recovered sufficiently to go fishing and sailing at L'Arcouest the following summer and early fall.

Meanwhile, Irène taught her grandchildren to swim and occasionally rowed in the bay. One evening she joined in the dancing in the village hall—to the music of Breton bagpipes and a violin—at the annual benefit for the local school. Another evening she spent writing a message for an International Congress of Mothers, in which she applauded their initiative in preparing to defend their children against the danger of an atomic war.

Joliot had a change of heart while hunting in the woods on that vacation. With a bird in his sights, he watched it fluttering around its young for a moment, and then couldn't bring himself to squeeze the trigger. He never went hunting again.

Joliot told his friend Biquard that he was sure he had not long to live and would die before Irène. But he was wrong. Early in 1956 Irène was being cared for in the Curie Hospital, where doctors told her that her tuberculosis was under control, and that her frequent bouts of fever and weight loss were due to leukemia. They treated her with the latest medications, including one sent from Japan by Tosiko Yuasa, who had once worked with Joliot as a lab researcher, when he taught her how to use a Wilson cloud chamber. There was no hope and Irène seemed to know it, telling a childhood friend, Aline Perrin Lapique, that she didn't fear death because she had had a beautiful life.

She died of leukemia on March 17, 1956, aged fifty-eight. Almost everyone agreed that it had been caused by her work with X-rays during World War I and subsequent years of proximity to radioactive substances. It was named a day of national mourning in France.

Irène's death was a terrible blow to Joliot, who had lived and worked with her for thirty years. His friend Ilya Ehrenburg saw theirs as "a happy marriage although they were very unlike each other. Irène was reserved and rather taciturn and Joliot, who was generally talkative, often fell silent in her presence." Joliot told Ehrenburg, " 'Irène died from what we call our occupational disease. We're more careful nowadays but in the thirties . . .' He paused and then murmured, 'I'm not finding this easy.' "

Irène was given a state funeral, her coffin first taken to the Sorbonne's main hall, where for twenty-four hours professors and students from the Faculty Sciences stood on guard in fifteen-minute shifts. Because of her pacifist views the family prevailed on the government to do without the customary military honors and guards. Following a service in the Sorbonne's courtyard, she was buried in the cemetery at Sceaux not far from her parents. There were no prayers: Irène was deeply atheist.

James Chadwick, who had beaten the Joliots to the discovery of the neutron, agreed to write Irène's obituary and asked Kowarski for help. Kowarski replied, in part: "Contrary to the current belief, she never was a Communist. She never shared her husband's thirst for a church — preferably one in which he would be a cardinal. On the other hand, no mind-controlling party or movement could tolerate Irène as a member. She found it simple to . . . distinguish between right and wrong, to know and to speak her mind. She found the main tenet of the Communist propaganda in her ideas of right. She decided that European initiatives such as CERN were wrong, and in 1954 she was quite prominent in the attack against the French ratification of CERN [European Council for Nuclear Research, at Geneva, Switzerland]. At the time Joliot was rather more subtly beginning to concede that CERN might be all right, if sufficient funds were given simultaneously to French Institutes. [Kowarski was employed at CERN.] I know little of the cause of her death. She certainly had for several years some form of anemia or lack of resistance to infection. This looks like a chronic disturbance of her blood tissues and there may have been some connection with prolonged irradiation."

To his friends and colleagues Joliot now seemed like a man racing against the clock to make sure the extensive laboratories at Orsay, near Paris, which Irène had envisioned, were completed. He frequently visited the site to discuss the progress with architects and contractors. He filled almost every waking moment with work, although he fulfilled a few political commitments with the increasing help of his secretary, Mayer. He took over Irène's positions as professor of the Faculty of Science of Paris, and director of the Curie Laboratory and the Radium Institute.

He had naturally been interested to hear the views expressed at the Twentieth Congress of the Soviet Communist Party in February 1956, as it was the first congress since Stalin's death. Then Khrushchev, in what was first a secret speech but soon became known, had exposed the excesses of Stalin's dictatorial rule and the wrongful executions during the Great Purge of the 1930s, and characterized Stalin himself as intolerant and brutal. It disillusioned many formerly true believers in Communism, some of whom left the party.

Soon after, Joliot invited Ehrenburg to visit him at Antony and was eager to discuss Stalin. "After the 20th Party Congress a lot of our intellectuals wavered," he told his Russian friend. "But I believe that our cause has made a step forward. I never deluded myself as some others did who talked about Stalin as if he were a demi-god. I remember telling [a mutual friend]: 'Take care. We mustn't believe in infallibility, we can leave that to the Catholics.' I saw many faults in the Soviet Union, but the people there were the first to make a start—it's not surprising." As they were about to enter the house, Joliot said, "Please talk about the good things going on in your country in front of the children."

At the Fourteenth Congress of the French Communist Party at Le Havre in July 1956, Joliot again referred to Khrushchev's account of Stalin's reign of terror, saying: "Certainly men are not perfect. Mistakes have been made, some of them very serious ones. And everyone can see how we judge them when they are the work of a man as important as Comrade Stalin. But these are matters which concern neither the doctrine of Marxist Leninism nor the socialist system. They are matters which concern men and one can avoid their repetition by relying on the system and referring to the doctrine. We will then be able to avoid their happening to us. This is not an excuse—far from it—but how many crimes are committed, I ask you, each day in the countries which boast of their freedom and which, on the pretext of pacification, for example, kill thousands of human beings?"

On July 6, 1956, Joliot returned to L'Arcouest with his children for the first time since Irène's death, when he noted in his diary: "House in perfect order. Dine and listen to radio with Hélène . . . Must write to Guy Mollet [recently appointed Socialist premier of France, a former English teacher and member of the Resistance. And an outspoken anti-Communist]. But is it worth the trouble! I miss Irène very much. Bed at 9:30. Depressed. Go to sleep at 10."

He sent Hélène and her husband to represent him in China in 1957 for a celebration organized by the peace movement to honor Pierre Curie and Benjamin Franklin. Joliot gave them a friendly message to deliver to Kuo-Mo-Jo. It was during a period known as "The Hundred Flowers," and there were high hopes—not realized—that China would avoid the mistakes made by the Soviet Union. During their later tour of physics labs in Shanghai and Beijing, they met Chinese physicists just returned from the United States who had brought various pieces of apparatus with them.

Joliot attended a meeting of the Bureau of the World Peace Council in Moscow in April 1958, when he also inspected several Russian laboratories, and thought that his own were every bit as good. At Dubna he was pleased to meet his former student Bruno Pontecorvo, and told him that he would quit teaching in a year and return to experimental work. He had several conversations with fellow physicists and spent an evening with his writer friend Ilya Ehrenburg.

On that same visit, Premier Khrushchev welcomed Joliot to the Kremlin, where they spoke through an interpreter for two and a half hours about how to achieve worldwide disarmament and peace. Khrushchev had told an aide to hold all telephone calls, and when the phone rang he ignored it and continued talking. The phone kept ringing. Then someone entered and whispered a few words to Khrushchev, who then answered the phone. It was obviously great news because he was soon smiling broadly. He replaced the phone, tapped Joliot on the shoulder, and made circular motions over his own head. The interpreter explained that a third Sputnik was now circling the earth.

Early in 1958 Joliot told thirteen Nobel Prize–winning chemists, who were with him at a conference at Landau near Lake Constance, that many scientists were already engaged in fundamental research in the new Orsay laboratories. Irène's dream had been fulfilled.

In the summer when Ilya Ehrenburg visited Joliot at Antony, Joliot showed him around the garden, indicating a wall of the house covered with climbing roses and a spot where tulips had once grown. "Irène had a knack of massing the colours of tulips," Joliot said. "They flowered this spring but she was no longer here to see them." A little later, he said, "I'm gripped by the feeling that I must hurry. I want to get things done. It's not that I'm over-anxious about my health, but one shouldn't take it too casually." Ehrenburg was reminded of Victor Hugo's *Art of Being a Grandfather* as he watched Joliot romping with his grandchildren, noticed the photographs of Joliot's friends in the study, and had the impression, he wrote, of "clarity, light and happiness in everything."

After going to Paris to preside over the International Congress of Nuclear Physics, Joliot returned to L'Arcouest. On a Sunday night he helped the local fishermen to bring in and mend their nets, then visited friends, sitting on the floor among children—his own, Hélène (with her husband), and Pierre were on a week's cruise—and listened to someone play guitar music. On Monday he rose at four to go fishing and on his return his boat was inspected—the inspector congratulating him on the fine condition of his medicine chest.

On Tuesday night Joliot had a sudden hemorrhage, crying out that he was done for. His housekeeper went for help and an ambulance took him to the railroad station, where he was put on a train to Paris. He received emergency surgery in the Saint-Antoine hospital, and spent the next several days sitting up in bed writing the final pages for a course of lectures on radioactivity and proofreading a piece for *The Nuclear Age*. When Hélène learned that her father was hospitalized, she hurried back to Paris by train.

Joliot was in good spirits on August 14, 1958, but he needed a blood transfusion because of postoperative septicemia. When the news reached the outside, hundreds offered their blood, but despite the doctors' efforts they were unable to save him. Hélène was at his bedside discussing laboratory problems when he died. After Joliot's death, British scientist C. F. Powell described him as "the man whose work in the field of nuclear physics won him a place among the greatest scientists of the world and whose work as a man ensured him a place in history." Like Irène's death, it was a day of national mourning. Although doctors were unable to provide a diagnosis,

Dr. Raymond Latarjet of the Radium Institute believed that Joliot died of cirrhosis of the liver caused by overexposure to polonium.

Ilya Ehrenburg flew from Moscow to Paris for Joliot's funeral with D. V. Skobeltsyn, who had worked in Joliot's laboratory in the 1930s. "We had known two different men," Ehrenburg wrote, "but the one we loved was the same."

President de Gaulle had decreed that Joliot, like Irène, should be given a state funeral, but after discussions with Joliot's family, again two ceremonies were arranged. His coffin was first placed in the Sorbonne courtyard near the seventeenth-century chapel, between memorials to Victor Hugo and Louis Pasteur, and guarded by uniformed men of the Republican Guard. A large crowd attended the funeral service: members of the governing body of the Sorbonne in red robes trimmed in ermine, ministers of state, ambassadors, academicians, and senators. Paris is invariably deserted in August, the population having escaped to the sea or the countryside, but over the next two days, thousands of people came to pay their last respects.

Braving a rainstorm, Joliot's friends, colleagues, and students, members of the peace movement, laboratory assistants, workers, and ordinary men and women gathered in the street at the entrance to the cemetery at Sceaux, where he was to be buried in a simple ceremony his family had wanted. It was the same cemetery where Pierre, Marie, and Irène were buried. Some of the crowd were in tears. Among the official wreaths on the coffin were, as Ilya Ehrenburg noticed, "flowers from the little back gardens of France." Eulogies were delivered by his friend and biographer Pierre Biquard, and members of the peace movement, the Federation of Scientific Workers, and the French Communist Party.

That evening, having been at Joliot's funeral, the British scientist J. D. Bernal; French Communist leader Laurent Casanova; Italian Communist Velio Spano; Isabelle Blume, a Belgian Socialist member of parliament; and Ilya Ehrenburg, all members of the World Peace Council, met to discuss the future of the movement. "We could not speak, our grief was too fresh," Ehrenburg wrote later. "I could see Joliot as if he were present and could not grasp the fact that he was no more. And even now, five years later, I still see him alive, and everything in me rebels against the idea that he is dead. He had said that every human being leaves a trace on this earth, but it is difficult to call his memory a trace, rather it is a wound and a landmark."

The Soviet Union named one of its ships, a mountain, and a crater detected by Luna 3 on the far side of the moon after him.

The *New York Times* summarized his life in a column and four headlines:

JOLIOT-CURIE DIES;
FRENCH PHYSICIST
Famed Nuclear Scientist
Won Nobel Prize with Wife
—Communist Leader
RECEIVED STALIN AWARD
Co-Producer of Radioactive
Element Was Ousted as
Atomic Energy Director

Le Monde reported: "News of the death of the eminent nuclear physicist, resistance hero, and distinguished public servant, Frederic Joliot-Curie, has been received by this newspaper. His death occurred on August 14 in Paris following surgery for internal hemorrhaging . . . His death is a great loss to the Republic of France. Joliot was above-average in height with dark hair and dark eyes. He was very athletic and an avid skier, sailor, tennis player, hunter, and fisherman. With Joliot's skill in conversation and abundant charm, he will be greatly missed in scientific circles as well as in Parisian society."

Nobel Prize–winning physicist Georges Charpak said: "I was with Joliot-Curie for twelve exciting years. He was a charming extrovert, but not as some say, a womanizer. Ladies ran after him, but he never encouraged them. He sometimes invited me to his home, where I met his wife and children. They were very independent people and not at all bigoted. They had lively arguments, because they didn't all share his political convictions. I, too, was a Communist in those days. Now I am a Social-Democrat. Being a member of the Communist Party he had a tendency not to deny what was official Communist propaganda. There he made a mistake. The French Communist Party was not independent of the Soviet Communist Party It was like a big and a little church."

In his brief, affectionate biography of his friend Frédéric Joliot, Pierre Biquard described him as "a man who was profoundly human and profoundly good."

Pierre Radvanyi, who had been Joliot's student and was destined to be codirector of the national laboratory "Saturne," at Saclay, recalled: "Once inside his study one forgot the people who might be waiting their turn outside the door. I must say that, for my part, I never entered his study without my heart beating faster and I never left it without having been given food for thought for several days."

CHAPTER 23

The Curie Legacy

1954–2005

Today Eve Curie Labouisse, the writer in the Curie family, lives in New York City near the United Nations building where she once worked. She is still interested in world affairs and especially in the welfare of the world's disadvantaged children.

Eve married American attorney-diplomat Henry Labouisse in November 1954. They met when he was working for the United States as chief of the Marshall Plan Mission to France, part of the effort to help Europe recover from the ravages of World War II. Then he took on what was regarded as a dangerous and thankless task as director of the Relief and Works Agency for Palestinian Refugees (UNWRA) headquartered in Beirut, where some nine hundred thousand refugees were on its rolls. Eve went with him on all of his many journeys—at his expense—and visited some of the fifty-seven refugee camps her husband inspected. He led an emergency team to enter the Gaza Strip to resume UNWRA operations in the fall of 1956 while fighting was still under way, and from there the couple went to the Congo during the 1960 crisis.

Later in 1960, as consultant for the World Bank, Labouisse led an economic survey mission to Venezuela, where he advised using "the country's funds to make services available for all classes of people, including those in remote rural areas, rather than for the construction of more sophisticated hospitals."

He was the U.S. ambassador to Greece from 1962 to 1965, when he and Eve donated a parcel of land they owned there for a city park, and constructed a kindergarten behind it with the last of the Marshall Plan funds.

Labouisse then became the executive director of UNICEF, a United Nations organization devoted to helping children and families in developing countries to get social services such as health and education. One of his first tasks was to receive the Nobel Peace Prize medal on behalf of UNICEF in Oslo on December 10, 1965.

Over the next fourteen years he and Eve traveled to over one hundred countries for UNICEF, including Tanzania, where they were made elders of the Wahehe tribe. Their last mission was to Cambodia, where UNICEF had initiated a vast emergency relief program. This entailed visits to Vietnam and to the Cambodian refugee camps along the Thailand border.

Over the years, in helping her husband, Eve had been working—like her brother-in-law, Joliot—for world peace. As Labouisse said in accepting the Nobel Prize for UNICEF, "To all of us, the Prize will be a wonderful incentive to greater efforts, in the name of peace. . . . You have reinforced our profound belief that each time UNICEF contributes, however modestly, to giving today's children a chance to grow into useful and happy individuals, it contributes to removing some of the seeds of world tension and future conflicts."

He also warned: "The longer the world tolerates the slow attrition which poverty and ignorance now wage against 800 million children in developing countries, the more likely it becomes that our hope for lasting peace will be the ultimate casualty."

Although Labouisse retired in 1979, he and Eve retained a vital and affectionate interest in the American Farm School in Thessalonika. This was a vocational training school for Greek rural youth, of which Labouisse was a trustee, and chairman of the board from 1980 to 1985, and for which he contributed a gymnasium and youth center.

He died of cancer at Memorial Sloan-Kettering Hospital on March 25, 1987, aged eighty-three. Eve Curie Labouisse continued to live and work in New York City. The Joliot-Curies' children, Hélène and Pierre, both developed into brilliant scientists. Hélène's son, Yves, is an astrophysicist mainly interested in planetology and asteroids. Hélène herself is one of the world's experts in low-energy nuclear physics and was a member of the scientific advisory committee to the French Parliament for several years. In 1957 she joined the Institute for Nuclear Physics at Orsay, which was essentially created by her parents, as a researcher paid by the National Center for Scientific Research (CNRS). There she focused in her research on a few nucleon problems and then on nuclear structure.

"The essential message I got from my parents," she told interviewer J-F Picard on June 11, 1986, "was that research first of all must be a game and a pleasure. Nothing annoyed my mother more than the martyrs-to-science image applied to her parents, Pierre and Marie Curie. I also learned that obstacles are not overcome by force but, on the contrary, by going around the difficulties, by trying multiple approaches and using the maximum of fantasy. In other words, 'playing' with the problem."

Interviewed by L'Humanité in March 2001, she said: "My parents' discovery of artificial radioactivity has had extraordinary and unexpected applications in biology. Most of modern biology is founded on the use of tracers developed by the use of artificial radioactivity. If somebody had launched a problem to obtain tracers, they certainly would not have come up with the idea of resorting to radioactivity!"

In July 2003, when asked by a reporter for the Research News of the U.S. Department of Energy, "What is your message to the public regarding fear of radiation?" she replied: "Earth is naturally radioactive; otherwise it would already be a dead planet. We live in a bath of radiation from rocks, gas and space, with some 7,000 Becquerels [the number of nuclei that decay per second] inside our [bodies]. We get enormous benefits from the use of radiation, especially in medicine. Nuclear energy, whose wastes are highly radioactive, has the advantage of producing no carbon dioxide. I regret that the necessary efforts to handle nuclear wastes properly have been underestimated for many years. New programs are developing seriously now and I am convinced that safe answers could be found to the problem."

Hélène's brother, Pierre Joliot, a biophysicist and international expert in photosynthesis, is a professor at the Collège de France and chairman of the department of cellular biology, as well as a member of the French Academy of Sciences and of the American National Academy of Science. In his 2001 book La Recherche Passionnément ("The Passionate Research") he writes: "It is moving for me to remember that shortly before his death my father spoke to an assembly of Nobel Prize–winning chemists at Lindau, when he expressed his nostalgia for a recent era when the basic nuclear physics experiments could be done on a wooden table in a small laboratory. Then, the time necessary from conception to the realization, and then to the interpretation of an experiment, was days, not years."

During that speech Joliot also said: "Hardly twenty-five years ago, the artillery used to explore the atomic nucleus could be contained in a flask of a few cubic centimeters . . . The researcher, whose mentality must be very similar to that of the artist, felt himself close to the phenomenon he was studying . . . The worker could give a free run to his creative originality . . . Sometimes as the poet sees the beat of a bird's wings, so he was carried to the discovery." As for his own work, Pierre Joliot wrote: "I always find renewed pleasure in discovering the complex and unexpected figures which come on my computer screen and which translate symbolically the multiple readings happening when in contact with the photosynthesis apparatus, which is the object of my investigation. Such was the pleasure of Pierre and Marie Curie admiring in the darkness of their laboratory the strange luminosity emitted by a receptacle containing radium."

In 1994 the Curie Museum in Paris was renamed "The Museum and Archives for the Radium Institute, Pierre and Marie Curie, and Frédéric and Irène Joliot-Curie," which includes a public museum, an archival service, and a library of photographs. The museum at 11 rue Pierre et Marie Curie is on the ground floor of the oldest building in the Curie Institute. And it is where Marie Curie and Irène and Frédéric Joliot-Curie did much of their research. In the garden outside the buildings are busts of Marie and Pierre. Visitors can see a sheet of paper with Pierre and Marie's calculation of the atomic mass of radium and handwriting samples of both scientists. Visitors can also see one of their thumbprints, which dates from 1902 and is still radioactive.

In April 1995, when Pierre and Marie Curie's ashes were to be reinterred in the Panthéon, France's national mausoleum, scientists found that the level of radium emanations within Marie Curie's coffin was significantly lower than the maximum accepted safe levels of public exposure and concluded that, considering the very long half-life of radium (1,620 years), her final illness and death was caused not by extended exposure to radium but as a direct result of her overexposure to X-rays in World War I.

Marie Curie would be the first woman whose achievements earned her the right to be buried alongside France's greatest men, among them Louis Braille, Jean-Jacques Rousseau, Voltaire, Emile Zola, Victor Hugo, Jean Perrin, Paul Langevin, and World War II Resistance hero Jean Moulin.

On the day of the Curies' reinterrment in the flag-draped Panthéon, thousands lined the streets, which were covered in white carpeting, along which Republican Guardsmen led the way to the music of "La Marseillaise." Faculty from the Curie Institute followed with the cortège, and after them came high school students carrying banners bearing Greek letters in red, white, and blue, representing alpha, beta, and gamma rays.

Seated on a platform under the Panthéon's dome were the Curies' daughter Eve, and their grandchildren, Hélène Langevin-Joliot and Pierre Joliot.

As Marie Curie biographer Barbara Goldsmith recalled: "Pierre-Gilles de Gennes—the director of the school . . . where Marie and Pierre had discovered . . . radium and polonium—spoke first, saying that the Curies represented the collective memory of the French people 'and the beauty of self-sacrifice.'"

Poland's president, Lech Walesa, then praised Marie as both a Polish patriot and a French one.

Dying of cancer, French president François Mitterrand made what would be his last speech, which he dedicated to the women of France. He said: "The transfer of Pierre and Marie Curie's ashes to our most sacred sanctuary is not only an act of remembrance, but also an act in which France affirms her faith in science, in research, and we affirm our respect for those whom we consecrate here, their force and their lives. Today's ceremony is a deliberate outreach on our part from the Panthéon to the first lady of our honored history. It is another symbol that captures the attention of our nation and the exemplary struggle of a woman who decided to impose her abilities in a society where abilities, intellectual exploration, and public responsibility were reserved for men."

The crowd in the street roared its approval.

In April 2005, France 2 Television, the main state network, invited viewers to vote for "The Greatest Frenchman of All Time." The viewers did not restrict themselves to men. Charles de Gaulle topped the list, with Louis Pasteur second. Number four, and the first woman on the list, was Marie Curie.

Notes

Chapter 1: Pierre Curie

2   *"What shall I become?"*   Eve Curie, *Madame Curie*, trans. Vincent Sheean (New York: Pocket Books, 1964), 132–133; Marie Curie, *Autobiographical Notes*, (New York: Macmillan, 1924), 45.

3   *"During 676 days he treated"*   Julian Winston, review of *Homeopathy in the Irish Potato Famine*, by Francis Treuherz, *New England Journal of Homeopathy* 5, no. 1 (winter 1996): 66.

3   A *fervent practitioner*   "To you—whose lives are devoted to the application of scientific knowledge—whose interests are involved in the embracing Truth and rejecting Error—whose feelings are often tortured at the bed of sickness, by the inefficiency of your present remedial means—to you I venture to dedicate this work, in the earnest hope that it may attract your attention to the practical and all-important truths contained in the doctrines of Hahnemann—truths which it is the object of the following pages to illustrate. . . . I ask you to test by actual experiment the homeopathic doctrines, instead of contemptuously rejecting them without trial, and condemning them without proof."
    Dr. Samuel Hahnemann was the founder of homeopathy. Partly from fear of losing customers, conventional doctors and chemists greeted the new treatment with scorn and derision. Curie responded to them vigorously in his book: "Thunder and lightning were observed hundreds of years before our knowledge of electricity enabled us satisfactorily to explain their origin, yet no one, on that account, doubted their existence. The heavenly bodies moved in their orbits, and ponderous substances were attracted to the earth, thousands of years before Newton arose to discover and explain the laws which regulated their motions; so likewise, the law, 'Similia Similibus,' co-existent with electricity and gravitation, remained unknown till the genius of Hahnemann discovered, developed, and applied it to the cure of disease." P. F. Curie, M.D., *Practice of Homeopathy* (London: Medi-T, 1838).

4   *"It is clear,"*   Marie Curie, *Autobiographical Notes*, 34–35.

4   *"Pierre's intellectual"*   Ibid., 34.

6   *"Yesterday," he reported,*   Phillip Knightley, *The First Casualty: The War Correspondent as Hero, Propagandist, and Myth Maker* (New York: Harcourt Brace Jovanovich, 1975), 49–50.

7   *Though, strangely, he wrote*   Eve Curie, *Madame Curie*, 132.

8   *The big difference*   Pierre to Marie, July 29, 1897, Robert Reid, *Marie Curie* (New York: New American Library, 1975), 42.

8   *Though nominally a Protestant*   Susan Quinn, *Marie Curie: A Life* (Reading, Mass.: Addison-Wesley, 1996), 107.

9   *These were therapeutic*   Marie Curie, *Autobiographical Notes*, 42.

10   *"When I was twenty"*   Pierre to Marie, September 7, 1894, Eve Curie, *Madame Curie*, 139.

10   *"Women, much more than men,"*   Marie Curie, "An Intimate Picture of Pierre Curie," *The Living Age* 149 (June 9, 1923): 584.

10   *He confided to his diary*   Marie Curie, *Autobiographical Notes*, 44.
11   *"Their experiment," she wrote*   Ibid., 46.
12   *But in time, though still shy*   Quinn, *Marie Curie*, 112–113.
13   *As he explained*   Marie Curie, *Autobiographical Notes*, 70–71.
13   *"Thanks to you Lyon"*   Quinn, *Marie Curie*, 112.
13   *"I pray you do not do so"*   Marie Curie, *Autobiographical Notes*, 71–72.
14   *"I thank you very much"*   Eve Curie, *Madame Curie*, 130.
14   *Had Kelvin claimed*   Marie Curie, "An Intimate Picture of Pierre Curie," 557–558.
15   *"What difference is there,"*   Ibid., 588.

Chapter 2: Marie Salomea Sklodowska

18   *As she later explained*   Eve Curie, *Madame Curie*, 22.
19   *Then, at his prompting*   Ibid., 20.
20   *Marie's happiest times*   Marie Curie, *Autobiographical Notes*, 161.
20   *"Her influence over me"*   Ibid., 157–158.
21   *Although Marie still went*   Eve Curie, *Madame Curie*, 28.
21   *She hated its denigration*   Marie Curie, *Autobiographical Notes*, 159.
21   *And she expressed her ambivalence*   Eve Curie, *Madame Curie*, 35.
22   *As Marie stared down at her*   Ibid., 33.
23   *In letters to Kazia*   Ibid., 39–40.
24   *Several weeks later*   Ibid., 43.
24   *Marie also recited a poem*   Ibid., 45.
25   *To help out, Joseph*   Ibid., 50.
25   *"I shouldn't like my worst enemy"*   Ibid., 60.
26   *As she later wrote*   Marie Curie, *Autobiographical Notes*, 164–165.
26   *After a month*   Eve Curie, *Madame Curie*, 64.
27   *Some girls she met*   Ibid., 67–68.
28   *According to Marie's daughter Eve*   Ibid., 70.
28   *"In one instant the social"*   Ibid., 75.
29   *Marie wrote to their brother*   Ibid., 79
29   *Disillusioned and disheartened*   Reid, *Marie Curie*, 20.
29   *"That tale has been spread about"*   Eve Curie, *Madame Curie*, 79.
29   *"Ah, if only I could"*   Ibid., 90.
29   *In October 1888*   Ibid., 80–81.
30   *"Everybody says that I have changed"*   Ibid., 82–83.
30   *By July 1890*   Ibid., 84.
31   *"I dreamed of Paris"*   Ibid., 87–88.
32   *There, on free evenings*   Marie Curie, *Autobiographical Notes*, 167.
32   *"A scientist in his laboratory"*   Eve Curie, *Madame Curie*, 91–92.
32   *"[Marie] has a secret"*   Quinn, *Marie Curie*, 82–83.
33   *"The letter's melodramatic hints"*   Rosalynd Pflaum, *Grand Obsession: Madame Curie and Her World* (New York: Doubleday, 1989), 18.
33   *"It would restore me spiritually"*   Eve Curie, *Madame Curie*, 92.
33   *"Warsaw citizens still remember"*   Reid, *Marie Curie*, 24.
34   *"Dear and Honored Sir"*   Eve Curie, *Madame Curie*, 102.
35   *And Bronia recalled with a laugh*   Ibid., 105.
35   *Her usual state of mind*   Marie Curie, *Autobiographical Notes*, 171.
36   *"Higher, higher, up she climbs"*   Quinn, *Madame Curie*, 91–92.
37   *But "the next day she began again"*   Eve Curie, *Madame Curie*, 115.
38   *By September 1893*   Marie to Joseph, September 15, 1893, ibid., 120.
38   *Marie again wrote*   Marie to Joseph, March 18, 1894, ibid., 121.

Chapter 3: Pierre and Marie in Love

40   *He had auburn hair*   Marie Curie, *Autobiographical Notes*, 73–74.
40   *His slow, calm speech*   Eve Curie, *Madame Curie*, 128.
41   *Pierre, she wrote*   Ibid.
41   *Mine "was a poor little"*   Marie Curie, *Autobiographical Notes*, 74.
41   *In an adoring biography*   Eve Curie, *Madame Curie*, 124–125.
42   *For seven years she had avoided*   Ibid.
42   *Lamotte longed to see her*   Lamotte to Marie, June 1894, Quinn, *Marie Curie*, 101.
42   *Marie sensed that he meant*   Eve Curie, *Madame Curie*, 135.
43   *"We have promised each other"*   Ibid., 136–137.
43   *Then a step forward*   Ibid., 139–140.
44   *There, Marie felt immediate*   Marie Curie, *Autobiographical Notes*, 29.
44   *When Pierre first mentioned*   Eve Curie, *Madame Curie*, 141.
44   *If Marie was not yet in love*   Ibid., 142.
44   *As her daughter Eve*   Marie Curie, *Autobiographical Notes*, 67.
44   *News of Marie's engagement*   Reid, *Marie Curie*, 39.
44   *Her brother, Joseph, agreed*   Joseph to Marie, July 16, 1895, Eve Curie, *Madame Curie*, 142–143.
45   *Marie explained her difficult*   Marie to Kazia, July 1895, ibid., 143.

Chapter 4: Mutual Adoration

46   *As Pierre's mother had assured*   Eve Curie, *Madame Curie*, 145.
48   *Discussing it with a woman*   Reid, *Marie Curie*, 67.
49   *Though she wanted a child*   Marie to Kazia, March 2, 1897, ibid., 155.
49   *And she wrote to her brother*   Marie to Joseph Sklodowski, March 31, 1897, ibid., 156.
49   *This was the first time*   Pierre to Marie, July 1897, ibid.
49   *To which she replied*   Marie to Pierre, ibid.
49   *She thought of him*   Marie Curie, *The Literary Digest* 149 (June 9, 1923): vol. 149, 50, 52.
50   *Their daughter Eve explained*   Eve Curie, *Madame Curie*, 157.
50   *Their work was "precious"*   Marie Curie, *Autobiographical Notes*, 179.
51   *He made himself useful*   Eve Curie, *Madame Curie*, 159.
51   *The London correspondent*   Denis Brian, *Pulitzer: A Life* (New York: John Wiley & Sons), 2001, 226–228.
51   *Students paraded*   Ibid., 228.
51   *And Marie explained why*   Eve Curie, *Madame Curie*, 150.
52   *Later, asked by a reporter*   H. J. W. Dam, *McClure's Magazine* 6, no. 5 (April 1896).
54   *In 1897 a U.S. Army doctor*   Abraham Pais, *Inward Bound* (New York: Oxford University Press, 1982), 98.
54   *A contemporary English magazine*   History of X-Rays, University of Dundee, Museum Collections, p. 1, www.dundee.ac.uk/museum/xray.htm.
54   *Edward Reid, professor of physiology*   Ibid., 3.
54   *As his wife told a relative*   Walter C. Alvarez, *American Man of Medicine*, comp. David H. Scott (New York: Pyramid, 1976), 318.
55   *On March 1*   William Crookes, *Proceedings of the Royal Society* 83, no. 20 (1910).
55   *According to Robert L. Wolke*   Robert L. Wolke, "Marie Curie's Doctoral Thesis: Prelude to a Nobel Prize," *Journal of Chemical Education* 65, no. 7 (July 1988): 563.
56   *Marie hoped "to determine"*   Mme. Sklodowska Curie, "Radium and Radioactivity," *Century Magazine* (January 1904): 462.
56   *As she later explained*   Marie Curie's Nobel lecture, December 11, 1911 (New York: Elsevier, 1996), 202–212.
56   *After several weeks*   Marie Curie, "Radium and Radioactivity."

57   Then she "simply put"   Reid, Marie Curie, 62.

57   Because neither she nor Pierre   Les Comptes rendus de l'Académie des sciences (official journal of the Academy of Sciences) trans. Carmen Giunta 126 (1898): 1,101–1,103.

57   Biographer Robert Reid pointed out   Reid, Marie Curie, 63.

58   She confided this daring hypothesis   Eve Curie, Madame Curie, 166.

59   Their joint report   Comptes Rendus 127 (1898): 175–178.

59   On July 20, 1898   Eve Curie, Madame Curie, 172.

60   Because of Irène   Marie Curie, Literary Digest (June 9, 1923): 50.

60   Demarçay died a few years later   Reid, Marie Curie, 71.

60   Despite her preoccupations   Eve Curie, Madame Curie, 171.

60   The most powerful radioactive   F. E. Close and others, The Particle Odyssey: A Journey to the Heart of the Matter (New York: Oxford University Press, 2002), 21.

61   To satisfy the skeptical   Nanny Froman lecture at the Royal Swedish Academy of Sciences in Stockholm, February 28, 1996, trans. Nancy Marshall-Lundén, http://www.nobelprize.org.

Chapter 5: Spirits, Radioactivity, and the Price of Fame

62   Determined to get it   Hélène Langevin-Joliot correspondence with author, October 29, 2002.

62   However, Professor Suess   Eve Curie, Madame Curie, 176.

63   German chemist Wilhelm Oswald   Reid, Marie Curie, 76.

63   Cornell University physics   Naomi Pasachoff, Marie Curie and the Science of Radioactivity (New York: Oxford University Press, 1996), 41.

64   Yet, she wrote   Eve Curie, Madame Curie, 179.

64   As Marie told her sister   Marie to Bronia, 1899, ibid., 181.

65   Meeting fellow physicist   Pflaum, Grand Obsession, 91.

67   In July 1900, Pierre wrote   Pierre Curie to Charles Guillaume, July 31, 1900, Curie Papers, Bibliothèque Nationale (BN).

68   According to former student   Sevriennes d'hier et d'aujourd'hui 50, December 1967, to celebrate the one hundredth anniversary of Marie Curie's birth; Quinn, Marie Curie, 213.

68   Biographer Susan Quinn   Ibid., 214.

69   A reproach, as their daughter   Eve Curie, Madame Curie, 185.

69   "seemed to violate the first law"   Rapport présenté au Congress international de physique, Paris, Gauthier-Villars, 1900.

69   In 1901 in their joint paper   Comptes rendus, March 25, 1901.

70   As he wrote to his mother   Reid, Marie Curie, 83.

70   In fact, wrote biographer Pflaum   Pflaum, Grand Obsession, 72.

70   Or, as Paul Langevin speculated   The Sorbonne's Faculty of Science online.

71   She stayed beside his coffin   Eve Curie, Madame Curie, 198–199.

71   He asked Appell   Ibid., 195.

72   She pointed out   Marie Curie, Autobiographical Notes, 115–116.

72   Pierre's longtime physicist   Georges Gouy to Pierre Curie, July 27, 1903, Bibliothèque Nationale.

72   "by his luminous expression"   Quinn, Marie Curie: Of Matter and Forces in the Physical World, 215.

73   When Thomas Alva Edison's   Abraham Pais, Inward Bound (New York: Oxford University Press, 1986): 35.

73   During the lecture   Pierre Curie, "Radium," in Smithsonian Treasury of Science, ed. Webster P. True (New York: Simon & Schuster): 265.

74   Pierre thought that radium   Reid, Marie Curie, 104.

74   Then the room at the Royal Institution   Eve Curie, Madame Curie, 216.

74   Twenty years later, Marie recalled   Ibid., 214.

75   *Finally, he turned to Marie*   Ibid., 212.
75   *And the audience broke*   David Wilson, *Rutherford* (Cambridge, Mass.: MIT Press, 1983): 254–255.
75   *The examining committee*   Nanny Froman lecture, http://www.nobelprize.org.
75   *"The chemical separations"*   Wolke, "Marie Curie's Doctoral Thesis," 572–573.
76   *However, three years previously*   At the annual public meeting of members of the Société de Secours des Amis des Sciences.
76   *She conceded that*   Wolke, "Marie Curie's Doctoral Thesis," 573.
76   *It was, however, as good as resolved*   Ibid., 572.
77   *Aware how indifferent or stubborn*   Georges Sagnac to Pierre Curie, Pflaum, *Grand Obsession*, 101.
77   *As she wrote to Bronia*   Marie to Bronia, August 23, 1903, Eve Curie, *Madame Curie*, 200.
78   *Hearing of it, Marie wrote*   Marie to Joseph, ibid., 201.
78   *Pierre impressed him*   J. J. Thomson, *Recollections and Reflections* (Toronto: Macmillan, 1937), 413.
79   *In it, they credited Pierre Curie*   Elisabeth Crawford, *The Beginnings of the Nobel Institution, The Science prizes, 1901–1915* (Cambridge: Cambridge University Press, 1984).
79   *He mentioned her role*   Pierre Curie to Mittag-Leffler, August 6, 1903, Mittag-Leffler Institute, Djursholm, Sweden.
79   *On the other hand*   Eve Curie, *Madame Curie*, 221.
81   *A day after the ceremony*   Ibid., 220–221.
81   *When a* La Liberte *reporter*   *La Liberté*, December 12, 1903.
81   *A* Le Temps *reporter*   *Le Temps*, December 10, 1903.
81   *Pierre complained to his friend*   Pierre Curie to Georges Gouy, January 22, 1904, Reid, *Marie Curie*, 112.
82   *Getting a comparatively warm reception*   Quinn, *Marie Curie*, 199.
82   *To them she was either*   *New York Herald*, December 21, 1903; *Nouvelles illustrées*; *Truth*, December 17, 1903.
83   *This caused Marie's bitter*   Eve Curie, *Madame Curie*, 250.
83   *The* New York Times *was pleased*   *New York Times*, December 11, 1903.
84   *To escape the demands of celebrity*   Eve Curie, *Madame Curie*, 231.
84   *Marie, true to her motto*   Ibid., 232.
84   *Confiding in a friend*   Pierre Curie to Charles Guillaume, January 15, 1904, Bibliothèque Nationale.
84   *A Philadelphia Evening Bulletin*   Eve Curie, *Madame Curie*, 230.
84   *Pierre also made clear*   Pais, *Inward Bound*, 99.
84   *As Pierre told his friend*   Pierre to Georges Gouy, March 20, 1904, *Curie Papers*, Bibliothèque Nationale.

Chapter 6: Psychic Researchers

88   *Marguerite was so excited*   Mindy Aloff, "Lights! Crepe! Action!" *New York Times*, September 7, 1997.
88   *Pierre's father invariably*   Eve Curie, *Madame Curie*, 240–241.
88   *Or, as Pierre put it*   Reid, *Marie Curie*, 117.
88   *He also told his audience*   Pierre Curie's Nobel lecture, "Radioactive Substances, Especially Radium," June 6, 1905, http://www.nobelprize.org.
89   *Having given his Nobel audience*   Ibid.
89   *Pierre had reason to fear*   Captain Ferrie to Pierre, January 29, 1900, Curie Papers, Bibliothèque Nationale.
89   *Henri Poincaré once*   Reid, *Marie Curie*, 117.

89   *What apparently did the trick*   Mascart to Pierre Curie, May 22, 1905, Bibliothèque Nationale.

90   *Hela recalled how*   Hela Szalay's memoir, Quinn, *Marie Curie*, 220–221.

90   *When the next woman stared*   Ibid., 223.

90   *He once told Marie*   Pierre to Marie, September 17, 1894, Bibliothèque Nationale.

91   *Neapolitan Dr. Ercole Chiaia*   Denis Brian, *The Enchanted Voyager: The Life of J. B. Rhine* (Englewood Cliffs, N.J.: Prentice Hall, 1982), 3.

91   *Harvard's William James*   Flournoy to James, March 15, 1910, Robert C. LeClair, ed., *The Letters of William James and Theodore Flournoy* (Madison: University of Wisconsin Press, 1966), 227.

91   *He wrote that the levitating table*   Anna Hurwic, *Pierre Curie* (Paris: Flammarion, 1995), 248–249.

92   *On July 24, 1905, he told*   Ibid., 249.

92   *Published reports of the Curies' tests*   John E. Coover, "Metapsychics and the Incredulity of Psychologists," in *The Case For and Against Psychical Belief*, Carl Murchison, ed. (Worcester, Mass: Clark University, 1927), 251.

93   *January 1906 started well*   *The Oxford Book of the Supernatural*, ed. D. J. Enright (New York: Oxford University Press, 1994), 43.

93   *The lab, he wrote*   Eve Curie, *Madame Curie*, 249–250.

94   *"Did I eat a beefsteak?"*   Ibid., 239–240.

94   *But, unlike Irène*   "I guess I was born with blue eyes but, ever since I could look at a mirror, they have been a mixture of green and brown." Letter to author from Eve Curie Labouisse, November 5, 2002.

94   *As her mother's eventual biographer*   Eve Curie, *Madame Curie*, 252–253.

95   *George Jaffe, a research assistant*   George Jaffe, *Journal of Chemical Education* 29 (1952): 230.

95   *In the spring of 1906*   Pierre to Georges Gouy, April 14, 1906, Bibliothèque Nationale.

95   *Danne had traded on*   Communication with author from Pierre Radvanyi, November 21, 2002.

95   *"The result is"*   Pierre to Gouy, April 14, 1906, Bibliothèque Nationale.

97   *Poincaré was skeptical*   Marie Curie, *Autobiographical Notes*, 147.

Chapter 7: Pierre Curie's Last Day

100   *"My son is dead"*   Eve Curie, *Madame Curie*, 259.

101   *As Eve wrote*   From Marie's journal, April 30, 1906. All these and subsequent quotes from Marie Curie's diary are from Marie Curie, *Pierre Curie* (Paris: Editions Odile Jacob, 1966), 169–188, trans. Martine Brian.

101   *"Prof. Curie, the discoverer"*   *New York Times*, April 20, 1906, 11.

102   *Paul Langevin, his former student*   Quinn, *Marie Curie*, 238.

102   *Lord Kelvin, among the first*   Marie Curie, *Pierre Curie*, 132.

102   *Jean Perrin: "His devotion"*   Ibid., 129–130.

102   *Ernest Rutherford: "Our scientific"*   Ibid., 147–148.

103   *"Sixty years later"*   Pflaum, *Grand Obsession*, 132.

103   *Marie recalled how*   Marie Curie, *Pierre Curie*, 169–188.

104   *After locking the door*   Francoise Giroud, *Marie Curie: A Life*, trans. Lydia Davis (New York: Holmes and Meier, 1986), 143–144.

105   *The day before Pierre's brother*   Pflaum, *Grand Obsession*, 134.

107   *To give herself courage*   Reid, *Marie Curie*, 130.

107   *As a prelude*   Pflaum, *Grand Obsession*, 141.

107   *And quipped that "if a woman"*   Reid, *Marie Curie*, 132.

107   *A Figaro reporter*   Pflaum, *Grand Obsession*, 142.

107   *Pierre had ended his last lecture*   Naomi Pasachoff, *Marie Curie and the Science of Radioactivity*. (New York: Oxford University Press, 1996).

108   *Yet he wrote, "I hope"*   Jacques Curie to Marie, April 18, 1907, Bibliothèque Nationale.

Chapter 8: Rescuing Langevin from His Wife

109   *As a child, intrigued*   Sharon Bertsch McGrayne, *Nobel Prize Women in Science: Their Lives, Struggles and Momentous Discoveries* (Washington, D.C.: Joseph Henry Press, 2000), 121–122.

110   *Dr. Curie never revisited*   Eve Curie, *Madame Curie*, 280.

110   *He enclosed a written*   Eugènie Cotton, *Les Curies* (Paris: Editions Seghers, 1963), 75–76.

110   *She recalled how Marie*   Quinn, *Marie Curie*, 250.

110   *But Marie admitted*   Eve Curie, *Madame Curie*, 279.

110   *Irène recalled that*   Irène Joliot-Curie, "Marie Curie, ma mère," *Europe* 108 (1954): 97.

111   *Eve explained how*   Information provided to author by Eve Curie Labouisse, November 5, 2002.

111   *Worried about their further education*   Françoise Giroud, *Marie Curie: Une Femme Honorable* (Paris: Fayard, 1982), 152.

112   *Should a student make*   Eve Curie, *Madame Curie*, 285.

112   *As Eve remembered*   Ibid., 287.

112   *"She toughened them"*   Giroud, *Marie Curie*, 153.

113   *Eve acknowledged*   Eve Curie, *Madame Curie*, 286.

113   *Rutherford quickly came*   Ernest Rutherford, *Nature* 74 (1906): 634.

114   *She saved all their letters*   Gilette Ziegler, ed., *Marie Curie–Irène Correspondence* (Paris: Les Editeurs Français Réunis, 1974), 26.

115   *"My dear Me"*   Ziegler, *Marie Curie–Irène Correspondence*, 27.

116   *When Dr. Curie died*   Marie Curie's Notebook, Bibliothèque Nationale.

117   *He had met Albert Einstein*   Denis Brian, *Einstein: A Life* (New York: John Wiley & Sons, 1996), 85.

118   *During the summer of 1910*   Irène to Marie, August 6, 1910, Bibliothèque Nationale.

119   *In another Letter Marie*   *L'Ouevre*, November 23, 1911, 1.

119   *And in one of his replies*   Ibid.

120   *"I will never forget"*   Hélène Perrin's court testimony in the French press.

120   *"Why should anyone"*   André Langevin, *Paul Langevin, Mon Père: L'Homme et l'ouevre* (Paris: Les Editeurs Français Réunis, 1971), 63.

121   *Comparing her with the lively*   Rutherford Papers, Cambridge University Library, undated.

121   *This, as she later explained*   Marie Curie, *Pierre Curie*, 201.

121   *Subsequently, Marie wrote*   Ibid.

121   *It was a friendly gesture*   Rutherford to Boltwood, December 14, 1910, Yale University Library.

122   *Marie also told Henriette*   Giroud, *Marie Curie*, 169.

123   *To prove her inadequacy*   Reid, *Marie Curie*, 157.

124   *"You are too noble"*   Georges Urbain to Marie Curie, January 23, 1911, Bibliothèque Nationale.

125   *"the election of M Branly"*   Charles Guillaume to Marie Curie, January 25, 1911, ibid.

Chapter 9: Battered by the Press

126   *Someone, he told her*   Marcel Brillouin Papers, American Institute of Physics Archives.

127   *She implored Marguerite to help*   Giroud, *Marie Curie*, 168–169.

127   *After their return*   Ibid., 169.

128   *It read: "Mathematical"*   Marie Curie to Professor Weiss, November 17, 1911, Zurich Polytechnic Archives.

129   *"For sentimental reasons"*   David Wilson, *Rutherford: Simple Genius*. (Cambridge, Mass.: MIT Press, 1984), 257.

130   *Obviously aimed at*   Giroud, *Marie Curie*, 171–172.

130   *She was quoted as saying*   Ibid., 173–174.

131   *As for "the horror story"*   Albert Einstein, *The Collected Papers of Albert Einstein: The Swiss Years, Correspondence 1902–1914* Vol. 5, Doc. 303, trans. Anna Beck (Princeton, N.J.: Princeton University Press, 1995), 219–220.

131   *Pierre's brother damned*   Quinn, *Marie Curie*, 311–312.

131   *"The woman who was once your*   Giroud, *Marie Curie*, 175.

131   *This scared* Le Journal's *reporter*   Ibid.

132   *She was quoted as saying, "The attack upon me"*   New York World, November 6, 1911, 6.

132   *"You have been awarded the Nobel Prize"*   Giroud, *Marie Curie*, 175.

132   *"We share your sadness"*   Karin Blanc, *Marie Curie et le Nobel*, Uppsala Studies in the History of Sciences, 26, trans. Martine Brian, 1999. 125–126.

133   *Literate, often witty, and always provocative*   Gordon Wright, *France in Modern Times: From the Enlightenment to the Present* (New York: W.W. Norton & Co., 1987), 264.

133   *One contributor, Léon Daudet*   Ibid.

133   *As André Debierne wrote to*   Blanc, *Marie Curie*, 95.

134   *They "will dumbfound people"*   Giroud, *Marie Curie*, 176, 177.

134   *He was an ugly, aggressive little man*   Reid, *Marie Curie*, 172.

134   *Boasting that he held his pen*   Giroud, *Marie Curie*, 177, 179.

135   *"Get the foreign woman out!"*   Pflaum, *Grand Obsession*, 174.

135   *"an ambitious Pole"*   Ibid.

136   *"All right," Borel replied*   Giroud, *Marie Curie*, 182.

136   *He interrupted her frantic protest*   Nanny Froman lecture at the Royal Swedish Academy of Sciences in Stockholm, February 28, 1996, 17; http://www.nobelprize.org and Marguerite Borel [Camille Marbo, pseud.] *A travers deux siècles, 1883–1967*, trans. Martine Brian (Paris: Bernard Grasset, 1968).

136   The New York Times *headed its account*   New York Times, Nov. 24, 1911, 3.

137   *"Another Curie Duel"*   San Francisco Examiner, November 25, 1911, 1.

137   *"Pistol Duel Pantomine [sic]"*   Los Angeles Times, November 26, 1911, part 1, 5.

138   *"A perfidious campaign"*   Eve Curie, *Madame Curie*, 293–294.

139   *"When these horrible accusations"*   Blanc, *Marie Curie*, 85–122. This letter and the rest of the correspondence about whether or not to award Marie Curie her second Nobel Prize are from this source.

141   *"Suffering though I was"*   Marie Curie, *Autobiographical Notes*, 203.

142   *"in recognition of the part"*   Nobel e-Museum, Official Web site of the Nobel Foundation, http://www.nobelprize.org.

142   *She acknowledged that she and Pierre*   Ibid.

143   *That same day, the* New York World *reported*   New York World, December 11, 1911, 11.

143   *"The Langevin divorce case"*   New York Times, December 17, 1911, part 3, 2.

143   *"Mme Curie's fever has gone down"*   Perrin to Rutherford, Rutherford papers, Cambridge University Library, undated letter.

Chapter 10: Surgery and Suffragettes

145   *illness as appendicitis*   London Times, January 5, 1912, 3E.

147   *"We are losing confidence"*   Eve Curie, *Madame Curie*, 296.

147   *"Yesterday I read in Le Matin"*   Marie Curie–Irène Correspondence, Irène to Marie, July 19, 1912.

148   *"Last evening André"*   Ibid., July 27, 1912, 59–60.

148   *Next day, Irène wrote*   Ibid., July 28, 1912, 61.

149   *Hertha explained, "I am a member"*   Ayrton to Curie, May 28, 1912, Bibliothèque Nationale.

149   *Marie replied*   Evelyn Sharp, *Hertha Ayrton: A Memoir* (London: Edward Arnold, 1926), 237.

149   *"We had to discredit the Government"*   Emmeline Pankhurst, *My Own Story* (New York: Hearst International Library, 1914), 282–283.

150   *"Errors are notoriously hard"*   Reid, *Marie Curie*, 190.

150   *While in England, Marie wrote*   Quinn, *Marie Curie*, 340.

151   *She explained to Rutherford*   Marie Curie to Rutherford, October 17, 1912, Cambridge University Library.

151   *Ramsey often denigrated*   Evelyn Sharp, *Hertha Ayrton: A Memoir* (London: Edward Arnold, 1926), 246.

151   *The condition of the country*   Eve Curie, *Madame Curie*, 283.

152   *After the visit, Einstein wrote*   Einstein to Marie Curie, April 3, 1913, Einstein, *Collected Papers*, 332.

152   *"The derivatives are coming along"*   Pflaum, *Grand Obsession*, 191.

153   *Eve's biographer wrote*   Ibid., 188–189.

154   *The letter included a trigonometry problem*   Marie to Irène, September 15, 1913, Bibliothèque Nationale.

154   *She was amused by the ceremony*   Ibid.

154   *A. S. Eve, who attended*   A. S. Eve, *Rutherford: Being the Life and Letters of the Rt. Hon. Lord Rutherford, O.M.* (New York: Macmillan, 1939), 223.

154   *Rutherford had said that the atom*   Marie Curie, "Sur la loi fondamentale des transformations radioactives," Ouevres de Pierre Curie (Paris: Gauthier-Villars, 1908), 507–510.

155   *Regaud, he recalled, listened to Marie*   Reid, *Marie Curie*, 196.

Chapter 11: "Little Curies" and World War I

156   *"It's all the more important for us"*   Marie–Irène Curie Correspondence, Irène to Marie, August 8, 1914, 108–109.

157   *He felt sorry for this exhausted woman*   Eve Curie, *Madame Curie*, 309.

157   *If that should happen*   Marie to Irène, August 28, 1914, ibid., 306.

157   *"I'm afraid you're going to worry"*   Marie–Irène Curie Correspondence, 126.

158   *to talk to "the boor"*   Marie–Irène Curie Correspondence, September 2, 1914, 130.

158   *"they say I'm a German spy"*   Ibid, September 3, 1914, 131.

159   *According to Winston Churchill*   Winston S. Churchill, *Great Contemporaries* (London: Fontana Books, 1965), 74.

159   *Now, as Marie walked*   Marie Curie, *Autobiographical Notes*, 206.

159   *Irène was almost frantic*   Marie to Irène, September 6, 1914, McGrayne, *Nobel Prize Women*, 126.

160   *Marie talked them into*   Eve Curie, *Madame Curie*, 310.

160   *"The day I leave is not fixed yet"*   Ibid., 313.

161   *"she would climb into the front seat"*   Ibid., 311.

161   *To be more self-reliant*   Ibid., 312.

162   *"Here we are at a semi-luxurious"*   Jean Perrin to Paul Langevin, January 25, 1915, Langevin, *Paul Langevin*, 79–80.

162   *"Dear friend, I have just read"*   Marie Curie to Paul Langevin, ibid., 80.

162   *"Some German aeroplanes"*   Eve Curie, *Madame Curie*, 314.

163   *As a pacifist he had "speculated"*   Brian, *Einstein*, 94.

163   *As Eve recalled*   Eve Curie, *Madame Curie*, 314–315.

164   *Her affectionate nephew*   Maurice Curie to Marie, February 23, 1915, Bibliothèque Nationale.

164   *"Dearest Aunt"*   Ibid., June 11, 1915.

164   *"doctors encased"*   Pflaum, *Grand Obsession*, 209.

164   *To Marie's great delight*   Eve Curie, *Madame Curie*, 318.

164   *Another student*   Reid, *Marie Curie*, 208.

164   *"Bullet in the forearm"*   Ibid., 202.

165   *"To hate the very idea of war"*   Marie Curie, *Autobiographical Notes*, 216.

165   *"The memory of the thousands"*   Eve Curie, *Madame Curie*, 320.

165   *When one day he arrived*   Irène Joliot-Curie, "Marie Curie," 103.

166   *"My mother had no more doubts"*   McGrayne, *Nobel Prize Women*, 117.

166   *"slept [in a tent] under"*   Irène to Marie, September 13, 1915, *Marie–Irène Curie Correspondence*, 171.

166   *At Hoogstade, for example*   Marie Curie, *La Radiologie et la Guerre* (Paris: Alcan, 1921), 107.

167   *"I asked for curtains"*   Irène to Marie, October 1916, *Marie–Irène Curie Correspondence*, 190.

167   *After making the Channel crossing*   Eve, *Rutherford*, 377.

167   *That afternoon he went*   Ibid.

Chapter 12: A Gift of Radium from the United States

171   *With those who had not signed*   Hurwic, *Pierre Curie*, 219.

171   *"Either the Germans have to be"*   Eve Curie, *Madame Curie*, 324.

171   *"I entirely share your aspirations"*   Marie to Rolland, June 26, 1919, Quinn, *Marie Curie*, 378–379.

172   *"Don't you agree that Israel"*   Brian, *Einstein*, 374.

172   *Irène's participation*   Marie Curie—War Duty (1914–1919), "A Military Radiotherapy Service," Naomi Pasachoff, AIP History, http://www.aip.org/history/curie/war2.

172   *To Eve, who had an*   McGrayne, *Nobel Prize Women*, 127.

172   *"had to have limitless space"*   Eve Curie, *Madame Curie*, 377.

173   *"I hope our Evette"*   Marie to Irène, September 3, 1919, ibid., 326–327.

174   *"She will see no one"*   Marie Curie, *Autobiographical Notes*, 12–13.

174   *"in the small bare office"*   Ibid., 16.

175   *"You have only one gram?"*   Eve Curie, *Madame Curie*, 338.

175   *"There were no patents"*   Marie Curie, *Autobiographical Notes*, 17–18.

177   *"What extraordinary event"*   Marie Curie, *Pierre Curie*, 21–22. "[Marie Curie] expressed regret that her husband had not lived to receive the honors due him. She said that the primitiveness of their laboratory and the difficulties under which they worked gave an air of romance to the discovery, but that this romantic element had not been an advantage. 'It exhausted our strength and delayed our success,' she declared."

178   *"I am closely related"*   *New York Times*, February 23, 1921, 12.

179   *"I left France to go on this"*   Marie Curie to Henriette Perrin, May 10, 1921, Eve Curie, *Madame Curie*, 341.

179   *"Show me where that switch is"*   Reid, *Marie Curie*, 227–228.

180   *"Radium is a positive cure"*   *New York Times*, May 12, 1921, 1.

181   *"Naturally you've brought your"*   Eve Curie, *Madame Curie*, 344.

181   *"she seemed dazed"*   *Springfield Republican*, May 17, 1921.

183   *"first among women"*   *Daily Hampshire Gazette*, May 14, 1921.

183   *"I am very grateful"*   Ibid.

183   *"Doubt has been expressed"*   *Springfield Republican*, May 16, 1921.

183   *"When radium was discovered"*   Ellen S. Richards, "The Discovery of Radium," address by Madame M. Curie at Vassar College, May 14, 1921, Monograph No. 2 (Poughkeepsie, N.Y.: Vassar College, 1921), n.p.

184   *"A quarter of a century"*   *Springfield Republican*, May 16, 1921.

185   *"Not next week. Not tomorrow."*   Eve Curie, *Madame Curie*, 347.

185   *"an adopted daughter of France"*   *New York Times*, May 21, 1921, 15.

185   *"the soul of radium"*   Giroud, *Marie Curie*, 241.

185   *"You, the chief"*   *Science*, "Mme. Curie's Visit to the United States," New Series, 53, no. 1378, May 27, 1921, 497–498.

187   *He certainly valued the product*   Ben A. Franklin, "U.S. Testing Workers for Effects of 13 Years Amid Atomic Wastes," *New York Times*, May 5, 1979, A1.

187   *"more than one hundred thousand dollars"*   Marie Curie, *Autobiographical Notes*, 228–229.

187   *"when they were not representing"*   Eve Curie, *Madame Curie*, 349.

188   *She began to leave trains*   Ibid.

188   *"I cannot go on there"*   Reid, *Marie Curie*, 233.

188   *"The three days on the train"*   Eve Curie, *Madame Curie*, 350.

188   *"surpassed all the others"*   Ibid.

189   *When he first met her in 1908*   Boltwood to Rutherford, October 11, 1908, Lawrence Badash, ed., *Rutherford and Boltwood: Letters on Radioactivity* (New Haven, Conn.: Yale University Press, 1969).

189   *Nevertheless, when she did visit*   Ibid., July 14, 1921.

189   *Her friend Albert Einstein*   Ibid., 346–347.

189   *"Let me look at you one more time"*   Giroud, *Marie Curie*, 243.

189   *"What do you think of the Carpentier-Dempsey match?"*   Reid, *Marie Curie*, 236.

190   *"Madame Curie," she wrote, "returned to France"*   Meloney to Stokes, July 27, 1921, Yale University Library.

190   *"I have suffered so much"*   Marie to Bronia, August 1921, Giroud, *Marie Curie*, 255.

190   *"I couldn't think of you more tenderly"*   Marie to Irène, September 10, 1921, Bibliothèque Nationale.

191   *"I'm happy that you think I'm good for something"*   Irène to Marie, September 11, 1921, Bibliothèque Nationale.

191   *"as a great scientist"*   Eve Curie, *Madame Curie*, 362.

191   *It recommended warning researchers*   M. Broca, "Au nom de la Commission du Radium," *Bulletin de l'Académie médicine* 111, no. 85 (1921).

192   *although a visiting Englishman*   Reid, *Marie Curie*, 240.

192   *"My eyes are very weak"*   Giroud, *Marie Curie*, 235.

192   *But when he revealed his interest*   Marcel Guillot, "Marie Curie-Sklodowska," *Nuclear Physics* A, 103 (Amsterdam: North-Holland Publishing Co.), October 23, 1967.

192   *"Bitch! Bitch!"*   Pflaum, *Grand Obsession*, 234.

192   *"You Camel!"*   Quinn, *Marie Curie*, 403.

192   *"Pig! Pig!"*   Giroud, *Marie Curie*, 259.

193   *"even laughed with a fresh, young laugh"*   Giroud, *Marie Curie*, 151.

193   *Danne was the assistant*   Communication with author from Pierre Radvanyi, November 21, 2002.

194   *Einstein accepted, aware of the risk*   Brian, *Einstein*, 137.

195   *"I am on the nationalists' list"*   Thomas Levenson, *Einstein in Berlin* (New York: Bantam, 2003), 270.

195   *"It is precisely because dangerous"*   Marie to Einstein, July 7, 1922, Stanley W. Pycior, "Marie Sklodowska Curie and Albert Einstein: A Professional and Personal Relationship," *The Polish Review* 17, no. 2 (1999): 131.

195   *"Since the hideous murder of Rathenau"*   Einstein to Solovine, July 16, 1922, Albrecht Folsing, trans. Ewald Osers, *Albert Einstein* (New York: Viking, 1997), 522.

195   *"I grant you willingly"*   Marie to Einstein, January 5, 1924, Quinn, *Marie Curie*, 382.

196   *They adopted her suggestion*   Stanley W. Pycior, "Her Only Infidelity to Scientific Research": *Marie Sklodowska Curie and The League of Nations* 41, no. 4 (1996): 456.

197   *Marie once confided*   Quinn, *Marie Curie*, 424.

197   *"We have seen Marie Curie"*   Eve Curie, *Madame Curie*, 363.

Chapter 13: Radium: Miracle Cure or Menace?

198   *"a lot of Mr. Einstein"*   Marie to Irène, July 23, 1924, Bibliothèque Nationale.

199   *She was "at her desk"*   Pierre Biquard, *Frédéric Joliot-Curie: The Man and His Theories* (New York: Fawcett, 1966), 21.

199   "'What! You don't have'"   Maurice Goldsmith, *Frédéric Joliot-Curie* (London: Lawrence and Wishart, 1976), 28.

199   "*Can you begin work*"   Biquard, *Frédéric Joliot-Curie*, 21.

200   "*This process*"   Ibid., 25.

200   "*an extraordinary person*"   Goldsmith, *Frédéric Joliot-Curie*, 31.

201   "*the bourgeois class*"   Ernest O. Hauser, "The Soviet's Friend in the Atom Camp," *Saturday Evening Post*, June 16, 1951, 141.

202   "*the manipulation of radium*"   *New York World*, "Bergonie Is Latest of 140 Martyrs to X-Ray and Radium," November 16, 1924, section 11, 1.

203   "*Like Professor Bergonie*"   *New York Times*, January 4, 1925, 1.

203   "*the same fate and mysterious malady*"   *Chicago Tribune*, January 8, 1925, 44.

204   "*she had always scorned*"   Eve Curie, *Madame Curie*, 394.

204   "*been invaded—yes, and pervaded*"   Eileen Welsome, *The Plutonium Files: America's Secret Medical Experiments in the Cold War* (New York: Dial Press, 1999), 47. Dr. Blum revealed his findings at a professional meeting reported in the *Journal of the American Dental Association* in September 1924.

204   "*five women had died*"   Shirley A. Fry, "Studies of U.S. Radium Dial Workers: An Epidemiological Classic," Radiation Research 150 (Suppl.) S21–S29 (1998): S23. *New York Times*, May 30, 1925, 13.

205   "*were in danger of snapping*"   Welsome, *The Plutonium Files*, 49.

205   "*No one has worked longer*"   *New York Times*, June 22, 1925, 17.

205   A *baby girl had been brought*   Los Alamos Science, Los Alamos National Laboratory, "Radiation Protection and the Human Radiation Experiment," no. 23 (1995): 226.

206   "*Dear, dear friend*"   Fuller to Marie, December 23, 1922, Reid, *Marie Curie*, 242.

206   "*The examinations for the bachelor's*"   *New York Times*, March 31, 1925, 3.

207   "*that she didn't fully understand*"   *Le Quotidien*, March 30, 1925, 359.

207   "*I even remember that you forgot*"   Eve Curie, *Madame Curie*, 359.

208   "*Oh, my poor darling!*"   Ibid., 375–376.

208   "*I have no objection*"   Ibid., 376.

208   "*It is unsatisfactory*"   Giroud, *Marie Curie*, 279.

209   Eve *recalled that it was*   Eve Curie, *Madame Curie*, 369.

209   "*What makes life interesting*"   Joliot-Curie Archives, Paris.

209   "*Does such discretion on your part*"   Ibid.

210   To *Eve Curie, words could not*   Eve Curie, *Madame Curie*, 312–313.

210   The *regulars called themselves*   Ibid., 314.

210   "*not obliged to keempany*"   Goldsmith, *Frédéric Joliot-Curie*, 218.

210   "*had an inferiority complex*"   Author's interview with Bertrand Goldschmidt, March 14, 2002.

211   "*Joliot was a complete outsider*"   Kowarski interviewed by Weiner, AIP, October 19–20, 1969, 61.

211   "*was not beyond removing*"   Reid, *Marie Curie*, 255.

212   "*the young man who married Irene*"   Per F. Dahl, *Heavy Water and the Wartime Race for Nuclear Energy* (Bristol and Philadelphia: Institute of Physics Publishing, 1999), 9.

213   "*The boy is a skyrocket!*"   Cotton, *Les Curies*, 114.

213   "*I would never have forgiven*"   Spencer R. Weart, *Scientists in Power* (Cambridge, Mass.: Harvard University Press, 1979), 3.

213   "*I have lived under oppression.*"   Ibid, 373.

214   "*The Polish radium*"   Meloney to Marie Curie April 20, 1928, Bibliothèque Nationale.

215   "*If ever a case called*"   Walter Lippmann, "Five Women Doomed to Die," *New York World*, May 10, 1928.

215   "*To dispute whether they can live*"   Ibid., May 19, 1928, 23.

215   "*Twelve women have died*"   Florence Pfalzgraph to Marie Curie, May 25, 1928, Bibliothèque Nationale.

215   "*affirmed the doom*"   Ethelda Bedford, "Radium Victims Too Ill to Attend Court Tomorrow," *Newark Ledger*, May 17, 1928.

215   "*I am not a doctor*"   "Mme Curie Urges Safety from Radium," June 4, 1928, United Press.

216   *"For the past two days"*   Goldsmith, *Frédéric Joliot-Curie*, 218.

216   *"Return home at dusk"*   Ibid.

217   *"Initially, it was thought"*   E-mail to author from Professor George Dracoulis, Chairman of the Department of Nuclear Physics, Australian National University, Canberra, July 22, 2003.

217   *"I haven't told M. Rosenblum"*   Marie to Einstein, August 30, 1929.

218   *"Representatives of three Governments"*   Elenore Kellogg, "World's Most Distinguished Woman Scientist, on Second Visit, Shrinks From Limelight," *New York Times*, November 20, 1929.

219   *"I came down the service stairs"*   Marie to Irène, October 20, 1929.

220   *"but his name would not"*   Pycior, *The Polish Review*, 465.

220   *"the funniest man"*   *New York Times*, July 27, 1930, 1, 2.

221   *"We've been here for a week"*   Frédéric to Marie, July 25, 1930, Goldsmith, *Frédéric Joliot-Curie*, 219.

222   *"In this chamber"*   Biquard, *Frédéric Joliot-Curie*, 28.

222   *"It was a pleasure"*   Goldsmith, *Frédéric Joliot-Curie*, 38.

Chapter 14: A Great Discovery—at Last

223   *"I just want to know"*   Robert Jungk, *Brighter Than a Thousand Suns* (New York: Harcourt, Brace and Company), 1958, 56.

224   *"Bohr insisted a good deal"*   Roger H. Stuewer, "The Discovery of Artificial Radioactivity," *Oeuvre et engagement de Frédéric Joliot-Curie*, eds. Monique Bordry and Pierre Radvanyi (Paris: EDP Sciences, 2001), 12.

224   *"A great discovery"*   Biquard, *Frédéric Joliot-Curie*, 36.

224   *"I admired the dexterity"*   Goldsmith, *Frédéric Joliot-Curie*, 40.

225   *"Their next step"*   Communication from Hélène Langevin-Joliot, January 5, 2004.

225   *"was as unlikely as"*   Rhodes, *The Making of the Atomic Bomb* (New York: Simon & Schuster, 1986), 162.

226   *"I don't believe it!"*   Albert Stwertka, *Guide to the Elements* (New York: Oxford University Press, 1998), 10.

226   *"It was quite the most"*   E. N. da C. Andrade, *Rutherford and the Nature of the Atom* (Garden City, N.Y.: Doubleday, 1964), 110–111, 117.

226   *Because most alpha particles*   Ibid., 169.

228   *"Now I want to be chloroformed"*   Rhodes, *The Making of the Atomic Bomb*, 165.

228   *"the basic physical rule"*   Ibid., 164.

228   *"someone remarked, 'Oh, that Englishman, Chadwick'"*   Transcript of Charles Weiner's interview of Lew Kowarski, March 20, 1969, Center for History and Philosophy of Physics, American Institute of Physics, 35–36.

229   *"Old laboratories"*   Stuewer, "The Discovery of Artificial Radioactivity," 14.

229   *"Gamma rays and protons"*   E-mail from Roger H. Steuwer to author, November 13, 2003.

230   *"I believe that Science has great beauty"*   Giroud, *Marie Curie*, 270.

230   *"It is very moving"*   Ibid.

230   *"brought the backward country"*   William L. Shirer, *The Nightmare Years: A Memoir of a Life and the Times* (Boston, Mass.: Little, Brown, 1948), 73.

231   *"Public health officials"*   Roger M. Macklis, "The Great Radium Scandal," *Scientific American*, August 1993, 94–95.

232   *"I felt so badly"*   Marie to Rutherford, September 12, 1932, Reid, *Marie Curie*, 268.

232   *"What was the good of it"*   Bertrand Goldschmidt, *Atomic Rivals*, trans. Georges M. Temmer (New Brunswick, N.J.: Rutgers University Press, 1990), 4.

232   *"We have trouble with the electrometer"*   Goldsmith, *Frédéric Joliot-Curie*, 51.

233 *"an exquisite technician"*   Charles Weiner, interview of Lew Kowarski, March 20, 1969, American Institue of Physics, 37, 39, 43, 48.

234 *"curved the wrong way"*   Spencer R. Weart, *Scientists in Power* (Cambridge, Mass.: Harvard University Press, 1979), 42–43.

234 *"On July 10, 1933"*   Stuewer, "The Discovery of Artificial Radioactivity," 14.

235 *"about 1933, the climate"*   Helge Kragh, *Quantum Generations: A History of Physics in the Twentieth Century* (Princeton, N.J.: Princeton University Press, 1999), 243.

235 *"I am afraid that the epidemic of hatred"*   Clark, *Einstein: The Life and Times* (New York: Avon, 1972), 473.

235 *"that between [Irène and Meitner]"*   Jungk, *Brighter Than a Thousand Suns*, 63.

236 *"I wish I were a movie comedian"*   Clark, *Einstein*, 333.

237 He was a *"merry and freakish soul"*   Jungk, *Brighter Than a Thousand Suns*, 27, 30.

237 *"It's as important an event"*   Ibid., 46.

239 After conducting more experiments   Stuewer, "The Discovery of Artificial Radioactivity," 16.

239 *"She seemed to her "to be afraid"*   Jungk, *Brighter Than a Thousand Suns*, 64.

239 *"Once more" as author Jungk pointed out*   Ibid, 65.

240 he felt *"a child's joy"*   Goldsmith, *Frédéric Joliot-Curie*, 54.

241 *"a telephone call"*   Biquard, *Frédéric Joliot-Curie*, 32.

241 *"the intense expression of joy"*   Goldsmith, *Frédéric Joliot-Curie*, 57–58.

242 *"For the first time it has been possible"* Weart, *Scientists in Power*, 46.

242 *"Nobody had ever dared to imagine"*   Communication from Hélène Langevin-Joliot, January 6, 2004.

242 an *"entirely new epoch"*   Niels Bohr, *Collected Works*, vol. 9, "Nuclear Physics: 1929–1952" (Amsterdam: North Holland, 1986), 174.

242 *"on a fine piece of work"*   Rutherford to Joliot-Curies, January 29, 1934.

242 His *"standard apology"*   J. L. Heilbron and Robert W. Seidel, *Lawrence and His Laboratory* (Berkeley, Calif.: University of California Press, 1981), 179.

242 *"especially beautiful" discovery*   Meyer to Marie Curie, January 25, 1934, Stuewer, "The Discovery of Artificial Radioactivity," 17.

242 She replied immediately   Marie to Meyer, January 27, 1934, ibid.

243 *"He is someone I frankly detest"*   Goldsmith, *Frédéric Joliot-Curie*, 219.

243 was *"a strange man"*   Author's interview with Bertrand Goldschmidt, March 14, 2002.

243 Water also contained plenty of hydrogen   Laura Fermi, *Atoms in the Family: My Life with Enrico Fermi* (Chicago: University of Chicago Press, 1955), 99.

244 *"It is conceivable that in the bombardment"*   Helge Kragh, *Quantum Generations: A History of Physics in the Twentieth Century* (Princeton, N.J.: Princeton University Press, 1999), 25.

244 *"Nodack was not taken seriously"*   Communication from Hélène Langevin-Joliot, January 6, 2004.

245 *"If the magnitude of a discovery"*   Stuewer, "The Discovery of Artificial Radioactivity," 18.

245 *"Don't worry," he said*   Charles Weiner interview with Lew Kowarski March 20, 1969, American Institute of Physics, 49.

245 *"They had used a very special source"*   Charles Weiner interview with Wolfgang Gentner, November 1971, American Institute of Physics.

246 *"veterans' groups and paramilitary leagues"*   Joel Colton, *Leon Blum: Humanist in Politics* (Durham, N.C.: Duke University Press, 1987), 94.

246 *"interpreted the riot as proof"*   Ibid.

246 *"led by reactionary and monarchist organizations"*   Joshua Rubenstein, *Tangled Loyalties: The Life and Times of Ilya Ehrenburg* (New York: Basic Books, 1996), 125.

246 *"certainly ten came from outside France"*   Charles Weiner interview of Wolfgang Gentner, November 1971, American Institute of Physics.

247 *"she was sitting in the garden"*   Ibid.

Chapter 15: Marie Curie's Last Year

248   *"On the following morning"*   Eve Curie, *Marie Curie*, 395.
248   *"I feel the need of a house"*   Marie to Bronia, May 8, 1934, ibid.
249   *"You must stay in bed"*   Professor Boulin to Marie, ibid, 296.
249   *"You've got an energetic soul"*   Jacques Curie to Marie Curie, June 19, 1934, Reid, *Marie Curie*, 276.
250   *"I can't express myself"*   Eve Curie, *Madame Curie*, 400.
250   *"It wasn't the medicine"*   Ibid., 400–402.
252   *"Mme Curie Is Dead"*   *New York Times*, July 5, 1934, 1.
253   *"Marie Curie is, of all"*   Pasachoff, *Marie Curie*, 103.
253   *"I have not related"*   Eve Curie, *Madame Curie*, introduction, x.

Chapter 16: Nobel Prizes, Spanish Civil War, and Fission

255   *"You are the one who knew her least"*   Goldschmidt, *Atomic Rivals*, 12.
255   *"the little chemistry room"*   Ibid.
256   *"I am hated"*   Ibid.
256   *Eventually Goldschmidt understood*   Author's interview with Bertrand Goldschmidt, March 14, 2002.
256   *"Why do they claim"*   McGrayne, *Nobel Prize Women in Science*, 131.
256   *"elegant, discreet, fluent"*   *Le Progrès*, February 4, 1935.
256   *"Joliot held forth"*   Weart, *Scientists in Power*, 49.
257   *"in an atmosphere of cordiality"*   Ibid., 9.
257   *"These experiments were carrried out"*   Biquard, *Frédéric Joliot-Curie*, 8.
258   *"If we look back"*   Ibid., 10.
259   *"would have been a very good actor"*   Charles Weiner interview with Chadwick, 71, 87, American Institute of Physics.
259   *"unsociable, slow moving, hard to approach"*   *Current Biography* (New York: H. W. Wilson, 1940), 436.
260   *"dominated by the Joliots"*   Goldschmidt, *Atomic Rivals*, 15.
260   *"Irene Joliot-Curie dislikes"*   Michael Troyan, *The Life of Greer Garson* (Lexington, Kentucky: University Press of Kentucky, 1999), 159.
261   *"as a sacrifice for the feminist cause"*   Irène to Meloney, February 9, 1937, Reid, *Marie Curie*, 279.
261   *"for her dry manner"*   Pflaum, *Grand Obsession*, 327.
262   *"to have a beautiful Irène with me"*   Ibid.
262   *"probably by going out"*   Ibid., 327–328.
263   *"in essence a class war"*   George Orwell, *Homage to Catalonia* (Harmondsworth, U.K.: Penguin, 1966), 240.
263   *"it was the hope of liberation"*   Kingsley Martin, *Editor* (Harmondsworth, U.K.: Penguin, 1969), 225.
264   *"The Germans in Spain"*   Edgar Ansel Mowrer, *Triumph and Turmoil: A Personal History of Our Time* (New York: Weybright and Tulley, 1968), 262.
264   *"A hundred percent victory"*   William L. Shirer, *The Rise and Fall of the Third Reich: A History of Nazi Germany* (New York: Simon and Schuster, 1981), 297.
265   *"Joliot" he explained, "was intensely French"*   Weiner interview with Kowarski, 1967, American Institute of Physics.
266   *"some four million francs"*   Weart, *Scientists in Power*, 47–48.
266   *"Normally in France"*   Weiner interview with Gentner, American Institute of Physics.
266   *"Our external interests"*   Weart, *Scientists in Power*, 58.
267   *"The partition of Czechoslovakia"*   Winston S. Churchill, *The Gathering Storm* (Boston: Houghton-Mifflin, 1948), 303–304.

267 *"Has not the minister"* Biquard, *Frédéric Joliot-Curie,* 50.

267 *"I was extremely fierce"* Ibid.

268 *"You are right, I agree with you"* Goldschmidt, *Atomic Rivals,* 19.

268 *Later Hahn ridiculed* Ibid., 26.

269 *"This damned woman."* Charles Weiner interview with Lew Kowarski, American Institute of Physics.

269 *We should continue working on it* Pflaum, *Grand Obsession,* 335.

270 *the danger for Meitner* Ruth Lewin Sime, *Lise Meitner: A Life in Physics* (Berkeley: University of California Press, 1996), 204.

270 *"The baby has arrived."* Ibid., 205.

271 *"physically absurd"* Ibid., 234.

271 *"it was possible to consider"* Biquard, *Frédéric Joliot-Curie,* 42.

271 *"Your radium results are very amazing"* Rhodes, *The Making of the Atomic Bomb,* 253.

271 *"Hahn is too good a chemist"* Goldsmith, *Frédéric Joliot-Curie,* 68–69.

271 *"Out of their calculations"* Margaret Gowing, *Britain and Atomic Energy: 1939–1945* (London: Macmillan,1965), 24–25.

271 *"Fortunately Lise Meitner"* Sime, *Lise Meitner,* 237.

272 *Hahn and Strassmann had, in fact, split the atom's nucleus* O. R. Frisch, "Physical Evidence for the Division of Heavy Nuclei under Neutron Bombardment, *Nature* 143 (1939): 276.

272 *"Binary fission"* Rhodes, *The Making of the Atomic Bomb,* 263.

272 *"Paul was electrified"* Arnold Kramish, *The Griffin: The Greatest Untold Espionage Story of World War II* (Boston: Houghton Mifflin, 1986), 50.

272 *"Joliot probably had his first glimpse"* Lew Kowarski interview, American Institute of Physics.

273 *"Maybe if we had worked"* U.S. Department of Energy interview with Hélène Langevin-Joliot, September 10, 2003.

273 *"Oh what assholes we've been!"* McGrayne, *Nobel Prize Women,* 139.

273 *"bitterly reproached Joliot"* Lew Kowarski, interview, American Institute of Physics.

273 *"Then he designed his experiment"* Moments of Discovery, *Discovery of Fission,* Spencer Weart, AIP History, 1.

273 *"brought this exciting piece of gossip"* Lew Kowarski interview, American Institute of Physics.

274 *"when Kowarski arrived in the lab"* Author's interview with Bertrand Goldschmidt, March 14, 2002.

274 *"A citizen of such a state"* Gowing, *Britain and Atomic Energy,* 27.

274 *"When Hahn's paper"* Weart, *Scientists in Power,* 7.

274 *It proved successful* H. von Halban, F. Joliot, and L. Kowarski, "Liberation of Neutrons in the Nuclear Explosion of Uranium," *Nature* 143 (1939): 470–471.

275 *"Why not secure priority?"* Pflaum, *Grand Obsession,* 341.

275 *"brings back the possibility of atomic power"* Weart, *Scientists in Power,* 88.

275 *"So important a matter"* Jungk, *Brighter Than a Thousand Suns,* 77.

275 *"we knew in advance that our discovery"* Ibid., 77–78.

276 *"I am presently engaged"* Leo Szilard, *Leo Szilard: His Version of the Facts: Selected Recollections and Correspondence,* ed. Spencer R. Weart and Gertrude Weiss Szilard (Cambridge, Mass.: MIT Press, 1972), 54.

277 *"the newest development in nuclear physics"* Richard Rhodes, *The Making of the Atomic Bomb* (New York: Simon and Schuster, 1986), 296–297.

277 *"Tempers and temperatures increased"* *New York Times,* April 30, 1939, 35.

277 *Bohr's telegram* Thomas Powers, *Heisenberg's War: The Secret History of the German Bomb* (New York: Knopf, 1993), 55.

278 *"Feather is not quite fair to you"* Meitner to Hahn, June 2, 1939, Sime, *Lise Meitner,* 275.

278   "Sir Henry took him by the arm"   Leslie R. Groves, Now It Can Be Told: The Story of the Manhattan Project (New York: Harper, 1962), 33.

278   They told him that "their work could eventually"   Weart, Scientists in Power, 102.

279   "trying to find a way"   Hauser, "The Soviet's Friend," 142.

279   Author Thomas Powers reports   Powers, Heisenberg's War, 55.

279   In July 1939 refugee physicists   Author's interview with Wigner, June 29, 1989.

280   "Some weeks ago one of the Sunday papers"   Churchill, The Gathering Storm, 386–387.

280   "Nor was it the Germans who found"   Ibid., 387.

280   "The curtain has been lifted"   Colton, Leon Blum, 336; Le Populaire, September 18, 1939.

281   Poland, in Churchill's words   Churchill, The Gathering Storm, 447.

281   "What is happening is sad"   Irène Joliot-Curie to her daughter Hélène, Curie archives.

282   "Unfortunately France was to be submerged"   Biquard, Frédéric Joliot-Curie, 46; Patrick Blackett, Jean Frédéric Joliot, 1900–1958: Biographical Memoirs of the Fellows of the Royal Society, London, 6, 1960, 64.

282   "if his work had not been interrupted"   Weart, Scientists in Power, 150.

282   The Soviet Union's lame excuse   Colton, Leon Blum, 337.

282   "We hope very much that the U.S. will"   Ibid.

Chapter 17: France Defeated

283   "Indispensable war industries."   Mowrer, Triumph and Turmoil, 297.

284   "France is proud"   New York Times, January 19, 1940, 8.

284   "The most terrible condemnation."   Ibid., January 20, 1940, 13.

284   "The President was very glad"   Eleanor Roosevelt, My Day, February 3, 1940.

285   The day after the team left   Weart, Scientists in Power, 136.

286   "it was off-loaded and stored"   Per F. Dahl, Heavy Water and the Wartime Race for Nuclear Energy (Bristol and Philadelphia: Institute of Physics Publishing, 1999), 108.

286   "Because he made a fuss"   E-mail to author from Per F. Dahl, March 18, 2004.

287   Apparently although it's still officially secret   Michael Smith, Foley: The Spy Who Saved 10,000 Jews (London: Houghton and Stoughton, 1999).

287   "Germans Occupy Denmark"   Ibid., New York Times, April 9, 1940, 1.

288   "Do not trust your best friend"   Cecil Beaton, The Years Between: Diaries 1939–1944 (New York: Holt, Rinehart and Winston, 1965), 20.

288   "The front at Sedan"   Goldsmith, Frédéric Joliot-Curie, 90.

288   "It was unheard of"   Winston Churchill, Their Finest Hour (Boston: Houghton Mifflin, 1949), 46–47.

289   "They were all haggard-looking"   Arthur Bryant, The Turn of the Tide: A History of the War Years Based on the Diaries of Field-Marshal Lord Alanbrooke, Chief of the Imperial General Staff (Garden City, N.Y.: Doubleday, 1957), 85, 89.

289   "Nothing but a miracle"   Ibid., 91.

290   "the loot of civilization"   Robert E. Sherwood, Roosevelt and Hopkins: An Intimate History (New York: Harper & Brothers, 1948), 141.

290   Churchill had "announced to his dismay"   Eve Curie, Journey Among Warriors (Garden City, N.Y.: Doubleday, Doran and Co., 1943), 20.

291   "We shall go on to the end"   Shirer, Rise and Fall, 738.

291   And if the worst happened   Mowrer, Triumph and Turmoil, 315.

291   "The Governor of the prison"   Jungk, Brighter Than a Thousand Suns, 108.

291   "Germany will overrun the whole of France"   Charles Weiner interview with Lew Kowarski, American Institute of Physics.

292   "That we are ordered to go"   Ibid.

293   "You are coming to England"   Ibid., 93.

294   *She had contempt for the Nazis*   Ibid., 96.

294   *"Should I accept?"*   Biquard, *Frédéric Joliot-Curie*, 54.

294   *"There was seasickness"*   Lew Kowarski, *Radio Times*, September 20, 1973.

294   *"there were plenty of Frenchmen ready to die"*   Bryant, *Turn of the Tide*, 126.

294   *"You take Hitler"*   Ian Ousby, *Occupation: The Ordeal of France 1940–1944* (New York: St. Martin's Press, 1998), 19.

295   *burst into my room"*   Bryant, *Turn of the Tide*, 143.

295   *"the anvil upon which French manhood"*   The New Encyclopaedia Micropaedia Britannica, 15th edition, s.v. "Verdun."

296   *"I declare that the French government"*   Shirer, *Rise and Fall of the Third Reich*, 744–745.

297   "The Germans are behaving very correctly"   Goldsmith, *Frédéric Joliot-Curie*, 97.

297   *"I wish to find my wife"*   Curie archives, Paris.

298   *"They asked Joliot about heavy water"*   Charles Weiner interview with Wolfgang Gentner, American Institue of Physics.

298   *"What happened to the heavy water"*   Biquard, *Frédéric Joliot-Curie*, 55–56. "Lord Suffolk, his secretary [Beryl Morden], his chauffeur [Fred Harts], an NCO and four sappers [Suffolk was training] were all killed at Erith [Kent] in May 1941 when a 250-kg S.C. [bomb] exploded," according to A. B. Hartley in his *History of the British Bomb Disposal Service in World War II.* Lord Suffolk appears as a character in the "In Situ" chapter of Michael Ondaatje's novel *The English Patient.* Halban and Kowarski continued their research at the Cavendish Laboratory in Cambridge where, in 1940, they did pioneering work on nuclear fission.

299   *"In June 1940"*   Joliot to Bichelonne, August 29, 1943, U.S. National Archives, folder 25, roll 2, 740-SH.

300   *"Certainly, Joliot's lab"*   E-mail from Spencer Weart to author, March 22, 2004.

300   *"the workroom [at Joliot's laboratory]"*   Philippe Burrin, *France Under the Germans: Collaboration and Compromise*, trans. Janet Lloyd (New York: The New Press, 1997), 314.

301   *"Last night [in London] we dined"*   Diana Cooper, *Trumpets from the Steep* (Harmondsworth, England: Penguin, 1964), 56–57.

301   *"For activities against National Socialism"*   Goldsmith, *Frédéric Joliot-Curie*, 102.

302   *"the glory and pride of France"*   Pflaum, *Grand Obsession*, 371.

302   *"I have learned today"*   Goldsmith, *Frédéric Joliot-Curie*, 102.

302   *"They thought they were isolating him"*   André Langevin, *Paul Langevin, Mon Père: L'Homme et l'oeuvre*, trans. Martine Brian (Paris: Les Editeurs Français Réunis, 1971), 178.

303   *"It is worth noting"*   Burrin, *France Under the Germans*, 314.

303   *"I don't know of anybody who did more"*   E-mail from Hélène Langevin-Joliot to the author, April 16, 2004.

Chapter 18: Joliot Keeps the Gestapo Guessing— Eve Curie Tours the Battlefronts

304   *"but [as] she left . . . to escape"*   New York Times, January 30, 1941, 6.

305   *"The deep suffering"*   Ibid., January 31, 1941, 10.

305   *"I've wished for you and Trude"*   Joseph P. Lash, *Eleanor Roosevelt and Her Friends* (Garden City, N.Y.: Doubleday, 1982), 334.

305   *"Mlle Curie has been"*   FDR Library archives.

306   *"No, thank you"*   New York Times, April 22, 1941, 6.

306   *"Since 1934 I have violently attacked"*   Ibid., May 5, 1941, 7.

306   *"The French government which Hitler destroyed"*   Ibid., May 6, 1941, 20.

307   *"the grand abettors"*   Les Nouveau Temps, February 15, 1941; Weart, *Scientists in Power*, 159.

308   that *"the German physicists"*   Goldsmith, *Frédéric Joliot-Curie*, 110.

309 *"helping the enemy"* Ian Ousby, *Occupation: The Ordeal of France 1940–1944* (New York: St. Martin's Press, 1997), 224.

309 *"Ten Nazi officers"* Ibid.

310 *"Collaboration, terror and repression"* Goldsmith, *Frédéric Joliot-Curie*, 104.

310 *"My husband, Aimé Cotton"* Ibid.

312 *"a huge beige-and-white city"* Eve Curie, *Journey Among Warriors* (New York: Double-day, 1943), 36.

313 *"had been landed from a submarine"* Ibid., 36; Kay Halle, ed., *The Grand Original: Portraits of Randolph Churchill by His Friends* (Boston: Houghton Mifflin, 1971), 116, 117, 118.

313 *"The word meant exactly what it said"* Ibid., 37.

313 *"When we get on both sides of an enemy"* Harold Nicolson, *The Wars Years: Diaries and Letters, 1939–1945* (New York: Atheneum, 1967), 192.

314 *"There are so many planes in the sky"* Eve Curie, *Journey Among Warriors*, 38.

314 *"Around me," she recalled* Ibid., 40–41.

315 *"Please . . . may I have your water?"* Ibid., 41.

316 *"The desert was a correspondent's paradise"* Quentin Reynolds, *Only the Stars Are Neutral* (New York: Random House, 1942), 247.

316 *"were sulking and speaking to no one"* Eve Curie, *Journey Among Warriors*, 41–45.

316 *"Cunningham was driving at Tobruk"* Reynolds, *Only the Stars*, 244–245.

316 *"seemed on the verge of a nervous breakdown"* Ismay, *The Memoirs of General Lord Ismay* (New York: Viking, 1960), 271–272.

316 *"Tobruk is as relieved as I am"* Nicolson, *The War Years*, 192.

317 *"Eve Curie was by far the most popular"* Cecil Beaton, *The Years Between: Diaries 1939–44* (New York: Holt, Rinehart and Winston, 1965), 191.

317 *"Japan has attacked Hawaii"* Eve Curie, *Journey Among Warriors*, 64.

317 *"almost drunk with happiness"* Ibid., 86.

317 *"None of the men would want"* W. L. White, "The Battlefronts of Freedom," *New York Times Book Review*, May 9, 1943, 1.

318 *"I could not help assuming"* Eve Curie, *Journey Among Warriors*, 99.

319 *"to avoid for Iran the fate"* Ibid., 109.

319 *"a nervous youngster"* Harrison Salisbury, *A Journey for Our Times* (New York: Harper & Row, 1983), 208.

319 *"the old and destitute"* Eve Curie, *Journey Among Warriors*, 144.

319 *"There have been two opposite propagandas"* Ibid., 145.

320 *"Russian suspicion of foreigners is immense"* Ibid., 186.

320 *She noticed that "their uniforms"* Ibid., 178.

321 *"after seeing the burned houses"* Ibid., 178–179.

321 *"been blind enough to follow"* Ibid., 193–195.

321 *"What kind of people"* Ibid., 195.

322 *"Today," she wrote, "when heroic"* Ibid., 195–196.

322 *"like many well-born Russian women"* Ibid, 197.

323 *Eve contended that "his moving efforts"* Ibid., 218.

323 *"The whole thing looked like a giant amusement park"* Ibid., 241.

324 *Eve did not know it, but the previous year* The Katyn Controversy: Stalin's Killing Field," Benjamin B. Fischer, History Staff, CIA's Center for the Study of Intelligence, CIA, Washington, DC.

325 *" 'Not unless you are a Jap' "* Eve Curie, *Journey Among Warriors*, 281–282.

Chapter 19: Joliot Becomes a Communist—Eve Curie Interviews Nehru, Gandhi, and Jinnah

326 *"had an agreement"* E-mail to author from Hélène Langevin-Joliot, June 7, 2004.

327 *"handsome, artificial smile"* Eve Curie, *Journey Among Warriors*, 320–321.

327 *Before boarding the train* Ibid., 321.

328 *According to historian* Barbara Tuchman, *Practicing History: Selected Letters* (New York: Ballantine, 1981), 74.

328 *"Everything was against us"* Eve Curie, *Journey Among Warriors*, 323, 324.

328 *"My idea of fighting"* Ibid., 384.

330 *"slim, smart, as neat as a Cartier jewel"* Ibid., 387.

330 *He had been exposed to* Theodore H. White, *In Search of History* (New York: Warner Books, 1981), 183.

330 *"an ignorant, illiterate"* Ibid., 180.

330 *Yet, "perhaps the most"* Eve Curie, *Journey Among Warriors*, 397.

331 *"But no," she wrote* Ibid.

331 *"as a football coach"* White, *In Search of History*, 104.

331 *On the contrary, Calcutta* Eve Curie, *Journey Among Warriors*, 401.

332 *"The old woman who sewed"* Ibid., 410.

332 *On the other hand* Ibid.

333 *"Whenever I heard such irresponsible"* Ibid., 411.

333 *"Some actually conspired"* Byron Farwell, *Armies of the Raj: From the Great Indian Mutiny to Independence: 1858–1947* (New York: W. W. Norton & Company, 1989), 309.

333 *"with a romantic face"* Eve Curie, *Journey Among Warriors*, 418.

333 *"a queer mixture of East and West"* *Encyclopaedia Brittanica*, 15th ed., s.v. "Nehru, Jawaharlal."

333 *"Brahman of Kashmir"* Eve Curie, *Journey Among Warriors*, 420–421.

335 *"quiet, shy and very pleasant"* Ibid., 435–436.

335 *"the great majority of the illiterate"* Ibid., 437–438.

336 *"great jungle feline"* Ibid., 445–447.

336 *"the world's most successful humbug"* Yogesh Chadha, *Gandhi: A Life* (New York: John Wiley & Sons, 1999), 390.

336 *"if the Jewish mind"* Ibid., 337.

337 *"Gandhi: I am against all wars"* Eve Curie, *Journey Among Warriors*, 450–451, 453–454.

340 *"Hitler killed five million Jews"* Larry Collins and Dominque Lapierre, *Freedom at Midnight* (New York: Simon and Schuster, 1975), 72–73; Chadha, *Gandhi*, 363–364.

340 *"a Peter Pan"* Collins and Lapierre, *Freedom at Midnight*, 116–117.

340 *"How can you ever dream"* Eve Curie, *Journey Among Warriors*, 463–464.

341 *"they were feverishly wondering"* Ibid., 466.

342 *"attacked post offices"* Farwell, *Armies of the Raj*, 310.

343 *"I cannot take you in my arms"* Madame Vaillant Courturier, in testimony at the Nuremburg Trial, January 23, 1946, *The Nizkor Project*, Trials of Major War Criminals, vol. 5.

343 *"Don't tell anyone you saw me"* André Langevin, *Paul Langevin*, 201–202.

344 *"Like many others in France"* Weart, *Scientists in Power*, 165.

344 *"resistance status was affirmed"* Lew Kowarski interview, American Institute of Physics.

344 *"worn by three young girls"* Ian Ousby, *Occupation: The Ordeal of France, 1940–1944* (New York: St. Martin's Press, 1997), 185.

344 *"It was not until he was close"* Ibid.

344 *"was the first anti-Semitic measure"* Ibid.

345 *"We were all here, as usual"* Michel Pinault, *Fréderic Joliot-Curie* (Paris: Editions Odile Jacob, 2000), 238.

345 *"Sleep with you until the end of the world"* E-mail to author from Hélène Langevin-Joliot, June 7, 2004.

345 *"I do not share your opinions"* Biquard, *Frédéric Joliot-Curie*, 61.

346 *Joliot's daughter* E-mail to author from Hélène Langevin-Joliot, June 7, 2004.

347 *"Sicily must be made into a Stalingrad"* C. L. Sulzberger, *American Heritage Picture History of World War II* (New York: Simon and Schuster, 1966), 370.

347 *"Politzer who had been shot"* Charles de Gaulle, *Speeches and Messages*, vol. 1.

347   *"The English are waging war"*   Joseph Goebbels, *The Goebbels Diaries*, ed. and trans. Louis P. Lochner (New York: Award Books, 1971), 613.

348   *"vivid personal portraits"*   W. L. White, "The Battlefronts of Freedom," *New York Times Book Review*, May 9, 1943, 1, 20.

348   *"When the time comes"*   Marjorie Avery, *New York Times Magazine*, November 28, 1943, 14, 41.

Chapter 20: The Battle for Paris

349   *"was bandaged and carried in the men's arms"*   Albert Parry, *Peter Kapitsa on Life and Science* (New York: Macmillan, 1968), 148.

349   *"at the University of Paris"*   Ibid. 147–148.

350   *"the small village seemed to exist"*   E-mail to author from Hélène Langevin-Joliot, June 7, 2004.

351   *"Once again I recognized"*   Goldsmith, *Frédéric Joliot-Curie*, 120.

351   *"You know how I like hunting"*   Ibid., 122; Joliot to Nine Choucroun, February 17, 1945.

353   *"the man who had discovered"*   Jungk, *Brighter Than a Thousand Suns*, 159.

353   *"saw one of Joliot-Curie's deadly bottles"*   Collins and Lapierre, *Is Paris Burning?*, 120.

353   *"Our only chance of survival"*   Ibid., 119.

354   *"Bradley, [with Eisenhower's approval]"*   C. L. Sulzberger, *World War II* (New York: American Heritage, 1966), 518.

354   *"During the truce"*   E-mail to author from Hélène Langevin-Joliot, June 7, 2004.

354   *"there was some shooting near us"*   Denis Brian, *The True Gen: An Intimate Portrait of Hemingway By Those Who Knew Him* (New York: Grove Press, 1988), 163.

355   *"so its ruins will block"*   Collins and Lapierre, *Is Paris Burning?*, 209.

355   *"He asked Holmes to get arms"*   Ibid., 326.

355   *"I always had a deep suspicion"*   Powers, *Heisenberg's War*, 501.

355   *"because I am afraid for my life"*   Boris Pash, *The Alsos Mission* (New York: Award House, 1969), 69.

356   *"Feeling him out with regard to his work"*   Ibid., 71–73.

356   *"'J' [Joliot] insists that no war work"*   National Archives, DOE report, roll 9, folder no. 107, 1945.

357   *"he has very strong political views"*   Ibid.

357   *"between all countries whose nationals"*   Ibid.

358   *"that nothing that might be of interest"*   Groves, *Now It Can Be Told*, 234.

358   *"He was regarded as a traitor"*   Jungk, *Brighter Than a Thousand Suns*, 159.

358   *"many Frenchmen were convinced"*   E-mail from Hélène Langevin-Joliot to author, June 21, 2004.

359   *"the fraternity and close relations"*   Goldschmidt, *Atomic Rivals*, 281.

359   *"straight into the arms of Russia"*   Ibid., 241.

Chapter 21: Joliot's Fight for Peace and Communism

361   *"its greatest expansion"*   Weart, *Scientists in Power*, 213.

361   *"to pressure scientists"*   Ibid, 214.

361   *"sooner or later"*   Biquard, *Frédéric Joliot-Curie*, 66.

362   *"with scissors in hand"*   Ibid., 67.

362   *"If the person you are trying to convince"*   E-mail from Hélène Langevin-Joliot to author, June 21, 2004.

363   *"We were like members"*   Weart, *Scientists in Power*, 219–220.

364   *"go to Moscow all the time"*   Ibid., 220.
364   *"To lunch at a little bistro"*   Shirer, *Nightmare Years*, 626.
364   *"I performed the same procedure"*   E-mail from Hélène Langevin-Joliot to author, June 21, 2004.
365   *"by the familiar* tu"   Ibid.
365   *"our pals the British"*   Weart, *Scientists in Power*, 220.
367   *"exhausted but exhilarated"*   Biquard, *Frédéric Joliot-Curie*, 100–101.
367   *"entirely directed"*   Goldsmith, *Frédéric Joliot-Curie*, 144.
367   *"and the sight of all the things"*   Ibid., 145.
367   *"It is madness"*   Ibid., 147.
368   *"he was thrilled to feel"*   Goldschmidt, *Atomic Rivals*, 344.
369   *"but that Ellis Island"*   Ibid., 341.
369   *"I am here to aid"*   Ibid., 430–431.
369   *"in freedom and friendship"*   Ilya Ehrenburg, *Post-War Years: 1945–54* (Cleveland, Ohio: World, 1967), 136.
369   *"The communist block displayed"*   Julian Huxley, *Memories II* (New York: Harper & Row, 1973), 62–63.
370   *"The culture of various"*   Joshua Rubenstein, *Tangled Loyalties: The Life and Times of Ilya Ehrenburg* (New York: Basic Books, 1996), 243–244.
370   *life in Soviet Russia was "terrible"*   Ibid., 428.
370   *"a fast-talking"*   Hauser, "The Soviet's Friend," 141.
371   *"which strengthens our role"*   Weart, *Scientists in Power*, 248.
371   *"a poignant episode"*   Goldschmidt, *Atomic Rivals*, 343.
371   *"Let me speak frankly"*   Hauser, "The Soviet's Friend," 141.
371   *"it is worthwhile to notice"*   E-mail from Hélène Langevin-Joliot to author, June 21, 2004.
372   *"he was pale with fatigue"*   Goldschmidt, *Atomic Rivals*, 344.
372   *"the Moscow show trials"*   Antony Beever and Artemis Cooper, *Paris After the Liberation, 1944–1949* (New York: Doubleday, 1994), 371; "Joliot-Curie on the Stand," *New York Times*, March 8, 1949, 6.
372   *"she was* really *convinced"*   McGrayne, *Nobel Prize Women*, 141; e-mail from Hélène Langevin-Joliot to author, June 21, 2004.
373   *"In that polarized atmosphere"*   Charles Weiner interview with Lew Kowarski, American Institute of Physics.
373   *"I think I overdid it"*   Goldschmidt, *Atomic Rivals*, 344–345.
373   *"the leaders of the Communist party"*   Ibid., 345.
373   *"all through 1949"*   Charles Weiner interview with Lew Kowarski, American Institute of Physics.
374   *"my recent experience"*   Groves, *Now It Can Be Told*, 234.
374   *"The Americans, however"*   Weart, *Scientists in Power*, 258–259.
375   *"It seems that the Russians"*   Ibid.
375   *"Before taking any action"*   Biquard, *Frédéric Joliot-Cuie*, 86.
376   *"at the end of the meal"*   Goldschmidt, *Atomic Rivals*, 347.
376   *"French Remove Joliot-Curie"*   Michael Clark, *New York Times*, April 29, 1950, 1, 32.
376   *"Senator Joseph McCarthy"*   *New York Times*, April 29, 1950, 32.
376   *"They could have forgiven me"*   Biquard, *Frédéric Joliot-Curie*, 126.
377   *"His desk was piled high"*   Goldsmith, *Frédéric Joliot-Curie*, 169.
377   *"Joliot's family background"*   Ibid.
377   to *"use the atomic weapon"*   Frédéric Joliot-Curie, "A Proposal Toward the Elimination of the Atomic Danger," and "The Three Points of Professor Joliot-Curie," *Bulletin of the Atomic Scientists*, E.R. 6, no. 6 (June 1950): 163–167.

Chapter 22: Joliot Launches Peace Offensive and Charges the United States with Using Germ Warfare in Korea

380 *"Physicists are like poets"* Ilya Ehrenburg, *Post-War Years*, 73.

380 *"I feel as if I've spent the summer"* Ibid., 186.

380 *"Do you ever think about death?"* Ibid., 180.

381 *"captured Chinese from the small island"* Kuo-Mo-Jo 1952 address to the World Peace Council on U.S. bioterrorism.

381 *"You charge me with prostituting science"* Goldsmith, *Frédéric Joliot-Curie*, 190–191.

382 *"To every scientist"* Bruce Bliven, "How Did the Communists Take Over One of France's Greatest Scientists?" *Saturday Evening Post*, January 17, 1953, 41.

383 *"Just as neither Christian love"* Sidney Hook, *Out of Step: An Unquiet Life in the 20th Century* (New York: Harper & Row, 1987), 478–483.

383 *"Ten Commandments for a Liberal"* Bertrand Russell, *The Autobiography of Bertrand Russell, 1944–1969* (New York: Simon and Schuster, 1969), 71.

383 *"fabricated a campaign"* AP report, November 1998.

384 *"the only chance of peace in our time"* Ismay, *The Memoirs of General Lord Ismay*, 461.

384 *"his wife, his children"* Biquard, *Frédéric Joliot-Curie*, 107.

385 *"based on such clues"* C. L. Sulzberger, *A Long Row of Candles: Memoirs and Diaries, 1934–1954* (New York: Macmillan, 1969), 1008.

385 *"Maybe a Yugoslavian visitor"* E-mail from Hélène Langevin-Joliot to author, June 21, 2004.

386 *"the signatories should have"* Goldsmith, *Frédéric Joliot-Curie*, 193.

386 *"I am an anti-Communist"* Ibid., 112.

387 *"To die is not fortunate"* Russell, *Autobiography*, 94.

387 *"Limitations of national sovereignty"* Biquard, *Frédéric Joliot-Curie*, 112.

387 *"The French Government did not"* Goldsmith, *Frédéric Joliot-Curie*, 172.

388 *"Joliot wasn't a scientist anymore"* Author's interview with Bernard Goldschmidt, March 14, 2002.

389 *"a happy marriage"* Ehrenburg, *Post-War Years*, 186–187.

389 *"Contrary to the current belief"* Chadwick to Kowarski, April 6, 1956, American Institute of Physics.

390 *"After the 20th Party Congress"* Kowarski to Chadwick, April 17, 1956. American Institute of Physics.

390 *"Certainly men are not perfect"* Biquard, *Frédéric Joliot-Curie*, 174.

391 *"House in perfect order."* Ibid., 139.

392 *"Irène had a knack"* Ehrenburg, *Post-War Years*, 187.

392 *"clarity, light and happiness in everything"* Ibid., 188.

392 *"the man whose work"* Biquard, *Frédéric Joliot-Curie*, 124.

393 *"We had known two different men"* Ehrenburg, *Post-War Years*, 188.

393 *"flowers from the little back gardens"* Ibid.

393 *"We could not speak"* Ibid.

394 *"Joliot-Curie Dies"* *New York Times*, August 15, 1958, 21.

394 *"News of the death"* *Le Monde*, August 15, 1958.

394 *"I was with Joliot-Curie"* Author's interview with Georges Charpak, March 24, 2002.

394 *"a man who was profoundly"* Biquard, *Frédéric Joliot-Curie*, 140.

394 *"Once inside his study."* Ibid., 133.

Chapter 23: The Curie Legacy

395 *"the country's funds"* A eulogy by E. J. R. Heyward, former senior deputy executive director of UNICEF, at a memorial service for Labouisse at the Church of the Holy Trinity, New York on April 2, 1987.

396   *"The essential message I got"*   E-mail from Hélène Langevin-Joliot to author, June 2, 2004.

397   *"My parents' discovery"*   *L'Humanité*, March 14, 2001.

397   *"It is moving for me to remember"*   Goldsmith, *Frédéric Joliot-Curie*, 214.

397   *"I always find renewed pleasure"*   Pierre Joliot, *La Recherche Passionnément* (Paris: Editions Odile Jacobs, 2001), 48–49.

398   *"Pierre-Gilles de Gennes"*   Goldsmith, *Obsessive Genius*, 14.

399   *"The transfer of "*   Ibid., 14–15.

Selected Bibliography

Alvarez, Walter C. *American Man of Medicine*. Compiled by David H. Scott. New York: Pyramid, 1976.

Badash, Lawrence, ed. *Rutherford and Boltwood: Letters on Radioactivity*. New Haven, Conn.: Yale University Press, 1969.

Beaton, Cecil. *The Years Between: Diaries 1939–44*. New York: Holt, Rinehart and Winston, 1965.

Biquard, Pierre. *Frédéric Joliot-Curie*. New York: Fawcett, 1966.

Blanc, Karin. *Marie Curie et le Nobel*. Uppsala Studies in the History of Sciences, 1999.

Borel, Marguerite [Camille Marbo, pseud.]. *A travers deux siècles, 1883–1967*. Paris: Bernard Grasset, 1968.

Brian, Denis. *Einstein: A Life*. New York: John Wiley & Sons, 1996.

———. *The Enchanted Voyager: The Life of J. B. Rhine*. Englewood Cliffs, N.J.: Prentice Hall, 1982.

———. *Pulitzer: A Life*. New York: John Wiley & Sons, 2001.

Brillouin Papers, American Institute of Physics Archives, College Park, Maryland.

Burrin, Phillippe, *France Under the Germans: Collaboration and Compromise*. New York: The New Press, 1996.

Churchill, Winston S. *The Gathering Storm*. Boston: Houghton-Mifflin, 1948.

———. *Great Contemporaries*. London: Fontana Books, 1965.

Clark, Ronald W. *Einstein: The Life and Times*. New York: Avon, 1972.

Close, F. E., Michael Marten, Christine Sutton, and Frank Close. *The Particle Odyssey: A Journey to the Heart of the Matter*. New York: Oxford University Press, 2002.

Collins, Larry and Dominique Lapierre. *Is Paris Burning?* New York: Simon and Schuster, 1965.

Colton, Joel. *Leon Blum: Humanist in Politics*. Durham, N.C.: Duke University Press, 1987.

Cooper, Diana. *Trumpets from the Steep*. Harmondsworth, England: Penguin Books, 1964.

Coover, John E. "Metapsychics and the Incredulity of Psychologists." In *The Case For and Against Psychical Belief*. Edited by Carl Murchison. Worcester, Mass.: Clark University, 1927.

Cotton, Eugénie. *Les Curies*. Paris: Editions Seghers, 1963.

Crawford, Elisabeth. *The Beginnings of the Nobel Institution: The Science Prizes, 1901–1915*. Cambridge: Cambridge University Press, 1984.

Crookes, William. *Proceedings of the Royal Society*. London, A83, 20, 1910.

Curie, Eve, *Journey Among Warriors*. New York: Doubleday, 1943.

———. *Madame Curie*. Translated by Vincent Sheean. New York: Pocket Books, 1964.

Curie, Marie. *Autobiographial Notes*. New York: Macmillan, 1924.

———. File, Manuscript Division, Library of Congress, Washington, D.C.

———. *Marie Curie's Nobel Lecture*, December 11, 1911, Nobel Foundation, Stockholm, Sweden. http://www.nobelprize.org.

———. *Notebook*. Curie Archives, Paris.

———. *Pierre Curie*. Paris: Editions Odile Jacob, 1966.

Curie, Mme Sklodowska. "Radium and Radioactivity." *Century Magazine*, January 1904.

Curie, P. F., M.D. *Practice of Homeopathy*. London: Medi-T, 1838.

Curie, Pierre. "Radium." In *Smithsonian Treasury of Science*. Edited by Webster P. True. New York: Simon & Schuster and Washington, D.C.: The Smithsonian Institution, 1960.

Einstein, Albert. *The Collected Papers of Albert Einstein:* Vol. 5, *The Swiss Years, Correspondence 1902–1914,* Translated by Anna Beck. Princeton, N.J.: Princeton University Press, 1995.

Enright, D. J., ed. *The Oxford Books of the Supernatural.* New York: Oxford University Press, 1994.

Eve, A. S. *Rutherford: Being the Life and Letters of the Rt. Hon. Lord Rutherford, O.M.* New York: Macmillan, 1939.

Franklin, Ben A. "U.S. Testing Workers for Effects of 13 Years Amid Atomic Wastes." *New York Times,* May 5, 1979.

Giroud, Françoise. *Marie Curie: Une Femme Honorable.* Paris: Fayard, 1982.

Goldschmidt, Bertrand. *Atomic Rivals.* Translated by George M. Temmer. New Brunswick, N.J.: Rutgers University Press, 1990.

Goldsmith, Barbara. *Obsessive Genius: The Inner World of Marie Curie.* New York: W.W. Norton & Company, 2005.

Goldsmith, Maurice. *Frédéric Joliot-Curie.* London: Lawrence and Wishart, 1976.

Goudsmit, S. *Alsos: The Failure of German Science.* New York: Signet, 1947.

Gowing, Margaret. *Britain and Atomic Energy: 1939–1945.* London: Macmillan, 1965.

Groves, Leslie R. *Now It Can Be Told: The Story of the Manhattan Project.* New York: Harper, 1962.

Hauser, Ernest O. "The Soviet's Friend in the Atom Camp." *Saturday Evening Post,* June 16, 1951.

Hurwic, Anna. *Pierre Curie.* Paris: Flammarion, 1995.

Jaffe, George. *Journal of Chemical Education* 29 (1952).

Joliot-Curie, Irène. "Marie Curie, ma mère," *Europe* 108 (1954).

Jungk, Robert. *Brighter Than a Thousand Suns.* New York: Harcourt, Brace and Company, 1958.

Knightley, Phillip. *The First Casualty: The War Correspondent as Hero, Propagandist, and Myth Maker.* New York: Harcourt Brace Jovanovich, 1975.

Kramish, Arnold. *The Griffin: The Greatest Untold Espionage Story of World War II.* Boston: Houghton Mifflin, 1986.

Langevin, André. *Paul Langevin, Mon Père: L'Homme et l'ouevre.* Paris: Les Editeurs Français Réunis, 1971.

LeClair, Robert C., ed. *The Letters of William James and Theodore Flournoy.* Madison: University of Wisconsin Press, 1966.

McGrayne, Sharon Bertsch. *Nobel Prize Women in Science: Their Lives, Struggles and Momentous Discoveries.* Washington, D.C.: Joseph Henry Press, 2000.

Martin, Kingsley. *Editor.* Harmondsworth, U.K.: Penguin, 1969.

Mowrer, Edgar Ansel. *Triumph and Turmoil: A Personal History of Our Time.* New York: Weybright and Tulley, 1968.

Orwell, George. *Homage to Catalonia.* Harmondsworth, England: Penguin Books, 1969.

Pais, Abraham. *Inward Bound.* New York: Oxford University Press, 1982.

Pash, Boris. *The Alsos Mission.* New York: Award House, 1969.

Pasachoff, Naomi. *Marie Curie and the Science of Radioactivity.* New York: Oxford University Press, 1996.

Pflaum, Rosalynd. *Grand Obsession: Madame Curie and Her World.* New York: Doubleday, 1989.

Powers, Thomas. *Heisenberg's War: The Secret History of the German Bomb.* New York: Knopf, 1993.

Quinn, Susan. *Marie Curie: A Life.* Reading, Mass.: Addison-Wesley, 1996.

Reid, Robert. *Marie Curie.* New York: New American Library, 1975.

Rhodes, Richard. *The Making of the Atomic Bomb.* New York: Simon & Schuster, 1986.

Richards, Ellen S. "The Discovery of Radium," address by Madame M. Curie at Vassar College, May 14, 1921. Monograph No. 2. Poughkeepsie, N.Y.: Vassar College, 1921.

Rolland, Romain. *Journal des Années de Guerre.* Paris: Albin Michel, 1952.

Rutherford, Ernest. *Letters*. Yale University Library.
——. "The Recent Radium Controversy." *Nature* 74 (1906): 634–635.
Sharp, Evelyn. *Hertha Ayrton: A Memoir*. London: Edward Arnold, 1926.
Shirer, William L. *The Rise and Fall of the Third Reich: A History of Nazi Germany*. New York: Simon & Schuster, 1981.
Sime, Ruth Lewin. *Lise Meitner: A Life in Physics*. Berkeley: University of California Press, 1996.
Stuewer, Roger H. "The Discovery of Artificial Radioactivity." In *Ouevre et engagement de Frédéric Joliot-Curie*. Edited by Monique Bordry and Pierre Radvanyi. Paris: EDP Sciences, 2001.
Szilard, Leo. *Leo Szilard: His Version of the Facts: Selected Recollections and Correspondence*. Edited by Spencer R. Weart and Gertrude Weiss Szilard. Cambridge, Mass.: Harvard University Press, 1973.
Thomson, J. J. *Recollections and Reflections*. Toronto: Macmillan, 1937.
Weart, Spencer R. *Marie Curie and the Science of Radioactivity*. AIP History, American Institute of Physics, College Park, Maryland.
——. *Scientists in Power*. Cambridge, Mass.: Harvard University Press, 1979.
Wolke, Robert L. "Marie Curie's Doctoral Thesis: Prelude to a Nobel Prize." *Journal of Chemical Education* 65, no. 7 (July 1988).
Ziegler, Gilette, ed. *Marie Curie–Irène Correspondence*. Paris: Les Editeurs Français Réunis, 1974.

Index